"A brilliant and timely examination of one of the most important presidencies in American history. Avoiding narrow-minded critique and uncritical celebration, this book masterfully analyzes the unheralded victories and unexamined contradictions of the Obama presidency."

—Marc Lamont Hill, author of *Nobody: Casualties of America's War on the Vulnerable, from Ferguson to Flint and Beyond*

"This is a smart, timely collection of essays that will serve as an important first assessment of the Obama administration. It will be useful to scholars of modern American politics, but also to journalists and policy makers, as well as many politically minded general readers."

—Joseph Crespino, author of *Strom Thurmond's America*

THE PRESIDENCY OF BARACK OBAMA

The Presidency of Barack Obama

A First Historical Assessment

Edited by Julian E. Zelizer

PRINCETON UNIVERSITY PRESS
PRINCETON AND OXFORD

Published by Princeton University Press,
41 William Street, Princeton, New Jersey 08540

In the United Kingdom: Princeton University Press,
6 Oxford Street, Woodstock, Oxfordshire OX20 1TR

press.princeton.edu

Cover photograph: President Barack Obama campaigning in Ohio,
July 8, 2012 / EDB Image Archive / Alamy Stock Photo

Library of Congress Catalog Number 2017957812
Cloth ISBN 978-0-691-16028-3
Paperback ISBN 978-0-691-18210-0

British Library Cataloging-in-Publication Data is available

This book has been composed in Adobe Text Pro and Gotham

Printed on acid-free paper. ∞

Printed in the United States of America

10 9 8 7 6 5 4 3 2

*To Harav Hanoch and Bayshe Zelizer, my great-grandparents,
who arrived on these shores in the early twentieth century and
embodied the promise of our immigrant nation*

CONTENTS

ACKNOWLEDGMENTS

I would like to thank the many people who made this book possible. Most important, all the contributors of this book have been incredible colleagues. They put their energy and passion into these essays, producing work that captures essential aspects of this presidency. They have been a pleasure to work with.

The Center for Collaborative History, the Woodrow Wilson School, and the American Studies program all contributed funds that allowed our workshop about the Obama presidency to take place in November 2016. Bernadette Yeager was instrumental to making the conference, where this book started, a reality with her organizational efficiency. This was part of the annual Princeton University–Boston University–Cambridge University Conference, which Bruce Schulman, Anthony Badger, and I started many years ago, joined by new colleagues like Andrew Preston and Gary Gerstle.

I would also like to thank Eric Crahan, our editor at Princeton University Press, who has been a strong supporter of the project from the beginning. Jill Harris has been a superb production editor, moving the project along at a brisk pace. Marilyn Campbell provided terrific copyediting. Madeleine Adams assisted me with some editorial work, while Jake Blumgart and Nathaniel Jiranek assisted with the timeline.

Julian E. Zelizer

TIMELINE

2008

November 4   Barack Obama is elected president.

2009

January 20   Inauguration of Obama as forty-fourth president of
               the United States.

January 22   Obama promises to close Guantánamo Bay
               detention facility.

January 29   The president signs the Lilly Ledbetter Fair Pay Act.

February 17   Obama signs $787 billion American Recovery and
               Reinvestment Act.

February 18   Administration commits to doubling U.S. military
               presence in Afghanistan.

February 19   On Chicago trading floor, CNBC's Rick Santelli calls
               for "Tea Party" rallies.

February 29   Obama sets firm date for the end of America's
               "combat mission" in Iraq.

March 31   Government takes control of General Motors and
               Chrysler.

May 26   Sonia Sotomayor is nominated to the Supreme Court.

June 26   The House passes "cap and trade" bill to combat
               climate change.

June 30   Minnesota governor signs election certificate
               declaring Al Franken as senator, giving Democrats a
               filibuster-proof sixty-seat majority.

July 11   First presidential visit to Africa.

July 25	The $4.35 billion Race to the Top initiative is begun, largely using funds from ARRA.
July 30	Obama holds "beer summit" with Henry Louis Gates Jr. and the white police officer who arrested him.
October 9	Nobel Peace Prize is awarded to Obama.
October 28	Obama signs Matthew Shepard and James Byrd Jr. Hate Crimes Prevention Act.

2010

January 27	Obama's first State of the Union speech.
March 23	The president signs the Patient Protection and Affordable Care Act.
April 8	Obama signs the Strategic Arms Reduction Treaty (START) with Russia to decrease nuclear stockpiles.
April 20	The Deepwater Horizon oil rig explodes.
May 10	Elena Kagan nominated to the Supreme Court.
July 21	Congress passes Dodd-Frank Wall Street Reform and Consumer Protection Act.
August 3	Obama signs Fair Sentencing Act.
October 30	Comedian-led Rally to Restore Sanity and/or Fear attracts huge crowds.
November 2	Republicans win control of the House in the midterm elections.
November 28	WikiLeaks releases 250,000 American diplomatic cables.
December 13	Obama signs Healthy, Hunger-Free Kids Act.
December 17	Bush-era tax cuts extended.
December 18	Arab Spring begins with protests in Tunisia.
December 18	DREAM Act killed in the Senate.
December 22	Obama signs repeal of Don't Ask, Don't Tell policy.

2011

| January 8 | Gunman in Tucson kills six and badly wounds Representative Gabrielle Giffords. |

February 2	Ratification of the START treaty with Russia, to wind down nuclear arms stockpiles.
March 23	Donald Trump takes up "birther" conspiracy on *The View*, the beginning of a month-long media blitz.
April 4	Obama announces his plans to seek reelection via a web video.
April 27	Obama releases his long form birth certificate to prove that he is a native-born U.S. citizen.
April 30	At White House Correspondents' Dinner, Obama mocks Trump over birther conspiracy.
May 2	Osama bin Laden killed by U.S. special forces.
August 2	Obama signs Budget Control Act, raising the debt ceiling.
August 5	United States loses AAA credit rating.
September 17	Occupy Wall Street protests begin in Manhattan's Zuccotti Park.
October 20	Muammar Gaddafi is killed as a result of Arab Spring uprisings.
December 15	Obama formally declares that the Iraq war is over.

2012

February 26	Trayvon Martin is murdered.
May 9	Obama announces his support for legalizing gay marriage.
June 15	Obama releases Deferred Action for Childhood Arrival executive order.
September 11	U.S. consulate and annex in Benghazi, Libya, is attacked.
November 6	Obama wins reelection.
December 14	Twenty-six people are murdered at Sandy Hook elementary school in Connecticut.

2013

January 2	Obama signs American Taxpayer Relief Act raising taxes on the top bracket back to where they were before President George W. Bush took office.

January 21   Obama's second presidential inauguration.

February 1   Hillary Rodham Clinton steps down as secretary of state.

June 5   Edward Snowden leaks reveal massive NSA
                 domestic spying operation.

June 26   Supreme Court, in *U.S. v. Windsor*, invalidates key
                 provision of the Defense of Marriage Act.

June 27   Senate passes comprehensive immigration reform
                 bill, which dies in the House.

August 9   Obama signs the Bipartisan Student Loan Certainty Act.

August 31   Obama asks Congress to approve military action
                 against Syria.

October 1   The federal government shuts down because
                 Congress refuses to pass legislation lifting the
                 debt ceiling.

October 1   HealthCare.gov launches, disastrously.

November 21   The Senate votes to limit the use of filibusters on
                 executive branch nominees.

2014

January 1   Medicaid expansion and insurance subsidies under
                 ACA go into effect.

February 12   Obama signs executive order to increase the
                 minimum wage for workers on federal contracts.

February 20   In response to Ukrainian Revolution, Russia begins
                 invasion of that nation.

March 6   Obama demands sanctions against Russia for
                 invasion of Ukraine and Crimea.

June 2   EPA reveals new rules for power plants to limit
                 effects of climate change.

June 16   Obama sends small military detachment back to Iraq
                 to fight new Islamic radical movement known as ISIS.

July 31   Obama signs Fair Pay and Safe Workplaces executive
                 order.

August 9   Michael Brown is killed in Ferguson, Missouri.

September 17   Republicans hold first hearings on the Benghazi attack.

September 30   Obama allows unaccompanied migrant children to apply for refugee status.

November 5   Republicans take control of Senate in midterm elections.

November 19   The Child Care and Development Block Grant signed into law.

November 20   Obama executive order to allow immigrants living within the United States to legally stay.

December 28   Obama declares an end to the "combat mission in Afghanistan."

2015

February 24   Obama vetoes bill that would allow construction of the Keystone pipeline.

March 2   It is revealed that Clinton used a personal email server for official business.

April 12   Baltimore police arrest Freddie Gray, who falls into a coma while in custody, sparking civil unrest; Gray dies on April 19.

June 2   Obama signs a renewal of the Patriot Act.

June 25   The Supreme Court affirms most of the Affordable Care Act and maintains an individual mandate.

June 26   The Supreme Court rules on *Obergefell v. Hodges* and makes same-sex marriage legal in all states.

June 29   Obama expands eligibility for overtime pay for millions of workers.

July 1   Cuba and the United States restore diplomatic relations.

July 14   The Iran nuclear deal is brokered.

August 3   The EPA releases the Clean Power Plan.

October 5   TPP negotiations are completed.

October 22   Clinton testifies before the Benghazi Committee for over eight hours.

November 30   Obama speaks at the Paris climate conference.

December 10   Obama signs Every Student Succeeds Act.

2016

January 17	The Obama administration lifts sanctions on Iran.
February 13	Antonin Scalia dies.
March 16	Obama nominates Merrick Garland to fill Scalia's seat on the Supreme Court.
May 4	Obama visits Flint, Michigan, in wake of water poisoning scandal.
September 20	Keith Lamont Scott is fatally shot by police in Charlotte, stirring civil unrest.
November 8	Donald J. Trump defeats Clinton, winning the presidency.
November 10	Obama meets with President-elect Donald Trump in the Oval Office.

2017

January 10	Obama delivers his farewell address.

THE PRESIDENCY OF BARACK OBAMA

1

Policy Revolution without a Political Transformation

THE PRESIDENCY OF BARACK OBAMA

Julian E. Zelizer

When the contributors to this book gathered in a seminar room at Princeton University just three days after the 2016 presidential election, almost everyone in the room seemed to be in a state of shock. "Historians Assess Obama's Legacy under Trump's Shadow" read the headline of a *New York Times* article covering the conference.[1] Donald Trump's stunning victory over Hillary Clinton loomed over our discussions. Certainly, few participants had predicted that one of the most inexperienced and unconventional candidates in the history of modern presidential campaigns would defeat someone with one of the most impressive résumés imaginable. Whereas many of the historians had submitted draft essays focusing on the accomplishments and limitations of President Barack Obama with the expectation that the next president would probably preserve much of his legacy, the discussion turned to how quickly his programs might be dismantled now that Republicans controlled the White House as well as Congress. Trump's election appeared to symbolize a direct rejection of the basic meaning of 2008, when the country elected its first African American president.

Obama seemed to demonstrate—simply through his victory—that the possibility of genuine change in American politics was real. When he took office in January 2009, his ambitions were grand. Even in the middle of a severe financial crisis and turbulence overseas, the new president sought to remake the social contract within the bounds of what was politically possible. Not only was his election widely perceived as a mandate for a new era of governance—and a repudiation of Republican economic and foreign policy, given President George W. Bush's miserable approval ratings—but Obama also enjoyed Democratic control of the House and the Senate. With Nancy Pelosi, a liberal Democrat, as Speaker of the House, he had strong allies on the Hill. Conditions seemed ripe for the president to move forward with a bold agenda.

This was an unusual situation. Although Americans often yearn for earlier eras when governing was easy, there were not many moments in the twentieth century when liberal Democrats who believed in activist government could make much progress on their goals. The only true exceptions to the rule of congressional gridlock and conservative legislative power had come in the 1930s, when the crisis of the Great Depression led to a disavowal of small-government ideology, and the mid-1960s, when a vibrant civil rights movement and a landslide Democratic election in 1964 created enormously favorable conditions for enacting new federal policies. With 295 Democrats in the House and 68 in the Senate, Lyndon Johnson could realize much of his vision of the Great Society.

The opportunities for massive liberal government expansion had vastly diminished in the succeeding decades, which is why so many progressives were excited about Obama. There had been a sharp rightward turn in national politics as a lively conservative movement took hold throughout the United States. Since Ronald Reagan's election in 1980, the conservative revolution had seemed to be entrenched. Although Reagan was not able to reverse as many policies as he hoped, the regressive tax cuts that he put in place in 1981 took a big bite out of the federal government's fiscal muscle. He weakened a number of key federal agencies by cutting their budgets and staffing them with appointees who were unsympathetic to the policies they were supposed to implement. The anti-environmentalist James Watt served as secretary of the interior. Clarence Thomas, who openly opposed affirmative action, headed the Equal Employment Opportunity Commission.

When the electorate finally voted for another Democratic president in 1992, they chose someone, the Arkansas governor Bill Clinton, who tended to stay within the framework established by conservatism. To be sure, Clinton made a major push for a bold national health care program that would have cut costs, reduced premiums, and expanded access to health insurance. But many of his policies during the rest of his tenure—the North American Free Trade Agreement, welfare reform, budget cuts—were softened versions of what the increasingly conservative Republicans on Capitol Hill were trying to achieve. Clinton, one of the founders of the centrist Democratic Leadership Council, believed that jettisoning some party traditions was the only way that Democrats could survive. Because of his failed efforts on health care, the Republican takeover of Congress in 1994, and his own political inclination to move toward the center, Clinton's presidency did not offer Democrats anything nearly as robust as the policy initiatives of Franklin D. Roosevelt and Johnson. Democrats stood by Clinton when the House Republicans moved to impeach him for perjury about an affair with an intern. But their fervor for Clinton was more a response to the zealous partisanship of Republicans than an expression of enthusiasm for the president.

Though he came of age in the Reagan era, Barack Obama remained committed to the liberal political tradition that had shaped his party for so many decades, updated to fit the realities and experiences of the late twentieth century. Obama's background in community organizing and the time he spent studying at the nation's elite universities had exposed him to the animating ideas that shaped the presidencies from these earlier periods. Although Obama was an intellectual pragmatist who understood that some of his predecessors had overstated the potential of government, a person who was also very calculating about how he positioned himself in public,[2] there was little question among those who knew him that he embraced many of the fundamental liberal traditions of his party.[3]

Obama is part of a generation of liberals who have been lost in the historiographical focus on the "rise of the right" after the 1960s. He is one of many liberal leaders who remained alive and well—and politically active at all levels of government—in the conservative era that followed Ronald Reagan's victory in 1980. Whereas some attention has been paid to the grassroots activists who challenged the nation's rightward drift, we know much less about the politicians who took up this challenge.[4] The contributors to this book look at Obama as one of the most influential figures of this cohort. As president, he attempted to remake liberalism by finding a new role for government in postmanufacturing society and by crafting programs that would be viable within a polity that had shifted far to the right since Johnson's tenure.

Throughout his presidency, Obama proved to be a skilled policymaker, much more than most people realized at the time. Although critics complained that he didn't have enough Johnson in him, his policy output in 2009 and 2010 was remarkable. Unlike Johnson, he didn't love the wheeling and dealing that took place on Capitol Hill, but Obama did have a keen sense of how the institutions of government work and the ways that his team could design policy proposals so that they could survive the political vicissitudes of the period. Faced with the intransigent conservative opposition that I document in my opening essay (chapter 2), Obama was forced to build policies that made an end run around his opponents and created incentives to win over the support of powerful stakeholders, either through the strategic design of legislative programs or the blunt exercise of executive power.

The results were sometimes breathtaking, as journalists Mike Grunwald, Peter Baker, and Jonathan Chait, as well as the political scientists Theda Skocpol and Lawrence Jacobs, have argued in their books.[5] In the first two years of his presidency, Obama obtained support for the Affordable Care Act (ACA), the Dodd-Frank financial regulation, and an economic stimulus bill, a burst of domestic legislation unlike anything the nation had seen in years. Although not all the authors in this volume agree on how much change occurred, some believe it was much more significant than many people realize. As Paul Starr writes, the cumulative effect of Obama's policies was to make great progress in diminishing the inequality that was so rampant in the modern economy. The economic stimulus program, as Eric Rauchway recounts, was very successful at ending the economic crisis conditions under which Obama took office. It may not have been a new New Deal, but it moved the nation out of a deep recession.

Several of the other authors demonstrate how Obama was able to move policy forward, in ways that often were stifled in previous administrations, by using the power of the executive branch. When Congress proved resistant to any further change after Republicans took control in 2010, the president found other means of making an impact. Meg Jacobs, for example, analyzes the notable progress on climate change through executive action. Jeremi Suri reveals the profound changes in foreign policy that occurred under Obama's leadership with the advance of a liberal internationalist agenda that resisted the use of military power, offering an important turn away from the policies of President George W. Bush. Executive power enabled Obama to move the nation away from using military force so readily and to enter into treaties, such as the Iran nuclear deal, that diminished the threat of international conflict.

Besides Obama himself, robust social movements also checked the Supreme Court justices who wanted to undo the New Deal settlement that greatly expanded federal power. Risa Goluboff and Richard Schragger document that the limits to how far conservative justices could rule against policies such as same-sex marriage reflected the dramatic evolution that had taken place in many core social and cultural values since the 1960s. On gay rights, ethnic pluralism, and even racial tolerance, there is much deeper support in the electorate than the success of the conservative revolution would indicate. A vibrant grassroots movement checked reactionary elements seeking to block progress on legislative and judicial changes, as Timothy Stewart-Winter recounts in his essay. The election and the reelection of an African American to the presidency by large portions of the population, Gary Gerstle reminds us, were both historic moments, despite the victory of a reactionary candidate as his successor. It is significant that the candidate running as a defender of Obama's legacy, Hillary Clinton, won more than two million more popular votes than Trump in 2016; Democrats improved their standing in red states like Georgia and Texas. The Obama years likewise helped inspire new groups of progressive social activists— such as Black Lives Matter, Occupy Wall Street, and the Bernie Sanders primary campaign—even if, as Michael Kazin explains, they were often born out of frustration that Obama did not fulfill many of his promises.

The Obama presidency offered a powerful counterweight to the political legacy of Reagan and the conservative movement. The president offered—with a rhetorical vigor we have not seen since the 1960s—a renewed commitment within the Democratic Party to using the federal government as a tool to alleviate social and economic problems. In addition, many of the actual policies he put in place will be hard for the Republicans to undo. A united Republican government has already encountered strong resistance to revoking the Medicaid coverage that twelve million Americans enjoyed under the ACA when Obama left office.

To be sure, there were many ways in which the policy revolution that Obama's supporters envisioned fell short of expectations. In several areas, authors in this volume point out, there was great continuity, either by choice or by political necessity, between the administrations of Obama and President George W. Bush. With regard to education policy, Jonathan Zimmerman recounts, Obama stood behind the federal standards-based approach to reform adopted by Bush, which generated bipartisan opposition. In the realms of counterterrorism, policy in Africa, and urban programs, as Kathryn Olmsted and Jacob Dlamini show, Obama stuck to the path set by his predecessor or other leaders who came before. In other areas, such as immigration, criminal justice reform, and institutional racism, Tom Sugrue, Sarah Coleman, Peniel Joseph, and Matthew Lassiter argue, Obama failed to find ways to advance significant policy change. Nowhere was this more frustrating and disappointing than in race relations. Although many observers celebrated the idea that his election in 2008 was the culmination of the civil rights struggle, the frustration Obama felt, over the succeeding years, with ongoing racial conflict and continued evidence of racial inequality, often deeply inscribed in national institutions, belied that optimism.

A number of policy failures hurt Democrats politically. During Obama's presidency, Democrats did not make much headway in the fight against middle-class insecurity. Some liberals criticized the president's decision to put these economic issues on the back burner as he prioritized health care in his first year. The structural problems inherent in the postmanufacturing economy continued to worsen even as the administration made substantial progress in reducing the divide between the very rich and the poor. In foreign policy, there were certain areas of the world, such as Syria, where the crises that unfolded between 2009 and 2017 seemed to be in part a result of Obama's detached and restrained style. His critics argued that the president was unwilling to spend enough of the nation's international capital on crucial challenges that did not immediately threaten the national interest.

The defining paradox of Obama's presidency, a theme that shapes many of the essays in this volume, is that he turned out to be a very effective policymaker but not a tremendously successful party builder. During his presidency, even as he enjoyed reelection and strong approval ratings toward the end of his term, the Democratic Party suffered greatly. While Republicans reaped huge rewards from the investments they made in congressional and state politics, Democrats watched as their power—as measured in numbers of legislative and gubernatorial seats—dwindled.

To be sure, some of the dilemmas that Democrats faced were not a result of President Obama's strategic choices. The problems that challenged the Democratic Party at the state and local level were not new in 2009. Democrats had been struggling to rebuild the party since the 1980s, and had never fully regained the strength they enjoyed from FDR to LBJ. The reason that President Obama shone so brightly in the 2008 campaign was that he offered such a fresh and distinctive voice for Democrats, one that seemed absent throughout much of the party apparatus. He also mounted a very effective campaign against former Massachusetts governor Mitt Romney in the 2012 election, connecting his Republican opponent to the regressive economic policies of his party at a time when millions of middle-class workers were struggling to get by. Obama was also able to rekindle the excitement of his 2008 election by reminding them that, despite all of the shortcomings of his first term, he had worked hard and made progress on a number of pertinent issues that had been ignored by his predecessor as well as the Republican Congress. And of course, when looking at Capitol Hill it is important to note that the party of the person who occupies the White House usually suffers over the course of a two-term presidency.

But some of the problems that Democrats encountered, which made possible the election of one of the most inexperienced, controversial, and unorthodox Republicans in American history, were connected to Obama's decisions. The fact that Republicans were doing so well in state government and had amassed such a sizable majority in the House was not unconnected to the president. This, too, is part of his legacy, as much as any policy he pushed through Congress.

President Obama's programs were designed in such a way that they did little to strengthen the standing of Democrats as a whole. Congressional Democrats frequently complained that his strategies and policy choices put them at risk. Seeking to expand government with a hidden hand, his policies were crafted in a way that made it hard for the party to claim credit with voters. At the same time, some, such as the ACA, were enormously controversial. In public, Obama tried to deflate his partisan opponents by downplaying the scale and scope of policies such as the economic stimulus package so that they did not attract too much public attention. Whereas most Americans could never miss a bridge or road built by FDR's Public Works Administration, they traveled past projects from Obama's stimulus program without noticing a thing. The subterranean state-building strategy came at the cost of claiming credit for big accomplishments, as Paul Starr argues in his piece. Programs like financial regulation and health care depended on complex regulatory mechanisms that dampened the ability of conservatives to brand them as "big government" and won the support of private interest groups who saw ways to benefit from government. When he couldn't win support for legislation, Obama relied on executive power to achieve his goals, a strategy that could be easily undone by future presidents.

The design of many programs also left them vulnerable. The Dodd-Frank regulations, for instance, created significant space for financial institutions to curtail the impact of the programs. The reforms did not do enough to undercut the power of the interests they were meant to regulate; they provided only a framework for governance rather than more specific rules. The flexibility built into the law gave the financial industry more than enough room to maneuver to weaken its effects. Although some risky activity has been curtailed, Wall Street investors continue to engage in speculative behavior. These frameworks created regulatory programs that could be dismantled by a president and cabinet leaders who were not interested, as is now the case, in carrying out the laws. The programs were not well designed to withstand counterattack.

As historians look back at what happened, some of the blame for the condition of the Democratic Party will have to fall on the former president's choices. The organizational strength of the Democrats at the state and local level has withered under bad leadership, as Theda Skocpol and Vanessa Williamson have argued.[6] Shortly after the 2008 election, Obama's top advisors made a crucial decision when they shifted control of the political machine they had built, with thirteen million email addresses, eight hundred thousand registered users, and three million donors, to the Democratic National Committee. Some advisors, like Christopher Edley, wanted to build on the campaign to energize Democrats to engage in the governance process. Once in the DNC, however, much of the operation was left to languish. "Killing OFA [Obama for America] reduced the possibility of competing for the hearts, minds, and votes of the Tea Party disaffected," one political scientist concluded, and it "killed the one entity possible for institutionalizing the raw energy created by the Obama campaign in 2008."[7] When the national Republican Party and conservative donors made a decision to invest heavily in state and local races in 2010 through Operation REDMAP (Redistricting Majority Project), with the intention of winning control of state legislatures and thus to be able to shape congressional redistricting the following year,[8] President Obama did little to counteract this. The Democrats subsequently lost badly in redistricting battles across the nation. To the dismay of congressional Democrats, the president did not always work hard enough to help the party amass the resources that it needed to fight an aggressive GOP. His Democratic critics complained that Organizing for America, the political campaign operation that he rebuilt in 2012, had always focused on Obama over the interests of the party in the states and localities. Unlike President Franklin Roosevelt in the 1930s and 1940s, Obama did not leave behind a coalition that, at least in the short term, has the muscle to protect what he built.

By the time Obama's presidency ended, Republicans had regained control of the House in 2010 and the Senate in 2014, as well as controlling thirty-four state legislatures. Democrats lost more than one thousand seats in state legislatures, governors' mansions, and Congress during his time in office. Democrats complained that the president pushed them to handle controversial issues without giving them adequate political support in exchange, and without being tough enough against a Republican Party that was moving sharply to the right. And in 2016, the Republican Donald J. Trump was elected president.

When the outcome of the 2016 campaign became clear, Democrats understood the precarious state they faced. Given that the party would be defending more seats than the GOP in 2018, they were even pessimistic about the potential midterm backlash they would normally hope to enjoy. Within the states, the situation was even worse.

Although the full story has yet to be understood, initial evidence indicates that President Obama's political caution may have played a role in shaping the outcome of the election that brought Donald Trump to power and gave Republicans united control of the federal government. While Democrat Hillary Clinton was being pilloried by the Republicans and the press for her email scandal, President Obama was reluctant to disclose anything in the summer of 2016 about the ongoing investigation by the FBI of Russian intervention in the election—as well as contacts between the Trump campaign and the Russians—because he feared that the administration would appear to be meddling in the campaign. When the FBI director James Comey proposed to Secretary of State John Kerry, Attorney General Loretta Lynch, Secretary of Homeland Security Jeh Johnson, and National Security Advisor Susan Rice that he publish an op-ed in the *New York Times* revealing that the FBI was investigating Trump officials for links to the Russian intervention, they shot down the idea.[9] When the White House later revisited the idea of making public the investigation in October, Comey had changed his mind and opposed the idea.[10]

Following the election, Obama understood the damage that his party had suffered. The Republican Party had changed dramatically while he was in the White House. He saw how this was happening, and he was able to overcome its opposition at times, but he could not hold back its electoral success. "We've seen this coming," Obama said as he reflected on the election outcome.

> Donald Trump is not an outlier; he is a culmination, a logical conclusion of the rhetoric and tactics of the Republican Party for the past ten, fifteen, twenty years. What surprised me was the degree to which those tactics and rhetoric completely jumped the rails. There were no governing principles, there was no one to say, "No, this is going too far, this isn't what we stand for." But we've seen it for eight years, even with reasonable people like John Boehner, who, when push came to shove, wouldn't push back against these currents.[11]

The question historians must ask is why this caught Obama by surprise. Why wasn't he more aware? Why didn't he do more to work with the Democratic Party and activists to fight these currents as he saw them gradually building strength? Was he even correct in attributing Trump's victory to the new tactics and strategy of the Republican Party or did he grossly understate the responsibility of Democratic policy failures, such as not doing enough to alleviate middle- and working-class insecurity? In the following pages, some of the nation's best historians offer a preliminary assessment of the Obama presidency.

2

Tea Partied

PRESIDENT OBAMA'S ENCOUNTERS WITH THE CONSERVATIVE-INDUSTRIAL COMPLEX

Julian E. Zelizer

When Illinois state senator Barack Obama delivered his famous keynote address to the Democratic National Convention in 2004, he was full of hope and optimism about moving the nation beyond the partisan divide that separated Republicans and Democrats in Washington. He insisted that the divisions creating gridlock were artificial. "The pundits like to slice-and-dice our country into red states and blue states; red states for Republicans, blue states for Democrats. But I've got news for them, too: We worship an awesome God in the blue states, and we don't like federal agents poking around in our libraries in red states. We coach Little League in the blue states, and, yes, we've got some gay friends in the red states. There are patriots who opposed the war in Iraq and there are patriots who supported the war in Iraq."[1] When one looked at the feelings of most voters, Obama argued, the idea that there was a red and blue America made no sense. Since the partisan divide was artificially constructed, Obama believed it could be overcome. The speech he delivered in Boston inspired many Americans who heard this young African American Democrat speak at a time when the nation seemed mired in bitter and intractable partisan divisions over how President George W. Bush had handled the war on terrorism.

After defeating Senator John McCain in the 2008 presidential election, Obama continued to express this sentiment despite the intensity of the opposition he had encountered on the campaign trail. He still believed that much of the vitriol that emerged when Alaska governor Sarah Palin joined McCain as the vice-presidential nominee was an aberration. This surprised many Democrats, given what they had witnessed. At one point in the campaign, the situation became so heated that Senator McCain had to grab away the microphone from a supporter at a town hall meeting, who questioned the religion and background of McCain's Democratic opponent. These incidents, according to Obama, did not reflect any broader reality. The president-elect resolutely insisted that through an incessant appeal to reason and logic, combined with a healthy dose of pragmatic compromise, it would be possible for a Democratic president to win over substantial numbers of Republicans voters, and to secure votes from the other side of the aisle on key pieces of legislation.[2]

The warning signs turned out to be harbingers. Even during the first two years of his presidency, when Obama enjoyed the distinct advantage of having a united Democratic government and the public perception of a mandate following his historic election victory—combined with the lingering effects on the GOP of President Bush's disastrous approval ratings at the end of his term—Republicans remained steadfast in their opposition to the president. What was more important was that they had a number of institutional bases of power from which to fight him.

Throughout his tenure in the White House, Obama and his supporters gradually discovered just how institutionalized the conservative movement had become over the past few decades. Conservatism had moved beyond the kind of grassroots mobilization that historians such as Lisa McGirr and Kevin Kruse have examined to become an entrenched force in national politics.[3] As a result, the once optimistic Obama found himself to be a president constantly playing partisan defense, presiding over a nation where his opponents maintained immense political power regardless of his approval ratings, popularity in the media, or reelection victory.

Even an election as dramatic as 2008's did not have the capacity to remake the political landscape. Just as Ronald Reagan discovered, after trouncing Jimmy Carter in 1980, that liberal policies and ideas remained entrenched despite the rightward drift of national politics,[4] Obama, who some hoped would have a transformative presidency, learned the same lesson from the opposite political perspective. Since the 1970s, conservative Republicans had been able to build a strong political infrastructure that could not easily be knocked down even if the GOP lost control of the White House. After Richard Nixon resigned from the presidency amid a scandal in 1974, many conservatives felt they needed to construct bases of power in Congress, in the news media, and in the world of interest groups, think tanks, and universities. Although President Bill Clinton encountered the political universe that conservatives had built during his tenure between 1993 and 2001, which culminated in the House voting to impeach him on nearly strict party lines, Obama was the first Democratic president to confront these conservative institutions and organizations after they reached full maturation. When asked by the *New Yorker*'s David Remnick about whether he was less effective at wheeling and dealing than Lyndon Johnson, Obama responded: "When he lost that historic majority, and the glow of that landslide victory [in 1964] faded, he had the same problems with Congress that most presidents at one point or another have."[5] The president could take Speaker of the House John Boehner out to play as much golf and drink as much bourbon as their hearts desired, but it wouldn't make one iota of difference.

Congressional Power

Obama could never figure out a way around the conservative forces in Congress. The legislative branch had been the base of power for conservative Republicans since the 1994 midterm elections, when the GOP, led by Georgian Newt Gingrich, won control of the majority for the first time in forty years. Gingrich had been part of a maverick group of Republicans who in the 1980s argued that for conservatives to influence policy debates they needed to break the Democratic monopoly on congressional power and use the legislative process to advance their goals. Controlling the presidency, he said, would not matter unless conservative Republicans established themselves on Capitol Hill and were willing to use whatever tactics were necessary to win. Gingrich and his allies in the Conservative Opportunity Society (an informal caucus that he formed in 1983) pursued a strategy that centered on challenging the legitimacy of the Democratic Party, which he characterized as corrupt and dictatorial.[6] Following the 1994 elections, House Republicans chose Gingrich to serve as Speaker of the House. Under his leadership, the Republicans successfully pushed the national agenda toward the right and mastered the use of legislative procedure to undercut Democrats. While they controlled the majority until 2006, House Republicans prevented Democrats from participating in legislative deliberations and stacked the process so that Republican bills were in a stronger position to pass. Congressional Republicans centralized power with the Speaker and Senate majority leader, using their control of campaign funds and the distribution of committee chairmanships to ensure party discipline and prevent Democrats from finding any pockets of bipartisan support.[7] House Republicans were also willing to use ethics rules and investigations to bring down vulnerable Democrats and tie up the legislative process with scandals.

Although Republicans lost control of Congress from 2006 to 2010, during this interregnum they continued to demonstrate their ability to aggressively employ legislative procedure to counteract the Democrats. In the Senate, the tools available to the minority could be powerful if a party was willing to use them. Both parties had relied on the filibuster as a normal weapon in partisan combat since the 1960s, but Senate Republicans were willing to do this in new ways. Reviewing the steady rise of Senate obstructionism since the 1970s, the political scientist Steven Smith concluded: "The surge in obstructionism since the election of 2006, when the Democrats regained Senate and House majorities in the second midterm election of President George W. Bush, deserves special notice."[8] The Republicans launched an unprecedented number of filibusters in these years against all kinds of legislation, big and small.[9]

In short, Senate Republicans made it a virtual requirement for Senate Democrats to obtain a supermajority of sixty votes in the upper chamber (the number of votes needed to end a filibuster through cloture) if they wanted anything to pass. As a result, many items did not receive discussion because it was clear there would never be sixty votes of support for legislation. Other measures died in the upper chamber despite majority support. Senate Republicans also stood their ground on judicial and administrative appointments, refusing to agree to selections by President Bush and then President Obama unless the nominees fit the exact criteria that they were looking for. Few did. Federal courts and agencies remained severely understaffed during President Obama's first few years.

Policies such as the minimum wage diminished in value simply because Congress did nothing. By preventing Congress from updating programs to meet new economic conditions, Senate Republicans cut benefits. Obstructionism tended to hurt liberals more than the right.[10]

Few Republicans were willing to buck the party line. When the president repeatedly reached out to Republicans to support him on pressing legislation such as the economic stimulus package and financial regulation, both of which seemed to command strong popular support in the middle of a severe economic meltdown that had depleted the nation's wealth and left millions unemployed, most Republicans refused to go along with any deal. And even though much of his response to the financial crisis built on the policies of President Bush, including the Troubled Asset Relief Program (TARP, which Eric Rauchway calls the "Bush-Obama financial rescue program"), many Republicans acted as if Obama were virtually a socialist.

The driving engine behind the Republican Party in the Obama years was known as the "Tea Party." The Tea Party consisted of a cohort of conservative grassroots activists and Washington insiders who were angry in the aftermath of President George W. Bush's financial bailout of Wall Street in 2008, when they believed that the Republican president had betrayed libertarian principles by using government to save wealthy financial interests as well as homeowners from their own mistakes. They believed that Washington was a corrupt town where members of both parties caved in to the powerful interest groups who inhabited the city. But the main target of this nascent movement was President Obama. Some activists were motivated by unhappiness about having an African American president, but most of them were simply furious that a liberal Democrat and former professor had been victorious over McCain and Palin. The movement gained its name following a televised tirade by the CNBC reporter Rick Santelli who on February 19, 2009, on the floor of the Chicago Mercantile Exchange, called for a "tea party," a reference to the Boston Tea Party, to oppose the Obama agenda. The Tea Party movement was not a coherent entity but rather an amalgam of local chapters, protests, and organizations that took shape in community centers, churches, and diners, and through social media and websites such as Breitbart.com, to express their anger about Washington. Tea Party Republicans tended to be white, elderly, and middle class, with many of them, ironically, depending on government services like Social Security or veterans' benefits. The movement, as Theda Skocpol and Vanessa Williamson argued, gained its power by simultaneously being a top-down and bottom-up phenomenon.[11] The local chapters found national organizational support from FreedomWorks, a Washington-based libertarian advocacy group that was led by former House Republican Majority Leader Richard Armey.

Those who identified as being part of the Tea Party tended to be concerned about big-government spending, federal regulations of the environment and economy, and deficits; they were less interested in social issues such as abortion, which had animated the culture wars of the 1980s. On one issue, they were all in agreement: President Obama and the Democratic Congress had to be stopped in their tracks at all costs. The activists, and the legislators who supported them, believed that radical action was necessary to prevent the administration from pushing through programs that would endanger the country. While Obama remained in their crosshairs, they were also determined to bring down Republicans who were part of the "Washington establishment."

When confronted with opposition from increasingly strident Republicans, the president adopted a strategy that frustrated liberals in his party. He would start with a compromise, in the hope of sealing an early bipartisan deal, only to give away more of the provisions in the bill without Republicans ever showing any signs of interest in negotiation. In the best circumstances, the dance would end with Obama pushing watered-down legislation through Congress that barely received any Republican votes anyway. "Mr. Obama and Democrats in Congress have to hang tough—no more gratuitous giveaways in the attempt to sound reasonable," wrote the economist Paul Krugman in the *New York Times*.[12] "Bipartisanship" in 2009 and 2010 meant the president's ability to secure a handful of Republican votes (two or three) rather than what happened in the 1960s, when Lyndon Johnson was able to swing large numbers of Republican votes in the House and the Senate to his side. Obama's greatest domestic victory, the Affordable Care Act, took place only because the administration listened to congressional Democrats under the leadership of Speaker Nancy Pelosi and included the measure in the budget reconciliation process, which prohibited Senate Republicans from employing a filibuster. The healthcare legislation did not receive a single Republican vote, the first time that a major domestic initiative of this scale and scope passed Congress on a strictly partisan basis.

Building on the backlash against President Bush's financial bailout and President Obama's Affordable Care Act, Republicans retook control of the House in the midterm elections. The Republican campaigns focused on attacking the president's Affordable Care Act and criticizing the administration for failing to revive the economy. Many Republicans connected President Obama and Speaker Pelosi, who they said were symbols of big-government liberalism and were pushing the country in a socialist direction. Republicans were exuberant on election night, when the short period of Democratic rule came to an abrupt end. Congressional Republicans, who had already caused trouble in Obama's first two years, now had the benefit of majoritarian power in the lower chamber. In the Senate, the powers afforded to the minority party enabled disciplined and dogmatic Republicans to tie up legislation and appointments even without having a majority. On the eve of the 2010 midterm elections, Senate Minority Leader Mitch McConnell told one journalist, "We need to say to everyone on Election Day, 'Those of you who helped make this a good day, you need to go out and help us finish the job.'" When asked what the job was, McConnell responded: "The single most important thing we want to achieve is for President Obama to be a one-term president."[13]

During the 2010 midterm elections, Republicans had also solidified their prospects for maintaining and expanding their House majority by investing heavily in state legislative races shortly before redistricting was to occur in many states. Their goal was to capture a large number of the state legislatures that would be redrawing congressional lines so that they could gerrymander districts in ways that favored the GOP. Republican political operatives had worked hard to institutionalize this advantage in the House. Chris Jankowski, a tactician for the Republican State Leadership Committee, came up with a plan to target campaign money toward regaining control of state governments where reapportionment would take place. The operation, called REDMAP (Redistricting Majority Project), was never secret. Karl Rove outlined in the *Wall Street Journal* exactly what the GOP planned to do. In a local race in Pennsylvania, for instance, Democrat David Levdansky, a thirteen-term state representative, found himself under assault. He faced a barrage of nationally funded advertising claiming in misleading television spots and home mailers that he had voted to spend $600 million on a library to honor Arlen Specter, the controversial U.S. senator who had left the Republicans to join the Democrats. This didn't sit well with local voters in the middle of a deep recession. He paid the price: Republican Rick Saccone narrowly defeated him. "The f—ing Arlen Specter Library," Levdansky commented after losing.[14] Once Republicans flipped this seat, they gained control of the state's lower chamber. The scene played out all over the country. Republicans won majorities in ten of the fifteen states that would be redrawing their districts.

Following the 2010 election, in which Obama admitted to taking a "shellacking," congressional Republicans immediately went to work using their newfound power. From the start, the GOP made clear that the administration would find no support for any domestic initiative. The Republicans who were entering Congress had no interest in working with the president, regardless of whether he was willing to abandon his own base by reaching agreements with them. The brief period of liberal legislating was over. The new generation of Republicans was not hesitant about using its power to keep this promise and to make sure that older Republicans did not accede to any compromises. Fueled by the freshman class of Tea Party members, Republicans in the House and Senate were determined to prevent the president from moving forward with any of his legislative agenda. They were the children of Newt Gingrich and took his tactics to new extremes. The Tea Party members constituted approximately forty votes in the House Republican Caucus, enough to make them impossible for Speaker John Boehner to ignore. Representative Tim Huelskamp, who held a Ph.D. in public administration, won a seat in Kansas by stressing his roots in farming and staunch opposition to big government. South Carolina Republican Mick Mulvaney, who studied economics in college, decided to enter politics when he concluded that Republicans were spending too much money in the Bush era. He ran for office as a firm opponent of abortion, family planning, and federal deficits. More than anything, he gained a reputation for being someone who had absolutely no tolerance for Republican leaders who were willing to compromise. There were members who had been in office for a few years that provided leadership to this group. Ohio Republican Jim Jordan, who represented a rust belt district that was 89 percent white and the proud home of three radio stations that broadcast Rush Limbaugh's show, voted as a solid conservative. He believed that he was on a mission to change Washington and to change the Republican Party. A former champion wrestler in high school, Jordan proved to be a master of the technical side of public policy and understood how to play the legislative game. He believed firmly in using obstructionist techniques to advance his cause. Although there was no filibuster in the House, he learned that there were several procedural tools available to House members, particularly in the majority, to block a president.[15]

Speaker John Boehner, a chain-smoking midwestern conservative who thought that the new Republicans were too extreme and didn't know how to govern, entered into an uneasy alliance with the Tea Party caucus. The Speaker concluded that the Tea Party Republicans had enough members to block any of his legislative priorities that they did not approve of. At the same time, he felt that the Tea Party could offer the kind of political energy the Republican Party needed to rebuild itself after the defeats it had suffered in 2008 and to mobilize opposition to the president. The Republican Party as a whole quickly shifted rightward after the midterms as a result of this post-2010 alliance.

To complement the committed conservative Tea Party citizens who came to town hall meetings to stir up trouble for Democratic legislators and who went to the voting booth to elect a different kind of Republican politician, there was an influential network of donors who were funding these efforts and backing candidates who stayed to the right. The multibillionaires David and Charles Koch, who had founded the political advocacy group FreedomWorks and created the Americans for Prosperity, worked with a network of wealthy allies to distribute a sizable campaign war chest, bringing together fellow donors, conducting seminars to spread their libertarian ideas, and devising campaign strategies to assist conservative Republican candidates who were loyal to their agenda.[16]

Whereas Gingrich and his colleagues had been willing to shut down the federal government during a high-stakes confrontation with President Clinton over entitlement spending in 1995 and 1996, the Tea Party Republicans were willing to close the government over the most mundane budget disputes and to send the entire federal government into default if necessary. The budget battles in 2011 shocked the Obama administration by providing a clear sense of just how far to the right congressional Republicans had moved. House Republicans, who were intent on repealing Obamacare, as the ACA health care program came to be called, insisted that President Obama agree to a deficit reduction package far more draconian than the administration was willing to accept. The Speaker no longer controlled his own colleagues. To force the president's hand, the House Republicans threatened that they would not raise the federal debt ceiling, which enabled the federal government to pay for obligations that Congress had made. Although there had been other moments since the 1980s when members of both parties had voted against raising the debt ceiling, the protests had always been symbolic and the votes were taken with full knowledge that the other side had sufficient support to keep the government afloat.

This time the situation was different. Tea Party Republicans were prepared to block the increase, which would send the government into default. When the Speaker proposed a compromise, his fellow Republicans refused to budge. Their zeal became clear on May 31, 2011, when House Republicans surprised many observers by voting against legislation to raise the debt ceiling without deficit reduction (the authorization failed, 318–97). Two hundred thirty-six Republicans present voted against the bill. The crisis did not reach a conclusion until July 31, two days before the Treasury would no longer have the borrowing authority it needed. The resolution came only after the president acceded, over the opposition of House Democrats, to the Budget Control Act of 2011. The legislation, which President Obama accepted for fear of another financial meltdown, was a huge blow to liberals. The legislation cut spending by $1.2 trillion over ten years. It also established a joint committee to produce deficit-reduction proposals. If this committee and Congress could not reach agreement on specific spending cuts to achieve the stated goals of the bill, the legislation stipulated there would be automatic across-the-board cuts in all spending, including on defense (a mechanism called sequestration). The sequestration would take effect in January 2013.

Any Republican who strayed from the party line faced the threat of a primary challenge from the Tea Party. This was where the redistricting plan of 2010 took effect. With control of so many state governments, Republicans had launched the second phase of their plan. Using sophisticated software, GOP party operatives crafted favorable districts packed with conservative white voters, using the kind of psychographic data available to companies like Amazon.[17] National conservative funders were willing to provide money to challengers in these and other Republican districts when any incumbent diverged from the party line on an issue like the budget. Republican incumbents would be forced to raise gigantic emergency campaign funds to fight off primary challengers. The easier solution, which most of them adopted as they scrambled for money, was simply to avoid angering the right.

Republican congressional obstructionism would not end in the coming years. Indeed, it would become the norm. Before and after Obama's decisive reelection victory in 2012 against Mitt Romney, congressional Republicans continued to engage the administration in budget battles and refused to allow any legislation to make it through the chamber. Republicans were realizing that the political incentives at work in congressional politics differed from those in presidential politics, which were sensitive to long-term demographic changes, such as the growth of Latino populations, single women, educated suburban voters, and the emergence of millennials, who tended to be liberal on social and cultural issues. But for members of Congress retaining their majorities was central, and they pushed the party to continue its rightward drift. In 2013, they would force a sixteen-day shutdown of the government during a budget impasse. Many of the party's top leaders emerged from this Tea Party generation. Texas senator Ted Cruz, elected in 2012, was a Princeton- and Harvard-educated champion debater, married to a banker at Goldman Sachs, who had no hesitation at all about raising the temperature on Capitol Hill to pursue a conservative agenda. He worked with House Republicans to build support for draconian threats like not raising the debt ceiling in order to achieve their goals. He denounced senior leaders like Mitch McConnell as liars and thieves who told voters one thing about their right-wing beliefs and then cut deals that enabled the party to enjoy the benefits of government pork. Cruz believed that there was an establishment in Washington that had destroyed both political parties. His views on issues like immigration, gay marriage, the budget, and race were on the extreme end of the political spectrum and far off-center of the electorate. Other leaders, like Speaker Boehner, would be forced to leave when they no longer served the needs of the Tea Party. "Garbage men get used to the smell of bad garbage," Boehner explained in an interview about how he had been able to deal with the younger members of his caucus.

Even when a bipartisan group of senators that included Republicans such as John McCain and Marco Rubio attempted to move forward on immigration reform, House Republicans stood firm. In the Senate, the judicial appointment process ground to a halt. Once the Republicans retook control of the Senate in the 2014 midterm elections, their grip on the legislative branch was complete. Although some politicians said that the midterms signaled that Americans wanted the parties to work together, the gridlock only worsened. When President Obama nominated Judge Merrick Garland to replace the deceased Supreme Court justice Antonin Scalia in 2016, Senate Republicans said right away that they would not hold confirmation hearings on any nominee. The next president should fill the vacancy on the Supreme Court. The president spent much of his energy using executive power on issues such as immigration reform and climate change because the power of congressional Republicans blocked any opening for achieving his objectives through legislation.

Back in the House, North Carolina Republican Mark Meadows, a former businessman elected in 2012, had joined forces with Jim Jordan to establish the Freedom Caucus in 2015, which organized Tea Party Republicans into a cohesive and efficient group that could speedily whip up the vote of their members via a novel app-based vote-counting system. The Freedom Caucus had enough members and organizational savvy to prevent the Republican leadership from moving forward without them.

A Conservative Echo Chamber

Congress was not the only place where the infrastructure of the right became a major obstacle to the president. The conservative media had become a formidable force, too.[18] During the age of cable television, the Internet, and talk radio, conservatives had made a massive effort to build media outlets that were sympathetic to their views. They believed that during the era of "objective" journalism in the early Cold War and the 1960s, most reporters had in fact supported liberal views, which biased their stories. The effort of movement activists to build a distinct media world dated back to the Cold War, with radio personalities such as Clarence Manion, whose show was a must-listen for right-wing warriors.[19] Most conservatives believed that the information that Americans read or heard about was tilted decidedly to the left.

Technological innovations had created opportunities for conservatives to change the dynamics of media coverage. Most important, cable television increased the bandwidth available for new kinds of networks that had a more pointed outlook. The end of the Fairness Doctrine in 1987 allowed broadcasters to showcase hosts and guests who had very specific points of view, without inviting everyone to the taping.[20] The result of these changes was a proliferation of conservative-oriented news channels. The main force in the new conservative media was the Fox News Network, created in 1996. The network, which was funded by Rupert Murdoch and run by Roger Ailes, became a major source of conservative information.[21] The stories were often connected to and coordinated with Republican congressional themes. There were also websites such as Breitbart.com and the *Drudge Report* that offered twenty-four-hour online outlets for the dissemination of conservative ideas and links to right-wing stories regardless of their validity or source. The comments sections also offered space for readers to "talk back" to the journalists and each other. In this world, misinformation spread quickly, and a Democratic administration had to spend a substantial amount of time responding to and rebutting claims that had little basis in fact. The liberal equivalents in the media, such as MSNBC and the *Huffington Post*, did not command the same kind of audience in terms of loyalty or size.

By the time Obama became president, conservatives were primarily listening to their own sources of news. According to Matt Grossman and David Hopkins, Republican voters trusted only Fox News and openly conservative media outlets, in contrast to Democratic voters, who still read and watched a more diverse and eclectic range of sources. The line separating Republican politics and the media was no longer clear, with figures moving back and forth (seven congressional Republicans in 2016 had been radio hosts, while ten entered that business after leaving Capitol Hill).[22]

During his presidency, Obama found himself continually struggling to shape the national conversation by rebutting the kinds of stories and information that this media produced. One of the most frustrating and bizarre stories had to do with his birthplace. Rumors had been circulating since his speech at the Democratic Convention in 2004, when some bloggers claimed that he was a Muslim who received his education at an Indonesian madrassa. During the 2008 election, rumors emerged from fringe groups that Obama had not been born in the United States. Some Democratic supporters of Hillary Clinton in the primaries circulated emails reiterating this claim. The emails made their way to various conservative blogs, which pointed to the accusations as evidence that Obama's might not be a legitimate presidency. The first time the story appeared in an official outlet was on June 9, 2008, when one columnist wrote in the *National Review Online* that Obama should show the public his birth certificate. The implication of the attacks on his origins was that since he was not (they claimed) a natural-born citizen, he did not fulfill the requirements of Article Two of the Constitution. The rumors claimed that his birth certificate had been forged and that he had been born in Kenya, not Hawaii. When a fact-checking site (FactCheck.org) inspected the document and reported that it was legitimate, the *National Review* was satisfied but most of the birthers ignored the findings.[23]

After the 2008 election was over, the accusations did not stop. There was now a vast media world to keep the conversation alive. One prominent antitax advocate in Chicago named Robert Schultz purchased an ad in the *Chicago Tribune* that claimed that Obama had been born in Kenya and had rejected becoming an American citizen.[24] Schultz ran a website called *We the People Foundation for Constitutional Education*, which was devoted to building support to prevent Obama from being officially confirmed by the Electoral College as president. Various conservative radio talk show hosts such as Rush Limbaugh and Michael Savage spent significant parts of their broadcasts in December and January ruminating about the issue. There were even celebrities like the Hollywood film actor Charlie Sheen who in interviews made statements about the question. Republican Alan Keyes, a conservative radio talk show host who had unsuccessfully run for his party's nomination, filed a lawsuit based on these claims to block Obama from becoming president.

The charge intended to discredit the legitimacy of the first African American president. The birther movement played directly into racially charged opposition to the presidency of an African American that had been barely below the surface since he ran. In 2009 and 2010, more prominent voices within the GOP gave expression to these claims and they found more than ample opportunity in the right-wing media to discuss this conspiracy theory. Senator Jim Inhofe of Oklahoma claimed that birthers "have a point" and should pursue the issue. Although Obama had posted a copy of his birth certificate on a website during the campaign to rebut the accusations, the birthers claimed that the document had been digitally forged. The charges were repeated by more and more mainstream politicians in the GOP. Senator Richard Shelby, a former Blue Dog Democrat turned Republican, said in a town hall meeting when asked about the rumors: "Well, his father was Kenyan and they said he was born in Hawaii, but I haven't seen any birth certificate."[25]

Each statement found its way into the conservative media, where the topic was discussed, rehashed, and debated. The hosts of these shows could spend every minute in between commercial breaks discussing whether the rumors were true. In July 2009, Lou Dobbs demanded on his syndicated radio show, "Just produce [the birth certificate] and be done with it." During an interview with a conservative radio talk show host named Rusty Humphries, Sarah Palin said that she thought this was a "fair question, just like I think past associations and past voting records—all of that is fair game." Newt Gingrich told Fox News that Obama's policies could only be understood by those who grasped "Kenyan, anticolonial behavior." The new governor of Georgia (elected in the Republican victories in 2010), Nathan Deal, gained some instant national media attention by announcing, "I am joining several of my colleagues in the House in writing a letter to the president asking that he release a copy of his birth certificate so we can have an answer to this question." Senator David Vitter explained to one crowd: "I know all the information I've been able to get my hands on through the media. But obviously with the mainstream media as a filter, that's not a whole lot. I personally don't have standing to bring litigation in court. But I support conservative legal organizations and others who would bring that to court. I think that is the valid and most possibly effective grounds to do so." One Tea Party leader, Judson Phillips, lent his support to an investigation conducted by the sheriff of Maricopa County, Arizona, Joe Arpaio, saying, "The person who forged the document is the easiest target and as a matter of criminal law, a prosecution of him or her would be pretty easy."[26] The topic received extensive airtime on national radio and television shows hosted by Dobbs, Sean Hannity, Rush Limbaugh, and others.

The worlds of the conservative news media and presidential politics melded together around the birther issue in 2011 when real estate mogul and reality television star Donald Trump took up the issue. Trump, who was considering a presidential run, started to become interested in the birther comments. He had not previously opposed Obama. But as the 2010 midterms approached, he started to map out a plan of attacking the president and gaining national attention for his own political views. The birther issue would be front and center. Trump called Joseph Farah, a fringe writer who had been promoting birther ideas on his far-right conservative website WorldNetDaily.com, founded in 1997. Farah, a one-time leftist who had been arrested in a May Day antiwar demonstration against Vietnam in the 1970s, was now a culture warrior for the right. The former reporter for the *Los Angeles Herald Examiner* was a conservative aggregator who devoted much of his website's space to these stories, along with dramatic click-bait headlines. Trump and Farah discussed different strategies they could use to gain mainstream attention for the birther issue. Trump, according to one account, was willing to send private detectives to Hawaii to investigate the claims and dig up material for his appearances.[27]

For Trump, the key would be to raise these concerns outside the conservative media. He wanted to bring the conversation that had been nurtured on right-wing television, radio, and Internet networks to the rest of the broadcasting world. In March, he went on the popular morning show *Good Morning America* to talk about whether Obama had released a forged birth certificate. He admitted to being a "little skeptical" about whether Obama had been born in Hawaii. Trump said: "Growing up no one knew him. The whole thing is very strange." Given his prominence as the star of the reality show *The Apprentice*, which had millions of viewers, Trump instantly became a major figure in the birther movement. He went on another morning talk show, *The View*, where he told the panel of female hosts that he wanted Obama to show Americans his birth certificate: "I want him to show his birth certificate. There's something on that birth certificate he doesn't like." And then on NBC's *Today Show* on April 7, 2011, Trump repeated that he was dubious about the president's citizenship. "Three weeks ago when I started, I thought he was probably born in this country," Trump said. "Right now, I have some real doubts." Even if some of the hosts sat aghast as he made these claims to mainstream audiences, there he was on the air saying what he wanted to enormous audiences.

When the administration decided to release a copy of the birth certificate on April 27, 2011, Trump declared victory. "I am very proud of myself," he boasted. The campaign had brought him immense attention. African American leaders like Jesse Jackson condemned Trump for stoking racial fears.

During the White House Correspondents' Dinner in 2012, the president took some shots at Trump. The real estate mogul had caught on to the power of Twitter that year when he blasted out a statement that there was "an 'extremely credible source'" who told him the president's birth certificate was a "fraud." Obama joked to the reporters at the dinner that "no one is happier, no one is prouder, to put this birth certificate matter to rest than the Donald." When the audience started laughing, Obama delivered his punch line with the force of a comedian: "And that's because he can finally get back to focusing on the issues that matter: Like, did we fake the moon landing."[28]

But good jokes and official documents could not quell the stories. Even after the release of the birth certificate, the story continued and doubters found space to talk about these rumors. In 2012, Breitbart.com published a story about a document that falsely challenged the validity of Obama's defense. The story featured a copy of a promotional booklet in 1991 by Obama's literary agency, Acton & Dystel, which claimed that he had been "born in Kenya and raised in Indonesia and Hawaii."[29] Although the founder of the website, Andrew Breitbart, claimed that he was not a birther, the website was willing to run with the story. Republican political consultant Roger Stone praised Trump for what he had done. Stone said that many core Republican voters believed "the president is foreign-born," as a result of the birthers' campaign, "and Trump has an ability to interject any idea that is outside of the mainstream into the mainstream."[30]

The accusations had their effect. According to one study in the *American Journal of Political Science*, "birtherism" was one of the most well known and popular conspiracy theories by 2010 and 2012. Eric Oliver and Thomas Wood found that 94 percent of the people they surveyed in 2011 knew about the birther arguments, more than any of the other conspiracies they had asked about. Although only 11 percent strongly agreed with the claims and 13 percent agreed, a striking number of people had heard about this fringe argument. Republicans and persons identified as conservatives were more likely to support birther arguments than Democrats and liberals, so there was a strong partisan dimension.[31]

The administration tried to reach out to a greater number of voters by using new forms of media. President Obama, for instance, appeared on the online show *Between Two Ferns* to promote his healthcare program. He traveled to the comedian Marc Maron's basement in California to speak about gun control and money in politics on Maron's popular podcast, entitled *WTF?*, a name that seemed to capture some of the sentiment that the president felt about the state of politics. But none of these media outreach efforts could match the powerful force shaping the news that was coming from the right.

Interest Groups, Think Tanks, and Big Money

After his reelection victory against Romney, Obama hoped that he might be able to use some of the momentum from the victory, even with Republicans in control of Congress, to make progress on key issues on which he had not gained much traction in his first term. Most experts believed that the election proved that Republicans had to move to the center if they hoped to remain a viable national party in presidential elections. The growing power of suburban voters as well as the demographic changes that were making the nation more ethnically and racially diverse meant that a staunchly right-wing party could not survive. It was inevitable, the experts said, that the Republican Party needed to change. But Obama found that, in many areas, powerful interest groups and think tanks had the ability to prevent any kind of serious legislative progress on wedge issues regardless of changing political circumstances, crises, or shifts in public opinion.

Nowhere was this clearer than on the issue of gun control, where the president was desperate to make progress on imposing more legislative restrictions on the ability of Americans to purchase assault weapons. A horrendous school shooting in Newtown, Connecticut, on December 12, 2012, shocked the nation. A twenty-year-old shooter named Adam Lanza killed first his mother and then twenty students and six staffers at the Sandy Hook Elementary School before committing suicide.

The shooting, like others that had come before it, led to public outcries for Congress to impose stricter gun-control measures. The sentiment was so strong that the president, who believed in such restrictions, moved forward with a proposal. The polls showed that there was strong public support for legislative action, which gave the White House confidence. The national gun lobby blamed gun-free schools for creating a dangerous environment. Disagreeing with the lobby, California senator Dianne Feinstein introduced legislation to ban assault weapons one month after the shooting took place.

When her colleagues in the Senate considered the assault weapons ban, as well as compromises that were floated by centrist Democrats, it looked as if something might pass. One of the biggest changes was that there were more congressional Democrats willing to push back against the gun-rights lobby and, more important, a president championing the cause.

But despite the public outcry, the National Rifle Association, combined with even more conservative groups like the Gun Owners of America, stood their ground and intensified their pressure on legislators to hold firm. They threatened to withhold campaign funds from any legislator who bolted. They mobilized local chapters to contact their representatives and senators to warn them of the consequences of voting in favor of any bill. They would also be willing to finance primary challenges against Republicans who decided they wanted to move to the center. Speaker Boehner warned that there was little chance of the legislation passing in the House, given that the Freedom Caucus had no appetite for the measure, which created a strong disincentive for any Senate Republican to be too bold. The vice president of the National Association for Gun Rights sent a letter to all of its members when a compromise plan emerged from West Virginia Democrat Joe Manchin that would impose tougher background checks and limit sales at gun shows: "I've warned you from the beginning," he said in his email, "that our gravest danger was an inside-Washington driven deal."[32] The organization instantly jammed the telephones and filled the email inboxes of senators, including Republican Pat Toomey, who was cosponsoring the bill, demanding that they drop their support for it.

When the legislation died in the Senate in March 2013, with Senator Harry Reid admitting that proponents could not muster the sixty votes necessary for passage, President Obama considered this to be one of his greatest defeats, and a symbol in his mind of why Washington was broken. Even Machin's compromise went down to defeat. With 92 percent of the public favoring universal background checks, Machin's bill had seemed destined for victory. It was not. The president called the defeat a "shameful day" in Washington. He would repeat this process several times in the coming years, each time in the aftermath of a horrific shooting and each time walking away without any legislation. During the podcast interview with Marc Maron, Obama lashed out against the power the gun-rights lobby wielded despite these tragedies. "This is unique to our country," the president said. "There is no other advanced nation on earth that tolerates multiple shootings on a regular basis and considers it normal. And to some degree that's what's happened in this country." He blamed the failure on the political process. "Unfortunately, the grip of the NRA on Congress is extremely strong," Obama said.[33]

The gun-rights issue was only one example where a powerful array of interest groups, think tanks, and donors prevented a liberal Democratic president from putting pressure on Congress. He saw the same story repeated on issues such as immigration reform and climate change, where "inevitable" reforms and electoral pressures on Republicans to move toward the center went absolutely nowhere when confronted with the powerful organizational forces that defended the policy status quo.

A Sobered Pragmatist

When President Obama completed his second term in office, he sounded like a very different man than the person who spoke in Boston in 2004. He was sobered and frustrated, understanding much better the political world that he had entered after his historic election. He was much more willing to use executive power to achieve his goals, although even there he found many of his directives tied up in the courts when conservatives mounted instant legal challenges to any of his efforts to circumvent the legislative process. Trump's presidential campaign built directly on this infrastructure, revealing to much of the nation just how much the Republican Party had changed over recent decades. Trump found a way, at least in the short term, to turn the conservative strategy into a winning presidential campaign.

In his farewell address to the nation, even while warning of the ways that polarization threatened the nation's democracy, Obama still held onto his optimistic faith in the "power of ordinary Americans to bring about change—that faith has been rewarded in ways I couldn't possibly have imagined."[34] Yet when Obama left office in 2017, he did so with a tempered spirit, understanding how entrenched conservatism had become on a number of fronts so that the swings that occurred in elections were incapable of really remaking the political world, and his legislative successes would remain tenuous once he left office.

3

Neither a Depression nor a New Deal

BAILOUT, STIMULUS, AND THE ECONOMY

Eric Rauchway

The economy overtook Barack Obama's presidency before he assumed office. By the time voters chose him to become the forty-fourth president on November 4, 2008, a financial crisis had already reached sufficient magnitude to prompt comparison to the disaster of 1929–1933, and reckoning with it became the principal duty for both the outgoing administration of George W. Bush and the embryonic Obama White House. As *New York Times* columnist David Leonhardt noted, Democrats had spent years thinking about how to remedy structural problems afflicting the American economy: health care, inequality, and the budget deficit among them—but the emergency superseded their hopes and plans. Austan Goolsbee, an economist and an Obama advisor, observed, "Unfortunately, the next president's No. 1 priority is going to be preventing the biggest financial crisis in possibly the last century from turning into the next Great Depression." Invoking the first term of Franklin D. Roosevelt was apt: in 1933, the president-elect also had to set aside his immediate plans for reform to reverse a catastrophic failure of the U.S. banking system. Roosevelt's policies in his inaugural winter of 1933 became the basis for his New Deal, and recovery from the Great Depression began the moment he took office. Obama's policies of his inau-

gural winter of 2009 might well have averted an economic crisis of comparable severity to the Great Depression and begun a recovery, but they also
ensured the absence of anything much resembling another New Deal, and
the effects of these efforts to thwart a global catastrophe would hang over
the rest of his presidency.[1]

With a scant six weeks to go before the 2008 election, astute observers
felt a sense of historic occasion, not just because then-senator Obama stood
a chance of becoming the first African American president, but because the
country was increasingly obviously beset by, as Obama said, the "most serious financial crisis since the Great Depression." In September, Obama's
Republican opponent and fellow senator John McCain first declared, "the
fundamentals of the economy are strong," and then announced he would
suspend his campaign, devoting himself to work in Congress to address the
financial crisis. Obama conferred with congressional Democrats while continuing his own campaign for the White House. At that moment, one journalist reported, both presidential contenders were being treated in Washington as the "leaders of their respective parties."[2]

And unlike McCain, it appears Obama's intervention had important consequences, both immediate and lasting. Lawmakers told reporters that, despite the dramatic suspension of the Republican campaign in the name of
financial rescue, "no McCain imprint appears to be on the final bailout package moving through Congress." McCain would vote for the bill (as would
Obama) but his apparent influence extended no further than his "aye."[3]

By contrast, some congressional Democrats said privately that Obama
himself had persuaded them to support the bill. Indeed, on its first outing
before Congress the bill had met stiff opposition from both Democrats
and Republicans. Chris Dodd, Democratic chairman of the Senate Banking Committee, said, "This proposal is stunning and unprecedented in its
scope—and lack of detail," going to on to say it put "not just our economy . . . at risk, but our Constitution as well," while his Republican col-
league Richard Shelby complained the bill was "aimed at rescuing the same
financial institutions that created this crisis." The serving Treasury secretary, Hank Paulson, and his ally, president of the Federal Reserve Bank of
New York Timothy Geithner, had not assiduously courted members of
Congress, instead asking a grant of emergency authority immediately and
without legislative hindrance—or as Geithner said, "I just wanted Congress
to pass it as fast as possible while screwing it up as little as possible."[4]

Obama exhibited a characteristically more emollient approach—he was
not evidently more scrupulous than Bush administration officers about the

substance of a broad and unprecedented grant of executive power that might disregard constitutional barriers, but he was more sensitive than they to the niceties of getting Congress to support such a law. He contacted the White House to express his willingness to assist in getting the bill through; he spoke likewise to Democrats in Congress. The bill initially failed in the House of Representatives, where the Democrats voted for it by a majority, but Republicans overwhelmingly opposed it. Then, after extensive lobbying from Obama, among others, enough lawmakers changed their mind to pass the bill. Congressional Republicans ultimately split almost evenly, with 91 of the 202 GOP members supporting the bill. For Obama, it was proof of his often-asserted belief that Americans of both parties could cooperate in the national interest.[5]

The passage of the Emergency Economic Stabilization Act of 2008 on October 3, with the support of the Bush administration, both candidates for president, and a bipartisan majority, gave the secretary of the treasury (then Paulson, soon to be Geithner) authority to spend $700 billion to relieve financial stress through the Troubled Asset Relief Program (TARP). For the Bush administration, the win inspired little enthusiasm. The Bush White House had long supported financial deregulation. For the congressional Republican Party, too, it was a source of ambivalence; the House minority leader, John Boehner of Ohio, supported the bill, but had to endure sniping from colleagues who said it forced the taxpayer to "pick up the tab for Wall Street's party." With the GOP divided between establishmentarians willing to pay that check lest disaster ensue, and outsiders content to let the system collapse, ownership of the policy devolved on the Democratic Party, and specifically Barack Obama. At least one prominent Democrat comprehended the risk of adopting this policy birthed by a Republican administration and Wall Street: the former Treasury secretary, Lawrence Summers, a man "known for being blunt, to put it mildly," as Federal Reserve Chair Ben Bernanke said. Summers told Fed officials that bank bailouts might well fail, and even if they succeeded, it would "invite legitimately all kinds of charges of 'helping friends.'" Summers's concerns were borne out, as the Obama campaign's promise of hope and change was overtaken by events and the new president's implementation of what became known simply as "the bailouts" grew into an immediate and ongoing irritant to critics on both the left and right.[6]

The bailouts encompassed more than just TARP's activities after its official creation, and included ad hoc decisions made by the Bush administration earlier in 2008, including notably the rescues of investment bank Bear

Stearns, insurance company American International Group (AIG), and the government takeover of the Federal National Mortgage Association and Federal Home Loan Mortgage Corporation (Fannie Mae and Freddie Mac) through which the U.S. Treasury assumed liabilities in mortgage guarantees and related obligations exceeding $7 trillion. In the first spring of the Obama administration, the bailouts extended beyond financial firms to the auto manufacturers General Motors and Chrysler. Bailout proponents justified the public assumption of risk by saying that otherwise the entire financial system—not only in the United States, but around the world—would otherwise collapse, destroying much of the economy. It would become nearly impossible to borrow money. Business would stop expanding and start to contract. Rising unemployment would mean unpaid debts, foreclosures, and further collapse. As vile as it might seem to rescue businesspeople and bankers from their own greed and shortsightedness, it would be worse to cheer on their discomfiture if it meant severe pain for many others.

Despite these arguments, the bailouts tended to remain unpopular. Geithner said "we hit the political sweet spot where the right, the left, and much of the middle disapproved of our actions." Many Americans went past disapproval to rage. From the right came the live, spittle-flecked television tirade of CNBC journalist Rick Santelli, railing from the floor of the Chicago Mercantile Exchange against mortgage relief, saying it was wrong to "subsidize the losers' mortgages," proposing a "Tea Party" revolt for "capitalists" while traders cheered him on. This moment was often credited with inspiring the subsequent "Tea Party" movement in the Republican Party. Activists adopted Santelli's rhetoric, using it to organize protests both online and in person, ultimately mounting primary challenges that pulled the Republican Party to the right.[7]

From the left came the print campaign of journalist and bestselling author Matt Taibbi, who described the argument for the bailouts as "one of the biggest and most elaborate falsehoods ever sold to the American people. We were told that the taxpayer was stepping in—only temporarily, mind you—to prop up the economy and save the world from financial catastrophe." Instead, Taibbi wrote, the bailouts indefinitely propped up and promoted an overly centralized, ungovernable, and little-regulated financial sector, encouraging increased risk rather than saving the system. Taibbi objected specifically to the vast sums of money used as "capital injections," scoffing at the notion that "certain Wall Street banks only took the bailout money because they were forced to."[8]

As for what Geithner called "the middle," the nonprofit and nonpartisan news organization ProPublica initially took a skeptical view of the bailouts but later came to regard them more tolerantly. Keeping a public scorecard of the expenditures and profits of the program, ProPublica showed the mortgage relief program that so offended Santelli and the traders was tiny—initially budgeted at $50 billion, later reduced to $29.9 billion—compared to the sums used for direct assistance to banks. And as for Taibbi, ProPublica's reporters found, he misstated the case: "People think: 'Oh, we gave all this money to the banks' and we did, but a lot of it was in the form of investments where we eventually get money back from it." By the end of Obama's presidency, ProPublica's bailout scorecard showed the U.S. government had turned a profit of some $71.7 billion, or 11.6 percent.[9]

Scholars have tended to view the bailouts differently than the critics have. One analysis found the U.S. bailout compared favorably to those of other nations. The financial collapse was after all international, and the United States was not the only country to conclude that it was better to save even the odious banks than to sink alongside them. And the U.S. government drove a better deal than others, precisely because of capital injections going to banks that did not actually need or even want them.

The financial collapse of 2007–2008 could have caused another Great Depression largely because, as was true in the 1920s, the U.S. financial system was deeply involved with major banks around the world. The bundling of U.S. mortgages into financial instruments with unwarranted triple-A credit ratings had enticed overseas investors into the American market. If it went down, so would they. Indeed, they started to—whereupon their governments stepped in to save them.

In Britain, the government acquired ownership of troubled banks, nationalizing Bradford & Bingley while buying large stakes in Lloyds and the Royal Bank of Scotland. The relatively healthier Barclays and HSBC chose to remain outside the plan. This system—where failing banks took public capital while successful banks did not—put the U.K. government in the position of holding only bad assets in the banking sector.[10]

The U.S. government, by contrast, forced the nine largest banks to take public capital. And some did need forcing: while the banks were happy to have emergency aid in the form of lending, they resisted capital injection, which reduced the value of existing shareholders' stakes in the firm. Geithner and Paulson had a weapon to compel healthy banks to participate: "If a capital infusion is not appealing, you should be aware your regulator will require it in any circumstance." Indeed, the CEO of Wells Fargo tried to refuse only to be told, "Your regulator is sitting right there. . . . And you're going to get a call tomorrow saying you're undercapitalized." The threat of regulatory compulsion worked in the American case and not in Britain because unlike British banks, American banks depended almost entirely on their domestic market and thus were at the mercy of the regulators who licensed them to operate in the United States. The more inclusive U.S. bailout thus let Washington turn a profit, while the U.K. bailout left Westminster suffering a loss.[11]

On another comparison, this one in time rather than in space, the bailout looked markedly more aggressive and interventionist: the Bush-Obama financial rescue program was larger, swifter, and more comprehensive than its counterpart in the Great Depression. Like the 2008–2009 bailout, the earlier effort straddled the period of an outgoing Republican administration and incoming Democratic one: the Reconstruction Finance Corporation (RFC) was created in 1932, under Herbert Hoover, and endowed with new, more expansive powers in 1933, under Roosevelt. But the RFC only gradually invested in the U.S. financial sector, reaching its peak in 1938. And the U.S. government's overall burden in the Great Depression amounted to 19 percent of precrisis GDP and about 10 percent of precrisis private sector debt. By contrast the TARP and related bailouts took only about a year and a half to reach their peak, and they were much larger than the comparable efforts in the 1930s, reaching a total potential exposure of 97 percent of GDP and 59 percent of private sector debt. Thus the Obama administration was by the end of 2009 involved in a financial rescue program that was, proportionally, about five times the size of the one undertaken by Roosevelt over his first two terms.[12]

The dramatically larger speed and size of the bailouts under Obama were owed to several factors. First, the economists of 2008–2009 had the Great Depression in mind. Bernanke and the chair of Obama's Council of Economic Advisers, Christina D. Romer, had each devoted considerable portions of their scholarly careers to studying the Depression and how to avert another one. Together with a consensus of mainstream economists they thought that speedier and larger intervention in terms of both monetary and fiscal policy after the crash of 1929 could have avoided, or at least lessened the severity of, the Depression.[13]

Second, because the institutions of the New Deal existed in 2008 (as they had not in 1929) policymakers did not have invent them. Once they secured money for bailouts, they had the anti-Depression instruments they needed and could wield them without waiting. The Federal Reserve Board had interventionist powers resulting from Depression-era legislation, and Bernanke used them. The Federal Deposit Insurance Corporation (FDIC), created in 1933, assured ordinary savers that their money would not vanish in a bank failure, and therefore in 2008–2009 could deal with defunct banks without panicking depositors and causing further failures. To inspire greater depositor confidence, the bailout programs increased FDIC's depositor insurance from $100,000 to $250,000 (allegedly temporarily; as of this writing the higher limit remains). Federal unemployment insurance (a creation of 1935) exerted an automatic stabilizing influence on the economy.

The speed and size of the bailout program when compared to that of the 1930s ensured its relatively swifter success—which perhaps also ensured that the Obama administration would not undertake anything like a New Deal. After all, Roosevelt's programs were born of a sense that civilization was in genuine peril, with unemployment approaching 25 percent and fascist movements arising around the world. Righting the financial ship quickly might render such a response unnecessary in the Obama administration—and, many public figures believed, it was a good thing, too. For by 2009 public discussion of comparisons to the 1930s had turned decidedly against repeating anything like the New Deal, and to a peculiar extent this shift owed to a single, unusually successful book.

Three weeks before the presidential election of 2008, the popular satirical *Daily Show with Jon Stewart* featured the author Amity Shlaes and her book *The Forgotten Man: A New History of the Great Depression.* Shlaes's book became that rare phenomenon: a book about history that had an important impact on policymakers. As Stewart exhorted his audience, Americans could learn from it how not to deal with a financial crisis: "Buy it and learn what we did wrong!"[14]

Shlaes argued that the New Deal was bad for business, a case she made by ignoring the rapid economic growth of the Roosevelt era and deliberately using misleading unemployment data discarded by economists more than a decade before. As Romer noted, Roosevelt's first two terms in office saw average annual economic growth rates of near 10 percent; "spectacular," she wrote, "even for an economy pulling out of a severe depression." Another economist noted that Roosevelt's first term saw the "strongest growth . . . of any four-year period in US history outside of wartime." Shlaes also used unemployment data that overstated unemployment in the late 1930s, thus making it appear as if the New Deal had done little to alleviate the effects of the Great Depression. Economists had reached a consensus by 1992 that these figures did not accurately reflect the overall jobless rate, and by the time Shlaes was writing her book, this consensus was reflected in the authoritative reference work, *Historical Statistics of the United States*. Nevertheless, she used these data that gave a false impression of the New Deal's effects, saying, "I have gone with the traditional numbers." The unemployment data were only one of several ways in which the book was misleading.[15]

Shlaes did not do what she did alone—she relied on anti–New Deal and anti-Keynesian work stretching back to the Depression itself—but she vividly summarized these long (and long-debunked) critiques. By the time Obama became president, Shlaes's insistence that the New Deal failed became doctrine in much of official Washington, with conservatives "carrying around *The Forgotten Man* like it's Mao's *Little Red Book*," as one journalist observed. Senator John Barrasso (Republican of Wyoming) mentioned in a Senate hearing that "members of the Senate are reading a book called *The Forgotten Man*, about the history of the Great Depression . . . as we look at a stimulus package." George Will promoted the book. "The New Deal did fail," a conservative guest insisted on CNN's *Larry King Live*; ". . . as told very well by Amity Shlaes . . . at the end of the thirties, we had just as high unemployment as the average of the entire ten years of the Depression." Shlaes herself drew the same lesson in a newspaper column, warning legislators that "Roosevelt . . . is unworthy of emulation." Shlaes's anti–New Deal testament became the guide for conservatives not only in the United States but overseas.[16]

Nor were these views limited to Republicans. At least one Democrat prominent in the Obama administration—Geithner—echoed some myths from Shlaes's account about Roosevelt's taking an irresponsible approach to the Depression. It appears the prevailing understanding of the New Deal among Washington policymakers in the early Obama presidency was ill informed and uncomplimentary. The consequences for economic policy cannot have been expansive.[17]

A sound critique of the Roosevelt administration might have improved public debate. The New Deal featured a variety of experiments before the administration settled on fiscal stimulus, or what the economist John Maynard Keynes was then calling "governmental expenditure which is financed by loans and is not merely a transfer through taxation"—that it was the way to "increasing aggregate purchasing power." If the government borrowed and spent, particularly on public works that put money in otherwise poor people's pockets, those previously unemployed and poverty-stricken would start an economic turnaround with their purchases.[18]

The mainstream scholarly consensus held that any failing of Keynesianism under the New Deal was "not because it did not work but because it was not tried." This might have been an exaggeration: a closer look would suggest that federal fiscal policy was expansionary throughout Roosevelt's first two terms; it just should have been more so. The logical inference was that the government in 2009 should more aggressively pursue Keynesian fiscal stimulus than it had in 1933. Instead, readers of Shlaes, or those who had merely heard vaguely about the argument, took it to mean that fiscal stimulus was a failed policy. The historical and economic knowledge informing the debate over how to spur recovery in 2009 was of poor quality.[19]

The proponents of fiscal stimulus in the Obama administration therefore found themselves at a tremendous intellectual and political disadvantage, despite having a Democratic president, a Democratic House, and a Democratic Senate. At the start, political aides were discussing what sounded to them like large figures for a stimulus—$500 billion, or even $600 billion. But of course the effect of a stimulus is not determined by what sounds large, but by arithmetic and data. When Romer got the data and did the arithmetic, she found that a stimulus of the proposed size would prove inadequate. It would take, she figured, $1.8 trillion to get the economy back on track by 2011. Among economists, the notion that the proposed figure was too small was not a matter of political affiliation: Romer got support on that score from the conservative economists John Taylor and Martin Feldstein, each of whom proposed something in the neighborhood of $1 trillion.[20]

But when officials within the administration began talking seriously to the president, they suggested no such number. Summers, now head of the White House National Economic Council, rejected Romer's $1.8 trillion out of hand: it was too high, he said—not for economic, but for political reasons. Congress would not take it seriously. Romer then proposed $1.2 trillion, together with lower options of $800 billion and $600 billion—believing these reductions would mean millions of lost jobs and lost income to Americans. In the end the economists dropped the already too-low $1.2 trillion estimate, leaving only the two smaller choices—the larger of which was already less than half of what Romer thought necessary. But Romer believed Summers was probably right that even $800 billion was a lot to ask of a Congress captivated by anti–New Deal and anti-Keynesian sentiments.[21]

In addition to the scholarly consensus on stimulus—more—and the presumed congressional consensus—less—there was another figure of considerable importance in the calculation: the new president, whose views were, and to an extent remain, unknown. That Obama wanted to work with congressional Republicans is sure. He hoped to repeat with the stimulus what he believed he had done with the bailout bill even before his election. He seems genuinely to have thought he could transform Washington by defining a national interest beyond party and rally reasonable Republicans and Democrats alike. It was difficult to overstate what one journalist later described as "the sincerity of Obama's desire to govern in concert with a loyal opposition."[22]

Republicans had no intention of becoming Obama's bipartisan partners. Early in drafting a stimulus, the Democratic chair of the House Appropriations Committee, David Obey, sought the cooperation of Jerry Lewis, the committee's ranking Republican member. Obey asked Lewis what Republicans wanted to see in the bill, which Democratic measures they could live with, and which they could not, so the two parties could find common ground in the national interest. Lewis laughed. He had orders "from on high" that Republicans must not cooperate. A few Senate Republicans were interested in Obama's offer: Susan Collins and Olympia Snowe of Maine as well as Arlen Specter of Pennsylvania indicated they could support the stimulus—if it included more tax cuts and less spending. The White House obliged, even though such cuts were less efficient at boosting the economy than public works spending that would put money quickly into the pockets of needy Americans. Another Republican senator, Charles Grassley of Iowa, negotiated the inclusion of a major tax cut for high earners, then voted against the bill anyway. House Republicans remained firmly uncooperative. Notwithstanding the White House's conciliatory concessions, no Republicans in the House of Representatives voted for the bill.[23]

Clearly, too, Obama regarded the bailout and stimulus as necessary projects that nevertheless could not cement his legacy the way his preferred issue, healthcare reform, could. Geithner told the president that preventing another Depression would be his major accomplishment, only to be told "that's not enough." Romer implored the president to focus on jobs, saying that increasing employment would be "enough of an accomplishment"—but Obama believed that if he did not seize the moment and shift public attention toward healthcare reform, he would lose a rare, if not unique, opportunity. So he reserved political capital and other resources to expend on the longer-term project of extending health coverage to millions of uninsured Americans.[24]

In the event, the American Recovery and Reinvestment Act (ARRA) that emerged from Congress allowed for $787 billion in stimulus. The president's hope of changing Washington's partisan culture and uniting lawmakers to support the national interest had foundered, yielding a stimulus one commenter called "puny." Romer thought likewise. When rehearsing for the Washington talk shows, she fielded the practice question of whether the stimulus was big enough by retorting with an unbroadcastable "Absofucking-lutely not."[25]

Still, the United States was immediately better off for having a small stimulus than none. The economy began to recover with ARRA's passage. The stock market bottomed out in March 2009, beginning a years-long trek upward. GDP also stopped its plummeting early in 2009 and began rising. Most important for most Americans, the rate of job loss reached its worst point in March 2009 and by the end of the year the U.S. economy was creating jobs again. Overall unemployment reached its peak, at 10 percent, in October 2009, and began a long slow decrease so that six years later, in the fall of 2015, it at last reached a tolerable 5 percent. Economic recovery helped debtors resume payment on their obligations, reducing pressure on the creaking financial system. Later studies estimated that the stimulus ensured that two to three million Americans who would not otherwise have had jobs enjoyed the benefit of an income and the dignity of work owing to ARRA.[26]

Perhaps more important in the longer run was the second "R" in ARRA, "reinvestment." If the Obama administration did not emulate the spectacle of New Deal public works, it nevertheless plowed enormous sums of money into obscure fields of American endeavor that might eventually yield valuable results. ARRA funded energy efficiencies, weatherizing the homes of low-income families and paying for the installation of smart electric meters, as well as investments in methods to derive energy from the wind and the sun. It paid for cities to install low-consumption LED streetlights and traffic signals. ARRA projects improved flood-control measures as well as wastewater treatment and disposal. The program paid for improvements in public housing and for the extension of high-speed Internet access to poorer Americans. It pushed money into initiatives applying information-technology improvements to medical treatment. It extended tuition aid for low-income college students.[27]

But the administration did less to claim credit for its interventions than the Roosevelt administration had done. Modern political polarization and a conservative media environment surely posed obstacles to declaring a new New Deal. But it is worth noting that Roosevelt faced similar obstacles. The Democratic congressional majorities of the 1930s depended on southern conservatives who frequently opposed or weakened New Deal proposals. And Roosevelt had to promote liberalism in a media environment dominated by anti–New Deal publishers and newsreel producers like William Randolph Hearst. Obama clearly did not share Roosevelt's view of how to reckon with such barriers. He believed, like his advisor Cass Sunstein, that it was easier and more effective for government to remain invisible while subtly "nudging" citizens to do desirable things. So the promotion of public goods that characterized the New Deal was absent in the twenty-first century.[28]

However prudent ARRA's investment would prove, it could yield real results only in the long run. In the near term, ARRA was still providing insufficient stimulus. If the economy turned the corner sharply with the financial rescue and the stimulus, it then dawdled back to prosperity. After the end of the recession, U.S. economic growth averaged an annual rate of about 2 percent, for the weakest recorded expansion since 1949.[29]

Moreover, even this moment of lamely Keynesian action soon passed: as one scholar wrote, "We all became Keynesians for about eight months from October 2008 to June 2009," after which policymakers began turning to the notion that government penny-pinching—austerity—would inspire confidence among shell-shocked private investors, who would take heart at miserly policy, emerge from shelter, and deploy capital in job-creating ways once more—a belief that the economist Paul Krugman referred to as a faith in the "confidence fairy." Snark did not kill the fable of restoring prosperity through austerity, which informed a practice of budget cutting in governments around the world.[30]

In the United States, the Republican opposition to anything resembling the New Deal intensified after the stimulus debate. In the summer of 2010, the president did obtain the enactment of financial regulation meant to prevent some of the activities that had caused the crisis in the Dodd-Frank Wall Street Reform and Consumer Protection Act, but with only a few Republican votes—and then only after the many of bill's provisions had been weakened or left vague. The large and complicated law required considerable legal interpretation, and implementation of one of its most prominent provisions, the Volcker Rule (named for former Federal Reserve Chair Paul

Volcker), limiting banks' ability to make riskier investments, was delayed until 2015.[31]

In the fall of 2010, the Republicans gained a congressional majority and afterward refused to raise the legal debt ceiling, threatening an unprecedented default on U.S. debt unless Obama agreed to cut spending. While the president resisted short-term cuts, which would surely have damaged the halting recovery, he did agree to longer-term austerity. A similar episode occurred again in 2013. It was clear that in the United States, as elsewhere, further stimulus was not forthcoming, and the recovery would have to lean on its original, inadequate support. As Democratic Senator Evan Bayh said, ARRA "is going to be the last stimulus we see for a long time."[32]

So slow indeed was the recovery from the crisis of 2008–2009 that before the end of Obama's presidency it had been outpaced, in relative terms, by the recovery from the Great Depression. Although the world economy had fallen much further by 1933 than by 2009, its recovery under expansionary policies was more robust in the Roosevelt era than in the twenty-first century. By August of 2015, industrial output relative to the start of the recession was lower than industrial output at the same relative time under the New Deal, seven and a half years after the crash of 1929.[33]

The slow recovery put Obama's legacy at political risk. For decades, political scientists had been modeling the effect of economic performance on U.S. elections. The longest-established predictor was Ray Fair, whose equation took into account a series of variables including economic good news. In the waning weeks of the 2016 presidential election, the Fair model predicted the Democrats would narrowly lose the presidency. Challenged on his forecast, Fair conceded the possibility that "people who would otherwise vote for the Republicans because of the sluggish economy and a desire for change will vote for the Democrats because of Donald Trump's characteristics that they don't like." But it was impossible to say in advance of the November 8 canvass.[34]

If the economists were right that a better stimulus would have produced a faster economic recovery with more widespread prosperity, and the political scientists were right that lackluster economic performance gave Republicans favorable odds of taking the White House in 2016, then Obama's decision to deemphasize stimulus in favor of pressing for health insurance reform was a gamble of immense, if unknowable, magnitude and consequence. The opportunity to craft the largest missing piece in the ramshackle American welfare state was surely unique. But for the adoption of healthcare reform to prove meaningful to American lives in the long term, the new program would have to remain in place, and indeed be improved in later years. The Obama health insurance reform barely survived a legal challenge in the Supreme Court in 2015, and its further survival would depend on the willingness of congressmen and -women and judges to defend it. The parlous recovery made the election of such congressmen and -women, and a president who would appoint such judges, uncertain indeed. Even at the end of Obama's presidency it was unclear whether he had won his gamble, owing in large measure to the dramatically changed character of the Republican Party in 2016.

It is possible the political effects of the weak turnaround were not limited to Obama's legacy, Democratic electoral chances, or the future of reformed health insurance provision. They may have extended to the legitimacy of the U.S. political system itself. A recent international study of the early twentieth century illustrated the risk of permitting an economic recovery to move slowly. Examining the economic and political fortunes of twenty-eight countries between the world wars, the economic historians Alan de Bromhead, Barry Eichengreen, and Kevin H. O'Rourke found that "when economic bad news continues beyond a certain period of time and negative expectations become firmly entrenched, some people reach for extreme solutions." As the limping recoveries of the interwar period extended into a period of years, it became ever more likely that these conditions would lend strength to fascist parties whose leaders and constituents did not want merely to reform existing institutions, but to destroy them.[35]

The disappointments that followed the brief moment of hope in 2009 yielded similar boosts to right-wing parties and movements in many nations. Five years onward, in the European Parliamentary elections of 2014, the National Front of France increased its share of the vote from 6.3 to 24.9 percent, the U.K. Independence Party likewise rose from 16.5 to 26.8 percent, and the Freiheitliche Partei Österreichs went from 12.7 to 19.7 percent.[36] British voters in the throes of nationalist enthusiasms and angered at the effects of austerity on their institutions chose to depart the European Union, or "Brexit," in 2016. The United States has an institutional bias against minor parties, but taking account of that constraint, the political effects of the weak recovery looked similar. Trump gained the Republican nomination and Trumpism—a mix of nationalism, nativism, and contempt for constitutional limits and parliamentary norms, among other resentments—gained a purchase on the Republican Party.

As the worldwide trends of the twenty-first century indicate, economic malaises and rightward shift cannot owe solely to decisions made in the

Obama White House or even within the United States. These trends owe to a decades-long effort to discredit Keynesianism and the New Deal in favor of leaner budgets, lower taxes, and fewer public services. But it is worth noting that in the 1930s, the United States diverged from a global trend toward right-wing extremism owing in large measure to the rapid and visible successes of the New Deal. In the years after the 2008 crash, it did not.

Achievement without Credit

THE OBAMA PRESIDENCY AND INEQUALITY

Paul Starr

Like global warming, the growth in economic inequality poses a challenge to progressive presidential leadership that would be daunting under the best of political circumstances. The trends in both the climate and the economy are by their nature difficult to reverse, and in an era of partisan polarization and nearly constant gridlock, presidents seeking to meet those challenges are unlikely to be able to claim decisive victories. When change fails to match expectations, the disappointment that many people feel may lead them to disparage what political leadership has accomplished. That reaction, however, would be a mistake in the case of Barack Obama's record on economic inequality. Despite relentless Republican opposition, Obama made significant progress in mitigating and reducing inequality. What he did not receive is much political credit for that achievement—and why he failed to get credit is as important a question as how he was able to do as much as he did.

With Donald Trump as president, Republicans in control of Congress, and a conservative majority on the Supreme Court, most of the progress Obama made on inequality is likely to be eroded or entirely wiped out. But it is all the more important to take the measure of what Obama accomplished and to ask why the gains under his leadership were not better entrenched. Substantively, the choices that Obama made were often well reasoned and reasonably successful. But the policies brought only limited support chiefly because of compromises at their inception and choices about their design that blocked the public from connecting positive results with the president and his party.

The historical moment when Obama took office put economic inequality in a new light. Although income inequality had been on the rise in the United States since the 1970s, most liberals and Democrats had long understood the problem as primarily involving the declining fortunes of people in the lower half of the income distribution. The financial crisis and Great Recession redirected attention. Instead of focusing almost entirely on lagging incomes at the bottom, critics increasingly pointed to soaring incomes at the top along with stagnant incomes for everyone else. The Occupy movement popularized the idea of the "1 percent" benefiting at the expense of the 99 percent. Social science research, particularly the work of Thomas Piketty and Emmanuel Saez, culminating in Piketty's book *Capital in the Twenty-First Century*, helped to substantiate the claim that breakaway gains among the superrich were the cardinal change of recent decades.[1] In the 1960s Lyndon Johnson had called for a war on poverty; in the 1990s Bill Clinton had promised to end "welfare as we know it." Neither had talked about inequality as such. When Barack Obama went to Osawatomie, Kansas, in December 2011 to give a speech on inequality and called it "the defining issue of our time," he was registering a shift in the framing of the problem and seeking to put inequality at the center of his 2012 reelection campaign.[2]

But could Democratic policies do much about inequality? Doubts have come from three directions. Conservatives have generally seen redistribution as both illegitimate and futile—illegitimate because government has no right to transfer income from those who earn it to anyone else, and futile because doing so will only reduce the incentives to be productive. Among economists, the prevailing view of the causes of rising inequality has, at least until recently, emphasized seemingly impersonal market forces: skill-biased technological change (inherently favoring those with greater human capital), and more efficient global markets. But if these were the chief causes, policy would likely be ineffectual in reducing inequality, except by depressing economic growth. Disagreeing with this analysis, other economists as well as sociologists and political scientists have argued that rising inequality has political and institutional sources and pointed to cross-national evidence that greater equality does not, in fact, come at the expense of growth. But many who have offered this interpretation have also

insisted that more radical policies than Obama's would be necessary to reduce inequality in the United States.

The constraints of American politics are severe, but which party controls the presidency has nonetheless made an enormous difference in the
extent of economic inequality. Building on the work of Douglas Hibbs,
Larry Bartels finds that from 1948 to 2014 income inequality increased
sharply under Republican presidents but decreased somewhat under Democrats. While affluent families at the 95th percentile of income have done
about equally well under presidents of both parties, middle-income families have seen their incomes grow twice as fast under Democrats, and the
working poor (at the 20th percentile) have seen their incomes rise ten
times faster under Democrats. In fact, Bartels notes, "income inequality
would have been no greater in 2014 than it was in the late 1940s" if the patterns of income growth under Democrats had prevailed for the entire period. Yet even Bartels is skeptical about any recent rollback of inequality
under Obama. Referring to Bill Clinton as well as Obama, he writes that
"recent Democratic presidents have not managed to *decrease* income inequality—as their Democratic predecessors did—but have merely stemmed
the rate of increase."[3]

This judgment, however, depends on how income is defined and inequality is measured. Three different definitions of inequality are com-
monly used in estimating changes in inequality. "Market income" consists
of income from labor (wages and salaries) and from capital (interest, dividends, capital gains). "Pretax income," as defined by the Census Bureau,
consists of all forms of money income before taxes—market income plus
government transfer payments such as Social Security and unemployment
benefits—but still excludes in-kind benefits such as food stamps and health
care. Posttax, disposable income consists of pretax money income less
taxes.[4]

Among these three measures of income (none of which includes in-kind
benefits), the more inclusive the definition, the greater is the equalizing effect of public policy. Since market income excludes all government benefits
and taxes, it yields the highest measure of inequality and the least effect of
public policy. This is the definition used by Piketty and Saez in their work,
which draws on tax data. Although they are clear about their definition,
many others cite Piketty and Saez to make broad and misleading claims
about income inequality returning to the level in the 1920s or increasing
under Obama, as if taxes and government benefits made no difference.[5]
Most of Bartels's research on partisanship and income inequality relies on

Census data on pretax money income, which provides a more complete picture than market income but still leaves out in-kind benefits (including health care and food stamps) as well as taxes. Those omissions are a problem in evaluating change over the course of a presidency in which health care, food stamps, and taxes accounted for a great deal of redistribution. There is a similar problem in measuring the changes in "extreme poverty" highlighted in recent work by Katherine J. Edin and H. Luke Shaefer; since the passage of welfare reform in 1996, extreme poverty has risen—but the broader the definition of income, the less of an increase appears to have taken place.[6]

Policies of almost every kind affect economic inequality, many of them indirectly in hard-to-measure but consequential ways over the long run. Among the many critical determinants of economic inequality are the rules that govern labor relations, finance, antitrust, trade, and immigration. A complete account of how presidential leadership affects inequality would have to deal with the consequences of new legislation and executive rule-making in these and other domains, as well as the influence of judicial appointments on court decisions. The more tractable questions about presidential leadership involve changes in policy with an immediate and direct impact. During Obama's presidency, these changes came in three areas: 1) the response to the Great Recession, particularly through the Recovery Act in 2009; 2) healthcare reform, mainly through the Affordable Care Act (ACA) in 2010; and 3) changes in taxation, chiefly through tax provisions of the Recovery Act and the ACA and legislation adopted during the lame-duck session after the 2012 election, which repealed earlier Republican tax cuts on the top brackets and extended permanently the Recovery Act's tax cuts for the poor.

These policies substantially mitigated the effects of the Great Recession on poverty and inequality. Once the healthcare and tax reforms were carried out in 2013 and 2014, they significantly reduced inequality from the level it had reached before Obama became president. But these achievements might as well have been declared state secrets. Many of them involved policies that were low in visibility and high in complexity and therefore inherently difficult for ordinary citizens to understand even when they were beneficiaries.[7] When policies succeed objectively, they can still fail politically if they are not well designed to win credit from the public, and that failure can limit a president's ability to move ahead further. Failures to win credit were evident in all three of the areas of immediate impact on inequality—the Recovery Act, healthcare reform, and tax policy—but nowhere more so than in the response to the Great Recession.

The Great Recession, the Recovery Act, and Inequality

Any assessment of Obama's record on inequality has to take into account the conditions under which he became president. During 2008, unemployment had risen from 5 percent to nearly 8 percent (it would eventually peak at 10 percent). The collapse of the housing market had set off a financial panic in the fall of 2008, imperiling major financial institutions and raising the specter of a depression on the scale of the 1930s. As of January 2009, the economy was in free fall: nearly 750,000 jobs were being lost each month, and real GDP was dropping at an annual rate of about 6 percent.[8]

A declining economy typically has disparate implications for people depending on their socioeconomic position and how much of a cushion they have against adversity. Recessions increase inequality in market incomes chiefly because of higher unemployment rates and the increased duration of unemployment. So, at the inception of Obama's presidency, inequality was set to increase substantially from its already high levels. Instead, federal policies cut short the recession and limited the impact on both inequality and poverty.

The federal government's response to the recession had three different aspects. The first consisted of standing countercyclical policies—automatic stabilizers such as unemployment insurance and food stamps. The second aspect comprised measures taken to stabilize financial markets, beginning under George W. Bush. In September 2008, the Treasury and Federal Reserve Board had rescued major banks and other financial institutions, and in October Congress passed the Troubled Asset Relief Program (TARP), which authorized up to $700 billion to buy distressed assets or equity in financial institutions. By the end of 2008, the Federal Reserve had reduced interest rates to zero, and it continued to support the economy through quantitative easing under Obama. The continuity of these financial-market policies from the Bush to Obama administrations highlights the short-lived bipartisan support those policies enjoyed at the height of the financial crisis. Obama did, however, use the TARP funds in one way that many Republicans opposed—to bail out the auto industry, an unambiguous success. And in 2010, Obama signed the Dodd-Frank Wall Street Reform and Consumer Protection Act, passed by Congress almost entirely on party lines.

Fiscal stimulus, the third aspect of the federal response to the Great Recession, was chiefly the work of Obama and the Democrats, except for a tax cut adopted under Bush in early 2008. Obama's stimulus program, enacted less than a month after he took office, served in part as a vehicle for his larger agenda. As its full name indicated, the American Recovery and *Reinvestment* Act included provisions for long-term investments in public infrastructure and technological innovation. Indeed, with its provisions for the financing of green technology and a new program in the Energy Department to support breakthrough discoveries, it would turn out to be the only major piece of legislation that Obama was able to get through Congress to address climate change (all his other measures would be through executive action). The Recovery Act also financed improvements in roads, bridges, water and sewage systems, and other aspects of public infrastructure, emphasizing "shovel-ready" projects to create jobs and get money into circulation as quickly as possible.

But, partly because of the difficulty in using public investment to boost short-term demand and target support to those hit hardest by the recession, most of the Recovery Act's more than $800 billion in funds went to three other purposes: tax cuts, expanded benefits for the unemployed and the poor, and fiscal relief to the states. The first two of these were unambiguously aimed at mitigating inequality and poverty as well as stimulating the economy. The legislation created or enlarged three tax credits: a new Making Work Pay tax credit, which went to low- and middle-income people, and increases in the earned income tax credit and child tax credit, which went to those with low incomes. The expanded government benefits in the Recovery Act were also structured to favor people in greatest distress. The legislation increased the duration and generosity of unemployment benefits and, in an unprecedented step, paid for a substantial portion of health insurance for the unemployed. It also temporarily expanded food stamps (Supplemental Nutrition Assistance Program [SNAP]), welfare payments (Temporary Assistance for Needy Families), and assistance for housing (Homelessness Prevention and Rapid Rehousing Program). SNAP assumed particular importance: one in four children and one in eight adults were receiving food stamps by 2010, as the program functioned, in effect, as a minimum basic income.[9]

The final part of the Recovery Act—fiscal relief to the states—was more uncertain in its distributive implications. The rationale for federal aid to the states was to reduce cutbacks in public services and layoffs of teachers and other public employees as states saw their revenues fall. But the federal money was fungible. Even when the federal aid was tied to a program like Medicaid, states might use the funds to reduce their own spending in that area. So there was no guarantee that federal aid would end up as stimulus, much less as progressive stimulus.[10]

Altogether—taking into account later extensions of the Recovery Act's temporary tax cuts and spending measures—the total discretionary stimulus from 2009 to 2012 amounted to $1.2 trillion and averaged about 2 percent of GDP.[11] Republicans called it the "failed stimulus," but the evidence (and the consensus among economists) is that it worked.[12] The combined effect of the automatic stabilizers and stimulus, as data from Gary Burtless and Tracy Gordon show, was to give disposable income "extraordinary stability" despite the sharp decline in market income between 2008 and 2010.[13] The Recovery Act alone reduced the impact of higher unemployment on inequality in wages by about half as measured by the Gini coefficient, according to a 2016 estimate from the Council of Economic Advisers.[14] The automatic stabilizers and the stimulus together, according to the CEA, "offset nearly 90 percent of the increase in poverty that would have occurred otherwise, even without accounting for any impact they had in moderating the recession itself." Without government transfers, the poverty rate would have increased by 4.5 percentage points; it actually rose only by half a percentage point.[15] The United States made a stronger recovery from the Great Recession than the countries in the Euro area or Japan.[16] But this was not the frame of reference for public opinion.

When surveys at the time asked people about the "stimulus program," the public judgment was harsh. In a January 2010 CNN poll, 63 percent said the stimulus funds had been spent "for political reasons," while only 36 percent said the funds had been spent on projects "to benefit the economy." According to 45 percent of respondents, "nearly all" or "most" of the money had been wasted; another 29 percent thought that half the money was wasted. Other responses in the same survey suggest, however, that many of the respondents had something else in mind when responding to these questions. Asked who benefited from the stimulus, 54 percent said it helped bankers and investors. As the CNN polling director suggested, many people seemed to be confusing the stimulus with the bailout of the financial industry. In fact, 70 percent or more of the respondents favored government spending to help unemployed workers, cut taxes, and build roads and bridges—just the things the stimulus had done.[17]

The mix-up of the stimulus and the bailouts in public understanding cast a shadow over the stimulus. Although the federal government ultimately made back almost all the money it spent in TARP by selling its equity holdings in financial institutions for a profit, the bailout created the sense that the government was favoring Wall Street to the exclusion of ordinary people suffering from the recession. The Justice Department's use of deferred prosecution agreements in cases of Wall Street fraud reinforced the belief that the Obama administration allowed those responsible for the financial crisis to escape with impunity. Companies paid financial settlements, but none of the individual executives faced any punishment.[18]

The choices that Obama made about the stimulus program contributed to the public confusion about what he was doing on behalf of people suffering from the recession. Each of the elements of the stimulus had a low profile. Consider the difference in how Bush and Obama delivered their tax cuts. In early 2008, the Bush administration had sent taxpayers lump-sum rebate checks with a letter signed by President Bush. In contrast, the Obama administration distributed its tax cuts through reduced withholding, averaging so small an amount, $16 a week, that most people would hardly notice it. Obama's economic advisers had a well-reasoned rationale for this choice. Research in behavioral economics had shown that the recipients of a lump-sum check would be more likely to save it, whereas the aim was to get them to spend the money to support aggregate demand. But unobtrusiveness had a political cost. As Michael Grunwald notes in his history of the stimulus program *The New New Deal*—tellingly subtitled *The Hidden Story of Change in Obama Era*—surveys indicated that fewer than 10 percent of Americans were aware Obama had cut taxes. In fact, more people thought Obama had raised their taxes.[19]

The expansion of unemployment insurance, food stamps, and other existing benefits also made sense as a quick way to shore up the economy and the position of the vulnerable. But channeling money through existing programs conveyed no message about what Obama was doing. Similarly, the Recovery Act's billions in aid to the states did help to limit cutbacks in services and avert public employee layoffs. But it was invisible to the public. Republican governors used the federal money to balance their budgets, while castigating Obama and the Democrats for increasing the federal deficit.

Unlike the New Deal, which conspicuously built new dams and bridges, the Recovery Act devoted most of its spending on infrastructure to repairs and renovations. Obama envisioned a smart electric grid or high-speed rail as high-visibility projects, only to find that quick progress was impossible.

The *removal* of a closed nuclear plant on the Savannah River was the stimulus program's single biggest project.

The majority who believed that the government had spent the stimulus on projects "for political reasons" rather than to benefit the economy had it backward. Obama repeatedly chose substance over politics, which hardly seems like a fault in a president—except that the failure to get credit later limited what he was able to do. By mid-2010, some of the president's economic advisers were convinced that the stimulus package had been too small and Obama needed to go back to Congress for a second round. "Look, I get the Keynesian thing," Obama told them. "But it's not where the electorate is."[20] In fact, a Gallup poll at the time indicated majority support for stimulus policies, but anything that could be called "stimulus" would lose the votes of moderate Democrats in Congress.[21] Hemmed in by the failure to win credit for the Recovery Act, Obama was unable to build on it. Healthcare reform would have that same problem.

Healthcare Reform as Redistributive Policy

The ACA was the most important redistributive reform of the Obama presidency that involved institutional change—rewriting the rules of a central institution in American society. Although Obama had little to do with the original formulation of what came to be called "Obamacare," he provided the leadership to pass it. The framework had emerged from discussions among liberal reformers, healthcare interest groups, and congressional Democrats; the immediate model came from a Massachusetts program enacted, ironically enough, under Governor Mitt Romney in 2006. But Obama made healthcare reform a priority and repeatedly rescued the legislation when it seemed on the brink of defeat.

Healthcare reform became a priority for Obama, as it had been for Bill Clinton at the beginning of his presidency, because it could serve an unusual combination of goals and constituencies. By coupling universal coverage with cost containment, comprehensive legislation could simultaneously address problems of the poor, the middle class, and government itself. Universal coverage would not only benefit the low-wage workers who made up a majority of the uninsured but also many in the middle class who were underinsured, at risk of losing coverage when unemployed, or denied insurance altogether because of preexisting conditions. Moreover, by reducing the rate of cost growth in existing federal health programs, legislation could offset the cost of expanded coverage for the uninsured and over the long run produce budget savings. Even with those provisions, a reform package could win significant support from some healthcare providers. No other form of redistributive policy could promise long-term budget relief with so little need of new taxes, while extending social protections to both the poor and the middle class.

The political barriers to reform were nonetheless formidable: healthcare interest groups anxious to protect the status quo; a protected public consisting of many people with good employer benefits as well as seniors on Medicare, veterans, and others who believed they had earned their health care and objected to paying for people who hadn't; and a long tradition of ideological opposition from conservatives, who, unlike their counterparts in other democracies, have for nearly a century equated a public program to provide universal health insurance with a loss of individual freedom.[22]

Obama and the Democrats sought to overcome each of these sources of potential opposition with a program of minimally invasive reform, relying on two forms of coverage—Medicaid and private insurance—that earlier advocates of national health insurance had hoped to replace. Passed in March 2010, the law expanded Medicaid to serve more of the poor and near-poor (up to 138 percent of the federal poverty level), and it enabled others to obtain private insurance through a new structure of rules and subsidies in the individual insurance market. The new rules required insurers to cover all applicants, including those with preexisting conditions, at rates not based on an individual's health status. The new subsidies for insurance premiums, offered in state-based marketplaces, went to people with incomes up to four times the federal poverty level; those with incomes up to 250 percent of the poverty line received additional subsidies for deductibles and co-pays. To prevent people from opportunistically buying insurance only when sick, the ACA imposed a financial penalty on individuals for failing to carry a minimum level of coverage, unless the cost of that policy would create financial hardship. Although the Supreme Court upheld the individual mandate in 2012, it made the Medicaid expansion voluntary for the states.

The main provisions of the ACA went into effect in 2014 and immediately affected insurance coverage, access to medical care, and financial security among low-income families. The number of uninsured dropped from 49 million in 2010 to 28 million in 2016, or from 16.0 percent to 8.8 percent of the population, an all-time low. If all states had expanded Medicaid, the number of uninsured would have fallen by an additional three to four million.[23] The law also gave many of the previously insured added protection, abolishing exclusions of preexisting conditions, capping out-of-pocket costs, and requiring insurers to cover preventive services of demonstrated effectiveness at no charge to the consumer. At a minimum, a health insurance policy now had to cover 60 percent of actuarial costs—a criterion previously met by policies covering less than half of the enrollees in the individual market.[24] The newly insured gained in access to treatment; for example, according to one survey, three out of five of the newly insured who had used their coverage to get care said they previously would have not have been able to afford it.[25] Studies comparing states that expanded Medicaid with non-expansion states showed that the extension of coverage brought significant gains in both healthcare access (for example, more regular treatment of chronic conditions such as diabetes) and financial security (reductions in debts turned over to collection agencies).[26]

While the law expanded access to care and financial protection, the predictions of opponents of the ACA that it would be a budget-buster, job killer, and general source of economic havoc were not borne out. From 2010 to 2015, national health expenditures grew at a subdued rate, and the costs of Medicare, Medicaid, and the new affordability subsidies fell far below the original projections by the Congressional Budget Office.[27] The unemployment rate dropped over the same period, and the law had little or no effect on the share of Americans with job-based health insurance.[28]

Nonetheless, public opinion about the ACA, which was sharply divided from the outset, did not turn more positive after the major provisions were carried out. Tracking polls by the Kaiser Family Foundation continued to show the public split about evenly between approval and disapproval of the law; as of June 2016, the share of the public who wanted to see the ACA repealed or scaled back was just about equal to the share who wanted to see it maintained or expanded.[29] Only a minority recognized Obama's achievement in reducing the number of uninsured. Asked in a September 2016 Kaiser survey whether the rate of Americans lacking health insurance was at an all-time high or all-time low, only one-quarter (26 percent) were aware that it was at an all-time low. Almost as many (21 percent) said the number of uninsured was at an all-time high, and about half (46 percent) said it was just about the same as it had been.[30]

Partisan affiliation strongly colored opinions about "Obamacare" and its effects. But an additional reason lay in the compromises made to pass the ACA. Despite the substantial subsidies they received, many of the enrollees in the exchange plans still resented the costs they were left to bear. The ACA also did not protect those who previously had employer-provided insurance from reductions in coverage. Deductibles, which had begun rising sharply in the early 2000s, continued to increase in employer-sponsored plans; from 2006 to 2015, the average deductible rose from $303 to $1,077.[31] By imposing requirements for minimum levels of health insurance, the ACA did raise the standard of protection for people who had the least adequate policies, and it required all plans to cover preventive services and eliminate annual and lifetime caps. After the ACA went into effect, the increases and reductions in private coverage just about cancelled each other out. The net effect was to reconfigure private insurance, which provided more coverage of both preventive and catastrophic costs but typically less coverage of routine medical care because of higher deductibles. Thanks to the ACA's increased protection against the costs of serious illness, health care was less likely to cause personal bankruptcy. But because more people needed to pay more of their regular medical expenses out of pocket, they saw their insurance as doing less for them than it had in the past.

Like the stimulus program, the ACA reflected well-reasoned policy choices but little attention to how it would be experienced. Obamacare was not a discrete program like Medicare; it revised the rules of the insurance market and federal programs, and most people could not be expected to distinguish what the law regulated from what it didn't. The state-based insurance marketplaces, which served about twelve million people or 3.7 percent of the U.S. population in 2015, were the one distinct new organization directly affecting the public. But many of the states gave the marketplaces names of their own ("Covered California," "Connect for Health Colorado," "AccessHealthCT"). Beneficiaries in those states did not necessarily see the connection to the federal law. Learning about Kentucky Kynect at a state fair in 2013, one prospective enrollee is reported to have said, "This beats Obamacare, I hope."[32] The federal government did operate healthcare.gov for people in states that chose not to run their own exchanges, and the media therefore took the federal exchange to be synonymous with Obamacare—the source of a public relations disaster for the program when technical glitches in healthcare.gov's debut set off a media frenzy.[33]

The ACA's failure to generate strong public support had political consequences. Republicans not only felt free to vote repeatedly to repeal the law; they also obstructed any legislative effort to fix its shortcomings as those became apparent. Indeed, they succeeded in passing an amendment re-

stricting one of the protections the law had given insurers with disproportionate numbers of high-cost enrollees in the state-based marketplaces. In
2016, after suffering significant losses, several major national insurers pulled
out of the marketplaces, and in some states the remaining plans announced
large rate increases for the following year. These increases brought the rates
into line with the original CBO projections; whether they indicated a one-
time upward adjustment or a long-run trend was unclear at the time. Most
people did not appear to understand how limited the scope of the rate increases was. According to a Kaiser survey, a majority of people believed the
increases applied to all health insurance or to employer plans (where rates
in 2016 increased by an average of only 3 percent); only one out of ten understood that the increases applied only to the individual insurance market.[34] In fact, more than 80 percent of the twelve million enrollees in the
ACA marketplaces received subsidies that capped their premiums as a percentage of income, so the higher rates did not affect most of them.

In a normal political environment, Congress and the president might
have worked out solutions for the difficulties in the marketplaces (as they
had previously done with private insurance plans in Medicare). When the
ACA passed, many of its supporters compared it to Social Security and
Medicare. After 1935 and 1965, however, Democrats retained control of
Congress for years and consequently amended those programs as problems
emerged. When Democrats lost control of Congress in 2010, they lost the
ability to make course corrections in the ACA and to address emerging
sources of public dissatisfaction. By any reasonable standard, the ACA was
a policy success, but like the economic recovery program, it failed to produce the political return to Democrats that Social Security and Medicare
had generated.

Tax Reform in the Obama Presidency

The progressivity of tax policy has long depended on the party in power
and especially on presidential leadership. Democrats have raised taxes on
top incomes, while Republicans have cut them. When Democrats have cut
taxes, they have cut them for different groups. The tax cuts at the beginning
of Reagan's and George W. Bush's presidencies were skewed toward the
upper brackets, whereas Obama's tax cuts were targeted toward low- and
middle-income people. The two temporary tax cuts in the Recovery Act
that were later made permanent both benefited people at the bottom of the
income distribution.

Obama also raised taxes on those with high incomes. The ACA included an increase in the Medicare tax rate of 0.9 percent on earnings over $200,000 for individual taxpayers and $250,000 for married couples. Even more significantly, in a break with the tradition in social insurance, the ACA extended the full Medicare tax of 3.8 percent to income from capital (dividends, interest, and capital gains) for the same high-income taxpayers. Legislation in 2012 repealed the Bush tax cuts for high-income individuals and families, pushing the top rate back up to 39.6 percent. It also increased taxes on capital income and made a variety of other changes, including reinstatement of the estate tax, that fell primarily on the rich. Obama was able to secure these changes in 2012 only because the Bush tax cuts were set to expire; progressives believed he should have driven a harder bargain with Republicans. Nonetheless, under Obama, the capital gains rate rose from 15 percent to 23.8 percent; tax rates on the superrich returned close to the levels they were before Reagan. The Foreign Account Tax Compliance Act, passed by Congress in 2010, was also intended to increase tax collections on top incomes. Under the law, aptly abbreviated as FATCA, taxpayers must report accounts held abroad worth more than $50,000, and foreign financial institutions must report on the accounts of their U.S. clients.

A Treasury Department analysis sums up the impact of the Obama tax changes on income inequality:

> The enacted policies made the tax system much more progressive than it was under pre-existing law. The increase in tax burden is highly concentrated at the very top of the income distribution. The average effective federal tax rate for the top 0.1 percent of families increased by 6.7 percentage points (from 31.0 to 37.7 percent), and after-tax income was therefore reduced by 9.7 percent. This is equivalent to an average tax burden increase of nearly $550,000 per family. . . .
>
> By contrast, lower-income families experienced proportionately large reductions in tax burden, and middle-income families had relatively small changes in tax burden. For example, families in the lowest 10 percent of the income distribution saw their average effective tax rate fall by 9.7 percentage points (from −0.6 to −10.3 percent) and experienced a reduction in their annual tax burden of almost $850—equal to an increase in disposable after-tax income of 9.7 percent.[35]

According to these Treasury estimates, changes in tax law during the Obama administration offset between 8 and 29 percent of the increase in income inequality since 1979, depending on the measure of inequality. The low estimate of an 8 percent rollback uses the Gini coefficient as the measure; the high estimate uses changes in the ratio of income at the 90th percentile to income at the 20th percentile. The tax changes under Obama rolled back 22 percent of the gains in shares of after-tax income made by the top 1 percent from 1979 to 2013.[36]

The increases in taxes on top incomes went into effect in 2013, while taxes on the middle class and the poor remained near historic lows. As of 2014, according to an analysis by the Urban-Brookings Tax Policy Center, a family at the middle of the income distribution paid only 5.3 percent of its income in federal income taxes. (This is the effective rate, not the marginal rate.) Just as impressive, families at half the median income (a level often used as the cut-off point for relative measures of poverty) received net credits equal to 8.52 percent of income—in effect, a negative income tax. Except for the Great Recession, these were historic records going back to the 1950s. Under Obama the federal income tax was exceptionally light on the middle class, and it had never been more favorable to the poor.[37]

None of this seems to have registered in public opinion. Gallup surveys indicated a slight increase from 2009 to 2016 in the proportion of Americans saying they pay too much in taxes.[38] While Republicans attacked Obama for something he did not do (raising taxes on Americans generally), Democrats gave him little credit for something he did do (making the tax system more progressive).

The Credit Conundrum

The Recovery Act, healthcare reform, and tax changes of the Obama presidency all followed the same pattern. The policies were progressive in their inspiration and impact, but they were nonetheless disappointing to progressives, who wanted stronger measures. They were also little appreciated or understood by the public at large, which saw them largely through partisan lenses. Republicans, of course, lambasted the policies, and conservative media portrayed them as unmitigated failures. To be sure, the economic recovery and healthcare reforms did help Obama win reelection in 2012, though at that time even opinion leaders who supported Obama did not believe that he had been able to do much about the growth in economic inequality.

Many of Obama's initiatives aimed to modify what Suzanne Mettler calls the "submerged state," policies lying beneath the surface of government that incentivize and constrain activities in the market. Such policies often benefit interest groups that fight hard to keep them, while making the government's role opaque to ordinary citizens. Writing in 2010 about Obama's early record, Mettler argued that even submerged-state policies benefiting low- and moderate-income people "may do little to engender positive attitudes among recipients toward such policies—or, quite likely, toward the political leaders who helped bring them into being." Progressive changes in the submerged state might amount only to a "submerged success"—a good description of Obama's record on inequality.[39]

Part of the reason Obama received so little credit for making progress on inequality through most of his presidency is that the major tax and healthcare reforms did not take effect until early in his second term, and the results took even longer to show up in official data. Data from Saez and Piketty on market income were also being widely reported from 2013 to 2015 as if they referred to a more comprehensive definition of income, including government benefits and taxes.[40] Many progressives cited those data on behalf of arguments for more radical change and may have resisted acknowledging what Obama had accomplished for fear of weakening their case. Bernie Sanders campaigned for the Democratic presidential nomination as if Obama had done nothing of significance about inequality. In September 2016, however, the Census Bureau reported that real pretax money income had risen an average of 5.2 percent the previous year. The gains in 2015 were greatest for those at the bottom. While incomes were up 2.9 percent for those at the 90th percentile, they rose 7.9 percent for households at the 10th percentile, and the decline in the poverty rate was the largest in decades.[41] To be sure, the increases for low-income families had not yet fully made up what they had lost in the Great Recession, although when data were reported for 2016 they showed median income increased another 3.2 percent, reaching an all-time high, with the poverty rate falling to 12.7 percent, back to the level it had been before the recession.[42] If the Census measure of income included food stamps, health care, and taxes, the distributive picture would have looked even better. The reports were a confirmation that an economy with a tight labor market can still generate a progressive distribution of gains from growth, as it had in the past.

Celebrating the progress at a rally for Hillary Clinton in Philadelphia, Obama recited some of the Census findings for the previous year. Then he added "Thank you, Obama," as if no one else was saying "thank you"—an expression perhaps of his frustration in failing to get recognition for the headway he had made on economic well-being despite coming into office

in the worst economic crisis in seventy-five years and receiving no cooperation from Republicans.

The historical memory of presidential leadership is inevitably affected
by what comes afterward. If Clinton had been elected and carried out key
items on her agenda, such as raising the minimum wage and taxes on top
incomes, Obama's record might have been seen as part of a longer wave of
progressive change. But as a result of the advent of unified Republican government in 2017, the Obama years will probably amount only to a parenthe-
sis in the rise of economic inequality. The lesson is likely to be lost that on
inequality as on so much else, even a politically constrained presidency can
make a big difference. But if presidents do not effectively convey their accomplishments in highly visible and readily understood ways, they will be
unable to generate the deep public support that their party can call on to
extend those achievements when in power and to defend them when power
changes hands. Achievements without public credit impair the achievements themselves.

5

Obama's Fight against Global Warming

Meg Jacobs

When Barack Obama came into office in 2009, he promised "change we can count on." Perhaps nothing presented as fundamental a challenge to politics-as-usual as Obama's pledge to solve global warming, as carbon emissions have caused temperatures to rise at an unprecedented rate. An issue so po-larizing that it was nearly absent in the 2016 presidential campaign, global warming has proven more resistant to reform than almost any other public policy. Fundamentally, the issue of climate change poses an insoluble prob-lem for politicians: the benefits of mitigating global warming reveal them-selves in the long term, well beyond any immediate or short-term payoffs for politicians who consider taking this on. And yet Obama insisted that confronting this challenge would constitute an important part of his legacy. "We will respond to the threat of climate change, knowing that failure to do so will betray our children and grandchildren," he boldly declared in his second inaugural address. A child of the 1960s, growing up on the islands of Hawaii, Obama embraced environmentalism as a progressive liberal who believed that he had an obligation to use the power of the presidency to place global warming at the center of public policy once and for all.

Progress on the issue was not for lack of trying. Since the environmental movement of the 1970s, activists and liberal politicians have sought sweep-ing regulatory powers to impose an environmentally friendly regime on

American industry and consumers. The passage of the National Environmental Policy Act (NEPA) in 1970 was an astonishing piece of legislation,
reading more like a manifesto from the 1960s for social change than a blueprint for public policy. At the time, the concern was with pollution and
damage to the health of citizens and nature. Starting with the 1973 Arab oil
embargo, presidents also worried about the security threat of energy dependence by making the United States and its allies reliant on imports from
insecure sources in the Middle East. Since the 1990s, climate change has
added urgency to the fear over a fossil fuel future. Without tough measures
to slow carbon emission, warn advocates of reform, we will reach a point of
no return.

In spite of these warnings, the advances have been mixed at best. Given
the heavy costs of reform, at pivotal moments, the oil, natural gas, coal, and
nuclear industries have shown themselves to be better organized and more
invested than environmentalists and liberal allies in blocking policies to
curb production and promote alternative energies and conservation. Even
in the 1970s, with skyrocketing gas prices and fears of depending on hostile
Arab OPEC producers, long-term, systemic reform proved elusive, in spite
of the enormous efforts of Jimmy Carter, who made solving the energy crisis his top priority. As much as Americans claim to support environmental
reform, their desires to maintain their energy-intensive lifestyles serve as a
roadblock to permanent and wide-reaching change. The public has supported regulation and reform when facing immediate and visible costs of
fossil fuel usage, such as smog, or polluted waters, or asthma attacks. But
they have shown resistance to altering their consumption habits or paying
more for energy for the long-term goal of saving the planet.[1]

Once in office, Obama started out slow, disappointing many of his followers. He understood that to bring about fundamental and lasting change
required pushing a sweeping bill through Congress to limit carbon emissions. That would take a massive commitment to crafting a winning political coalition to overcome the inherent obstacles. Investing in this issue on
Capitol Hill would mean placing it above, or at least on par with, other
important initiatives on the new president's agenda, such as economic recovery and health care. And it would require using the bully pulpit to rally
public opinion. Personally, Obama was a big believer in "doing what's
right," and he hoped that Americans would listen. In the media and in conservative think tanks, opponents had been successfully spreading doubts
about the reality of climate change despite the near unanimity within the
scientific community that this problem was real. On the campaign trail in

2007, the young idealistic senator from Illinois promised to implement a bold, ambitious, clean energy program as soon as he entered the presidency. "When the world arrives at the doorstep of the White House to hear about what America has to say about climate change, I will let them know that America is up to the challenge, that America is ready to lead again." Yet the obstacles to reform trumped the sincerity of Obama's commitment to this issue, and he made no rapid progress on the issue.

But, after two terms, as his time in office neared an end, there was greater respect for what President Obama accomplished, from his Clean Power Plan to the Paris climate accord to other regulatory reforms. He achieved those gains through executive action rather than through a legislative victory and without broad buy-in from the public. These successes suggest the strength and weakness of the Obama presidency as a whole. Specifically, Obama's environmental legacy highlights the role of the president to shape an agenda and use executive action to bring about reform while exposing the fragility of those very tools. With the election of Donald Trump in 2016, many of Obama's advances became vulnerable to rollback by the new GOP president who believes climate change is a "hoax." This reversal confirmed both the seriousness of the obstacles Obama had faced from Republicans when he was in office and, given the lack of real political alternatives, the necessity of Obama's reliance on executive power. In contrast to the image of Obama as politically tone-deaf, in fact, his handling of environmental issues demonstrates his astute maneuverings in an otherwise stalemated polarized system.

First-Term Jitters

In his 2008 primary campaign victory speech, Obama promised his would be the administration "when the rise of oceans began to slow and our planet began to heal." It was time, he said, "to end the tyranny of oil." During the campaign, energy prices were at a high—in August 2008, a gallon of gas peaked at $4.11 a gallon—so, despite how deep its environmentalism did or did not run, the public had good pocketbook reasons to respond to the promise of moving past a fossil fuel future.

Once elected, the Obama White House had to figure out if change was politically possible. In one respect, Obama had an auspicious beginning, winning the commitment of more than 10 percent, totaling $90 billion, of TARP funds dedicated to promoting energy from renewable sources including wind and solar. In addition, in a pivotal decision, the Supreme Court had recently ruled that the Clean Air Act and its amendments required the Environmental Protection Agency (EPA) to regulate emissions of carbon dioxide and other global warming gases. But the key battle would take place in Congress where the goal was to pass legislation to set a limit on carbon emissions and then auction off permission slips to pollute, which firms could buy and sell—a market-based system based on capping overall pollution levels that allowed flexibility for producers and states to reach the stated goal. The White House was not sure whether it could win enough votes, including from some Republicans, which it would need, to get a cap-and-trade bill through.

The idea of cap and trade as the solution to global warming had emerged as early as the 1980s as a conservative response to this policy challenge. Instead of the EPA mandating pollution levels for each industry and every firm, and the exact method of how to attain those goals, Congress would set an overall allowance and let each business decide whether it restricted output, switched to cleaner fuels, installed costly antipollution devices—or paid the money to pollute in excess of its allowances. Policymakers would create market incentives for businesses to protect the environment. Essentially, the idea was to give vouchers issued by the government to trade in the marketplace, providing incentives to manufacturers and power plants to buy and sell the right to pollute. Many environmentalists who had previously favored what its deriders called a "command and control" system of regulation came to see this market approach as preferable, especially after its successful adoption in 1990 to reduce the problem of acid rain. Cap and trade reflected a broader post-1970s liberal embrace of market-based policies over the liberalism of direct government intervention, which had been the basis of the New Deal and the Great Society.

In 2009, to get a bold new bill passed, this kind of market-based cap on carbon emissions, legislated through Congress, required a deal. Those in favor of carbon dioxide regulation would have to allow for greater offshore oil drilling, increased natural gas production, and greater nuclear power as the price for agreeing to an eventual and overall reduction in emissions. In addition, those states that were heavily reliant on coal as a power source for electricity (Pennsylvania, West Virginia, Indiana, Illinois, Ohio, Kentucky) would have to be compensated. Even with Democrats in control of Congress, party leaders would still need to win over members of their party from these extractive regions by offering economic aid to coal miners, for example, as the country moved away from this dirty energy source toward cleaner alternatives.

In June 2009, the House passed the Waxman-Markey bill by a vote of 219–212. It appeared that Obama's goal of cutting emissions by more than a quarter within fifteen years was within sight. As with the creation of healthcare exchanges, Obama seemed to be capitalizing on conservative ideas to achieve core liberal policy goals. Yet the narrow passage of this historic accomplishment did not bode well. Despite a majority of 75 members, the Democrats could not get 44 of its own to vote for the bill and had to turn to the support of a handful of Republicans. The battle would be even tougher in the Senate, where the representatives from fossil fuel states had disproportionate influence. The carrot would be scaling back the EPA's reach, newly empowered by the Supreme Court decision, and coming up with a compromise set of regulations, worked out through the legislative and lobbying process, that industry could count on and live with. For the regulated industries, a legislated deal—with allowance for agreed-upon time schedules, tax incentives, exemptions, all of which they could lobby for—was better than being subject to the EPA's rule-making authority.

The passage of this bill, as riddled with compromises as it was, would have been the most significant legislative environmental breakthrough since the 1970s. To push this through, Senators John Kerry, Lindsey Graham, and Joe Lieberman, each eager to position himself as a dealmaker and author of a major piece of legislation, reached across party lines and worked out an understanding among the leading environmental groups as well as the key affected industries, including oil, utilities, and nuclear power. In exchange for acceding to corporate demands, those in favor of environmental reform saw the measure as a game-changing step in the direction of capping carbon. If the National Environmental Policy Act of 1970 had begun the serious effort to rein in the ill effects of pollution, then this bill would mark the next chapter in which environmentalists took on climate change.

The compromise fell apart in the Senate as a result of bad timing for the White House and the rise of more aggressive climate change deniers on the right. Just as Obama was announcing his support for offshore drilling, a necessary move to get the bill through, the Deepwater Horizon explosion in April 2010 that left eleven men dead and set in motion a massive oil spill in the Gulf of Mexico made these kinds of deals seem unacceptable. As the *New Yorker* reporter Ryan Lizza concluded, "The White House's 'grand bargain' of oil drilling in exchange for a cap on carbon had backfired spectacularly."[2] Given that Obama was investing capital in health care and the bailout, he believed he could not afford to lend support to what now seemed to be an even bigger uphill battle. Groups like the Environmental Defense Fund and the Natural Resources Defense Council worked hard to build an effective coalition and lobby key Capitol Hill members. But absent pressure from constituents and a big White House push, the Senate Democrats from coal and gas states hesitated.

And in spite of early promises from a few like Olympia Snowe and Susan Collins, no Republicans lined up behind the bill. Partisan discipline remained strong on this issue, which commanded strong opposition from powerful corporate supporters of the Republican Party. The issue had also gained strong resonance among conservative activists, becoming a major test for elected officials as to whether they were committed to right-wing principles. Key GOP members who had earlier sponsored global warming bills, including John McCain and Lindsey Graham, were facing tough Tea Party challenges in their home states where any willingness to regulate climate change was a nonstarter at best and a political nightmare at worst. Tea Party supporters, a loose caucus of far-right Republican congressmen, denied the human-made causes of global warming, and a majority of their movement rejected the very idea of climate change, believing that it was another cover for big-government interventions, such as Dodd-Frank financial regulations, the Affordable Care Act, and the stimulus package, all of which helped to arouse and mobilize this conservative base. Even though the Tea Party was at the fringes of the Republican Party, its supporters, organized and well funded by oil and coal interests, including the Koch brothers, played an outsized influence in primary races.

According to the social scientist Theda Skocpol, the biggest problem for an effective legislative strategy for cap and trade came from the absence of a broad-based grassroots mobilization effort on the left. In 1969, an oil spill in Santa Barbara led to public outrage and galvanized the newly forming environmental movement, especially when President Richard Nixon appeared on the oily beaches and threw his weight behind environmental regulation, seeing this issue as a way to mute criticism over Vietnam and win over moderate and young voters. But in 2010, the BP spill, even as it underscored the hazards of continuing to rely on oil, did not push Obama to use this disaster as a clarion call for climate change legislation. At this point, as Skocpol observes, climate change was an insiders' game, based on an environmental-business lobbying alliance, with no grassroots mobilization. In contrast, she argues, healthcare legislation worked because it relied not only on an inside-the-Beltway strategy of working with insurance companies but also could draw on and point to center-left grassroots organization.[3]

The failure to mobilize popular support and backing for climate change legislation became particularly problematic given the successful climate change denial campaign in the 2010 midterms. In 2008, Obama had faced off against Republican candidate John McCain who had run ads supporting climate change legislation in his presidential bid. Two years later, few Republicans were willing to voice any support for legislation, let alone their belief that this was a human-made and very real problem. This was not the result of a change in opinion. During the intervening years, the scientific consensus became even stronger. Rather this Republican reversal resulted from a systematic campaign to require GOP members to sign a "no climate tax" pledge, funded by the oil and gas industry.

The well-funded effort to sideline climate change reform transformed electoral dynamics. Although there was general support for the idea that the globe was heating up and that this warming could cause problems, less than half of all Americans believe that the problem resulted from human activity. Those who rejected the science behind climate warming felt their convictions more deeply and were more vocal and politically engaged—and better financed than those who accepted the scientific consensus.[4] Even as political luminaries or celebrities on the left like Al Gore or Leonardo DiCaprio championed the environmental cause, right-wing groups were more successful at targeting and messaging, especially in Tea Party races. In swing districts, where Obama had won in 2008 by a narrow margin, public opinion polling revealed that support of cap-and-trade legislation cost Democrats their seats in the mid-term election.[5]

The chances for legislation became remote after Republicans won control of the House in 2010. The incoming class included Tea Party climate change deniers, making the future prospect of legislation dim. Eighty-three of the ninety-two new members had signed the "no climate tax pledge."[6] Their obstructionist tactics worked in tandem with the Koch brothers' lobbying efforts against any carbon bill. With a staff of 1,200 people employed by their advocacy group, Americans for Prosperity, they had more than three times the number of employees as the Republican National Committee. Their goal, according to University of Michigan law professor David Uhlmann, was to undo all the regulations since NEPA. "They and their allies want to take us back to 1970, before the regulatory state."[7] Their impact increased when the 2010 *Citizens United* Supreme Court decision eliminated restrictions on election spending by corporations and individuals. Since 2010, campaign contributions from the oil and gas industry skyrocketed, including spending on soft and outside money.[8] In 2012, Richard Lugar, six-time elected senior senator, lost his reelection bid in part because of his moderate views on climate change, which, along with his ownership of a Prius hybrid car, made him vulnerable to a successful Tea Party primary challenge on this issue.[9]

Rallying public support also became harder as the energy market underwent nothing short of a technological revolution. The successful implementation of hydraulic fracking upended all previous assumptions about the availability of oil and natural gas. Through this process of extraction, by which drillers inject liquids into rock formations, they can reach farther underground and in harder-to-access places to release previously trapped fuels. Within a short period of time, these discoveries brought the prospect of energy independence within reach and also radically contributed to lowering the cost of fuel, especially natural gas. That decline had the effect of making more expensive coal plants uneconomical, which led to a decrease in coal use for generating electricity. With the reliance on coal slipping, the increased use of natural gas, which emits fewer greenhouse gases, promised to bring a decline in emissions.

The drop in fuel costs also reduced popular interest in conservation and alternative fuels. With gasoline at half the price it was during the 2008 election, Americans were not as motivated to consider making changes to their consumption patterns. The much-publicized failure of the solar manufacturer Solyndra, which the right pointed to as a case in point of why the government should not invest in solar energy, also led to a slippage in support for alternative fuels. History shows Americans don't care as much about moving beyond fossil fuels when these resources are readily available and cheap. In general, public opinion polls reveal more concern about immediate pocketbook issues and less about large-scale phenomena like global warming.

Calculating that the prospects for environmental reform were small, Obama pulled back for the rest of his first term. Under the radar, he took some actions, but did not seek an overhaul of policy. Nor did he expend a great deal of political capital building support for legislation. Whereas a year or two earlier, it had gained momentum, a cap-and-trade bill fell off the political agenda. Through executive action, Obama implemented more rigorous standards for energy efficiency in appliances, autos, and future power plants. With the auto industry in particular, where he called for more than doubling gas mileage, he understood he had leverage at a moment when the auto industry was receiving a bailout from Washington. This effort to increase gas mileage constituted a major advance since CAFE standards to improve fuel efficiency, which had first been introduced in the 1970s, had stalled with the expiration of these rules and the introduction of

SUVs in the 1990s. But these were not the kinds of high-profile, high-stakes reforms that would lead to a substantial slowing of emissions that the president had promised.

By and large, these moves were all out of the public's eye. Having watched the cost of environmental support in the midterm elections, the White House concluded that the time was not right to advance this cause. The president deliberately delayed controversial decisions at the EPA to propose more aggressive regulations that would have triggered fierce resistance until after his 2012 reelection bid.[10] In fact, in his campaign run against Mitt Romney, Obama routinely bragged about an energy all-of-the-above strategy, proclaiming, "We've added enough new oil and gas pipeline to encircle the Earth, and then some."

Perceiving the White House's tepid support and inaction, the most committed environmentalists sought to trigger a mobilization at the grassroots. They saw an opportunity around the Keystone pipeline issue, which, absent a more aggressive White House agenda, became a test case of Obama's environmental support. Keystone XL is a 1,700-mile pipeline that would transport oil from the tar sands in Canada to the refineries in the Gulf of Mexico. Opponents worried not only about the higher chance for spills and leaking, but also about the increased emissions from greater oil use as well as from the energy-intensive process to extract the oil from the Alberta tar sands. Because the pipeline would cross an international border, the decision for approval rested in the president's hands, and thus it seemed a perfectly designed litmus test, a way to force Obama to make clear the depths of his environmental commitment. Early in his first term, it looked as if Obama would lend support given high unemployment, high energy prices, and his all-of-the-above energy strategy. Based on pure political calculations, given that 60 percent of Americans favored the pipeline, approval seemed likely.

Bill McKibben, author of the 1989 book *The End of Nature*, which was an early attempt to popularize the threat of human-made climate change, took the lead. He formed a grassroots group, 350.org, the name deriving from the calculations of global warming scientist James Hansen, who warned that levels of carbon dioxide levels higher than 350 parts per million would be a point of no return for the planet. The group trained its sights on defeating Keystone. In the spring of 2011, Hansen issued his much-heralded assessment that if the pipeline went through it would be "game over for the planet." Clamping down on coal emissions was a necessity to prevent devastating global warming. But, according to Hansen, allowing for energy production from the tar sands would put the planet on an irreversible trajectory. At the White House, in August 2011, McKibben's group staged a protest with more than 1,200 arrests. In November, another 15,000 demonstrators made a human chain—a "solidarity hug"—around the White House to get Obama's attention. "We want him to live up to what he said he was going to do," said McKibben.[11]

These efforts received a big boost with the formation of a super PAC by California billionaire hedge-fund manager Tom Steyer. His organization, Next Generation Climate, sought to challenge Republican climate change deniers and exact a political cost for their position. He hoped to offer a financial counterweight to the Koch brothers who were continually pouring their resources into political and intellectual initiatives that aimed to discredit climate change and block regulatory action. In November 2011, after the White House protest, Obama announced a delay on the pipeline decision until after the 2012 election. If he opposed it, he feared hurting Democrats in key elections. Steyer successfully backed key environmentalists, including Terry McAuliffe for governor of Virginia and Ed Markey, who had authored the cap-and-trade bill in the House and was now running for the Senate. But he and his advisers also understood the need to change public opinion and mobilize. For that, he lent his support to the Keystone opposition. As Steyer's top policy adviser, Kate Gordon, put it, "The goal is as much about organizing young people around a thing. But you have to have a thing. You can't organize people around a tipping point."[12]

After Obama's 2012 reelection, the president became more outspoken on the environment, but was still hesitant. His rhetoric revealed his true position and in his second inaugural address, where he promised to act for the sake of future generations, he took on his opponents directly, declaring, "Some may still deny the overwhelming judgment of science, but none can avoid the devastating impact of raging fires and crippling drought and more powerful storms." In a June 2013 speech at Georgetown, Obama tipped his hand that he was leaning against Keystone. But the pressure mounted. Canadian officials took out more than $20 million in ads in Metro stations near the White House.[13] Uncertain about his ability to make his rejection of the pipeline stick, with Congress able to pass legislation to approve the pipeline and possibly override a presidential veto, Obama continued to delay his decision.

Obama, who had hoped to be a pioneer, leading not only the Democratic Party but also the entire country toward a fossil-free future, found himself stymied. He had not rallied Americans to the cause. None of the actions he took in his first term, done deliberately under the radar, helped to reshape the public dialogue. Even as the left had embraced this issue, they had not succeeded in triggering a mass mobilization. The only consequence of the Keystone fight was a further polarization on the issue and a ratcheting up on both sides, which in turn boxed the president in. Given the disconnect between environmentalism and the base of the party, where constituents were inclined to see energy as a pocketbook and jobs issue, Obama saw no successful path forward, especially not a big legislative push. On an issue like the pipeline, support alienated many constituents within the Democratic Party, including unions, who claimed that its defeat would lead to a loss of jobs. By the end of his first term and even into his second, it appeared that the president had failed to be the change agent he had promised to be.

Seizing the Mantle: Obama's Use of Executive Action

In truth, Obama was preparing to unsheathe his most powerful weapon—a dramatic use of executive action. In his 2013 State of the Union address, the president revealed his intention to have the EPA move forward on regulating climate change and carbon. "If Congress won't act soon to protect future generations, I will," he said. Corporate opponents of a cap-and-trade bill had come to the table early in Obama's first term with the hopes of delaying the EPA from taking aggressive action. In 2011, the Supreme Court had again affirmed the EPA's power to regulate. But Obama waited to deploy this agency. It was a deliberate political strategy, one that reflected both the realities of a polarized Congress and Obama's often underestimated skill.

Taking on climate change required confronting the coal industry. Coal-fired plants that generate electricity accounted for more than a quarter of carbon emissions, and Obama knew he had to reduce reliance on this dirty power source to reach his stated goals of emissions cuts. In the 1970s, when environmentalists first sought to rein in pollution under the Clean Air Act, they imagined that power plant operators would retire inefficient and ancient coal plants rather than install expensive pollution controls. Thus much of the legislation directed its aim at the construction of new power plants. However, the industry had discovered an unintentional loophole. Instead of building new plants, it could add capacity to existing facilities and argue that these new sources were exempt from regulations. Under George W. Bush the EPA interpreted the law so liberally that operators, in effect, built entire new plants within the body of existing plants while escaping pollution controls. Obama's Clean Power Plan aimed to substantially reduce carbon emissions from these polluting power plants.

Already the number of these coal-powered plants was declining. Since Obama had come into office, more than 200 of the 523 coal-fired plants had shut down as natural gas prices fell and made coal less competitive. Given the government-supported improvements in solar and wind, operators were not likely to build new coal plants. More than twice as many people were finding employment in the solar industry as in coal. And while the 2016 race made it clear that coal miners had a loud and angry voice, disproportionate to their actual numbers, public opinion polls showed that Americans were generally favorable toward regulating greenhouse gas emissions. While they had mixed feelings about Keystone and about global warming in general, they supported regulatory policies when framed as an issue affecting their health.

Still, Obama's strategy was risky and potentially costly. His Clean Power Plan, by which the country would see a fairly rapid decline in coal plants, escalated the fight over climate change. It also played into a larger narrative about Obama as an elitist, out-of-touch politician. His proposal served as exhibit A to his political opponents, particularly Tea Party Republicans, who portrayed Obama as a dictator bent on expanding the federal government's reach, even at the expense of the former base of the Democratic Party, the blue-collar coal miners. Climate change was an issue that resonated in large urban centers on the East and West Coasts, and in the capitals of Western Europe. It was not an issue that played well to working-class interests still suffering from the slow recovery and wage stagnation after the 2008 Great Recession.

As Obama became more resolute in his second term—he called climate change the single greatest threat to future generations in his 2015 State of the Union address—the other side also dug in. In the 2014 election, the GOP retook the Senate, which made Senator James Inhofe, Republican from Oklahoma, the chair of the Senate Energy and Environment Committee. In 2012, Inhofe had published a book called *The Greatest Hoax: How the Global Warming Conspiracy Threatens Your Future*. Newly empowered, from the Senate floor, he threw a snowball to demonstrate his claim that the Earth's temperature was not rising. For him, and for other like-minded conservatives, opposing climate change regulation was not just about representing the fossil-fuel industry, but rather a matter of ideological principle tied to a broader distrust of science. "It is as if the spirit of Rachel Carson—

author of *Silent Spring*—is occupying the Oval Office," remarked Gene Ko-proski of the conservative Heartland Institute.[14]

Now Obama moved with force. In August 2015, he formally announced his Clean Power Plan to cut the nation's carbon emissions from coal-fired power plants. It would take a year for the EPA to hold required public hearings before it could implement new regulations, but the regulations would take effect before he left office. In another dramatic move, in November 2015 Obama rejected the Keystone XL oil pipeline. With unemployment down and oil prices also down, it was easier for the president to eliminate this source of fuel and jobs. The upcoming Paris climate talks also motivated his timing on these actions. It would have been hard for Obama to attend an international summit and pledge a commitment to a worldwide effort to cut back on emissions if he had no credible plan for reducing carbon pollution in his own country. The lesson for Bill McKibben was "not to be as defeatist in the face of the richest industry on Earth as I think I was."[15]

In Paris, Obama seized the chance to act on the world stage, using his presidency as a global bully pulpit. If he faced intractable opposition at home, then he hoped he could find a warmer reception abroad. Throughout his administration, Obama had pledged his commitment to restoring American prestige abroad, which had suffered in the wake of the Iraq war. By embracing international efforts to address climate change, Obama advanced his goal of positioning the United States as a benign world leader committed to liberal internationalism. Moreover, he correctly understood that the United States shared a disproportionate responsibility for emitting heat-trapping greenhouse gases, even as less developed countries were likely to face graver environmental consequences. The only way to play a leadership role was to pledge the United States to an aggressive schedule of slowing emissions.

At the meetings in December 2015, 195 United Nations countries announced their intentions to limit global warming by taking measures to prevent rising temperatures. By design, the agreement was not a treaty, which meant it did not need ratification from the U.S. Senate. Instead it was a nonbinding pledge to take effect once fifty-five countries representing at least 55 percent of global emissions signed onto it. Together the United States and China accounted for 38 percent of global emissions and in September 2016, these two countries signed the climate deal. "Someday we may see this as the moment when we decided to save our planet. History will judge today's efforts as pivotal," Obama announced upon their mutual acceptance.

The signing of this accord, even as it shored up Obama's environmental credentials, caused him further political trouble. Acting unilaterally on an international agreement without submitting it to the Senate, where it was sure to meet its death, offered proof to the president's enemies of yet another dictatorial overreach. Along with the president's support of the Trans-Pacific Partnership, this international accord seemed to suggest a lack of concern with the needs of some working-class voters. Even as Obama suggested that the Asian trade agreement and an embrace of renewable energies would create greater prosperity for Americans, he failed to communicate that message effectively to the broader public. Critics of the Paris accord quickly jumped in to argue that the agreement would cost Americans in the coal industry jobs and would result in a slowing of overall growth. The Paris accord was a sign of Obama's out-of-touch, heavy-handed elitism.

Finally, in another unprecedented move, as his time in office came to a close, President Obama protected millions of acres of public lands and waters from development. In doing so, he had plenty of examples from Theodore Roosevelt to Jimmy Carter, who also faced a hostile Congress toward the end of his time in office and moved to protect large tracts of Alaskan land from development. But Obama used his executive authority on an even grander scale, setting aside more than 253 million acres of land and water, which was more than any other president.

The more Obama took deliberate action, the more he triggered greater resistance. Obama's opponents turned to the courts to prevent implementation of the Clean Power Plan. Not only did the fossil-fuel industry depict Obama as an imperious dictator, but it successfully mobilized state attorneys general to resist and challenge the expansion of federal power. Scott Pruitt, the attorney general of Oklahoma who received millions of dollars in campaign contributions from the fossil-fuel lobby, took the lead in refuting the EPA's constitutional power, which he and other AGs denounced as the actions of "radical bureaucrats." In February 2016, the Supreme Court issued a stay on Obama's Clean Power Plan as an appellate court heard a challenge from Republican-led states and industry groups.

Green Legacy?

By the time Obama left office, the United States surpassed Saudi Arabia as the greatest producer of oil and a massive exporter of coal, which effectively meant exporting emissions to other countries. Emissions fell under

Obama in part because of the 2008 recession and the decline in economic activity. But with the return of growth, those gains threatened to be lost. "At the moment when physics tells us we should be jamming on the carbon brakes, America is revving up the engine," said Bill McKibben, who remained a staunch critic of the president, denouncing the United States as a "global-warming machine." From his point of view, it was simple: "Most of the coal and gas and oil that's underground has to stay there if we're going to slow climate change." It is not enough, he said, to invest in green technologies. Even as wind-power generation had doubled and solar power had soared six times over, the United States was poised to become the biggest producer of oil and a major exporter of coal. "It's like eating a pan of Weight Watchers brownies after you've already gobbled a quart of Ben and Jerry's."[16]

Yet Obama had taken aggressive executive actions to slow emissions and force a substantial change in policy. The story of Obama's environmental policy reshapes how we think of his presidency. Rather than aloof or politically unskilled, his moves in this area show him to be both deeply committed and deeply political. For example, his choice before the 2012 election to delay on new EPA rules reflected a political decision to save congressional seats in order to ensure Democratic elections, including his own. And his decisive moves after his reelection and his choice to accelerate the use of executive action after 2014 demonstrate his willingness to deploy his political capital when he believed it would be most effective.

The most pressing uncertainty, though, both for the environment and for Obama's green legacy, was whether his executive actions would stick. With the loss of Hillary Clinton and the victory of Donald Trump in the 2016 election, the prospects of a reversal of Obama's actions became very real. Trump gave voice to a full-throated climate change denial position, denouncing it as a "hoax." Moreover, his embrace of coal miners with his promise to block Obama's Clean Power Plan and pull out of the Paris accord played well in the swing states of Pennsylvania, Ohio, West Virginia, and Michigan. After coming into office, Trump appointed Scott Pruitt as the head of the EPA and he lived up to his promise to reject the Paris agreement. Only a legislative solution to limit emissions and invest in clean technologies would have guaranteed Obama's legacy.

The question remains whether Obama could have done more to shore up his gains. Obama himself did not change the political calculus on climate change. Even as he jumped into the international spotlight in Paris, he did not push hard from the beginning to sell the need for a climate bill to the public. Under his watch, in part as a reaction against his timidity, an ongoing and expanding grassroots movement began to form. As Bill McKibben himself remarked after the Keystone decision, "All I ever wanted to see was a movement to stop climate change and now I've seen it."[17] The movement evolved from organizing against Keystone to a demand on college campuses for divestment from fossil-fuel corporations.[18] Since 2012, organizations formed on more than two hundred college campuses, especially in the Northeast, and Stanford University decided to divest. But, if anything, the political prospects for legislative reform grew dimmer during Obama's time in office. As much as Obama maneuvered within the confines of what was politically possible and will likely be remembered for his bold embrace of executive action, his environmental accomplishments are at best fragile. Executive action without political support will probably prove a thin reed upon which to build a lasting legacy.

6

Obama's Court?

Risa Goluboff and Richard Schragger

When Barack Obama became the forty-fourth president of the United States in 2009, the Supreme Court was not high on his list of priorities. A Harvard-trained lawyer himself, Obama had long thought social change more likely to come from the grassroots than decisions the Court would hand down from on high.[1] In 1991, when Obama graduated from law school—after serving as the first African American president of the *Harvard Law Review*—he eschewed the prestigious and well-worn path to a federal clerkship or an elite, national legal organization like the NAACP or ACLU. Instead, he returned to Chicago, where he had been a community organizer before law school, accepting positions with the University of Chicago Law School and a prominent local civil rights litigation firm.

No doubt, Obama's views on the efficacy of the courts had much to do with the time in which he came of age. Twenty years earlier, young lawyers who held Obama's views would have embraced the heroically liberal Supreme Court that had dominated the mid-twentieth century. By 1991, conservatives had already held a majority on the Court for twenty-three years. The trend looked likely to continue, and it did. In fact, Obama's law school years coincided with a burgeoning conservative attack on both liberal constitutional doctrines and liberal approaches to constitutional interpretation more generally. When Obama took up the presidency, the Court was more conservative than ever, and it seemed poised to succeed in its transformational ambitions.

The big surprise during Obama's presidency was that it did not. The constitutional bedrock those earlier liberal Courts had built proved far more resistant to change than anyone had predicted. To be sure, Obama and the liberals on the Court lost many a case over the eight years of the Obama era. But even before the Court lost its most powerful conservative with Antonin Scalia's death a year before Obama left the presidency, the predicted constitutional realignment had not come to pass. In the battle between a liberal president and a conservative-majority Court, Obama prevailed when it came to blockbuster cases on new issues, like the Affordable Care Act and same-sex marriage, as well as the defense of longstanding doctrines like affirmative action and abortion. Despite the conservatism of the Court's majority, it has been Obama's Court, which is to say a twenty-first-century Court that continues to reflect—even if imperfectly—the central preoccupations of the second half of the twentieth century.

With the election of Donald Trump to the presidency in 2016, that equilibrium was precipitously threatened. Trump quickly made his first appointment to the Supreme Court in 2017—an appointment that Democrats claimed was stolen from Obama by the Republicans' refusal to consider his nominee. And while Trump's appointment of federal appellate judge Neil Gorsuch was relatively conventional, Trump's ascendancy and governing style has been anything but. With the help of an intransigent Republican Senate, Trump has already reshaped the Court. Given the age of some of the remaining justices, that transformation seems likely to continue. Obama can only watch as his judicial legacy threatens to wither to almost nothing, as a Court that looked as though it might have a solidly liberal majority returns yet again to the cusp of conservative control.

The Mid-Century Settlement

The constitutional doctrine the Supreme Court elaborated in the middle of the twentieth century had two essential features: the broad legitimacy of the federal administrative state, especially in the realm of economic regulation, and the judicial protection of civil rights and civil liberties. The legitimacy of the administrative state had its origins in the New Deal era of the 1930s. Though the Supreme Court had initially thwarted President Franklin D. Roosevelt's responses to the Great Depression, by the latter part of the decade the Court had placed its imprimatur on a vastly expanded federal administrative apparatus. For the following fifty years, the Court allowed the political branches virtually free rein to regulate the economic and social spheres.

As it evolved, the mid-century settlement became as much about carving out a space for judicial protection of minorities and fundamental rights as it was about protecting the administrative state from the judiciary.[2] The first African American president of the United States was possible because of a civil rights movement that had received the Court's blessing in *Brown v. Board of Education* in 1954, a movement that forced the adoption of the civil rights acts of the 1960s and fundamentally changed the American electoral calculus.[3] Beginning with *Brown*, the Warren Court became synonymous with the judicial expansion of a certain kind of liberal constitutional rights, from racial equality to privacy to freedom of speech and religion. Taken together, the constitutional developments that characterized the 1930s to the 1960s established both the enormous power of the federal government and the judicial protection of individual and minority rights.

Even before the justices put the finishing touches on this mid-century settlement, however, Republican appointees to the Court began proliferating. Beginning with Richard M. Nixon in 1969, Republican presidents seemed to have all the Supreme Court vacancy luck. Over the course of just three years, Nixon appointed four new members of the Court: Chief Justice Warren Burger and Associate Justices Lewis F. Powell, Harry A. Blackmun, and William H. Rehnquist. Though the Burger Court was less liberal than its predecessor, it nonetheless continued expanding individual rights, most notably where women's rights were concerned. In 1986, the Burger Court gave way to the identifiably more conservative Rehnquist Court. Even after Bill Clinton appointed Ruth Bader Ginsburg and Stephen G. Breyer to the Court in the 1990s, that conservative dominance continued with seven Republican-appointed justices. The Rehnquist Court was the most stable in 150 years. Breyer remained the junior justice—speaking last at conference, responsible for ministerial tasks when the justices convened—for eleven long years.[4]

The conservatives who increasingly populated the Court toward the end of the century did not accept the evolved equilibrium of a vast administrative state combined with judicial protection of liberal rights. Justices Antonin Scalia and Clarence Thomas, appointed in 1986 and 1991 by Republicans Ronald Reagan and George H. W. Bush respectively, were unafraid of enforcing their version of the Constitution whether or not it challenged established political settlements. In fact, they were part of a more fundamental challenge to the method of constitutional interpretation itself. Articulated most powerfully on the Court by the charismatic Justice Scalia, this conservative challenge strategically embraced an approach to the Constitution that emphasized the text of the document and its original understanding. The goal was to limit judicial discretion to protect liberal causes and produce more conservative constitutional outcomes. With the assistance of Reagan's attorney general, Edwin Meese—perched at the center of the government's prosecutors—lawyers, scholars, and ultimately judges were enormously successful in making textualist and originalist arguments.[5]

That interpretive victory did not translate directly into doctrinal successes, however. Despite several decades of a majority of Republican appointments, the Court had not delivered as conservatives had expected by 2000. Too many Republican-appointed justices had turned out to be less than reliable. Justices John Paul Stevens (Nixon, 1975), Sandra Day O'Connor (Reagan, 1981), Anthony M. Kennedy (Reagan, 1988), and David H. Souter (George H. W. Bush, 1990) were all disappointments. Stevens and Souter came to be closely aligned with the Court's left flank. O'Connor and Kennedy became swing justices, sometimes moving across the political aisle to join the liberals on key issues like abortion, affirmative action, church-and-state, and LGBTQ rights.

It was against this backdrop that, in 2005, George W. Bush appointed John G. Roberts to replace Rehnquist as chief justice and Samuel Alito to replace O'Connor. Roberts was a 1979 graduate of Harvard Law School and a scion of the conservative legal establishment. Even more important for the balance of the Court, the appointment of Alito, a judge and former prosecutor with impeccable conservative credentials, enabled Bush to replace a swing voter with a consistent conservative.

With Alito and Roberts at the Court, conservatives saw a better chance to remake the Constitution. Some years earlier, conservative appellate Judge Douglas Ginsburg had bemoaned that the New Deal Court had "exiled" the crucial provisions of constitutional federalism—most prominently the Commerce Clause—by failing to heed meaningful limits on federal power. Reestablishing the "Constitution-in-Exile" would undermine the legitimacy of the regulatory state that had been insulated from constitutional challenge since the New Deal.[6] Conservative justices were equally committed to rolling back the protection of individual rights in areas like affirmative action and abortion, and stopping the evolving protection of sexual orientation in its tracks. This more reliable 5–4 Court seemed poised to deliver on promises not kept—a wholesale remaking of the mid-century constitutional settlement seemed achievable.

Obamacare and the Persistence of the Administrative State

The opportunity came with the constitutional challenge to President Obama's Affordable Care Act (ACA, or "Obamacare," as it was quickly dubbed), the signal achievement of his domestic policy and the most significant expansion of the regulatory state in a generation.[7] Though the Court had imposed almost no limits on Congress's power to regulate in an area of nationwide concern for the fifty years following the New Deal, the Rehnquist Court had flirted with reimposing such limits. During the 1990s, the Court for the first time since 1936 struck down a few federal laws as exceeding Congress's power to regulate under the Commerce Clause (though none involved the regulation of a national marketplace or the invalidation of a national entitlement program).[8] By the time Obama succeeded in making the Affordable Care Act law, then, longstanding precedent suggested it would be constitutional, but more recent trends made it vulnerable.

Reviled by the entirety of the Republican Party, especially its Tea Party wing, and offensive to the very notion of a federal government with limited powers, the ACA precipitated a severe political backlash as soon as it was signed into law on March 23, 2010. The following fall, Republicans regained control of the House; in 2014, they gained a majority in the Senate. Health care was both the beginning and end of Obama's grand domestic policy successes.[9]

States with strong conservative governments swung into action to challenge the law in court. An empowered political movement presented the resurgent conservative Court a unique opportunity to strike down a comprehensive social welfare statute on the order of Social Security or Medicaid, to establish a potent principle of limited federal government, and to reset the mid-century settlement for decades.

None of those things happened. In a splintered decision handed down in June 2012, the Court upheld the part of the statute most offensive to those hoping for a return of the Constitution-in-Exile. This was the individual mandate—the requirement that all citizens buy health insurance or face a financial penalty.[10] A federal government that could force a person, or millions of people, to buy health insurance that they did not want was a federal government that could do anything. Roberts wrote an opinion for himself. He agreed with the four other conservatives—Kennedy and Alito, in addition to Scalia and Thomas—that the individual mandate could not be upheld as a valid exercise of the federal government's power to regulate commerce, and that it was invalid under the Constitution's Necessary and Proper Clause. He nonetheless saved the mandate by treating the penalty as a tax and therefore as a valid exercise of Congress's taxing powers. Congress could not order people to buy health insurance, but it could tax people for not having it.[11]

The remaining conservatives authored a bitter dissent that, in an unusual move that highlighted their solidarity, they all signed jointly. Conservative commentators savagely attacked the chief justice they had held up as their champion just a few years before.[12] Roberts might have been surprised by the vitriol. After all, he had been careful to salvage the jurisprudentially important issue—the Commerce Clause—despite validating the law. He also significantly expanded the Court's conditional spending clause doctrine by holding that states could opt out of the federal government's proposed Medicaid expansion without losing preexisting federal Medicaid funding. Many conservative states opted to do just that.

The political implications of the case were clearly more salient to the public, and perhaps to the conservatives on the Court, than the constitutional ones. Roberts's vote saved Obama's leading domestic initiative, at least for the remainder of Obama's presidency. But the decision also lent energy to the Tea Party wing of the Republican Party. A Republican Congress voted repeatedly to dismantle Obamacare.[13] And in 2016, Obama's successor, Donald Trump, would ride the wave of popular discontent all the way to the White House by promising repeal.

Rumors abounded as to both the cause and timing of Roberts's apostasy. The structure and substance of the opinions suggested that he had abandoned his usual bedfellows late in the game. It is difficult to say what motivated the chief justice. Predictably, he asserted that his fidelity to the rule of law dictated his vote. But that begged the question of what exactly the rule of law meant and which way it pointed, clearly a question in some dispute. There is no way to know whether he had other motivations. Aware of the Court's limited political capital, Roberts might have decided not to spend it here—instead choosing to embed doctrinal bombs that could be detonated in future years. Indeed, for many commentators, the fact that five justices agreed that the ACA violated the Commerce Clause signaled a dangerously out-of-touch and radical Court. It portended the kind of judicial activism last seen when the Court regularly struck down Progressive and New Deal era social welfare legislation in the decades before the New Deal.[14] One could also speculate that Roberts might have calculated that in an election year, the backlash against invalidation from an energized Democratic base would undermine his longer-term political interests. Even if he was the target, an organized right might prove more productive for his views in the long run.

Regardless of Roberts's motivation, the New Deal agreement that economic regulation would be committed to the political branches persisted at a moment that could have seen its dramatic undoing. Though that settlement is more about Congress's formal powers than the president's, the initiative here was clearly the president's. Moreover, Chief Justice Roberts, who had been thought of as the standard-bearer of the conservative revolution, had ensured the ACA's survival. Momentary political winds notwithstanding, the man ultimately seemed no match for the long-term equilibrium of the mid-century settlement.

The Rights Revolution Extended and Defended

If the ACA represented the counter-revolution that failed to undermine the administrative state, same-sex marriage tells an even more dramatic story in the realm of individual rights. The drama of this latter story inheres in both the fact that the Roberts Court extended individual rights to people and areas beyond the Warren and Burger Courts and the rapidity with which it did so.

By 2008, LGBTQ Americans had been fighting openly for their rights for more than sixty years.[15] Over the course of the 1950s and 1960s, gay rights organizations proliferated and flourished, and the movement grew in size, assertiveness, and visibility. Even so, judicial and political victories were a long time coming. In 1986, the Supreme Court upheld 5–4 a sodomy statute selectively applied to gay men.[16] It was not until 1996 that the Court visibly, if partially, protected sexual orientation in an opinion that struck down a Colorado statute barring local governments from extending antidiscrimination protections to gay men and lesbians.[17] Seven years later, Justices Kennedy and O'Connor joined the liberals in *Lawrence v. Texas*, which reversed the 1986 sodomy decision and established an individual right to sexual privacy.[18]

Lawrence led Justice Scalia to complain in dissent that a constitutional right to same-sex marriage was now only a matter of time. In fact, state supreme courts in Massachusetts and Hawaii began articulating the case for marriage equality around the turn of the century as well.[19] If courts embraced gay rights in some form by the 1990s, it took far longer even for Democratic political leaders. In 1996, Democratic president Bill Clinton signed the Defense of Marriage Act (DOMA), which prohibited the federal government from recognizing same-sex marriages validly performed under state laws. In 2008, Obama the candidate took the position that marriage should be restricted to opposite-sex couples, with civil unions for gay men and lesbians.

That position threatened to put Obama out of sync with much of his constituency. By the time the Supreme Court addressed the question in 2013 and 2015, most Americans thought that marriage equality was a foregone constitutional conclusion. In the twenty years between 1996 and 2016, Americans' views on same-sex marriage flipped, from close to 70 percent disapproval to over 60 percent approval.[20]

Indeed, within five years of his campaign, Obama the president put his weight behind the LGBTQ movement. When the Court considered DOMA in *United States v. Windsor* in 2013, Obama's Justice Department refused to defend the law.[21] In 2015, his solicitor general argued before the Supreme Court on the side of full marriage equality in *Obergefell v. Hodges*.[22] The Court agreed, requiring the states to recognize same-sex marriages.[23] Kennedy made the fifth vote in the 5–4 cases, and his majority opinion in *Obergefell* offered a paean to the importance and sanctity of marriage.[24]

As Timothy Stewart-Winter highlights,[25] the rapidity of these developments over the course of the Obama presidency was astonishing and unprecedented. Especially given Obama's earlier doubts about same-sex marriage, it seems apt to say that social forces pushed elected officials and the Court toward marriage equality. Yet the culture wars—which Obama sought so desperately to overcome—continued unabated. Even *Obergefell*, the most fulsome of the Kennedy opinions, did not explicitly extend the Equal Protection Clause to LGBTQ Americans beyond marriage. And the rise of same-sex marriage invited a host of state-level "religious freedom" laws permitting businesses to discriminate against gays and lesbians.[26] Similar federal laws were proposed, and the existing federal Religious Freedom Restoration Act (RFRA) was deployed to protect cultural conservatives in the face of a hostile Court and administration.

Indeed, for evangelicals and other religious traditionalists, same-sex marriage was only the latest in a long series of judicial onslaughts that they had worked for fifty years to overturn—either through the courts or through state legislatures and Congress. In *Burwell v. Hobby Lobby*, the Court held that a for-profit corporation could assert a religious liberty exemption under RFRA from the ACA's requirement that employer health plans provide contraception coverage for their employees.[27] *Hobby Lobby* was the perfect Obama storm: a federal mandate imposing contraception coverage requirements on religious traditionalists operating their business along religious lines. The Court's decision extending religious freedom rights to a corporate plaintiff was doctrinally significant and reflected the energy with which religious traditionalists continued to battle against a mid-century settlement that licensed such federal power and such a liberal assault on conventional morality.

Abortion, of course, had been and continued to be the über-issue. The Court decided twenty abortion-related cases after *Roe v. Wade* mandated access to the procedure in 1973.[28] Throughout the Reagan and two Bush administrations, presidents and their solicitors general asked the Court to overturn *Roe*, and the Court's abortion jurisprudence waxed and waned with the impulses of swing justices O'Connor and Kennedy. The Court always ultimately reaffirmed the basic right, even if its exercise lost a fair amount of protection in practice. In 2016, the final abortion decision of the Obama era concerned stringent Texas regulations that made it almost impossible for abortion clinics to remain open.[29] Justified on the grounds of maternal health, the laws required abortion providers to provide hospital-level facilities for an outpatient procedure. An eight-member Court, deciding 5–3, did not hesitate to identify the *real* intent of the regulations, which was to put clinics out of business. It invalidated the regulations as imposing an "undue burden" on the rights of abortion-seeking patients.[30]

To many, 2016 had seemed like the moment the Court would finally withdraw constitutional protection for abortion. Once again the counter-revolution failed to materialize. Along with same-sex marriage and school prayer (and perhaps going forward, transgender rights), abortion served as a litmus test for both sides in the political arena. The country has still not made peace with the sexual revolutions of the 1960s and 1970s. Abortion and LGBTQ rights are the long tail of that revolution—an outgrowth of the social and political movements that began with the baby boom generation and still exert outsized cultural and social influence.[31] Ironically, it was the allegedly conservative Roberts Court that put to rest, for the moment at least, the most aggressive claims against the fundamental rights that had been a critical part of the mid-century settlement.

Color-Blindness and Race Consciousness
in the Twenty-First Century

The record is more troubling on what is often considered the core issue of constitutional rights under the mid-century settlement: race. One of the central (and dismaying) realities of the Obama presidency was that the first African American president unleashed (perhaps predictably) a virulently racist countermovement. Whether Donald Trump's ascendancy to the presidency was the exclamation point to that movement or merely coincided with what appeared to be a white backlash will no doubt occupy historians for some time.

At the same time, Obama's electoral success gave cover for courts and policymakers to assert that we now live in a postracial world. Certainly, state-backed, de jure racial segregation has been impermissible since the dismantling of Jim Crow in the mid-twentieth century. The question that followed was whether the Constitution required, or at least allowed, governments to redress the racial inequalities that persisted despite the ban on legal discrimination.[32] Beginning in the 1970s and gaining traction in the 1980s, conservative justices became skeptical of such race-conscious remedies and affirmative action. Embracing the concept of "color-blindness," they contended that the government must be neutral as between the races, and that as the nation achieved such neutrality, civil rights remedies were no longer appropriate.[33]

That societal change obviates the need for racial remedies was the theme of the Roberts Court's most aggressive attack on race-based government action—the 2013 case of *Shelby County v. Holder*.[34] *Shelby County* struck down part of the Voting Rights Act of 1965 (VRA). Intended to hold state and local governments—especially in the South—accountable for the suppression of the black vote, the VRA had been a target of conservative ire for decades. Of particular concern were Section 5, which requires certain state and local governments to obtain federal preclearance before implementing any changes to their voting laws or practices, and Section 4(b), which contains the coverage formula that determines which jurisdictions are subjected to preclearance due to histories of discrimination in voting. Preclearance gave the Justice Department a potent tool to discourage state and local voting changes that undermined black (and consequently often Democratic) voting power. It was also an affront to the sovereignty of those places, for it signaled a certain kind of probationary status.

In *Shelby County*, the jurisdictions under the preclearance regime argued that the coverage formula in 4(b) was based on forty-year-old data that did not reflect significant changes that had occurred over that time. As Justice Roberts observed in his majority opinion, since the coverage formula was last modified in 1975, the country "has changed, and while any racial discrimination in voting is too much, Congress must ensure that the legislation it passes to remedy that problem speaks to current conditions."[35] Prior oversight based on past data impermissibly violated the principles of state sovereignty and limited federal power.

This takedown of a key provision of the Voting Rights Act was a significant incursion into the mid-century settlement, undermining both the power of the federal government's political branches and an earlier conception of equal protection and racial equality. The Voting Rights Act is a central component of the equal rights edifice that President Lyndon Johnson, at the urging of Martin Luther King Jr., helped to force through a somewhat recalcitrant Congress. Its passage came at great cost, most notably in the blood of lynched, tortured, and martyred African Americans. Its status as a super-statute, one with significant constitutional dimensions, had been unquestioned in both Republican and Democratic administrations and Congresses—which regularly renewed it with almost unanimous acclaim.

In the age of Obama, the Roberts Court brought down an important component of that edifice at least partly because of the success of the first black president. That many Republican-controlled states had adopted new voter suppression techniques in the aftermath of Obama's first victory (like voter identification laws intended ostensibly to fight "voter fraud") did not seem to matter to the Court. Though the four liberal dissenting justices predicted that *Shelby County* would lead to more of the same, Roberts asserted that there had to come a time when the country moved on from its race problem. In Justice Scalia's words, the Voting Rights Act constituted a "perpetuation of racial entitlement," and a "racial preferment"[36] that was no longer warranted.

Initially, the Roberts Court seemed poised to treat other claims for affirmative protections for racial minorities similarly—as simply past their prime. Prior to Obama's ascendancy, affirmative action had already been on the defensive. Though the 2003 case of *Grutter v. Bollinger* upheld the constitutionality of race-conscious admissions policies at the University of Michigan Law School, Justice O'Connor, writing for a 5–4 liberal majority, suggested a time limit of twenty-five years for such racial preferences.[37] In a companion case, the Court struck down the University of Michigan's undergraduate affirmative action plan for not providing the same individualized assessments as the law school did.[38]

The Court moved even more aggressively in *Parents Involved in Community Schools v. Seattle School District* in 2007.[39] That case considered the constitutionality of race-based primary and secondary school assignments. The Seattle and Louisville school districts had voluntarily adopted pupil assignment plans that considered race in an effort to maintain racial balance and ensure desegregation. The Court invalidated both plans. The chief justice, again writing for a divided Court, asserted famously that "the way to stop discrimination on the basis of race is to stop discriminating on the basis of race."[40]

Yet the swing justices continued to dictate outcomes in such cases. In *Parents Involved*, Justice Kennedy differed with his conservative colleagues in claiming that race could *sometimes* justify government action. Equal protection doctrine remained contested in the Obama era. Even more significantly, in the 2016 case of *Fisher v. University of Texas*,[41] Justice Kennedy, for the first time, joined an opinion upholding an affirmative action plan in higher education. Liberals had worried since the rise of the Rehnquist Court that affirmative action would fall, and the Roberts Court seemed surely poised to make that a reality. But even as the Court and some of the public remained hostile, the principle of "diversity" continued to gain traction in the larger society, with military and business leaders bolstering the universities' claims that race consciousness was necessary for the development of national leadership and international competitiveness in every sector. Unlike *Shelby County*, where racial and partisan politics converged to undermine a key mid-century protection, *Fisher* proved a notable victory for progressives. It was another indication of the staying power of the mid-century settlement, even in the face of a Court that had seemed poised to destroy it.

Conservative Victories and the New Rights Bearers

Even as affirmative action survived, *Shelby County* was hardly alone in moving constitutional doctrine in a more conservative direction. Though the Court largely failed to undermine prior liberal bedrock, it did succeed in establishing some new conservative principles within constitutional law. Consider the 2008 case of *District of Columbia v. Heller*, in which the Court, by a bare majority, struck down a Washington, D.C., gun regulation as a violation of the Second Amendment.[42] Enshrining the Second Amendment as an individual rights provision—against arguments that it only applied to gun possession in the context of militias—was a significant step. *Heller* buttressed the rights claims of a core constituency of the Republican Party, gave constitutional legitimacy to the National Rifle Association—one of the most powerful interest groups in the nation—and offered conservatives a rights jurisprudence that they could embrace.

That jurisprudence bolstered the politics that had partially created it. Despite the mass shooting of children in a Sandy Hook, Connecticut, elementary school, preceded and followed by numerous other mass shootings throughout the country, the gun rights answer was always more guns, not fewer. When Obama talked about passing more stringent gun laws, gun sales soared.[43] Obama reluctantly spent a great deal of political capital attempting to rein in the peculiar American penchant for violence—to no avail. The political support for gun rights now had constitutional support as well.

Heller also served as notice that rights claims could work against progressives as much as for them. Most dramatically, the new rights claims included rights for corporations. In a case Obama condemned in his 2011 State of the Union address—2010's *Citizens United v. Federal Election Commission*—the Court struck down campaign finance laws that limited the capacity of corporations to spend money on political advocacy.[44] The decision undermined a key tenet of campaign finance reform. Moreover, it appeared to do so by treating corporations as worthy of exercising First Amendment rights. As liberals defended the constitutionality of so much New Deal and Warren Court precedent, this is the case that liberal justices said they themselves most wanted to see overturned.[45]

That antipathy had two sources: the offensive notion of corporate rights and the larger problem of concentrated wealth. If the mid-century New Deal settlement had succeeded by allowing extensive regulation of the economic sphere while protecting liberal individual rights, the Roberts Court most radically undermined that settlement at the contact point between those two spheres: economic inequality. Ever since the Court decided in 1937 to leave debates over redistribution to the political branches and determined that racial inequality could be addressed separately from economic inequality, it had remained on the sidelines of economic debates.[46] This was so during the late New Deal, when Johnson pursued his War on Poverty, and as the Reagan revolution cut back on federal antipoverty programs. Though coming perilously close in the Obamacare case, the Court (mostly) stayed out of the way as successive Congresses and presidents fought over the contours of the social welfare state.

At the turn of the twenty-first century—in what some called a new "Gilded-Age"[47]—economic inequality emerged as a problem for the Court through a different, and not altogether direct, avenue: campaign finance. The dismantling of the post-Nixon campaign finance system, imperfect as it was, was one of the Roberts Court's greatest successes or most abject failures—depending on which side of the issue one was on.

The most visible import of *Citizens United*, however, was in its underlying principle that money equals speech at a moment when the richest 0.1 percent of Americans owned more wealth than the bottom 90 percent.[48] *Citizens United* reinforced an already existing perception that the political class was owned by the capitalist one—that concentrated wealth skewed policymaking. That *Citizens United* also asserted that corporations enjoy speech rights did not help matters. In the shadow of the Great Recession of 2008, when banks were bailed out and their managers were not held to account for the foolish (and sometimes criminal) things they did, treating corporations as persons with rights seemed to add insult to injury. The populist movements that produced a right-wing Donald Trump and a left-wing Bernie Sanders reflected a deeply held belief that the system was rigged.

Just as the Court in the original Gilded Age reinforced the growing inequalities of capitalism with what many viewed as its laissez-faire judicial doctrine, the Roberts Court was more generally characterized by its corporation-friendliness. The U.S. Chamber of Commerce certainly had a good run after Roberts and Alito were appointed: the Court sided with the Chamber close to 70 percent of the time.[49] Many of these cases are obscure to the ordinary citizen. They include decisions that force consumers to go to arbitration instead of litigation, that make it more difficult for plaintiffs to obtain class-action status, or that limit punitive damages or raise the bar to corporate liability.[50]

Pointing to *Citizens United*, *Shelby County*, *Heller*, and the Chamber of Commerce victories, commentators have asserted that the Roberts Court has been the most conservative in the Supreme Court's modern history. It is undeniable that during Obama's two terms, the Court's conservative wing was ascendant in many important areas and that the conservative justices made progress toward their counterrevolutionary agenda. Even so, many expected the Court to devastate the mid-century settlement. It did not. The Court ruled for progressives in a number of areas: affirmative action remained possible in higher education; the right to abortion was reaffirmed as one that states cannot unduly burden; and gay men and lesbians gained marriage rights. The outlines of a new conservatism are identifiable, but the real story is how much of the liberal standards of the mid-twentieth century stood fast against what had at the start seemed inevitable destruction. Whether that destruction was merely—and only briefly—postponed, however, remains a live question.

The Power and Politics of Appointments

A year before Obama was scheduled to leave office, the sudden death of seventy-nine-year-old Antonin Scalia gave him the opportunity to further entrench the mid-century settlement with his own appointment to the Court. Obama had already placed two justices there: Sonia Sotomayor replaced David Souter and Elena Kagan replaced John Paul Stevens. Sotomayor and Kagan joined Justice Ruth Bader Ginsburg, the eighty-three-year-old Clinton appointee, bringing the total number of women on the Court to an historic high of three—all of them liberal. During the Obama years, Ginsburg attained something of the status of a rock star in certain progressive and feminist circles—along with the nickname "Notorious RBG." Sotomayor became an outspoken voice, popular as the first Latina on the Court, and unafraid to articulate the new perspective her experience growing up in a poor neighborhood in New York gave her. Meanwhile, commentators anointed Elena Kagan—with her clear opinions directed not at the cognoscenti but at the public writ large and her considerable, William J. Brennan–like interpersonal savvy—the future intellectual center of a post-Roberts Court that was likely to lose its most senior liberals, Ginsburg and Breyer, in the next decade.

Obama's appointments solidified the liberal wing of the Court, but they did not change the number of votes on either side. Though he got off to a slow start, Obama's appointments in the lower courts were more transformative. His initial attempts to depoliticize the judicial nomination and appointment process failed. Just as obstruction and deadlock characterized Obama's relations with Congress for the last four years of his presidency, so too they characterized his judicial nominations.[51] Republican senators filibustered a significant number of his district court nominees, something that had happened only rarely in earlier administrations. Though thirty-five courts were sufficiently short-handed to be designated judicial emergencies, when Obama left office some fifty nominees remained stranded in the Senate.[52] Even so, Obama successfully placed 323 judges: 268 in district courts and 55 in the courts of appeals. They were the most diverse group of judges in history. In several circuit courts where conservatives had reigned, liberals began to prevail.[53]

Scalia's death in 2016 instantly changed the political calculus at the high court. Cases that might have been decided 5–4 with Scalia giving a conservative edge ended up tied at the end of the 2015 term. That split left lower court decisions in place. These included a case challenging compulsory union dues that had been decided for the union and an immigration case in which the lower court had invalidated Obama's executive order providing millions of undocumented immigrants some protection from deportation.[54] The latter issue became moot with the election of Donald Trump, as political events overtook judicial ones. Trump's anti-immigrant executive orders became the subject of new judicial challenges. Trump found himself at the beginning of his administration also facing resistance from the courts—this time from the other side of the political spectrum.[55]

Scalia's death might have given Obama an opportunity to further entrench the mid-century settlement with a fifth liberal vote at the Court. Obama chose Merrick Garland, a well-respected, moderate, sixty-three-year-old judge on the Court of Appeals for the District of Columbia. Garland was an uncontroversial pick in any presidential administration and a choice that would normally kick up little fuss even amid a polarized electorate. However, the Republican-controlled Congress refused to consider the nomination, betting that a future Republican administration would give them a more congenial choice. Senators argued that it was inappropriate for the sitting president to make an appointment with a presidential election looming—even if that election was almost ten months away. The refusal even to consider Garland was unprecedented and a significant breach of constitutional norms.

That delay ultimately proved consequential. Elections matter. With the presidential victory of Republican Donald Trump, and the subsequent nomination of conservative judge Neil Gorsuch, many on the left protested that the Republicans had robbed Obama, and the Democrats, of their rightful Supreme Court seat. Continuing to play hardball, the Senate dispensed with the filibuster to confirm Gorsuch, and he was seated quickly as the newest junior justice. Gorsuch's confirmation put Justice Kennedy back in the middle of the Court, with the balance of power between liberals and conservatives at 4–4–1.

As Obama left the White House, the question was how much the Obama Court would become the Trump Court, with two more specific questions looming: Would more liberal or moderate justices leave the bench, giving Trump further opportunities to truly shift the political balance? And would the mid-century constitutional settlement persist despite the ever-increasing conservatism of the Court? The most significant events in the life of the twenty-first-century Supreme Court would be dictated by the rightward lurch of American politics. Trumpism was unsettling American law and politics in myriad ways. Obama's judicial legacy—which had seemed so promising just a year earlier—would now be written by his successors' appointments.

7

The Gay Rights President

Timothy Stewart-Winter

Five months into his first term, President Barack Obama told the crowd at his first Pride Month reception, "I know that many in this room don't believe progress has come fast enough." For him to counsel patience, he said, would be no more just than it was for white liberals to ask for patience from African Americans in the 1960s. But, he added, "We've been in office six months now. I suspect that by the time this administration is over, I think you guys will have pretty good feelings about the Obama administration."[1] In retrospect, Obama was right: the two terms of his presidency decisively ended a half-century period during which antigay federal laws passed with overwhelming congressional backing, while progay proposals went down to overwhelming defeat. Although gay activists had launched their first formal political organizations in the 1950s, they had never previously achieved even a modicum of influence in Washington. During Obama's presidency, their movement—now broadened into a movement on behalf of lesbian, gay, bisexual, transgender, and queer people—won an unprecedented cascade of victories from all three branches of government. In the first term, Obama signed an LGBTQ-inclusive hate crimes law and a bipartisan measure to integrate gay and lesbian Americans into the U.S. military. In the second term, the Supreme Court legalized same-sex marriage nationwide, and the administration enacted a vast array of gay- and transgender-inclusive federal policies.

Of course, Obama's support for this cause was far from the only reason for its triumphs. Long despised, LGBTQ Americans had already in 2009 seen two decades of steadily increasing public support for their equal rights by the time of Obama's first inauguration. This shift in public opinion partly reflected cohort succession—the tendency of younger Americans to be more progay than the preceding generations. There was also a massive cultural shift *within* all cohorts, as gay Americans came out to their relatives and friends in dramatically increased numbers, and gay characters proliferated on television and in the movies. Especially striking was the dramatic shift in support for gay marriage, which rose in Gallup polls from 40 percent in mid-2009 to 64 percent in mid-2017.[2] As grassroots activists pushed for policy changes under Obama, they were buoyed by the fact that many of their key demands lacked major fiscal implications, and were thus well-suited to a political climate of austerity and to independent action by the executive branch and the courts.

Presidential leadership, too, played a role. As president, Obama legitimized and partially accommodated major demands made by the LGBTQ movement, much as Lyndon Johnson did in response to the black civil rights movement in the 1960s. Like Johnson, President Obama often clashed with movement leaders, whose foot soldiers and clout in the nation's capital were growing, and who pushed to accelerate change. But where many African American civil rights activists became disillusioned with Johnson over his handling of the Vietnam War, Obama's association with gay rights as a cause, and LGBTQ Americans as a constituency, continued to intensify throughout his presidency. In particular, Obama frequently used the bully pulpit, and his status as the first African American president, to affirm gay rights as an extension of the black civil rights struggle. He increasingly spoke of progress toward LGBTQ equality as his signature achievement in the field of civil rights.

Though Republican intransigence blocked further legislative progress after 2010, the executive branch took many steps to advance the status of LGBTQ Americans by administrative means and recognize them as a vulnerable minority deserving of protection. The Equal Employment Opportunity Commission began in 2012 to recognize Title VII of the 1964 Civil Rights Act as prohibiting discrimination based on transgender identity.[3] As we will see, the Justice and Education departments moved to address the practical needs of transgender Americans for respectful treatment and accommodation on the part of various institutions over which the president had some form of independent leverage, including public schools and private as well as public health insurance plans.

The implementation of the Affordable Care Act, after it was signed into law in March 2010, illustrates how the administration pushed toward progay policies even after losing control of Congress. As interpreted by executive-branch rulemaking, for example, the ACA prohibited discriminatory treatment by providers on the basis of sexual orientation and gender identity, and required most insurers to cover medical expenses associated with gender transition, such as hormones and surgery. People living with HIV benefited from the elimination of Medicaid's medical need requirement, which had previously required most childless HIV-positive adults to wait until their disease progressed to AIDS before becoming eligible. Yet the case of people living with HIV also highlights how seriously the ACA's impact was limited by the Supreme Court's 2010 decision to permit states to elect not to expand Medicaid. In the first half of 2014, when most of the law's provisions went into effect, the twenty-six Medicaid expansion states sharply reduced the proportion of people living with HIV who were uninsured, while no such improvement occurred in the remaining states.[4]

By the close of the Obama presidency, the most visible signs of progress toward LGBTQ equality seemed less vulnerable to rollback during the presidency of Donald J. Trump than other Obama-era policy changes. The integration of gay and lesbian citizens into the military took place relatively smoothly, as did the expansion of marriage equality to additional states and then nationwide, which occurred faster than many gay activists would have predicted a few years earlier. Both changes came to be broadly popular. Transgender rights, however, remained hotly debated, and as the Obama presidency wound down, many red-state legislatures began to take up "bathroom bills," dictating which bathrooms could be used by students in high schools and in public places.

A Legacy of Exclusion

Mid-twentieth-century U.S. policy treated gay and lesbian people as pariahs. In the New Deal era, conservatives nurtured fears that the expanding federal bureaucracy was riddled with individuals who were disloyal, deviant, or both. During World War II, the U.S. military began not only to prohibit same-sex acts, but also systematically to exclude homosexual persons from serving. The early Cold War saw gay federal employees subject to unprecedented purges, their logic memorably encapsulated by a 1950 Senate subcommittee report that solemnly declared, "One homosexual can pollute a government office." Federal agencies deemed homosexuals to be "security risks," and their presence as employees a threat to national security, both because of their purported mental instability and because they were thought to be at risk of being blackmailed by Soviet agents. In many cities, hidden police surveillance of gay male cruising areas—sometimes spying through peepholes, often using plainclothes officers—was widespread. The 1952 McCarran-Walter immigration law, in the words of Margot Canaday, "targeted the homosexual as an excluded figure against which a citizenry supposedly unified along racial and class lines could define itself."[5]

Gay people remained marginalized politically throughout the remainder of the twentieth century. In a 1953 executive order, President Dwight D. Eisenhower excluded all homosexuals from the federal civil service. Although the U.S. Civil Service Commission relaxed this policy in 1975, allowing gay and lesbian people to serve in civilian roles, they nonetheless were routinely denied security clearances well into the 1990s. When the Supreme Court liberalized many of the nation's laws concerning birth control, pornography, and abortion in the 1960s and 1970s, it explicitly reaffirmed that the new toleration did not extend to gay and lesbian people. In the 1967 case *Boutilier v. INS*, involving a Canadian-born gay permanent resident who had applied to be naturalized, the Supreme Court upheld his deportation, holding, "Congress commanded that homosexuals not be allowed to enter."[6]

Beginning in the 1970s, gender and sexuality became major aspects of partisan alignment, as two organized constituencies—social conservatives, a large majority of them evangelical Protestants, and feminist and gay and lesbian activists concentrated in major cities and university towns—became active in the Republican and Democratic Parties respectively. Yet even as activists demanded equality, they found virtually no supporters among national politicians. At the 1972 Democratic National Convention in Miami Beach, when a gay rights plank was placed before the convention and a gay man and a lesbian spoke from the podium on its behalf, the measure was defeated overwhelmingly on a voice vote. By contrast, a moderate abortion rights plank—the first ever adopted—was approved after a long and painful debate. The Supreme Court's decision in *Roe v. Wade* the following year appeared to most to be a decisive and permanent victory. Both issues became the focus of increasing polarization in subsequent decades, as activists on both sides gained clout within the two parties.

In the 1980s, as the AIDS crisis breathed new life into the public's fear of homosexuality, the deaths of tens of thousands of gay men went unmourned by the nation's president. In 1985, Ronald Reagan's health and human services secretary, Margaret Heckler, declared, "We must conquer AIDS before it affects the heterosexual population and the general population." By then, ten thousand Americans had been diagnosed, and half of those had died. Two years and fifteen thousand more American deaths later, when Reagan himself first gave a speech about the epidemic, he appalled many listeners by proposing mandatory HIV testing for some groups of Americans. The 1989 Helms Amendment, which banned federal HIV-prevention funds from being used for any materials that described or promoted gay sex, passed overwhelmingly. Even as it intensified antigay stigma, however, the AIDS epidemic led gay Americans to articulate new demands on the regulatory state. Particular targets of protest included the Centers for Disease Control and the Food and Drug Administration. Gay and lesbian people were among the AIDS activists who lobbied for passage of the 1990 Ryan White CARE Act, which funded health care for people living with HIV/AIDS and assisted the hardest-hit metropolitan areas.[7]

In the 1990s, gay and lesbian people became increasingly visible in popular culture, with television star Ellen DeGeneres becoming in 1998 the first high-profile celebrity to come out publicly as gay. But although activists in all of the nation's largest cities secured the enactment of legislation protecting gay and lesbian people from job and housing discrimination, all three branches of the federal government remained hostile.[8] President Bill Clinton used the word "gay" in his 1992 speech accepting the Democratic Party's presidential nomination, and ultimately named some 150 openly gay federal appointees, yet he signed legislation enacting new statutory prohibitions both on gay people serving openly in the military and on government recognition of same-sex marriages. The first law resulted when Clinton's attempt early in his first term to follow through on a campaign promise to allow gay people to serve in the military met unexpectedly strong backlash from the Pentagon and congressional Democrats, leading to a compromise that became known as "Don't Ask, Don't Tell" (DADT). Though Clinton portrayed DADT as an improvement in the status of gay service members, since it allowed them to remain in the military as long as they successfully concealed their gayness, it also for the first time codified in federal law the policy of discharging any who disclosed their sexual orientation to others, even inadvertently.

Even more important was the Defense of Marriage Act, enacted in 1996. The law was passed in response to a Hawaii state high court decision—reversed before going into effect by a state constitutional amendment—requiring that the legislature make civil marriage licenses available to same-sex couples. While the organized gay movement had long viewed access to civil marriage as an unattainable and perhaps even undesirable goal, both the lesbian "baby boom" and the AIDS crisis highlighted the plight of gay couples unable to secure equal treatment for their loved ones in high-stakes circumstances, such as hospital visitation.[9] Nationwide, religious conservatives pushed for legislation to block the practice before it could begin. Clinton signed DOMA, which stipulated that the federal government would not recognize any state-level same-sex marriages, while campaigning for reelection in 1996. DOMA appeared at first to have no meaningful immediate regulatory impact, since no states then allowed such marriages. However, like DADT, it enshrined antigay discrimination in federal law.[10]

The contested election of George W. Bush in 2000 dramatically increased the influence of the religious right, which vehemently opposed gay equality and whose agenda spanned many policy domains. To be sure, the gay movement saw important gains during Bush's first term: the breakthrough 2003 judicial invalidation of the remaining state laws prohibiting gay sex in the *Lawrence v. Texas* case, followed later that year by the legalization of same-sex marriage in a single state in *Goodridge v. Massachusetts Department of Health*. Republican governor Mitt Romney, invoking a 1913 law enacted to prevent out-of-state interracial couples from crossing into Massachusetts to marry, blocked nonresident couples from marrying there. Between 2004 and 2008, no other state followed suit in legalizing same-sex marriages. In the Bay State, activists worked quietly and successfully to stave off a state law authorizing a ballot measure to overturn *Goodridge*, which would have deprived the movement of the persuasive effect of having residents of other states observe that in Massachusetts, the sky was not falling.[11]

In the 2000s, the Republican Party moved rightward on gay rights, while their Democratic counterparts remained cautiously centrist, with progress coming exclusively from the courts. Bush appointed numerous antigay judges, including two Supreme Court justices. Moreover, *Goodridge* inspired a forceful—and nationwide—backlash: an ascendant Republican Party adopted a host of new antigay platform provisions, while Democrats, in defeat, treated same-sex marriage as politically radioactive. To many, Bush's reelection seemed to signify that Republicans could win at the polls by employing antigay policy proposals as a wedge issue to hurt their Democratic opponents. Bush had vocally opposed *Goodridge* and backed state constitutional amendments prohibiting same-sex marriage. Eleven states enacted such amendments by ballot referenda, most by overwhelming margins, in the November 2004 election in which Bush won a second term. He also gave his backing to the proposed Federal Marriage Amendment, which would have altered the nation's founding document to ban gay unions nationwide.

There was considerable disagreement within the organized LGBTQ movement about how to deal with the predicament posed by the political toxicity of same-sex marriage. A group of LGBTQ activists, writers, and academics issued a statement, "Beyond Marriage," offering a critique of marriage's checkered history as a patriarchal and heteronormative institution, calling for it to be delinked from welfare and benefit provision. Others, closely linked to the Democratic Party, pushed for abandonment of the "M word" on purely strategic grounds, especially as Connecticut, New Jersey, and Oregon enacted laws extending to unmarried gay couples certain benefits afforded to married spouses. Others still said only marriage would suffice. A group led by longtime activist Evan Wolfson held a series of private sessions with the goal of developing new strategies to cultivate political support for gay marriage from Democratic politicians.[12]

Obama, the Democratic Party, and Gay Rights

At the beginning of the Obama presidency, the gay rights movement remained marginal to electoral politics; indeed, not a single federal law protected the rights of LGBTQ people. As late as 2004, during his campaign for a U.S. Senate seat from Illinois, Obama, then a state senator, reportedly had not heard of the Stonewall uprising—the 1969 rebellion in which patrons of a Greenwich Village gay bar fought back against routine police harassment by New York City police, spurring a period of rapid growth in the American gay-rights movement during the 1970s.[13] Nine years later, Obama spoke of Stonewall during his second presidential inaugural address—and elevated it by linking it with the earlier struggles for voting rights on behalf of women and African Americans. "We, the people, declare today that the most evident of truths— that all of us are created equal—is the star that guides us still," he declared, "just as it guided our forebears through Seneca Falls, and Selma, and Stonewall." By the end of his second term, President Obama had designated the Stonewall Inn as a national historic site.

Yet Obama's relative youth and his liberal political background gave him a familiarity with gay and lesbian people. Obama came to the presidency as the first chief executive whose prior political career had taken place in an environment in which gay people were a well-organized constituency. During his first campaign for the Illinois state senate, in 1996, Obama's campaign returned by fax a questionnaire from a gay newspaper, on which he had written, "I favor legalizing same-sex marriages."[14] Obama wrote on another questionnaire that although he had no legislative track record, he had worked with gay groups on a voter-registration project.[15] Obama was elected that year alongside Larry McKeon, another new Democrat from Chicago, who had won election to the Illinois House as the state's first openly gay state legislator.

Obama's stunning electoral victories in both the 2004 U.S. Senate race and the 2008 presidential election each coincided with devastating blows for the gay movement, as voters passed state-level ballot measures to ban gay marriage by state constitutional amendments. He thus became nationally visible at the same time that gay rights—never a popular issue outside certain big-city neighborhoods—was reoriented toward the politically difficult terrain of marriage law. Even as prominent Democrats increasingly supported protecting gay people from job discrimination, they almost uniformly saw publicly supporting gay marriage as too risky. Obama distanced himself from his 1996 statement in the course of his meteoric rise. During the 2008 presidential primary campaign, Obama, like his opponent Hillary Clinton, took the position that he supported civil unions but believed "marriage is between a man and a woman."[16]

Only the third Democratic president since the Stonewall uprising, Obama took office at a moment of increasing polarization between red and blue states, with some progressive states increasingly challenging antigay federal policies such as DOMA. His historic election as the first black president coincided with the passage of Proposition 8, a statewide referendum in which Californians voted to rescind the state high court's legalization of gay marriage, six months earlier. Thus, at the time he took office in January of 2009, same-sex marriage was legal only in Massachusetts.[17]

The inability of gay couples to secure recognition of their relationships by legislation or referenda led some activists and commentators—not to mention Democratic strategists—to argue that marriage should be set aside in favor of more achievable goals. At the same time, the apparent contradiction between the breakthrough election of a black president and the rollback of gay rights in the nation's most populous state stimulated grassroots demonstrations nationwide in the final weeks of 2008, protesting the California referendum—which unlike previous antigay marriage referenda had eliminated an existing right.[18] Moreover, because Proposition 8 left in place more than 18,000 same-sex marriages enacted between May and November of 2008, while prohibiting any new such unions from occurring, it created an arbitrary division between two classes of citizens, leaving it potentially vulnerable to legal challenge.[19] Two prominent lawyers best known for opposing one another in *Bush v. Gore* a decade earlier now teamed up to have Proposition 8 invalidated by the federal courts. But major federal-level progress on the marriage issue would not occur until Obama's second term.

The Path to Repealing Don't Ask, Don't Tell

The signature gay rights achievement of Obama's first term—the enactment of a bipartisan law to allow gays and lesbians to serve openly in the U.S military—reflected the LGBTQ movement's increasing influence among congressional Democrats and the declining power of the religious right. The path to its enactment, however, was tortuous. Though Obama took office during a major economic crisis and two foreign wars, movement leaders felt tremendous pent-up frustration and growing militancy, partly as a result of Proposition 8. With public revulsion against Bush having given Obama control of both chambers of Congress, they saw a brief window of opportunity to enact a federal law extending to include sexual orientation and gender identity the 1964 law that had banned discrimination on the basis of race, gender, and national origin.

Five months into his first term, gay activists were already harshly criticizing Obama for his failure to act. Many were infuriated by a brief, submitted by the Justice Department in a federal court challenge to the Defense of Marriage Act by a California couple, that invoked decades-old precedents concerning the right of states to decline to recognize marriages between blood relatives.[20] The administration initially took only modest steps to mollify activists. Obama announced that the 2010 Census would for the first time attempt to quantify same-sex relationships (though not marriages). He signed an executive order reversing a longstanding ban, instituted by George H. W. Bush, on entry into the United States by people living with HIV.[21] In August he awarded the Presidential Medal of Freedom to gay icons Harvey Milk (posthumously) and Billie Jean King.

By the end of 2009, the gay movement adopted an increasingly militant tone. Hopes that the Democratic Congress might pass any antidiscrimination law protecting LGBTQ people—which had languished since they were first introduced in the 1970s—had faded. House Speaker Nancy Pelosi and Senate Majority Leader Harry Reid instead pushed a far less controversial and less consequential expansion of the federal civil rights apparatus: that of federal hate crimes laws. The Matthew Shepard and James Byrd Jr. Hate Crimes Prevention Act, which Obama signed in October of 2009, stretched existing federal protections against hate crimes, which covered categories such as race and religion, to cover sexual orientation and gender identity as well. It was the first federal gay rights statute ever enacted and the first federal policy that specifically afforded rights or protections to transgender citizens.

Yet the continued military discharges under DADT angered many gay Americans. During the first year of the Obama administration, 169 more women and 259 more men were discharged under the policy.[22] Several organizations worked to bring publicity to their plight, including Servicemembers Legal Defense Network, which assisted gay service members facing discharge. The Palm Center, a California university-based research institute that produced social science research supporting the case for repeal, released reports on the successful adoption of policies allowing gay service in the militaries of other nations, including Canada, Israel, and the United Kingdom.

When President Harry Truman decided in 1948 to end racially segregated units in the U.S. military, he did so by an executive order. Obama, by contrast, could not reverse DADT on his own, because Congress had enshrined it in a law signed by President Bill Clinton in 1994. Thus, the statutory ban could only be reversed by legislative enactment of another statute. Nonetheless, frustrated by the lack of progress, gay activists began to demand that the president act administratively to stop discharges under the policy. The notion that Obama held the power to issue such a "stop-loss" order put the White House on the defensive, and press secretary Robert Gibbs was asked numerous times in press conferences in the spring of 2009 why Obama was refusing to take this step.[23]

In spring 2009, the issue became more visible after news broke that the army would soon discharge 1st Lt. Dan Choi—also an Arabic linguist—who had recently come out as gay in an televised interview with MSNBC's Rachel Maddow.[24] Choi became the most visible face of the struggle to repeal DADT, and was arrested several times for chaining himself, while wearing his full-dress army uniform and medals, to the White House fence. In the spring of 2010, a new grassroots direct action group called GetEqual was founded by Robin McGehee, a young lesbian. The group organized highly confrontational protests in which activists chained themselves to the White House fence, effectively using the tactic of the "zap" that had been pioneered by the Gay Activists Alliance in the early 1970s and the AIDS Coalition to Unleash Power (ACT UP) in the 1980s.[25]

Drawing attention to the firing of service members with specialized expertise and training, particularly Arabic language specialists, proved an especially successful strategy. Focusing on the cost to the military of discharging patriotic Americans with highly specialized skills enabled gay activists to deprive the religious right of a key argument: the notion that military personnel policy should not be altered in wartime.[26] Yet military leaders warmed slowly to the issue. The chairman of the Joint Chiefs of Staff, Admiral Michael Mullen, testified before the House Armed Services Committee that he supported repeal. However, military leaders also made clear that they wanted Congress to empower *them* to change the policy, on their own schedule, rather than impose the terms of repeal on them. Democrat Ike Skelton of Missouri, who chaired the House Armed Services Committee, firmly opposed repeal.

By early 2010, as healthcare reform became the chief legislative priority, Obama also placed DADT repeal on the national agenda. A Pentagon memorandum, drafted by staff members for a meeting organized by Mullen, said "in time the law will change," but concluded that because of the strains imposed by the wars in Iraq and Afghanistan, "now is not the time."[27] However, in his first State of the Union address, Obama explicitly called on Congress to repeal DADT "this year," and he established a Comprehensive Review Working Group to study how it might be done. In May, the administration, the Pentagon, and lawmakers agreed on legislative language and a timeline that would effectively delegate to the Pentagon the task of deciding whether and how to change military policy on gay service members.[28] Defense Secretary Robert Gates—a Republican and a holdover from the George W. Bush administration—took administrative steps that sharply limited further discharges, if temporarily.[29] On November 30, the Defense Department report declared that the armed services would be capable of smoothly integrating openly gay service members.

Two other developments subtly paved the way for repeal. First, prominent Democratic politicians began to revisit the longstanding assumption—cemented in the Bush years—that forceful advocacy of gay rights would be politically disastrous. For example, Senator Kirsten Gillibrand of New York, who faced a special election in 2010 after being appointed to fill the seat vacated by Secretary of State Hillary Clinton, began to push vocally for repeal. Second, the prospect emerged that the courts might preempt Congress. In a lawsuit brought in 2004 that took many years to be heard, a federal judge ordered the military to stop administering the policy. Gates objected loudly.[30] While the Ninth Circuit held the status quo in place pending the Defense Department's appeal, the military's strong preference for a legislative repeal gave cover to wavering members of Congress, by enabling them to claim they were voting less for repeal than to impose order on a potentially chaotic process.[31]

DADT was finally repealed, amid complex and tense legislative maneuvering, during the lame-duck period following the 2010 November midterm elections, in which Republicans retook control of both chambers of Congress. Earlier, in May, House Democrats had inserted a repeal procedure into the National Defense Authorization Act, a must-pass defense bill—"a 'report-to-Congress' process locked inside military funding," as the political scientist Rick Valelly put it. Spurred by opposition to repeal both among a Republican base already angry about the Affordable Care Act and on the part of the Veterans of Foreign Wars and the American Legion, a majority of House Republicans voted *against* the broader defense bill—even though the nation was engaged in two wars.[32]

Following House passage, Majority Leader Harry Reid used aggressive parliamentary tactics to attempt a cloture vote in September, which failed. However, Reid voted against the bill himself, enabling him to bring up the measure again during the lame-duck session. In early December, following midterm elections in which Democrats lost Senate seats and control of the House, and Reid himself was narrowly reelected, he attempted a second cloture vote in early December on the omnibus defense bill containing the repeal measure. Again the tactic failed. An article in *Stars and Stripes*, the military newspaper, suggested that "gay rights advocates . . . may have to wait years for another chance" at repeal.[33]

Unexpectedly, however, after Reid's second failure to obtain cloture, two centrist senators—Joe Lieberman of Connecticut, then technically an independent but caucusing with the Democrats, and Republican Susan Collins of Maine—proposed taking the repeal out of the defense bill and passing it as a standalone bill. "Adjournment fever had reached the virulent stage," recalled Barney Frank, then the most prominent gay member of Congress. "The days that followed became a gruesome legislative duel." The standalone DADT repeal passed both chambers on December 18, 2010, with overwhelming support from Democrats and only five Senate Republicans. On the same day, Republicans succeeded in filibustering the DREAM Act.[34] The juxtaposition starkly highlighted that the LGBTQ movement—which had been for so long unable to achieve *any* federal-level policy success—now seemed to be benefiting more rapidly than other constituencies of the party from Democratic control in Washington. Obama signed the bill in a jubilant December 22 ceremony.

"Evolving" on Marriage

In the wake of DADT repeal, some gay rights activists turned their attention to legalizing same-sex marriage nationwide.[35] Indeed, the repeal itself drew attention to the inequalities imposed by the denial of access to civil marriage, as service members in same-sex relationships did not receive benefits equal to their heterosexual counterparts.[36] Obama remained publicly against same-sex marriage, but there were signs his opposition might be softening.[37] The administration had taken steps to recognize same-sex couples. In April 2010, Obama extended hospital visitation rights to same-sex partners, and the Justice Department "concluded that the Violence Against Women Act protects same-sex partners." In June he extended Family and Medical Leave Act (FMLA) benefits to same-sex couples administratively, "one of many actions taken by the Obama administration to respond to the concerns of gay men and lesbians within the constraints of the Defense of Marriage Act."[38] In a widely reported October 2010 interview with a group of liberal bloggers, he answered a question about same-sex marriage by saying, "Attitudes evolve, including mine."[39] Activists pushed the president hard. In an op-ed, the columnist Dan Savage reminded Obama of his onetime support for the right to marry, urging him to return to that position and enunciate it in that year's State of the Union address.[40] In a highly significant decision that nonetheless fell short of activists' demands, Obama's Justice Department decided to decline to continue mounting a legal defense of DOMA.

And then, in May 2012, Obama did it. Days after an alleged gaffe, in which Vice President Joe Biden said on *Meet the Press* that he was "absolutely comfortable" with gay couples marrying, Obama appeared in a recorded television interview with Robin Roberts of ABC News that immediately became a major news story. With his reelection campaign getting under way, the president declared, "It is important for me to go ahead and affirm that I think same-sex couples should be able to get married."[41] Gay activists and liberal celebrities showered praise on the president. His action challenged received wisdom. The two immediately previous presidents—Clinton and George W. Bush—had each cooperated with Congress, as they ran for a second term, to enact new laws codifying the illegality of same-sex couples marrying. Now, for millions of Americans, Obama modeled what it looked like to change one's mind about the issue.

Obama's televised interview received intense press coverage, which lent a sense of momentum to the issue that would continue to pervade his politics during his second term. Within days, the board of directors of the NAACP passed a resolution endorsing same-sex marriage.[42] The announcement reverberated throughout the fall campaign, as Obama benefited from enthusiasm and financial support from LGBTQ voters. Gay media executive Fred Eychaner, a campaign bundler, became the largest individual donor to the pro-Obama super PAC Priorities USA Action. (In his second term, Obama nominated four openly gay major campaign donors, all white men, to ambassadorships.[43]) In November, voters who self-identified as gay, lesbian, or bisexual backed Obama by over three-to-one; voters who did not identify as such were evenly split.[44]

Though proponents of gay marriage were increasingly confident that they could persuade many skeptical Americans to change their minds about the issue, few imagined how rapidly Obama's election-year embrace of extending marriage rights to gays and lesbians would be mirrored by decisions by federal judges. The administration's declining to defend DOMA in court contributed to a landmark victory in *Windsor v. U.S.*, a 2013 Supreme Court case involving taxation of a bequest that invalidated the core provisions of the Defense of Marriage Act. In a case decided at the same time, the Court ruled that Proposition 8 was unconstitutional. Immediately, gay residents of California once again could marry. *Windsor* left the executive branch to decide several issues of scope and implementation, which the administration used to make sweeping regulatory changes on the part of federal agencies.[45]

In the two years after *Windsor*, numerous federal appellate courts legalized gay marriage in additional states, and many Americans began to believe that nationwide legalization was inevitable. Early in 2015, the Supreme Court heard a case whose plaintiff, Jim Obergefell, was suing the state of Ohio for the right to be listed on his husband John Arthur's death certificate as the surviving spouse. Obergefell had chartered a medical jet to fly Arthur, who was dying of ALS, to a Maryland airport so they could marry on the tarmac. Some 379 employers, including many of the nation's largest corporations, filed a brief for the plaintiff, calling inconsistency in state marriage laws an onerous regulatory burden. In a bitterly divided 5–4 decision, the Court held that all states must permit same-sex couples to marry, and must also recognize same-sex marriages performed in other states. Justice Anthony Kennedy wrote for the majority that "far from seeking to devalue marriage, the petitioners seek it for themselves because of their respect—and need—for its privileges and responsibilities."[46] The two justices Obama appointed to the Court, Sonia Sotomayor and Elena Kagan, joined Kennedy.

Despite an unexpectedly hostile dissent by Chief Justice John Roberts, the *Obergefell* ruling was widely celebrated as a sign of national progress. Social media became an important avenue for both LGBTQ people and their allies to express their support for the decision. There was little backlash. To be sure, Republicans were able to constrain Obama's ability to reshape the judicial system, notably by Senate Majority Leader Mitch McConnell's unprecedented refusal in 2015 to even hold hearings on Barack Obama's nominee to replace Antonin Scalia, who in three decades had penned numerous passionately antigay opinions on the Supreme Court. But public opinion appeared to be moving in only one direction. In contrast to *Lawrence v. Texas*, which prompted a discernible drop in public support for legalizing gay sex, after *Obergefell* the policy of marriage equality became more widely supported by the public than ever before.

———

Some Obama campaign promises to the LGBTQ community remained unfulfilled, the most notable being a federal law prohibiting discrimination in jobs and housing on the basis of sexual orientation and gender identity. But the gay rights movement has seen more of its agenda successfully enacted under Obama compared to other groups that made up his political base. At Obama's 2015 Pride Month reception, Jennicet Gutiérrez, who is transgender and said she was in the country illegally, was removed after heckling the president, demanding the release of LGBTQ immigrants in Immigration and Customs Enforcement custody and an end to "all deportations." Gutiérrez was a founding member of Familia QTLM, an intersectional protest group advocating for LGBTQ immigrants.[47]

As corporate leaders and some prominent Republicans embraced LGBTQ equality, Obama took a series of executive actions during his final year in office that advanced the cause. The Justice and Education departments issued joint guidelines to school districts on how to ensure respect for the civil rights of transgender students, and the Pentagon began the process of lifting the ongoing ban—which had never been enshrined in law—on military service by transgender Americans.[48] But a court instituted a nationwide injunction against the former policy, and in February of 2017, in its first shift away from the Obama administration's pro-LGBTQ stances, newly installed Attorney General Jeff Sessions reversed course, abandoning the legal defense of the guidelines.[49] The surprise election of Donald Trump thus ushered in a period of uncertainty about the fate of Obama executive-branch actions. In July 2017, Trump announced via Twitter that he would ban transgender people from serving "in any capacity in the U.S. Military," a reversal that even many prominent Republicans immediately opposed. After weeks of debate, military officials had not reached final decisions about how to proceed.[50]

With progress stalled or reversed in many other areas of civil rights, including equal pay for women, housing and school segregation, police violence against communities of color, and the prospects for wage protections and retirement security, Obama pointed to military service and marriage equality as major civil rights achievements.[51] There was little historical precedent for these two major triumphs for gay equality—and among Obama's policy achievements, they appeared at the end of his term among those most likely to endure.

Education in the Age of Obama

THE PARADOX OF CONSENSUS

Jonathan Zimmerman

In 2002, the U.S. Congress enacted the most expansive federal education measure in American history. The No Child Left Behind (NCLB) law passed the House of Representatives by a vote of 381–41 and the Senate by 87–10. Eminently bipartisan, its sponsors included the Senate's liberal lion Edward Kennedy and future GOP House Speaker John Boehner. And the bill was signed into law by a Republican president, George W. Bush, whose party's most revered figure—Ronald Reagan—had called for the abolition of the federal Department of Education just two decades earlier. No Child Left Behind required every school district to test all students in grades 3–8 in reading and math, to disaggregate the results according to students' race, and to penalize schools that failed to show progress for each racial group as well as for the larger student body. It required districts to certify that all of their teachers were "highly qualified." Most audaciously, it declared that all of America's students—every single one—would perform at grade level on state tests by 2014.

Thirteen years later—and the year after NCLB's impossible deadline for universal proficiency—Congress reauthorized the law. The 2015 Every Student Succeeds Act (ESSA) passed by a nearly identical and profoundly bipartisan margin, 359–64 in the House and 85–12 in the Senate. The law continued to mandate annual testing—and the reporting of results according to race—but eliminated almost all of the punitive consequences that had been attached to them. Dropping the language of "highly qualified" teachers, the revised measure barred the federal government from influencing the evaluation of teachers; it also declared that the government could not encourage any given set of standards or curricula for students. The law was signed by a Democratic president, Barack Obama, who hailed it as a "Christmas miracle." In "a capital more often gripped lately by partisan gridlock," the *New York Times* added, ESSA was a "curiosity."[1]

To be sure, there were other areas of bipartisan agreement during Obama's presidency. Most notably, Obama continued or even ramped up the counterterrorism efforts he inherited from his predecessors. And on criminal justice, where Obama's rhetoric often diverged from Republicans, his policies hewed closely to their formulas. But few realms reflected the same degree of rhetorical *and* policy overlap as education. Part of the reason lay in the strong consensus around education that developed in the 1990s and early 2000s, which allowed Obama to build upon a shared federal framework that simply did not exist for health care, energy, and the many other issues that fractured Washington. Another factor, ironically, was the growing bipartisan dissatisfaction with that same federal education framework. Democrats and Republicans both objected to Obama's "Race to the Top" program, which used 2009 stimulus dollars to exert unprecedented influence over academic standards, charter schools, and teacher evaluation. Eventually, their concerns yielded the much more decentralized ESSA measure of 2015. But the fact that Obama's opponents came from both parties—just as supporters did—insulated his education policies from the white-hot, hyper-polarized atmosphere that inhibited many of his other efforts. It's always easier to fight a war—or to forge a truce—when your enemy isn't united. So Obama was able to sustain a bipartisan agreement around education, even as its substance shifted away from some of the policies he had promulgated.

In Washington, objections to Obama's education initiatives typically echoed attacks on his policymaking in other areas: instead of working with Congress, the argument went, Obama was governing by executive fiat. But out in the schools themselves, critics pointed to the practical, everyday effects of his reforms. Teachers denounced evaluation systems that tied their compensation to student test scores, a keystone of Obama's Race to the Top initiative; meanwhile, parents complained that schools devoted too much time to tests and—especially—to rote-style preparation for them. And while polls revealed strong support for the concept of test-based accountability, many middle-class citizens bridled when their own children were subjected to it. "It's fascinating to me that some of the pushback is coming from, sort of, white suburban moms who—all of a sudden—[realize] their child isn't as brilliant as they thought they were," Education Secretary Arne Duncan quipped, in a much-reported (and off-the-cuff) 2013 remark.[2] It elicited angry protests in some of the country's most affluent communities, where Duncan clearly struck a nerve. He had also violated the first commandment of contemporary politics: Thou Shalt Not Alienate the Broad Middle Class. Unlike many other federal policies, the Obama administration's educational directives reached directly into millions of lives. And many people decided they did not want the federal government there, at least not with such a heavy hand.

The term "education" does not appear in the U.S. Constitution. For most of American history, the federal government had almost no influence on American public schools. That began to change during the civil rights era, when *Brown v. Board of Education*—and subsequent court decisions—brought federal law and policy into the classroom. Indeed, education became a right that Washington could define, enforce, and expand. Democrats and Republicans united behind compensatory education for poor children, services for handicapped children, special instruction for English-language learners, and legislation barring discrimination in schools on the basis of sex. The focus of federal policy started to shift from rights to outcomes—or, as some observers put it, from equality to excellence—in the 1980s and 1990s, when critics across the political spectrum started to ask what kind of bang the government was getting for its educational buck. The result was a new consensus on "accountability," culminating in the No Child Left Behind Act of 2002. The agreement masked important divisions across and within the parties, which could never quite decide what they wanted the federal role to be. According to one well-worn Washington joke, nationally imposed tests were a nonstarter because Republicans don't like national directives and Democrats don't like standardized tests. But each party had a wing that embraced school reform, joining hands to rebut naysayers on both sides of the aisle.

Obama stood firmly on the proreform side of the Democratic Party, which generated new attention—and, eventually, new antipathy—for accountability, charter schools, and merit pay. By contrast, Obama's achievements in the higher-education realm made barely a blip on the political radar screen. Again building on campaigns by his predecessors, Obama established direct federal lending for student loans: bypassing the banks that had formerly served as intermediaries, the government plowed the savings into student aid. He also expanded tuition tax credits for nearly ten million students and their families. But most Americans were unaware of these efforts, which didn't affect their day-to-day lives in the same obvious ways that public school policies did. Obama's K–12 reforms led to testing and curricular changes that every American student, parent, and teacher could observe. By contrast, the effects of Obama's higher-education policies were buried deep inside citizens' loan statements and tax returns; indeed, many beneficiaries of his policies still don't know that he benefited them. Education remains a low-visibility matter in Washington, overshadowed by much more divisive issues like health care and taxes. That gave Obama the opportunity to shape it in new ways, which in turn exposed it to new political scrutiny. "We've done as much on education reform as any administration in the last 20 years, and nobody knows it," Obama declared, as his first year in office came to a close.[3] More people would come to know about the expanding federal educational role in the ensuing years, yielding a bipartisan consensus to scale it back.

Obama and Education Reform

In 2005, Senator Barack Obama stood on a chair in a crowded Manhattan apartment and pledged his allegiance to charter schools, merit pay for teachers, and turnaround plans for failing schools. The gathering was sponsored by Democrats for Education Reform (DFER), a set of hedge-fund managers and other well-heeled liberals who believed the party had missed the boat on these issues. It wasn't enough for the federal government to require states to test students, the reformers said, or to mandate ambiguous "remedies" for underperforming schools; sterner stuff was needed, to jolt the entire system out of its complacency and mediocrity. That would mean taking on the teachers unions, the key defender of the status quo and a longtime bulwark of the Democratic Party itself. But Obama seemed up to the task. "If someone can tell me where the Democratic Party stands on education reform, please let me know," Obama declared, from his perch atop the chair. "Because I can't figure it out. Our party has got to wake up on this!"[4]

Members of DFER and other education-reform allies would later support the young senator from Illinois in his successful 2008 presidential bid, invoking the analogy of Richard Nixon going to China: just as it took a longtime anticommunist warrior to establish relations with "Red" China, so would it require a devoutly liberal Democrat to execute lasting school reform.[5] But this comparison understated the divisions *among* liberal Democrats—who were hardly as united about education as Nixon's fellow Republicans were about China—as well as Obama's longstanding commitments to the reform wing of the party. Whereas Nixon had spent his career lambasting Communist China, which added shock value to his diplomatic reversal, no one who had observed Obama should have been surprised by his continued devotion to teacher accountability, charter schools, and the other verses of the ed-reform gospel. It was already clear in his 1995 autobiography, *Dreams from My Father*, where Obama—recalling his stint as a community organizer in Chicago—despaired over teachers and school leaders who put their own interests ahead of their students. Likewise, Obama's 2006 book *The Audacity of Hope* called on teachers to accept merit pay—based, at least in part, on their students' test scores—in exchange for higher salaries. That same year, Obama introduced Senate legislation to provide federal aid to school districts that linked teachers' pay to the performance of their students on standardized tests. The bill went nowhere, but it showed where Obama's ideas on education were going.[6]

So did Obama's behavior on the 2008 presidential campaign trail. He ran in the primaries as the "insurgent" Democrat, challenging Hillary Clinton—the party's establishment candidate—on health care, trade, and especially Clinton's Senate vote to authorize the war in Iraq. His education platform also defied the standard Democratic mantra on education, which focused mainly on providing more money for public schools. Obama insisted that any new resources be tied to reform, particularly in teacher evaluation and compensation. He was booed for his remarks about merit pay at the convention of the National Education Association, which loudly endorsed Clinton; so did the nation's other giant teachers union, the American Federation of Teachers, whose longtime president Randi Weingarten had served as cochair of Clinton's first campaign for the Senate. Closely following the union script, Clinton called Obama's comments on merit pay "divisive" and "insulting to teachers." But Obama stuck to his guns, predicting—correctly—that the unions would support him in the general election. As many accounts of the 2008 campaign have noted, voters tended to find what they wanted in the charismatic young candidate from Illinois. So there was some hope (to use Obama's own favorite mantra) that he would prove to be a union ally, especially after he appointed Stanford professor Linda Darling-Hammond—a frequent critic of his favored reforms—to head his presidential transition team on education. There were even rumors that he would make Darling-Hammond his secretary of education.[7]

The hope was audacious, and also short-lived. The first offer went to former secretary of state Colin Powell, who had broken with his fellow Republicans by endorsing Obama for president. After Powell turned him down, Obama turned to Chicago school superintendent Arne Duncan. A longtime basketball buddy of the hoops-crazy new president, Duncan had earned the enmity of teachers unions for closing failing schools and replacing them with charters. But he was also a diplomat rather than a detonator, much closer to Obama's own temperament than Washington, DC, school superintendent Michelle Rhee or New York chancellor Joel Klein (who were also rumored to be under consideration). Rhee had posed with a broom on the cover of *Time*, symbolizing her brash efforts to sweep away ineffective teachers and principals; Klein had instituted "report cards" for schools and closed ones with the lowest marks, angering New York's powerful United Federation of Teachers. Obama instructed Duncan and his staff to move full speed ahead with reform but to avoid alienating its most important opponent. "Just don't poke the unions in the eye with this," Obama said. "Let's engage, not attack."[8]

A Race to the Top

Obama's first big struggle would actually pit him against Democrats in Congress, reflecting fundamental divisions within the party as well as the scrambled nature of Washington educational politics. Taking office during the worst economic downturn since the Great Depression, Obama proposed an $800 billion stimulus package that included $100 billion for education. Most of the education money was designated to help cash-strapped school districts pay teachers and staffers who would otherwise have been laid off. But Obama's initial plan also included $15 billion for "Innovation Grants," which Obama and Duncan would use to promote reform of school practices. The idea won plaudits from Democratic legislators like California's George Miller, one of the original sponsors of No Child Left Behind, who flippantly described the fund as "applesauce" that would encourage states to "swallow some reform." But it was no joke to David Obey, Democratic chair of the House Appropriations Committee, who complained that Obama's innovation grants "scapegoated schools and teachers" instead of simply giving them what they needed: more money. Not surprisingly, Obey also objected to the fact that the Department of Education—not his own committee—would decide where the grants would go. For his own part, Obama enjoyed what the journalist Jonathan Alter called a "rare moment of leverage" on the issue. Public opinion polls consistently showed strong bipartisan support for school reform: in 2010, for example, 71 percent of respondents in a *Time* survey said they favored merit pay for teachers. And since the teachers unions had backed Obama's opponent in the primaries, he didn't feel beholden to them once he entered office. Obey and the White House eventually compromised by reducing the innovation fund to $5 billion, a third of Obama's original goal. But it was still the largest competitive grant program in American history. And it would be dispensed according to "criteria as the Secretary [of Education] deems appropriate," as the final version of the stimulus package declared.[9]

That made Arne Duncan the most powerful education secretary in U.S. history, by far. Renaming the grant competition "Race to the Top" (RTTT), Duncan called the program a "once-in-a lifetime opportunity to do something special, to drive change, to make our schools better." Indeed, Duncan wrote in a *Washington Post* op-ed, RTTT was nothing less than "education reform's moon shot." The Department of Education proceeded to lay out parameters for the competition, which included every major item in the reform playbook. States would get points for allowing charter schools to multiply, for compensating teachers based on student test scores, and for adopting higher academic standards. Under No Child Left Behind, states had devised their own standards; simply by setting a low bar, then, radically underserved states like Mississippi could report a much higher fraction of "proficient" students than wealthier (and, by all other measures, more educationally successful) states such as Massachusetts. To correct this glaring problem, RTTT incentivized states to establish "college- and career-ready" standards. For all practical purposes, that meant adopting the Common Core State Standards that had been developed by the bipartisan National Governors Association and the Council of Chief State School Officers (CCSSO). Rooted in state-level reforms that sprouted up in 1980s and 1990s, the standards "began with the idea that math in Massachusetts is not any different from math in Maryland," as the CCSSO's executive director stated. And now, thanks to Race to the Top, the federal government could pressure states into adopting shared ways for measuring what students learned.[10]

The political results of RTTT were astounding, both in speed and breadth. By the end of 2009, thirty-four states had changed their educational laws or policies to qualify for the competition. Some states lifted their "firewalls" on using student data to evaluate teachers; others removed their caps on charter schools. And by the following year, forty-three states and the District of Columbia had adopted the Common Core standards. It was an exaggeration to say that the Obama administration "forced" Common Core and other reforms on unwilling states, as critics would later charge. But with the country still mired in a serious recession, the RTTT money was—to borrow a line from *The Godfather*—an offer that most states could not refuse. "I'm pleased to announce this summer's blockbuster: from the creators of No Child Left Behind, it's 'NCLB 2: The Carrot that Feels like a Stick,'" jibed one observer in July 2009. Forty states and the District of Columbia applied for RTTT funds in the first year of the competition; and while the Department of Education made awards to only two states in the first round and just nine states (and D.C.) in the second, almost every state altered its policies to enter the RTTT sweepstakes. As another journalist noted, Race to the Top changed the game of education before the race even started.[11]

It also triggered celebrations among reform advocates within both parties, who happily noted their shared perspectives on the subject. "For the first time in my political life, there seems to be more consensus than disagreement across the ideological spectrum about education reform," noted Jeb Bush, who had championed charter schools and the Common Core as GOP governor of Florida. Leading Democratic enthusiasts included foundation titan Bill Gates—who proclaimed his "near-complete agreement" with Obama on education—and Davis Guggenheim, who had directed Al Gore's *An Inconvenient Truth* film on climate change. In 2010, Guggenheim's procharter movie *Waiting for Superman* would become a central talking point for Democratic and Republican reformers alike. The film took its name from a quote by Geoffrey Canada, whose Harlem Children's Zone—a broad social-service project that included a successful charter-school network—drew praise from liberal media superstar Oprah Winfrey and New York GOP mayor Michael Bloomberg; at one point, Bloomberg even tried to persuade Canada to become the city's school chancellor. On the pages of the *New York Times*, meanwhile, both Nicholas Kristof and David Brooks—the paper's liberal and conservative standard-bearers, respectively—heaped praise on the Obama administration's education achievements. Other press accounts focused on the strange-bedfellow forces arrayed behind RTTT, which made especially good copy in a capital otherwise suffused with partisan acrimony. The most bizarre alliance featured former GOP House Speaker Newt Gingrich and African American activist Reverend Al Sharpton, who both accompanied Arne Duncan on a multicity tour to pump up support for Race to the Top. "People that don't come together on anything else are coming together to say, we're going to do what must be done . . . to deal with education in this country," Sharpton told National Public Radio. The NPR web headline called Gingrich and Sharpton an "unlikely pair," which was an understatement par excellence.[12]

Similar stories dotted the newspapers and airwaves throughout Obama's first term, reinforcing the bipartisan flavor of federal education policy. Obama and Duncan shared the stage at a 2011 Miami high school with Jeb Bush, whom Obama praised as a "champion" of school reform. "It's time we came together—just like Jeb and I are doing today," Obama said, "not as Democrats or Republicans, as Americans, to lift up all of our schools, and to prepare students like you for a twenty-first-century education." The Common Core initiative proved especially popular with several GOP governors, including New Jersey's Chris Christie and Kentucky's Paul Patton. As the 2012 presidential elections approached, the differences between party leaders on education seemed to narrow even further. Campaigning for the GOP nomination, Newt Gingrich called education "the one area where I very much agree" with Obama; likewise, eventual Republican nominee Mitt Romney admitted that "some of [Obama's] education policies" have been "positive." Pressed on whether he would reappoint Arne Duncan as secretary of education, Romney dodged the question. But the line of inquiry spoke volumes about the shared presumptions of Romney and Obama, whom one reporter called "education twins." Less than 1 percent of questions and comments in their debates focused on education, because there were so few actual differences to discuss.[13]

Bipartisan Objections

But Romney did face criticism about education from other Republicans during the campaign, revealing the strong intraparty tensions that lurked beneath the bipartisan consensus on school reform. Grassroots GOP objections to federal education efforts were already apparent near the end of George W. Bush's presidency, when five Republican senators and fifty representatives called for the repeal of No Child Left Behind. Dissent stepped up under Obama, of course, when Republicans complained that his educational policies—like his efforts on immigration, gun control, and the environment—had concentrated new authority in the Oval Office. That's not to say Obama "abused executive power" to "blackmail" states into adopting Common Core and his other pet reforms, as GOP senator and presidential hopeful Ted Cruz charged. But no president had ever been able to shape K–12 schooling to the degree that Obama did, which inevitably raised the specter of executive overreach. "This is Washington Knows Best at its worst," warned Republican education writer Michael J. Petrilli in 2009. "Get ready for a backlash." Eight of the twelve governors or mayors leading states or districts that had won RTTT grants were replaced in the 2010 elections, when the GOP recaptured Congress. By the following year, as the 2012 presidential race heated up, Republican supporters of federal school reform were facing a full-scale revolt. Candidates Michele Bachmann and Rick Santorum both pledged to abolish the Department of Education, exactly as Ronald Reagan had demanded; Santorum even apologized for voting for NCLB when he was in the Senate. ("Sometimes you take one for the team," Santorum said, calling his vote an honest but unwise act of deference to Bush and the GOP leadership.) Romney stood by RTTT but eventually distanced himself from Common Core, which was a lightning rod for dissent at the 2012 Republican Convention. "We call it Obama Core," one delegate quipped, riffing on the "Obamacare" language from the healthcare debate. "It's been co-opted by the Obama administration. . . . We're Republicans and we're letting Obama take over our education system."[14]

At the same time, ironically, Democratic critics were grumbling that Obama had been co-opted by . . . Republicans. American Federation of Teachers chief Randi Weingarten told the *Washington Post* that Obama's RTTT looked like "Bush Three," an accelerated version of the policies put forth by the last president. The other major teachers union, the National Education Association (NEA), blasted "federal mandates . . . that usurp state and local government's responsibility for public education," sounding for all the world like Obama's GOP foes. Most union members continued to vote for Obama, who repeatedly reminded them that his stimulus had saved hundreds of thousands of school jobs. But the unions made no secret of their disdain for his educational reforms, particularly merit pay and charter schools; pay-by-test-scores insulted their professional authority, teachers said, while charters—most of which were not unionized—threatened their collective bargaining power. Neither Obama nor Duncan was invited to address the 2010 union conventions, where several speakers called for Duncan's resignation; at the NEA, meanwhile, delegates approved a vote of no confidence on RTTT. Tensions reached their peak during a 2012 strike in Chicago, where Arne Duncan had served as superintendent and Rahm Emanuel—Obama's former chief of staff—was mayor. The dispute centered not just on the teachers' salary scale and benefits but on merit pay and charters, both key elements of Obama's reform agenda. And while the president himself escaped direct censure, Duncan and Emanuel were lambasted mercilessly. Chicago Teachers Federation president Karen Lewis even mocked Duncan's alleged speech impediment, underscoring the astounding degree of hostility between her union and the White House. "This guy has the nerve to stand up and say, 'Education is the thivil rights ithue of our time,'" Lewis teased. "Now you know he went to private school because if he had gone to public school he'd have had that lisp fixed."[15]

Other pockets of Democratic dissent began to pop up within the civil rights community, an important strand of the bipartisan coalition that had built and sustained No Child Left Behind. Like Al Sharpton, some civil rights activists remained loyal to the Obama education agenda. But others started to express reservations about RTTT, which seemed to reward states with the greatest capacity; so it also threatened to leave poorer schools and communities behind, if their state leaders failed to capitalize on the competition. Other minority critics took aim at the goals of RTTT, particularly the expansion of charter schools; even when these schools succeeded, the argument went, charters harmed the regular public schools by depriving them of already-scant tax dollars and by skimming off the strongest students. To be sure, research has shown that charter schools can lead to reduced funding for other public schools. But there is scant evidence that charters worsen academic achievement in the other schools; indeed, a recent analysis suggested that the expansion of charter schools might actually improve outcomes in nearby noncharter public schools. Yet attacks on the reform agenda have continued to rise, especially in inner-city neighborhoods where schools were closed down. Citing low test scores and graduation rates, reformers replaced so-called failing schools with a menu of different options, including charters. But the mostly minority parents who supported these institutions saw things very differently. The school was a symbol of their community, and sometimes the only accessible public space within it; any attack on the school was perceived as an attack on local citizens, too, whether the reformers intended that or not.[16]

But the most vehement Democratic foes of Obama's reform framework came from universities, particularly from schools of education. Like union activists, most of these critics tended to mute their criticism of Obama himself. But they showed no such restraint about his reform agenda, which they reviled as a threat to public education writ large. Their best-known voice was historian Diane Ravitch, who embodied her own Nixon-goes-to-China story: a former advocate of national standards and charter schools, she switched sides and became their loudest critic. To Ravitch, standards—and the high-stakes exams that attached to them—replaced the richness and rigor of real education with the torpor and tedium of test preparation; charters, meanwhile, allowed a host of private vendors to rack up profits even as many of their students languished. She reserved her greatest disdain for what she called the "Billionaire Boys Club," the foundation executives like Bill Gates and Eli Broad whose contributions bankrolled charter networks as well as much of the research undergirding school reform. But as many scholars found, this research was highly contestable or—in a few cases—patently flawed. The scholarship on charter schools and academic achievement was like the elephant in the famous Indian folk tale, with each blind man (or, rather, each double-blind researcher) "seeing" the version he or she wanted. Nor was there solid evidence that student test scores could serve as a reliable indicator of teacher performance, even as RTTT incentivized states to base evaluations on these scores. The most basic premise of federally sponsored school reform—that test-based accountability systems would enhance student learning—was thrown into question by a nine-year National Academy of Sciences study, released in 2011. And so on. Obviously, it will take many years for us to know how these different reforms have affected students, teachers, and communities. But clearly some of the Obama-era reforms have been based on incomplete or faulty research, embraced by the same administration that proudly touted its scientific bona fides on questions like stem-cell research, drug policy, and climate change.[17]

Most citizens didn't keep tabs on the complexities of educational research, of course, any more than they monitored the back-and-forth of inside-the-Beltway politics. Instead, Americans rendered judgments based on their own immediate experiences. And there is no government institution that touches more Americans—directly, intimately, and consistently—than the public school. For most of U.S. history, education was almost entirely a state and local concern. The federal government didn't enter the picture in a sustained fashion until the 1965 Elementary and Secondary Education Act (ESEA), which aimed mainly at providing added services for poor students and communities. No Child Left Behind reauthorized ESEA in 2002, but also reoriented the act in two fundamental ways: it focused on outcomes instead of inputs, and on all students rather than the least advantaged ones. It thereby brought federal influence into every school, in ways that no other law had done. Starting before Barack Obama reached the White House and gaining steam after that, many voters began to indict the negative effects of the federal government in their educational lives. Ultimately, these local experiences and perceptions—not the machinations of Washington politics—fueled the bipartisan antipathy to No Child Left Behind and its Obama-era cousin, Race to the Top.[18]

In the suburbs and exurbs, especially, parents complained that high-stakes tests were narrowing the curriculum and "dumbing-down" its level of difficulty. With the advent of the federally encouraged Common Core exams, ironically, other parents said that the tests had suddenly become too hard. Most of all, parents objected to the growing number of school days and hours devoted to testing and preparation for it. Students in the nation's largest school districts take an average of 112 standardized tests between prekindergarten and twelfth grade, amounting to twenty to twenty-five hours per school year. But nobody knows how much time teachers spend readying children for the exams, which have sparked a new kind of civil disobedience: the "opt-out" movement. In 2015, an astonishing 20 percent of eligible students in New York State refused to take its Common Core exam; in Colorado and New Jersey, 5 percent of students did the same. Nationwide, however, less than 1 percent of students have opted out of tests. Centered mainly in well-to-do school districts, the movement was denounced by civil rights leaders who worried that it would prevent states from documenting the so-called "achievement gap" between different races; and if the gap couldn't be measured, they argued, it also couldn't be closed. So the testing controversy exposed yet another fissure in the fraying consensus over federally driven school reform. At the outset of the Obama years, reform united Democrats and Republicans across their myriad differences. Now it was dividing parents in tony liberal precincts like Brooklyn's Park Slope—a center of the opt-out movement—from their ideological allies in nearby minority communities.[19]

Every Student Succeeds

All of these cross-cutting tensions and objections set the stage for the 2015 Every Student Succeeds Act, which finally reauthorized No Child Left Behind. But whereas NCLB—and, especially, RTTT—dramatically increased the federal footprint in the schools, ESSA scaled it back. In a "direct rebuke" to the Obama administration, as one journalist called it, the new law explicitly barred the federal government from dictating or even encouraging a given set of standards, including Common Core; the measure also prevented the government from requiring states to evaluate teachers via test scores, perhaps the key feature of Obama's reform project. States still have to test all students each year and report the results by race. But they can now set their own goals and accountability systems, which need not rely solely on test scores. The lone exceptions involve schools scoring in the bottom 5 percent on tests or high schools graduating fewer than two-thirds of students, for which states will have to design explicit improvement plans. In that sense, Every Student Succeeds returns education policy to the spirit of the original Elementary and Secondary Education Act of 1965 and its focus on underprivileged children. Every student will still be tested, but only egregiously failing schools will require federally sanctioned interventions to monitor—and, ideally, to enhance—their academic success.[20]

Unfortunately, the federal government doesn't have a great track record when it comes to assisting the least privileged via education. Most studies of ESEA's Title I program—designed to address the "special educational needs of children of low-income families," as the act said—showed few lasting benefits for poor Americans. But the law *did* benefit middle-class Americans, in ways that still go unrecognized. Beyond Title I, ESEA's other chapters provided federal funds for libraries, textbooks, and educational television. And even Title I money was sometimes diverted away from its intended target—disadvantaged children—and into swimming pools, A-V equipment, and other facilities for middle-class or even upper-class schools. These features accounted for the political staying power of ESEA, which won successive reauthorizations—and enormous bipartisan support—in Congress. But the measure generated little interest or controversy inside the broad middle class, which remained mostly unaware of how it was affecting schools across the socioeconomic spectrum. Nor did most voters pause to consider the growing array of federal educational benefits they received, ranging from subsidized school lunches to special services for bilingual, disabled, and gifted children. Most of these benefits were "submerged," to borrow Suzanne Mettler's phrase; although they influenced millions of citizens, they generally didn't enter popular consciousness as forms of federal assistance or intervention.[21]

No Child Left Behind and Race to the Top augmented the federal role in education *and* brought that role to the surface, in a manner that almost everyone could recognize. Explicitly universal in scope, these measures stemmed from the perception that all American schools—not just the poorest ones—required systematic change. "The problems in our educational system aren't restricted to the inner city," Barack Obama wrote in *The Audacity of Hope*, citing statistics that showed American students trailing their peers in most other developed countries in math and science. Hence the need for "bold reform of our schools," Obama argued, not just piecemeal improvements. But it turned out that many Americans—probably, most Americans—did not want their schools to be reformed, at least not in the ways that reformers imagined. Just as citizens vilify "Congress" but continue to support their congressperson, so do citizens often condemn "American education" even as they praise their own school. So they also embrace an educational version of Not In My Backyard: test-based accountability systems might be a good thing for the school on the other side of town, but not for the one next door. Every Student Succeeds removed the most unpopular kinds of federal intervention but preserved myriad federal services, which will remain mostly unknown and unappreciated. They bring good things to schools, but almost no political advantage to their benefactors in Washington.[22]

Consensus Continues

That will also make the politics of K–12 schools a bit more like higher education, where reforms rarely resonate with American voters. Consider the fate of Obama's other large-scale educational initiative: the expansion of access to higher education, especially via direct government lending to students. Here, too, Obama built on a bipartisan consensus that preceded him. During the Bill Clinton years, when Democrats started to press for direct lending, Republicans rallied to the defense of the private banking industry. But near the end of his own presidency, George W. Bush signed a measure that reduced subsidies to the private lenders. The next step was to remove them from the equation altogether, which Obama did in his first year of office. Making the government the sole lender, Obama shifted the resulting savings into the Pell Grant program; he also expanded the tuition tax credit for students and capped loan repayments at 10 percent of a borrower's disposable income. Altogether, as the journalist Michael Grunwald wrote, it "added up to a revolution in how America finances higher education." But it also went mostly unheralded, Grunwald added, "completely overshadowed by the health care hoopla" that seized Washington in the early years of the administration. Obama mentioned higher education only nine times in public speeches during his first fourteen months in the White House; not surprisingly, then, only one in four Americans knew much about his higher-education package when he signed it into law. Buried deep in citizens' IRS returns, tuition tax credits proved especially hard to understand and appreciate. In a 2010 poll, nearly a quarter of Americans said their taxes had increased; only one-eighth knew that their taxes had actually gone down, often thanks to Obama's credits.[23]

Predictably, then, Obama himself got little credit for any of these efforts. Nor did they make many waves among Republicans, who had bigger fish to fry. Although House Speaker John Boehner initially derided direct lending as another "job-killing government takeover," just like the Affordable Care Act, no prominent Republican called for the repeal of direct lending as they did with Obamacare. (And direct lending really *was* a government takeover, while Obamacare wasn't; the first replaced private lenders, while the second let private insurance companies remain in place.) Republicans had more success in thwarting Obama's subsequent higher-education initiatives, which aimed to make community college free and to transform Pell Grants into an entitlement like Social Security or Medicare. Pell Grants would be guaranteed to anyone who was eligible, and it would also require Congress to fund the program for everyone who qualified. It's too early to predict the fate of these proposals. But they seem unlikely to make it through Congress, because their sticker price is so steep and undisguised. Programs that benefit the broad middle class live on, especially when (as in the case of tax credits) beneficiaries don't know about them. Extending those resources to a broader constituency makes them more visible but also more vulnerable, as Obama's stalemated student-aid efforts confirm.[24]

Most of all, the broader story of education during the Obama years reminds us how different it remains from most other issues in Washington. Americans have always argued deeply and passionately about education, of course, and the Obama era was no exception; indeed, the heightened role of the federal government made education perhaps more contested than ever before. But these debates occurred within a broader bipartisan consensus that survived across Obama's presidency, even as its contours veered away from the stronger federal presence he had created. There probably isn't another issue that could bring together Newt Gingrich and Al Sharpton—as Race to the Top did, in 2009—or Lamar Alexander and Patty Murray, the Republican and Democratic coauthors of Every Student Succeeds in 2015. That doesn't necessarily make our evolving education policies more rational or effective, especially for the least advantaged American students; "just because something is a compromise," wrote one jaundiced observer with the passage of ESSA, "doesn't mean that it will do good things for children." But it does mean that education is *different*, in ways that will continue to confound the fractured world of American federal politics.[25]

Barack Obama and the Movement for Black Lives

RACE, DEMOCRACY, AND CRIMINAL JUSTICE IN THE AGE OF FERGUSON

Peniel E. Joseph

Barack Obama's watershed election to the presidency on Tuesday, November 4, 2008, transformed the optics of American democracy. The victory of the first black man to be a major party nominee provided a dramatic, globally resonant, and symbolically powerful illustration of America's racial progress since the formal end of Jim Crow segregation in 1965. Obama's successful campaign for the presidency evoked an outpouring of nostalgia for the 1960s, echoing the charismatic but brief tenure of President John F. Kennedy and the passionate but truncated presidential campaign of his younger brother, the former attorney general turned New York senator Robert F. Kennedy.

The Obama campaign's main inspiration however, drew from the civil rights movement's heroic period, the years between the May 17, 1954 *Brown* Supreme Court desegregation decision and the August 6, 1965 passage of the Voting Rights Act into law by President Lyndon Baines Johnson. These years bookend one of the most tumultuous, violent, and important decades in American history where racial justice became enshrined, at long last, in our national consciousness and political and democratic institutions.[1]

As a young man of biracial ancestry, Obama was raised by his white mother, Ann Dunham, to respect and revere both his father's Kenyan identity and the long tradition of black political struggle that, to her, was exemplified in the activism and artistry of Harry Belafonte, the singer and actor she called "the most handsome man in the world." In his best-selling memoir, *Dreams from My Father*, Obama recounts his at times painful search for a usable racial identity while coming of age in Hawaii's multicultural social milieu. Black history, from the writings of the abolitionist Frederick Douglass to the *Autobiography of Malcolm X*, became sacred texts to the young Obama, ones that offered a hesitant and at times confused young man a blueprint to the African American experience.[2] A budding writer, voracious reader, and precocious intellectual, Obama analyzed and investigated the black experience on his way to experiencing black culture during his years in Chicago, marriage to Michelle Robinson, and work as a community organizer in the Altgeld Gardens section of the Windy City. In his early twenties he carried around a copy of Taylor Branch's Pultizer Prize–winning history of the civil rights era, *Parting the Waters*, referring to it as "my story."[3]

As a presidential candidate Barack Obama spoke of the civil rights movement in reverential and personal tones. He expressed open admiration for John Lewis, the civil rights legend turned Georgia congressman, identifying himself as part of the "Joshua Generation" of African Americans whose achievements, however towering, stood on the shoulders of longtime marchers for racial justice like Lewis. The personally fastidious Obama especially admired the early activism of the Student Non-Violent Coordinating Committee (SNCC), a group chaired by John Lewis that became the backbone of voting rights campaigns in Mississippi, Alabama, southwest Georgia, and Arkansas, among many other places. SNCC appealed to Obama's romantic conception of the civil rights era as being populated by young students, sons and daughters of sharecroppers and Jewish immigrants, united in the determination to change the world by placing their bodies on the line in organized acts of courageous civil disobedience strong enough to inspire movements around the world and topple empires.

Martin Luther King Jr.'s legacy loomed large in Obama's candidacy and presidential campaign. Obama frequently cited King as a source of inspiration and, during his Democratic Party primary showdown against New York senator Hillary Rodham Clinton, often relied upon King's words to provide ballast for his own audacious presidential run. Senator Obama utilized King's words about "the fierce urgency of now" repeatedly in his fight for the Democratic nomination. The phrase became an incantation capable of explaining why a forty-six-year-old junior senator from Illinois named Barack Hussein Obama thought himself capable of leading the most powerful country in the world.

Obama's "Yes We Can" speech, delivered in the aftermath of a New Hampshire primary loss to Clinton, conjured the civil rights era and its most important icon in a flush of rhetorical poetry that cited slaves, abolitionists, immigrants, and workers as composing the tapestry of hopes—real and imagined—that shaped the American story and ended with "a king who took us to the mountaintop and pointed the way to the promised land: Yes, we can, to justice and equality."[4]

Obama himself, during his election night acceptance speech, hailed America as a "nation where all things are possible," simultaneously upholding his presidential victory as both symbolism and substance of the nation's racial progress from slavery to freedom. Obama's resounding victory reverberated around the world as proof of the existence of things that remained unseen, most profoundly as illustration that America had not only achieved substantial racial progress but, in the spirit of domestic narratives of exceptionalism, had also achieved a new, unprecedented, "postracial" reality wherein institutional racism no longer disadvantaged a black community whose descendants were once considered a species of property rather than citizens. Yet this celebratory atmosphere also denied fundamental aspects of America's racial history that would be largely ignored during the Obama presidency until the eruption of the Black Lives Matter (BLM) movement. Namely, that American democracy, despite Obama's electrifying victory, has been built on institutional racism that continued to flourish long after the formal end of slavery and Jim Crow.[5]

If President Obama's election produced spasms of racial vertigo, the reality for millions of African Americans who cheered his victory continued to be contoured by the very forces of racial segregation, police brutality, poverty, and unemployment that, in some quarters, Obama's election had suddenly made irrelevant. Obama's personal commitment to civil rights for all Americans was reflected in his choice of Eric Holder to lead the Department of Justice as the nation's first black attorney general. Over the next six years Holder became Obama's more fervid racial alter ego, decrying America as a "nation of cowards" for refusing to publicly discuss racial injustice and pushing for substantive reform of a criminal justice system that disproportionately arrested, incarcerated, and punished black men, women, teenagers, and children.

The Age of Obama, instead of ushering in a postracial America, revealed long-simmering inequities most acutely, but not entirely, encapsulated by the criminal justice system. The death of Trayvon Martin, a seventeen-year-old black teenager shot and killed by a vigilante who successfully used Florida's "stand your ground" law to avoid jail, unleashed a massive wave of protests, demonstrations, and organizing that helped turn a hashtag, #BlackLivesMatter, created by three black feminist and queer-identified activists, into a social movement.

Black Lives Matter activists, inspired by roiling police community tensions in the aftermath of the shooting of unarmed black teenager Michael Brown in Ferguson, Missouri, in 2014, helped to expose America's criminal justice system as a gateway to a panoramic system of racial and economic oppression. From this perspective Obama's elevation to the nation's highest position of leadership, juxtaposed against racial unrest that turned violent in Ferguson and Baltimore in the middle of his second term, signaled not so much the end of racial injustice in America, but its evolution.

In many ways, Obama's election represented the success of one tier of African American life since the high point of the civil rights era. The rise of a thriving black middle and upper middle class, the creation of affluent black suburbs and parts of central cities, the growth of black entrepreneurs, business and thought leaders, sports icons, and music and entertainment moguls became embodied in the glamour and prestige of the nation's First Black Family. Michelle Obama, educated at Princeton and Harvard Law School, served as Obama's mentor during a summer internship in Chicago, where they started their courtship. Michelle's influence on Obama was both personal and political. In Chicago he attended Trinity United, the most influential black church in the city, whose fiery pastor, the Reverend Jeremiah Wright, became a liability during the 2008 campaign (after conservative news outlets ran excerpts of him saying "God Damn America" during one of his sermons), but provided ballast for the young Obama's search for personal faith. In fact, Obama took the title of his second book, *The Audacity of Hope*, from one of Wright's sermons. But Obama and Wright's close, almost familial relationship did not survive the presidential campaign. The young senator and would-be president delivered the speech of his life on March 18, 2008, in Philadelphia, where he dispassionately analyzed two centuries of race relations, finding moral equivalency in black anger over slavery and white supremacy with white resentment against affirmative action and perceptions of black entitlement. Obama's "race speech," lauded in the mainstream media as perhaps the best speech on race since Abraham Lincoln, featured troubling signs about his views of racial injustice, ones that BLM activists would highlight during his second presidential term.

Black Lives Matter demonstrators, like Obama, found inspiration in the civil rights era. They especially admired SNCC's grassroots organizing strategy, one that elevated a decentralized model of leadership, called for a restoration of democracy at the local level, and eschewed a cult of personality that surrounded presidents or movement leaders such as Martin Luther King Jr. BLM activists recognized SNCC as restless insurgents whose envelope-pushing political radicalism pulled no punches in speaking truth to power. On this score the group pilloried both the Kennedy and Johnson administrations' failure to protect civil rights workers in the Deep South, unwillingness to robustly support enforcement of the 1964 Civil Rights Act and subsequent voting rights legislation, and involvement in the Vietnam War. The group worked in creative tension with King, relying more on founder Ella Baker, a veteran organizer, feminist, and elder who appreciated King's prodigious talents even as she recognized the limits of his political vision during the early 1960s. SNCC chairman John Lewis revered King even as other activists, perhaps most notably Stokely Carmichael, pushed King to understand the limits of political reform and address the structural nature of racial and economic inequality.[6]

The Black Lives Matter movement has adopted the nonviolent disobedience of the civil rights struggle while embracing the structural critique of racial injustice most popularly associated with the Black Power era. In contrast to Obama's select utilization of King, the BLM movement continues the legacy of the later King, a prophet unrecognized in his own country, which he excoriated for its promotion of violence, racism, economic injustice, and war. International travel to Ghana and India, where he met with the nation's "untouchables," stoked King's empathy for political underdogs, yet he remained committed to working within a liberal framework of political reform until at least 1965. Earlier speeches, including the March On Washington "I Have a Dream" address, which called for reparations in the form of a long-overdue metaphorical check, touched upon the institutional nature of inequality that King began to focus on by 1966. Headquartered in a Chicago housing project, King mobilized a three-tiered movement calling for an end to racial segregation, slum housing, and institutional racism. On April 4, 1967, King broke with the White House, and severed his relationship with Lyndon Johnson, by calling for an end to the Vietnam War. Eleven days later he shared a stage with Black Power leader Stokely Carmichael and peace activist Dr. Benjamin Spock in New York City at the then largest antiwar demonstration in American history.

The civil rights movement, therefore, indelibly shaped Obama and BLM activists, albeit in different ways. Obama upholds the movement as an example of ordinary people compelling democratic institutions to achieve unprecedented levels of reform that helped lead to his election. From this vantage point civil rights helped to perfect a union that once held black people in generational bondage. The movement's diverse racial, class, gender, and religious makeup illustrates the power of America's multicultural roots.

Black Lives Matter activists, although no less inspired than the president, interpret the movement as exemplifying the destructive power of state-sanctioned violence, racial oppression, and economic injustice.[7] The movement's most radical edges were surveilled, harassed, imprisoned, even killed at the hands of white vigilantes working in concert with local, state, and federal authorities, with the FBI being the most well known offenders but far from the only ones. The continued persistence of racial segregation in neighborhoods and public schools, high rates of black unemployment, and continued assaults on voting rights by no less than the Supreme Court of the United States underscores the rank hypocrisy of a nation that annually celebrates a King holiday and Black History Month.

America's system of mass incarceration provides BLM activists with their most compelling evidence of contemporary racism in all of its tragically panoramic glory. The fact that this system continued to thrive under a two-term African American president is one of the great ironies of our time.[8]

The publication of legal scholar Michelle Alexander's *The New Jim Crow: Mass Incarceration in the Age of Colorblindness* during the second year of the Obama administration helped to catapult the issue of race and criminal justice into the public consciousness. In passionately lucid prose Alexander argued that the drug war had created a new racial caste system, one inaugurated by President Richard Nixon, ratcheted up by Ronald Reagan, and perfected under Bill Clinton with devastating consequences for the group of impoverished black Americans that the sociologist William Julius Wilson famously referred to as the "truly disadvantaged." African Americans, especially men and boys and increasingly women and girls, were arrested, convicted, and sentenced to felony drug convictions at disproportionate rates, a situation exacerbated by bipartisan anticrime bills passed in 1986 and 1988 that penalized users and sellers of crack cocaine far beyond (100–1 in federal law) predominantly white users of powdered cocaine. The Clinton administration turned Reagan era policies of punishment into practically a moral philosophy, passing a crime bill that turned mandatory minimums and three-strikes legislation (which required that three-time felony convictions, no matter the circumstances, earned twenty-five years to life in jail) into federal law. Clinton's welfare reform legislation offered new layers of punishment against the formerly incarcerated by denying ex-offenders access to food stamps, public housing, and any reasonable chance at reentering society.[9]

Millions of black men found themselves unable to vote even after completing their sentences, victims of Reconstruction era state laws designed to disenfranchise freedmen whose effects have carried over into two separate centuries. Stigmatized as criminals, forced to check the box on job applications, denied access to housing, education, even food, formerly incarcerated black felons found themselves embedded in an extensive system of surveillance through parole and probation for much of their lives. Local jails charged fees that caused former inmates to incur thousands of dollars in debt that could never be repaid.[10]

Blacks in the post–civil rights era, a putative age of color-blindness that Obama's election seemed to exemplify, found themselves under the cruel hand of a political and criminal justice system that paralleled the denial of voting rights, restrictions on movement, bleak job prospects, and public shame and humiliation that were some of the main features of a Jim Crow regime thought to have been relegated to history's dustbin. Alexander's *cri de coeur*, which became a *New York Times* bestseller in paperback, provides historical and political context for the racial fires that engulfed Ferguson, Baltimore, and the entire nation during Barack Obama's second term.

On August 12, 2013, Eric Holder, the nation's first black attorney general, addressed at least parts of the vast array of racial inequities in the criminal justice system outlined in *The New Jim Crow*, during a speech before the American Bar Association in San Francisco. The public admission from the nation's top law enforcement official that "too many Americans go to too many prisons for far too long and for no good law enforcement reasons" offered a political and moral framework for much-needed reform. Promising to "take bold steps" to end this injustice, Holder announced new proposals designed to ameliorate a criminal justice system the attorney general admitted was broken. Specifically, Holder announced new guidelines that provide U.S. Attorneys more discretion in applying federal charges to criminal defendants, update and innovate antiviolence strategies, and revise "zero tolerance" school policies that send too many young black children on a "school-to-prison pipeline." "A minor school disciplinary offense," explained Holder, "should put a student in the principal's office and not a police precinct."[11]

Holder also announced renewed efforts to provide every criminal defendant resources for a public defense and legal counsel through the DOJ's Access to Justice Initiative, and, through Justice's Civil Rights Division, to halt the flood of felony conviction pleas that many black criminal defendants accept (including those later proven innocent), without trial, documented by Alexander in *The New Jim Crow*.[12]

Holder underscored the high financial and moral cost of incarceration, with the former being a driving force behind reform efforts to reduce prison populations in several southern states. Black men, Holder acknowledged, received sentences that were 20 percent longer for the same crimes as white defendants, a situation he found to be "unacceptable" and "shameful." On this score Holder announced that the DOJ would no longer impose mandatory minimums on low-level drug offenders, would revise its guidelines to offer "compassionate release" to federal inmates, and would step up its efforts to enhance "diversion" programs focused on rehabilitation community development.

The attorney general's efforts to reform the criminal justice system at the federal level were extensive, thoughtful, and unprecedented in American history. Holder's speech before the ABA closely addressed criticisms made by the American Civil Liberties Union (ACLU), prisoners' rights groups, and Alexander.

One of the most underreported aspects of Holder's speech was his detailing of the conversations he had about the criminal justice system with Barack Obama. In the aftermath of Ferguson, when the attorney general, rather than the president, met with local activists and families impacted by police shootings and gun violence, many critics praised Holder as a strong "race man" at President Obama's expense. While understandable, such a view misses the complexity of the two men's close personal and professional relationship. Near the beginning of his speech Holder outlined Obama's views on criminal justice:

> These are issues the President and I have been talking about for as long as I've known him—issues he's felt strongly about ever since his days as a community organizer on the South Side of Chicago. He's worked hard over the years to protect our communities, to keep violent criminals off

our streets, and to make sure those who break the law are held account-able. And he's also made it part of his mission to reduce the disparities in our criminal justice system. In Illinois, he passed legislation that ad-dressed racial profiling and trained police departments on how they could avoid racial bias. And in 2010, this Administration successfully advocated for the reduction of the unjust 100-to-1 sentencing disparity between crack and powder cocaine.

Barack Obama's decision to name Holder (and later Loretta Lynch) as attorney general illustrated both a principled and pragmatic approach to law enforcement, one that confronted the practical realities of a federal sys-tem of law that could incentivize, but not directly control, the way in which individual states approached criminal justice. Even a relatively friendly Congress only reduced the disparities in the unjust sentencing reform Holder touted to 18–1, a glaring inequality that still ensures that racial bias remains entrenched in policy many still consider to be color-blind. The ad-ministration's pro–law enforcement worldview made it difficult to heed the policy advice of civil rights activists who urged the Obama Justice Depart-ment to radically transform the Byrne Grants, the largest federal aid to local law enforcement, by incentivizing rehabilitation, mental health services, and restorative justice rather than arrests, criminal stings, and drug busts that helped create the feedback loop that imprisoned two generations of blacks within America's vast system of mass incarceration.

On August 9, 2014, three days short of the first anniversary of Holder's watershed ABA speech, Michael Brown, an unarmed eighteen-year-old black teenager, was shot and killed by a police officer in Ferguson, Mis-souri. Brown's uncovered body lay in the street for four hours, sparking community anger and outrage. Dozens of protesters quickly turned into hundreds and then thousands of local people demanding answers that city officials were unable to give. In an age where cell-phone camera videos of police shootings of black people turned them into spectacles that recalled the era of lynching, Mike Brown's killing turned viral, helping to launch a national movement for social justice that reverberated far beyond Fergu-son, Missouri, a predominantly black (although firmly under the thrall of white political and economic power) city twelve miles outside of St. Louis.

In the summer of 2014 Ferguson became a metaphor for racial injustice in America, one that exposed the nation's tortured race relations before a stunned world audience. The Ferguson Police Department's mistreatment and arrest of journalists paralleled its rough handling of locals, resulting in

150 arrests in the week and a half after Brown's killing. Racial unrest and violence saw a QuikTrip gas station go down in flames produced by the kind of civil disorders, race rioting, or urban rebellions that marked the long hot summers of the 1960s.[13]

A growing contingent of national and international media documented Ferguson police outfitted in military gear, courtesy of Reagan era agreements to provide law enforcement with surplus Defense Department gear, which included camouflage uniforms, tanks, sniper rifles, and a posture of aggressive policing that made Ferguson look like a literal war zone out of Afghanistan and Iraq rather than a quiet American city.[14] Fresh rounds of violence greeted Ferguson in November, after a grand jury cleared the officer who fired six bullets into Brown, a ruling that came three days before Thanksgiving.

Ferguson revealed the depth and breadth of racial oppression in the Age of Obama. It did not so much undermine the Obama administration's efforts to ameliorate the criminal justice system, as expose them as neither far-reaching nor fast enough. President Obama, who would not find his voice on matters of racial justice until the following year, offered painfully disappointing efforts at moral leadership in Ferguson's immediate aftermath. The commander-in-chief who famously claimed that "if I had a son he would look like Trayvon Martin" in 2012 found no similar eloquence in the early days of Ferguson. Mike Brown joined a roll call of black Americans killed after violent encounters with police, including twelve-year-old Tamir Rice in Cleveland, Oscar Grant in Oakland, and Eric Garner in New York City.

A grand jury's decision not to indict police officers in the videotaped choking death of Eric Garner, a black man illegally selling cigarettes (a misdemeanor), ratcheted up national BLM protests at the end of 2014 that continued into the New Year. Eric Holder announced a DOJ investigation into Michael Brown's shooting, comforted Brown's parents, and presented the kind of robust empathy that many African Americans yearned for in Ferguson's aftermath. The Justice Department's investigation into Ferguson would reveal a pattern of racial injustice and inequality that went beyond racial profiling of blacks. They found a systematic criminal enterprise operated by the city that targeted black residents with tickets, warrants, and arrests for misdemeanors designed to boost Ferguson's municipal resources. In short, impoverished and working-class blacks were illegally targeted by law enforcement with arrests and warrants simply for being racially and economically vulnerable, the faces at the bottom of the well ruthlessly exploited by democratic institutions sworn to protect and serve them.

On December 1, 2014, the White House organized a hastily scheduled meeting with young political activists organizing around the broad energies unleashed by the BLM movement. "The first time I was tear-gassed was on the streets of St. Louis with an eighth grader," Missouri activist Brittany Packnett informed Obama. Other activists in attendance included Ashley Yates, Rasheen Aldridge, and T Dubb-O, who all hailed from Missouri; Jose Lopez and James Hayes from New York and Ohio; and Phillip Agnew, the founder of the Dream Defenders, a grassroots organization dedicated to violence prevention that had garnered national attention for its work.[15] The assembled activists shared their experiences of police brutality and harassment but went further than exchanging war stories with the former community-activist-turned-president. They pointedly demanded that Obama end the militarization of law enforcement around the country, deny federal resources to departments with long and brutal histories of racial bias and violence against black folk, discussed the need to track police killings in America, and, anticipating "A Movement for Black Lives" policy agenda that would be published the following August, requested federal resources be directed toward community investment rather than more cops.[16]

These were not representatives from your grandparents' civil rights movement.[17] Instead, they symbolized an insurgent movement for racial justice that placed them at odds with mainstream civil rights organizations ranging from the venerable NAACP to the upstart National Action Network (NAN). They embodied the spirit of radical dissent and revolutionary protest that found civil rights stalwarts such as Jesse Jackson and Al Sharpton being booed by local activists in Ferguson. When Sharpton's NAN organized a protest march in Washington, D.C., some of these same activists rushed the stage to protest against what they felt were efforts by more powerful groups to usurp their movement while silencing their voices.

Obama's meeting with young activists with scant ties to an older generation of civil rights activists followed on the heels of three earlier instances, the first and second, respectively, at August 14 and 18 press conferences in the immediate aftermath of Michael Brown's death, and the third during a live televised address from the White House on November 24, where he upheld the rule of law and spoke dispassionately about the counterproductive nature of urban violence.[18] Obama boiled down black anger at long-documented histories of police brutality as "perceptions," claimed that "young black men that commit crime" needed to be thrown in America's dungeons for the safety of poor black communities, and touted the racial progress exemplified by his own remarkable trajectory as a stand-in for

African Americans who face far more challenging obstacles to success than he ever did.[19] In these instances, Obama, the nation's first black president, seemed virtually indistinguishable from Lyndon Johnson, a president whose civil rights agenda faced daunting challenges from summers of racial unrest during the 1960s.

The April 25, 2015, death of Freddie Gray in Baltimore from an injury sustained in the back of a police van triggered another urban rebellion just months after Ferguson. A DOJ report published in August 2016, roughly on the second anniversary of Michael Brown's death, documented a pattern of institutional racism, harassment, arrests, and assaults against black residents of Baltimore.[20] *Time* magazine published a cover story on Baltimore's riots, striking the year 1968 and replacing it with the year 2015, accompanied by an image of young protesters running from an oncoming phalanx of police.[21]

A month before Gray's death President Obama delivered a remarkable speech on the fiftieth anniversary of the "Bloody Sunday" voting rights demonstrations that ended in violence after peaceful demonstrators were routed by Alabama state troopers on horseback.[22] Buoyed by the fiftieth anniversary of the Selma-to-Montgomery demonstrations that culminated in the passage of the Voting Rights Act, Barack Obama found his voice on issues of racial justice broadly and criminal justice in particular. Obama's inherent caution prevented him from advocating the kind of bold measures that social justice advocates might have hoped for, such as releasing all nonviolent federal prisoners on drug charges, but he more forcefully utilized the presidential bully pulpit to shine a light on institutional racism in the criminal justice system in a manner that no American president had done before.

Speaking with an unusual amount of candor, Obama traced the nation's civil rights history, reminding Americans of the extraordinary challenges that have faced champions of racial justice whom critics slurred as "communists or half-breeds or outside agitators, sexual and moral degenerates, and worse."[23] Obama's public recognition that Americans were too quick to sanitize a civil rights legacy that remained fraught a half century after the movement's heroic period offered a passionately lucid defense of social justice struggles and their wider meaning for American democracy that had been sorely missing from the president's comments in the aftermath of racially motivated police shooting and racial unrest the previous year.

The shooting massacre of nine black parishioners by a young white supremacist in South Carolina's historical Emanuel African Methodist Church in June forced Obama to once again confront issues of racial injustice, which he did during a nationally televised eulogy. The Charleston massacre, as it became known, thrust forward issues of gun violence, the Confederate flag (which the shooter apparently revered and displayed prominently in his social media profiles), and the meaning of racist symbols. Turning the eulogy into a seminar on race relations, Obama pointedly acknowledged the Confederate flag as a symbol of slavery, a moral and political "wrong" whose legacies continued to shape America's present reality. In a manner that BLM activists might have surely appreciated, Obama turned his Charleston eulogy into a history and policy seminar, one that highlighted the persistence of institutional racism. "Maybe we now realize the way racial bias can infect us even when we don't realize it," said Obama, "so that we're guarding against not just racial slurs, but we're also guarding against the subtle impulse to call Johnny back for a job interview but not Jamal."[24]

The next month, during a speech before the NAACP in Philadelphia, Obama took the gloves off, linking racial disparities in the criminal justice system to "a legacy of hundreds of years of slavery" that "did not happen by accident."[25] Obama's speech represented a robust call for criminal justice reform due in no small part to the escalating racial violence around the nation and the impact of Black Lives Matter protests that had transformed our national conversation about race into a full-throated call for social justice.[26] "Mass incarceration makes our country worse off and we have to do something about it," explained Obama. In this instance, like Lyndon Johnson's use of the words "We Shall Overcome" during a joint March 15, 1965, address to Congress, Obama incorporated the language of the prison abolition movement into his own. The president used his executive power, the day before his speech, to commute the sentence of forty-six nonviolent drug offenders, a practice he would continue until the end of his time in office.[27] Two days later Barack Obama became the first sitting U.S. president to visit a federal prison, in Oklahoma, where he again touted the need for criminal justice reform.[28]

By the fall of 2015, liberal politicians such as Massachusetts senator Elizabeth Warren were publicly embracing the Black Lives Matter movement as an example of moral political courage necessitated by the nation's tumultuous racial times.[29] Warren's wide-ranging speech argued that "economic justice is not—and has never been—sufficient to ensure racial justice," a point that another liberal firebrand and future 2016 Democratic Party presidential candidate, Vermont senator Bernie Sanders, could never seem to get during his groundbreaking campaign. BLM activists, most notably schoolteacher-turned-organizer DeRay Mckesson, embraced Warren's understanding of the movement's confrontation against economic, social, and political violence that were the pillars of the racial and economic oppression experienced by so many impoverished African Americans.[30]

The Obama administration, despite the Justice Department's continued efforts at criminal justice reform under the leadership of Loretta Lynch (a Harvard Law graduate who became the nation's second African American and first black woman attorney general), did not match the urgency of Warren's speech or grandeur of the BLM movement's political ambitions and policy goals. Under Lynch's stewardship the DOJ could proudly cite major victories in the struggle for racial equality and criminal justice reform, including consent decrees with the cities of Cleveland, Baltimore, and Ferguson, Missouri, which, as of August 2016, dismissed over 32,000 court cases and $1.5 million in fines that were imposed on its predominantly black and poor residents. The Civil Rights Division's efforts to reform how cities and states assessed fines, penalties, and fees and the use of bail, driving license suspensions, and "indigent defense" for the poor and homeless cast a blinding light on the intricacies of a legal system that structurally marginalizes its most vulnerable black citizens.[31]

Racial conflict, however, unfolded faster than the political vision behind the Obama administration's reforms. In 2016, Obama's last year as president, two police shootings of black men in Baton Rouge, Louisiana, and St. Paul, Minnesota, sparked BLM demonstrations around the country. The deaths of Alton Sterling and Philando Castile were followed by the killing of five police officers and the wounding of eight others during a memorial for the two slain black men in Dallas, Texas.[32] The horrific deaths of police officers sparked a predictable backlash against the BLM movement, which conservatives now caricatured as a violent anti-police force wreaking havoc against law enforcement. President Obama, while expressing sympathy for the slain black men, used the tragedy to defend law enforcement, producing the exact kind of political theater Black Lives Matter demonstrations purposefully sought to repudiate over the last several years.

BLM activists played a considerable role in shaping the 2016 presidential election, forcing both Democratic Party candidates Hillary Clinton and Bernie Sanders to address their concerns in detailed policy speeches and providing Republican nominee Donald Trump with a rhetorical scapegoat for his law-and-order rhetoric, which successfully resuscitated President Richard Nixon's silent majority and politics of racial division for a new generation. BLM activists did more than inject racial justice into the Democratic Party nominating process. They shaped its contours by publicly repudiating Hillary Clinton's past support for punitive criminal justice policies, her use of the term "superpredator" to describe young black men, and Bill Clinton's crime and welfare policies, which continue to make it virtually impossible for ex-offenders to reclaim citizenship long after they served their time in jail.

Barack Obama's record on criminal justice reform, racial equality, policing, and democracy remains a mixed one, perhaps the most contested part of his legacy and one that future historians, policy experts, and scholars will debate for many decades to come. A full assessment will not be possible until researchers have complete access to presidential papers that will be housed in Obama's presidential library in Chicago. Obama's memoir of his White House years will also shed much needed light on this issue.

Some things are clear, however.

President Obama cared deeply about issues of justice and fairness in the criminal justice system as a Harvard-trained lawyer who taught constitutional law at the University of Chicago, a former community activist, a father of two black daughters, a husband, and a black man. His appointments of Eric Holder and Loretta Lynch—perhaps the two most important and capable members of Obama's cabinet during his entire administration—attest to this fact.[33] Holder's forceful eloquence on race matters, his defiant stance against conservative critics, and his willingness to admit the past historical failings of American democratic institutions with regard to racial justice were all done with Obama's imprimatur. The attorney general spoke with a bracing candor about racial justice in America that Barack Obama felt he was unable to do politically, at times with good reason. Negative reaction to Obama's 2009 comments about the police "acting stupidly" after the mistaken arrest of Harvard University professor Henry Louis "Skip" Gates Jr. badly shook the White House, which vowed to never speak without thoughtful deliberation on racial matters again.[34] This was a vow that Obama kept until 2015 when history forced him to speak truth to power at the expense of his intrinsic caution. Obama, at his best, believes gradual reform of structures, no matter how unjust, is the only way to ensure the kind of lasting change activists called for.

Black Lives Matter activists exemplified Martin Luther King Jr.'s call for a "revolution of values," one that transcended the reform proposed by Obama's Justice Department and envisioned by the president himself. In doing so, BLM activists have exemplified what prisoner justice activist Bryan Stevenson has characterized as "just mercy," the unmerited grace that a humane society confers to all of its citizens irrespective of color or caste, wealth or status, innocence or guilt.[35] Confronted by a Congress that stymied his legislative agenda after 2010's watershed Affordable Care Act, the president was forced to rely on executive orders, his rhetorical bully pulpit, and the ability to bring public and private monies together in hopes of fostering social change, which he attempted to do through the "My Brother's Keeper" initiative designed to help young black at-risk youth better achieve their educational and professional dreams.

In contrast, BLM argued that the roots of Ferguson, Baltimore, and the continued shootings of blacks by police reflected systems of racial and economic oppression that required the kind of radical change the nation had last addressed during the 1960s. Black Lives Matter rejected the political philosophy of neoliberalism, one that argues for market-based solutions to a host of social, political, and economic problems and seeks to privatize, monetize, and militarize publicly owned spaces including housing projects, prisons, schools, playgrounds, and parks.

As laid out in its striking policy agenda, "A Movement for Black Lives," BLM argued that criminalization of black neighborhoods, the arrest of black children, the catastrophic rates of AIDS/HIV in the nation's capital and other cities, racial achievement gaps, unemployment rates, and mass incarceration represent nothing short of "A War against Black People," one that requires a political revolution to not only end, but to permanently transform.[36]

So while Obama and BLM activists each claimed legacies of the civil rights movement as their own, they spoke entirely different languages. The former community-organizer-turned-president urged young BLM insurgents to dream big but go slow, advice that contradicts his audacious and successful presidential campaign as a forty-six-year-old (he turned forty-seven that summer) black junior senator in 2008. Obama, even as he lectured the nation throughout 2015 on the messy, violent, and tumultuous history of the civil rights movement, failed to acknowledge the way in which BLM had revealed the halting, at time illusory, nature of racial progress in America.

BLM activists at times failed to recognize the magnitude of the federal government's efforts to roll back policies and legislation that took decades to fully implement. Despite its limitations, the DOJ made real progress on issues related to criminal justice in sentencing, reforming the Bureau of Prisons, aiding juvenile offenders upon reentry, and easing obstacles that prevented ex-offenders from returning to their communities as productive citizens. Of course Donald Trump's presidential election and the confirmation of former Alabama senator Jeff Sessions as attorney general place much, if not all, of these reforms in grave jeopardy. The pro–law enforcement rhetoric of Trump and Sessions not only dismissed the concerns and critique offered by Black Lives Matter activists, but also defined them as political subversives hellbent on destroying civilized society.

Ultimately, while many African Americans and political progressives whose lives have not been touched by the criminal justice system, unwarranted police stops, fines, and arrests will applaud Barack Obama's record in racial justice advocacy, those who fall outside of these parameters will think very differently.[37] Obama's election, with its lofty inspiring rhetoric about hope and change, healing this nation, and repairing this world, represents an opportunity found and frustratingly lost for advocates of criminal justice reform. Martin Luther King famously remarked that "riots were the language of the unheard." It is one of history's supreme ironies, and exemplifies the deeply structural nature of inequality in America, that those unheard voices demanding justice grew exponentially louder, while in many ways remaining invisible, during the time of the nation's first black president.

10

A Decent-Sized Foundation

OBAMA'S URBAN POLICY

Thomas J. Sugrue

For a time in 2009, it looked as if urban policy would move to the center of the national agenda for the first time in decades, finally rescued from the not-so-benign neglect that cities had suffered from the White House since the 1970s. Not even a month after Barack Obama was inaugurated, he signed an executive order creating a cabinet-level Office of Urban Affairs to implement "a comprehensive approach to urban development." He described the office in visionary terms: Obama's new urban team would reflect his "belief that our cities need more than just a partner; they need a partner who knows that the old ways of looking at our cities just won't do." For many urban analysts, the Obama presidency was a moment of extraordinary promise.[1]

Obama, the first urban born and raised president in decades, came into office at a transitional moment for American cities. Many observers celebrated the fact that "cities were back," pointing to new corporate headquarters rising in many downtowns, the gentrification of long-declining neighborhoods, and the expansion of an urban "creative class," which converted industrial lofts into tech incubators and art studios, and gritty storefronts into hip coffeehouses and brewpubs. Nearly all of the nation's ten largest cities had gained population between 1990 and 2010 after four decades of steady decline. Perhaps the most striking indicator of urban health was the dramatic drop in crime rates, which peaked at the height of the crack epidemic in the late 1980s and, by 2010, had fallen to pre-1960s levels.[2]

The visibility of empty nesters and hipsters reclaiming downtowns, however, obscured deep patterns of inequality that profoundly shaped the geography of metropolitan America. For all of the hype about the uptick in big-city population, urban growth was small in scale compared to suburban and exurban sprawl. Most Americans commuted suburb-to-suburb, because the majority of jobs in metropolitan America were outside central cities. Rates of black–white segregation fell modestly between 1990 and 2010, but nearly all of the nation's major metros remained highly segregated by race. More than half of African Americans lived in what sociologist Douglas Massey identified as "hypersegregated" neighborhoods, where more than 75 percent of their neighbors were black. Urban Latinos faced lower levels of segregation, but rates rose in the largest immigrant-receiving metropolitan areas, most notably Los Angeles, and East Coast cities with large Afro-Caribbean populations.[3]

Two other parlous long-term trends affected big cities. The first was the concentration of African Americans and Latinos in struggling school districts, with concentrated poverty, high teacher turnover, and decrepit facilities. In the late 1960s and 1970s, public schools had slowly desegregated, but by the 1990s, they began to resegregate by race and grow more stratified by class.[4] The second was the dramatic increase in the population of urban minorities entangled in the criminal justice system, the result of the strict enforcement of antidrug laws, the prevalence of stop-and-frisk police action, and especially the dramatic expansion of the incarcerated population.[5]

Whatever gains cities had made were imperiled by the Great Recession and, by nearly every measure, urban inequalities worsened in the aftermath of the crash. Millions of homeowners, disproportionately African American and Latino urbanites, held subprime mortgages, unable to pay the ballooning adjustable rate mortgages that banks had peddled to eager homebuyers. In the year before Obama took office, lenders foreclosed on more than 3.5 million homes, devastating neighborhoods and leaving families to fend for themselves, with bad credit ratings, in expensive rental markets.[6]

Finally, urban areas bore the brunt of federal and state austerity measures. Since the 1970s, big cities had suffered a steady decline of federal expenditures, including cuts in federal aid to housing (beginning in the 1970s), in infrastructure funding (beginning in the 1980s), and welfare (beginning with the bipartisan welfare reform act of 1996). As the federal government devolved spending to the states through block grant programs, and left discretion on spending priorities to state agencies and state legislators, cities took big hits. Since the middle of the twentieth century, once powerful cities had lost their clout in Washington and in state capitals as suburban and rural districts gained population and representation. Big cities had long struggled with fiscal constraints, aging infrastructures, huge criminal justice expenditures, impoverished populations, and massive pension and debt obligations. To make ends meet, nearly every major city cut municipal workforces and trimmed public services to the bone, and relied increasingly on revenue-generation gimmicks like increased service fees, fines, and (in many cities), casino gambling. Some, including Stockton and Vallejo, California, and, most infamously, Detroit, declared bankruptcy in the aftermath of the 2008 financial crisis.[7]

Obama's Urban Vision

Who better to address the challenges of American cities than a president who had spent his formative years in Jakarta and Honolulu, attended college in Los Angeles and New York, and lived nearly his entire adult life in Chicago? Who better to shift attention to cities than the man who spent three years as community organizer on Chicago's South Side, working with displaced steel workers and mobilizing the residents of a rundown public housing project to demand better living conditions? Who better to bring urban issues to the White House than a president who had launched his political career as a state senator representing a big-city district that included the University of Chicago and a large swath of surrounding, mostly African American poor and working-class neighborhoods, and after the 2000 redistricting, much of Chicago's wealthy Gold Coast? Who better to grapple with the challenges of urban inequality than a policy intellectual who counted among his influences the prominent urban sociologist William Julius Wilson, and who drew his policy prescriptions from the Brookings Institution's highly regarded Metropolitan Policy Program?[8]

No place influenced Obama more than Chicago, a city that embodied, in high relief, the tensions and contradictions of contemporary American urbanism. Chicago was a case study in urban deindustrialization and intense racial segregation. The nation's third largest metropolitan area, it had sprawled galactically nearly sixty miles to the north, west, and south. It was also a city that underwent substantial gentrification in the 1990s, as wealthy whites colonized formerly white working-class and lower-middle-class neighborhoods on the city's North Side. And in the fifteen years before Obama ran for the presidency, Chicago was a hotbed of experimentation for downtown redevelopment, affordable housing policy, and education reform, all overseen by liberal policymakers who embraced market-based solutions to urban problems over costly public investments.[9]

Many of Obama's closest advisors came out of the rough-and-tumble world of Chicago politics. David Axelrod launched his political career as an operative for Mayor Harold Washington and then as a chief of staff for Mayor Richard M. Daley, whose father had presided over Chicago's infamous political machine. During his twenty-two years as mayor, the younger Daley recast himself as the city's "CEO," built close alliances with Chicago's business elite, and worked to rebuild the city as a global economic center. Drawing from the market-based solutions that had migrated from Republican circles via the centrist Democratic Leadership Council, various think tanks, and the Clinton administration into the heart of liberal policymaking, Daley worked to create a business- and tourist-friendly urban environment. He also launched influential experiments in the expansion of public–private partnerships to beautify city neighborhoods and redevelop blighted commercial districts. And most consequentially, he reorganized Chicago's Housing Authority and Chicago public schools around the principles of privatization, competition, and innovation.[10]

Arne Duncan, Obama's first secretary of education, was Daley's appointee to run Chicago's public schools from 2001 to 2009. Valerie Jarrett, one of Obama's closest advisors, had been Daley's chief of staff. Obama's own first chief of staff, the abrasive Rahm Emanuel, had led Daley's fundraising efforts during his 1992 campaign and, with Daley's support, was elected to Congress, representing part of Chicago's North Side. Daley's brother William, a lawyer and investment banker who had served in the Clinton administration, replaced Emanuel as Obama's chief of staff. Even the First Lady, Michelle Obama, who grew up on Chicago's South Side, the daughter of a city employee, had spent two years early in her career working as a planner in the Daley administration. Chicago imprinted nearly every aspect of Obama's urban policy.[11]

During the long presidential campaign of 2007–2008, Obama mostly distanced himself from his Chicago roots for good reason. For all of the celebration of Chicago's reinvention, the Windy City could not escape its tawdry political past. When Obama's campaign assembled an urban advisory team early in 2008, it included academics, urban policy analysts, community organizers, and staffers at urban nonprofits and foundations, who mostly communicated through an unwieldy listserv, occasionally providing advice but mostly staging local events and helping with voter mobilization efforts. On the stump, Obama seldom discussed urban policy, saving the issue for just a handful of rallies with substantial African American audiences, a meeting of the U.S. Conference of Mayors, and a brief mention at the Democratic National Convention.[12]

Obama's reluctance to discuss urban issues was carefully calculated. A crucial part of his electoral strategy was fashioning a "postracial" identity that signaled to white voters that he was not beholden to black constituents (in popular discourse, the terms "urban" and "black" were often used interchangeably). Obama learned on the campaign trail that his mere mention of race could generate days or even weeks of controversy and headlines. He downplayed what many voters saw as distinctively "urban" issues like poverty and racial segregation. And his campaign team was careful to be sure that when he mentioned cities, he also highlighted programs that targeted entire metropolitan areas or even regions.[13]

What Obama offered was a hodge-podge of programs that appealed to the Democratic Party's base, including increased federal funding for urban infrastructure, public education, community policing, and job training.[14] But he also nodded toward market-based solutions to urban problems. Taking a leaf from Arne Duncan's school reform initiatives in Chicago, he pledged his support for charter schools and used education reform buzzwords like "innovation," "standards and accountability," and "competition." Inspired by urban reinvestment experiments in Chicago and other cities, he supported programs that provided incentives for corporations to locate their operations in central cities, including tax abatements and low-interest loans. Drawing from the work of Brookings Institution scholars, he supported "smart growth" strategies like investment and tax breaks for regional economic development. Urban policy advocates to sixties-era poverty warriors to liberal hedge fund managers could all project their images of a future urban America onto the candidate.[15]

In the White House

For all of his reluctance to discuss urban issues on the campaign trail, Obama sent out a strong signal that urban issues were near the top of his administration's priorities when he announced the creation of the new White House Office of Urban Affairs on February 19, 2009. Obama's announcement bore a striking resemblance to a long-forgotten urban initiative launched with great fanfare three decades earlier. In 1977, President Jimmy Carter created a high-level Urban Policy Research Group to advise him. Both presidents promised "comprehensive urban reform" and inter-agency cooperation. But Obama's office differed from Carter's group in one key dimension: his urban policy advisors did not consist of an ad hoc com-bination of domestic policy staffers and executive branch undersecretaries. Instead, Obama's appointees reported directly to him.[16]

Putting together a new executive branch office proved to be challeng-ing. Attracting and retaining first-rate, experienced leadership was difficult because the office lacked the power and perquisites of a cabinet-level posi-tion. Many urban policy advocates were surprised by Obama's appoint-ment of Bronx Borough President Adolfo Carrión as head and by his successor, Derek Douglas, a former aide to New York governor David Pa-terson. Both lasted about a year in their posts. Neither of them had sub-stantial urban policy expertise nor were they political heavyweights. The third head, Xavier de Souza Briggs, a city planner on the faculty at MIT, was a highly regarded scholar, but he lacked political connections and policymaking experience. Under them was a revolving group of young aides, few of whom brought extensive on-the-ground experience or stellar academic credentials to the job, like their counterparts in more prestigious offices like the Council of Economic Advisors or the Office of Management and Budget.[17]

Early on, the Office of Urban Affairs sponsored an "urban tour" to meet with local elected officials, planners, and policymakers and a "national con-versation" on cities and metropolitan areas. Most ambitiously, it created Urban Policy Working Groups to evaluate existing programs and eventually make recommendations to cabinet-level agencies on how to revitalize neighborhoods and spur regional growth. It also published an occasional newsletter on urban initiatives.[18]

The Office of Urban Affairs met with skepticism across the board. Con-servatives charged that it was an example of government overreach. "Cities improved dramatically in periods when the federal government backed off the most," argued Fred Siegel, a historian and former aide to New York mayor Rudolph Giuliani. Critics on the left were skeptical that the new agency had enough resources to make a difference. Brad Ladner, a special-ist in community economic development, worried that "it's not clear that the office, as established, has the tools or resources to make a lot of head-way."[19] By 2011, the Office of Urban Affairs was so invisible that the White House switchboard operator often could not find its phone extension.

When political scientists Theda Skocpol and Lawrence Jacobs gathered ten scholars to offer the first scholarly assessment of Obama's domestic policies, they left urban affairs out altogether.[20] Although the office remained in place through Obama's second term, seasoned observers dismissed the OUA as a lost opportunity. "The Office of Urban Affairs is [an] example of a grand idea that was implemented in a half-hearted way, and then lost its momentum over time," New York University sociologist Patrick Sharkey contended. The president, however, bore only some of the responsibility. Urban affairs had little congressional support: the Republican Party had long abandoned cities and, after its victory in the 2010 midterm elections thwarted the administration's entire domestic agenda. Even congressional Democrats, especially from suburban districts, concerned about taxpayer backlash, were reluctant to support programs that did not obviously benefit their constituents.[21]

Obama may well have intended his creation of the Office of Urban Affairs to be a symbolic gesture. During his first two years in office, the action was elsewhere. When the House and Senate were under Democratic Party control, the president directed his domestic policy toward addressing the Great Recession and winning passage of sweeping health insurance reform. Both the 2009 American Reinvestment and Recovery Act (ARRA, also known as the stimulus package) and the 2010 Affordable Care Act were, in effect, massive urban investment initiatives.

ARRA spending reached nearly every sector of the economy, and included substantial funds to rural areas, as part of a vain attempt to win the support of small-town Republicans. But many of its expenditures benefited cities. The emphasis on "shovel-ready" projects favored big municipalities that had public works departments, a large backlog of infrastructural needs, and the equipment and personnel in place to move quickly. For example, $27.5 billion went to port and rail infrastructure improvements, most in cities; another $20 billion went to improving airports, largely under municipal control; and $1.5 billion supplemented surface transportation improvement projects in both metropolitan and exurban areas. The stimulus also spent $97.5 million on public education at a moment when states were axing school spending and local tax revenues had plummeted, leading to massive layoffs, especially in big-city school districts. Based on grantee reports, the administration estimated that ARRA had saved or created between 275,000 and 300,000 education jobs between September 2009 and September 2010.[22]

Even seemingly minor stimulus expenditures sent federal dollars cascading into the coffers of financially strapped central cities. For example, ARRA funded energy-efficient streetlights and stoplights, a program that benefited small towns and suburbs, but had the greatest impact in cities dense with streetlights and highly trafficked intersections. ARRA funds also went to programs that subsidized the weatherproofing of low-income residents' homes, which likewise benefited cities, especially in the Northeast and Midwest, with older housing stock, neighborhoods with concentrated poverty, and municipal agencies and nonprofits that could easily identify needy homeowners and manage the program. White House advisor Van Jones argued that weatherization would "green the ghetto," while training urban workers for new environmentally friendly jobs retrofitting older homes.[23]

One urban economic sector was particularly well poised to benefit from Obama's domestic programs: health care. By the time Obama entered office, health care employed more than eighteen million people nationwide. More people worked in health care than in manufacturing. Hospitals comprised the fifth largest labor market in the country. And most of those jobs were urban, many clustered in or near minority-dominated neighborhoods. As industry decentralized and manufacturing moved to low-wage markets at home and overseas, hospitals had for the most part stayed rooted in cities. While commerce moved from downtowns to suburban malls and corporate offices fled to suburban office parks and corporate campuses, medical centers were sticky. As a result, the healthcare sector was at the top or near the top of the list of largest employers in nearly every major city, and the top employment sector for African Americans as well. Hospitals, in particular, provided a wide range of jobs, employing orderlies and janitors, nurses and neurosurgeons. And a growing number of healthcare jobs did not directly involve patient care. Major medical centers relied on an army of workers to enter data, ensure compliance with federal regulations, administer insurance policies, manage complex budgets, and procure supplies. In big cities that had hemorrhaged jobs, hospitals stanched the flow. Obama's stimulus program provided $155 billion for health care, including an $86 billion expansion of Medicaid, $25 billion to upgrade medical information technology systems, and $2 billion to bolster federal community health centers (a struggling, underfunded survivor of the Great Society), most of which were located in African American and Latino neighborhoods in central cities.[24]

Even more consequential for the healthcare sector was the Affordable Care Act. ACA substantially reduced the number of uninsured patients and it provided a predictable income stream for medical centers, including charitable hospitals and big-city research hospitals, which carried the burden of serving large numbers of uninsured patients. The impact on hospital employment was indirect but substantial: the healthcare sector grew at a faster rate than the economy. Obamacare was a de facto job creation program.[25]

The ARRA and ACA bolstered urban economies, at least temporarily. But the administration's efforts to deal with another dimension of the Great Recession—the collapse of the home finance market—were notably less successful. Between the late 1990s and 2008, banks, hedge funds, and insurance companies had profited immensely from the deregulation of financial markets and, in particular, the dramatic overextension of home credit through predatory lending and subprime financing. The home lending crisis affected a wide swath of American communities, but it hit hardest in cities and older suburbs, particularly those with large nonwhite populations. In 2006, more than half of subprime loans nationwide went to African Americans, who comprised only 13 percent of the population. And a recent study of data from the Home Mortgage Disclosure Act found that 32.1 percent of blacks, but only 10.5 percent of whites, got higher interest mortgages—that is, mortgages with an annual percentage rate three or more points higher than the rate of a Treasury security of the same length.[26]

The federal government—under both President George W. Bush and President Obama—oversaw the Troubled Assets Relief Program (TARP), which provided hundreds of billions to bail out failing financial institutions. Many Democrats argued that if the government salvaged banks, it should also provide aid to the victims of predatory lending. On the campaign trail, Obama promised to allow homeowners to modify their mortgages to prevent foreclosures and, in January 2009, the incoming administration pledged to set aside up to $100 billion in funds to help underwater households reduce their mortgage payments. In February 2009, the administration launched the Making Home Affordable Program (MHA), which oversaw the Home Affordable Modification Program (HAMP). President Obama pledged that HAMP would bail out at-risk homeowners, just as the White House had bailed out insolvent banks. But he oversold the program. HAMP provided incentives to banks and mortgage servicers to work with at-risk borrowers to modify mortgages by reducing interest rates and making other changes in the terms of their mortgages. But the application and qualification process was complicated and burdensome. Lenders retained control over the loan modification process and often arbitrarily turned down applicants. Government regulators provided little oversight over the program. Although the president promised that the program would protect as many as four million households from foreclosure, fewer than one million eventually benefited from HAMP.[27]

Between the onset of the Great Recession and the end of Obama's presidency, nearly nine million American households had suffered foreclosures, with devastating consequences. In many large cities and overbuilt suburbs, neighborhoods were pockmarked with abandoned houses. The foreclosure crisis fell particularly hard on people of color. The Obama years saw a dramatic decline in household wealth (which for most Americans consisted primarily of equity in real estate), particularly among African American and Latino homeowners who were more likely to have been the victims of both predatory lending and foreclosures. By 2011, the household wealth of blacks and Latinos reached a record low of only one-twentieth that of white Americans. The gap barely narrowed by 2013, the last year for which data are available.[28]

Thinking Big

In the two years when stimulus dollars were flowing to cities, Obama embarked on a mission to streamline urban planning initiatives through interagency cooperation. Getting federal agencies to collaborate has been the holy grail of good government reformers since the New Deal. Cabinet members often view their agencies as fiefdoms and have great discretion to set their own priorities. Pulling their staffs together to work even on small projects was usually a logistical nightmare. Because urban policy did not fall under the purview of any single executive branch agency, federal officials often worked at cross-purposes or created duplicative programs. In July 2009, Obama stated that "I've directed the Office of Management and Budget, the Domestic Policy Council, the National Economic Council, and the Office of Urban Affairs to conduct the first comprehensive interagency review in 30 years of how the Federal Government approaches and funds urban and metropolitan areas so that we can start having a concentrated, focused, strategic approach to Federal efforts to revitalize our metropolitan areas." Among journalists covering the event, Obama's statement surely drew a yawn: it went unmentioned in news accounts. But because Obama had appointed arguably the most competent cabinet in decades, achieving interagency cooperation was one of his noteworthy successes. For the next few years, the Department of Housing and Urban Development, the Department of Transportation, the Department of Education, and the Department of Labor collaborated to an unprecedented extent.[29]

Interagency cooperation was especially important because the Obama administration hoped to address economic development, job creation, and affordable housing at the regional level, rather than simply focusing on communities or neighborhoods. Since the 1950s, city planners had fairly consistently called for metropolitan-wide interventions to mitigate unemployment, improve infrastructure, and repair failing schools. And they just as consistently came up against huge obstacles. Most American metropolitan areas were hopelessly balkanized into dozens—sometimes hundreds—of municipalities and school districts that usually reinforced deep city–suburban political, economic, and racial divides. Suburbanites looked at the cities they left behind with a mix of horror and romance, unwilling to pay for public works, schools, or social services for "those people" whom they blamed for urban decline. Many urban politicians, especially African Americans and Latinos, feared that regional cooperation was a thinly disguised attempt to wrest away their hard-won political power. But while advocates of regionalism struggled to gain political traction, metropolitan areas were remade by economic shifts that respected no municipal boundaries. To deal with urban sprawl and environmental degradation required collaboration across city and county lines. To deal with the gap between where low-wage workers lived (mostly central cities) and where low-wage jobs were expanding (mostly suburbs and exurbs) required the expansion of affordable housing on the periphery and the improvement of surface transportation.[30]

By the time Obama was elected, a chorus of urban planners pushed the agenda of regional cooperation with urgency. Former Albuquerque, New Mexico, mayor David Rusk argued that the healthiest metropolitan areas were those with regional governance. University of Minnesota law professor Myron Orfield conducted studies of metropolitan areas throughout the country, arguing that municipal fragmentation was costly, that racial and socioeconomic segregation jeopardized urban labor markets, and that older cities and their nearby suburbs had many common political interests. Most influentially, a group of scholars at the Brookings Institution, led by former Clinton administration official Bruce Katz, promoted a new metropolitan policy, and produced influential books and reports documenting urban competitiveness, labor markets, business location, shifting demographic patterns, and housing needs. Their data pointed directly toward coordinated regional solutions. They made the forceful argument that urban problems were metropolitan problems, and vice versa.[31]

Obama listened. In his most detailed campaign speech on urban issues, Obama criticized "an outdated 'urban' agenda that focuses exclusively on the problems in our cities, and ignores our growing metro areas; an agenda that confuses anti-poverty policy with a metropolitan strategy, and ends up hurting both." He acknowledged the need to address urban poverty, but argued for "investing in the clusters of growth and innovation" in different metropolitan regions around the United States.[32]

By his first year in office, he grafted that policy onto a call for sustainable growth. "For too long," stated Obama, "Federal policy has actually encouraged sprawl and congestion and pollution, rather than quality public transportation and smart, sustainable development. And we've been keeping communities isolated when we should have been bringing them together." To that end, Obama hoped to build on a pilot Clinton administration program called Moving to Opportunity (MTO), which provided vouchers to public-housing-eligible urban residents to live outside of declining "inner city neighborhoods," where they would find better jobs and better schools.[33]

Obama pulled together Ray LaHood, his secretary of transportation and one of the few Republicans in his cabinet; Shaun Donovan, the secretary of Housing and Urban Development; and Lisa Jackson, the head of the Environmental Protection Agency to create an interagency group on sustainable cities to "make sure that when it comes to development—housing, transportation, energy efficiency—these things aren't mutually exclusive, they go hand in hand. And that means making sure that affordable housing exists in close proximity to jobs and transportation. That means encouraging shorter travel times and lower travel costs. It means safer, greener, more livable communities." HUD had a stake in bridging the gap between workers and job; Transportation had an interest in getting people to and from their workplaces; the EPA hoped to reduce carbon emissions. Obama hoped to provide incentives for transit-oriented development, namely dense townhouse and apartment projects and retail districts adjoining transit hubs.[34]

The stimulus package had included rail and highway transportation programs, but the funds needed to be spent down quickly to jolt the economy toward recovery. The ARRA specified that the stimulus funds be fully used by 2011. The time frame simply did not allow cabinet agencies to fully coordinate their investment strategies. Obama's vision of metropolitan planning had a somewhat longer horizon. But his ambitious plans were unfulfilled, put on the backburner when the administration channeled its energy toward health care, and then decisively crushed because of the obstructionist tactics of congressional Republicans who swept Congress in the Tea Party wave of 2010. Obama's hopes for urban light rail and high-speed intercity transit fell to austerity budgets; his plans for green and sustainable cities and suburbs found no Republican support. By 2012, Republicans had turned Obama's urban policy ideas against him. Conservative author Stanley Kurtz argued the president hoped to "force Americans out of their cars and into high-density urban centers, squeezing the population into a collection of new Manhattans. Obama also aims to force suburbanites to redistribute tax money to nearby cities while effectively merging urban and suburban school districts to equalize their funding." It was a nightmare scenario for suburban and exurban Republicans that echoed through the right-wing news media and on conservative websites through the 2012 election season.[35]

Thinking Small

With a major regional agenda in tatters, Obama turned to small-scale interventions. In fundamental respects, he revisited and reinvigorated community-oriented urban development strategies that dated back to the Nixon administration. Post–Great Society federal urban programs had several distinct features that reflected a turn away from "big government" and toward the market. They were small in scale; they devolved policy decisions to states and municipalities. They privileged public–private partnerships over direct federal spending. They deployed probusiness incentives, including tax cuts and deregulation to encourage urban investment. They demanded the reorganization of public-sector institutions so that they resembled private businesses. And they valued competition, individual initiative, and discipline. For all of Obama's rhetoric about change, his urban programs did not fundamentally deviate from these principles.

Obama, like all presidents, built on precedents, his options shaped and constrained by his predecessors' legacies. In particular, Obama offered an updated version of Enterprise Zones, an idea first hatched by British conservatives in the 1970s, imported to American think tanks in the 1980s, and baked into federal urban policy during the George H. W. Bush administration. EZs were carved out of rundown, usually old industrial sections of cities, and offered special incentives, loans, tax breaks, and laxer regulations to firms that located there. In the 1990s, the Clinton administration re-branded the program as Empowerment Zones, adding a nominal commu-nity participation requirement, but otherwise changing little. Some states, like Pennsylvania, offered their own version of EZs, creating tax-free zones as honey pots to lure corporate headquarters to declining downtowns; and some municipalities offered lucrative tax abatements to attract investors to rehabilitate older homes or build new ones in central city neighborhoods. What all of these programs shared in common was the use of government to spur market activity where it might not otherwise happen. The record of EZs and related programs was mixed at best: many zones attracted few em-ployers, and state and local tax abatement programs drained municipal tax coffers and transferred wealth to developers, corporations, and well-to-do homeowners, with few public benefits.[36]

Since his days as a community organizer, Obama had been attracted to community-based economic development initiatives and supported the principle of public–private partnerships and federal incentives behind the Enterprise and Empowerment Zones. But, befitting his emphasis on "com-prehensive" urban programs, Obama grafted antipoverty initiatives, hous-ing, social services, and education onto the EZ model. He took as his inspi-ration the Harlem Children's Zone, a program launched in New York in the 1990s by education reformer Geoffrey Canada. The Harlem Children's Zone combined education, social services, preschool and academic enrichment programs for students, and childrearing training programs for poor parents-to-be. Obama described it as "an all-encompassing, all-hands-on-deck ef-fort that's turning around the lives of New York City's children, block by block." Whatever its positive benefits (and those were intensely debated), the Harlem Children's Zone was small in scale, expensive to administer, and shaped by the vision of a single, charismatic leader.[37]

Whether Canada's experiment could be replicated on a nationwide scale was a doubtful proposition. It depended on hundreds of millions of dollars in support from hedge fund managers, investment banks, and private foun-dations in New York that only funded a program that covered a few dozen blocks in one city. No other city in the United States had New York's depth of wealthy donors. To replicate the program elsewhere would require mas-sive federal investment. But convinced that the model would work, Obama launched "Promise Neighborhoods," modeled on the Harlem Children's Zone, in the summer of 2009. The program would "make grants available for communities in other cities to jump-start their own neighborhood-level interventions that change the odds for our kids."[38] Promise Neighborhood grants (what he called a "community innovation fund") would provide seed money to nonprofits, but not sustained federal investment in disadvantaged communities. To assuage his critics—and attract private donors—Obama justified the program in market-friendly terms: its goal "was giving people the tools they need to pull themselves up." In method, rhetoric, and goals, Promise Neighborhoods were a far cry from the major interventions that the federal government had made in urban redevelopment and public education during the Great Society.[39]

Closely related to Promise Neighborhoods, but with a substantially larger financial commitment, was the Department of Education's support for the expansion of privately run, publically funded charter schools. Charter school experiments proliferated beginning in the 1990s, the result of a bipartisan push to bring "market discipline" to public education, by letting nonprofits, individual entrepreneurs, and educational corporations manage public schools. In most cities, like Chicago, where Obama's Secretary of Education Arne Duncan had run the public school system, charters were loosely regulated. Premised on the ideals of competition (parents were consumers with the right to choose the "best" school for their children), charters often skimmed higher-achieving students from neighborhood schools. Most charters did not provide special education services. Through strict disciplinary procedures, they regularly forced out troubled students. And charter school CEOs had authority to override teachers' collective bargaining agreements and food service and maintenance union work rules. In effect, many charters were de facto private schools that drained enrollment and funds away from neighborhood schools.[40]

Adolfo Carrión, the first head of the Office of Urban Affairs, singled out one project as exemplary of the administration's place-based programs: the construction of a new charter school on 129th Street in Harlem. The project required coordination across cabinet-level agencies and relied on elaborate public–private partnerships. The U.S. Department of Education provided $60 million. The remainder came from big investors. The investment bank Goldman Sachs, looking to burnish its image after the Great Recession, donated $20 million. Google added another $6 million. The school's general contractor donated $5 million of in-kind support. The Department of Housing and Urban Development oversaw the remapping of a city street through one of its housing projects there. It was a complicated venture, its small scope a reminder of the limits to the administration's efforts to reshape American cities.[41]

Like the Harlem Children's Zone, charter schools were a distinctive creature of the post–*Brown v. Board of Education* era. Rhetorically, Obama supported the principle of *Brown* that racially separate education could not be equal. But in practice, *Brown* was mostly a dead letter. In the aftermath of court decisions—from *Milliken v. Bradley* (1974) that rendered most metropolitan-wide school desegregation plans impermissible to *Parents Involved* (2007) that struck down even voluntary efforts to create racially balanced schools—most education policy took entrenched racial segregation as a given. The rationale behind charters was that if most minority and low-income children were to be concentrated in underperforming schools in troubled school districts, perhaps new forms of school administration or new curricula or loosened teacher hiring and firing procedures would solve the problem.[42]

Obama linked schooling, housing, and employment in his next place-based initiative, "Choice Neighborhoods," launched in 2011. Choice Neighborhoods built on HOPE VI, a federally funded program, which expanded rapidly in the Clinton years, to replace postwar urban public housing projects with mixed-income, low-rise developments usually with detached or semi-detached houses designed to resemble their suburban counterparts, often with porches overlooking fenced yards and driveways. Obama watched as neighborhoods near his own state senate district were transformed as the gloomy modernist towers fell. Chicago's mayor Richard M. Daley aggressively deployed HOPE VI funds to demolish and redevelop the city's infamous Cabrini-Green, Robert Taylor, and State Street Homes. HOPE VI was riddled with problems: it did not come close to meeting the demand for new, decent, affordable housing and it displaced many public housing residents, while enriching politically connected developers and community development organizations. In some neighborhoods, like the gentrifying North Side neighborhood around Cabrini-Green, the destruction of the projects fueled a massive boom in new luxury housing, adding to the city's affordable housing crunch.[43]

Obama mended but did not end HOPE VI. Choice Neighborhoods would provide grants to link residents of new, federally underwritten HOPE VI-type developments to anchor institutions, including universities, medical centers, convention centers, and downtown districts. Many HOPE VI communities—like the public housing projects they replaced—were geographically isolated, cut off from good public transit, and distant from jobs. Choice Neighborhoods provided relatively small grants to cities and civic groups, with hopes of leveraging additional funds from businesses, nonprofits, and foundations to connect impoverished residents with jobs.

Obama launched yet another place-based program, Promise Zones, in January 2014. A hybrid of Clinton's Empowerment Zones and the Promise Neighborhoods experiments, Promise Zones brought the federal government together in partnership with municipal economic development agencies, local nonprofits, and philanthropists to improve schools and incubate small businesses through grants and tax incentives, and to improve the delivery of municipal services. Using the language of small government and personal responsibility, Obama pledged that the federal government would support poor areas, "not with a handout but as partners with them every step of the way."[44]

Of the twenty-two Promise Zones, fourteen were located in impoverished urban areas (the remainder were rural communities and Indian reservations). Promise Zone grants were small, and so were the program's achievements. The administration used its website to highlight its modest successes: the opening of a community grocery store that employed forty workers in Sacramento, California; $2.1 million in federal funding to launch a recycling program that would hire ex-convicts in East Indianapolis; and $14.2 million from the U.S. Department of Education to seventeen schools in Los Angeles to prepare students for college by helping them develop "non-cognitive skills ... such as confidence and resiliency." On Atlanta's West Side, federal grants would support the construction of a new football stadium, with hopes that it would "catalyze commercial activity."[45]

Obama came into office with a mandate for change. His drew deep support from urban voters who hoped that his presidency would reverse the drift of federal policy from "benign neglect," through devolution, to market-based solutions. But the scope and scale of his urban programs was minuscule compared to the magnitude of social, economic, and educational problems that metropolitan America faced. Obama attempted to rebuild, expanding or retooling existing programs, and streamlining the federal agencies responsible for coordinating transportation, labor, housing, and education policy.

Obama bears some of the blame for the weakness of his urban policy. He was a product of the bipartisan neoliberalism of the 1990s and 2000s, too enamored of market-based solutions and public–private partnerships to fight for a more vigorous public sector. He was too cautious when it came to pushing pro-integration policies, particularly in public education and housing, fearful of firing up racial animosities and alienating white suburban and exurban voters. But, even more so, Obama was a captive of a climate of fiscal austerity and, after 2010, of bitter congressional hostility to any significant domestic policy initiatives. Perhaps, when it came to responding to persistent urban inequality and joblessness, Choice Neighborhoods and Promise Zones were the best the Obama administration could do.

Under Obama's watch, government took third fiddle to private capital and philanthropy when it came to setting an urban agenda. In cities, the federal government had become, in effect, a decent-sized foundation, providing grants to support urban demonstration projects, offering a flicker of hope at least until the grants dried up and the local philanthropic and business "partners" moved on. In the meantime, American metropolitan areas remain, with a few exceptions, deeply divided socioeconomically and still fragmented by race, still struggling with troubled schools. In Obama's last two years in office, American cities began to burn again, as protesters and the police clashed and as big cities like Baltimore, Milwaukee, and Ferguson, Missouri, exploded. Even the president's adopted hometown, Chicago, was rocked by tense protests, against the police, but also against charters and school closings, a process that began under Arne Duncan; against evictions and gentrification; and against a downtown-oriented mayor who left his office in the West Wing to move into Chicago's city hall just months later. American urban policy has only feebly responded to the ongoing crises.

11

"Tough and Smart"

THE RESILIENCE OF THE WAR ON DRUGS DURING THE OBAMA ADMINISTRATION

Matthew D. Lassiter

In July 2015, President Barack Obama toured the El Reno Federal Correctional Institution in Oklahoma and met with a multiracial group of six inmates, all serving lengthy sentences for drug offenses committed in their youth. The encounter, filmed for an HBO documentary called *Fixing the System*, represented the first time a current U.S. president had visited a federal prison. Obama identified the differing punishment for nonviolent drug cases as the primary evidence of racial bias against African Americans and Latinos in the criminal justice system, from arrest rates to prosecutorial discretion to sentencing outcomes. After exiting the cell block, the president told the assembled media that "a primary driver of this mass incarceration phenomenon is our drug laws—our mandatory minimum sentencing around drug laws. And we have to consider whether this is the smartest way for us to both control crime and rehabilitate individuals." Obama emphasized the $80 billion annual cost to taxpayers of maintaining the world's largest prison system and noted the bipartisan opening for criminal justice reform in Washington and in many state capitals. He then specifically distinguished "dangerous individuals who need to be incapacitated" from nonviolent drug criminals, "particularly young people of color," who should be diverted into treatment programs and provided with education and job training. Obama, who acknowledged marijuana and cocaine use in his 1995 memoir *Dreams from My Father*, sought to humanize the prisoners he had just met as "young people who made mistakes that aren't that different than the mistakes I made," except that their communities lacked the safety net of institutional resources and second chances. But the nation's first African American president also reiterated his tough-on-crime philosophy, because "there are people who need to be in prison, and I don't have tolerance for violent criminals. Many of them may have made mistakes, but we need to keep our communities safe."[1]

The Obama administration's "tough and smart" approach to drug and crime control largely operated within the political boundaries of bipartisan consensus and pursued a moderate reform agenda during an era of unprecedented activism against racially discriminatory policing and heightened consciousness about the broader system of mass incarceration. Many factors shaped Obama's cautious and incremental approach to drug policy reform, including the White House belief that an explicit "black agenda" promoted by an African American president would generate white backlash, the considerable power of "law and order" forces in the federal bureaucracy and in Congress, and not least the robust support for criminal prohibition and interdiction by most Democratic officials and the president himself.[2] Obama first deployed the "tough and smart" formulation during a 2007 campaign appearance at Howard University, where he rejected the "false choice between being tough on crime and vigilant in our pursuit of justice." The Democratic candidate endorsed the logic of criminalization—"if you're convicted of a crime involving drugs, of course you should be punished"—while emphasizing that even many Republicans agreed that nonviolent offenders should be diverted into treatment.[3] The 2008 Democratic Party platform likewise advanced a "smart on crime" blueprint that promised to be "tough on violent crime," prioritize treatment over incarceration for drug abusers, and maintain the longstanding federal interdiction campaigns against Mexican and Colombian traffickers.[4] In its first *National Drug Control Strategy* (2010), the Obama administration promised to move in a "new direction" through a "balanced public health and public safety strategy" that combined the traditional commitment to law enforcement and border interdiction with more funding for prevention and rehabilitation programs. The administration pledged to promote "alternatives to incarceration" for nonviolent drug offenders while disrupting trafficking networks and deploying law enforcement to "rid our streets of the drug dealers who infect our communities."[5]

President Obama's commitment to balanced policies of drug control, combining "smart" public health solutions for deserving victims with "tough" law enforcement crackdowns on predatory criminals, was nothing new and indeed closely resembles the rhetoric and blueprints of every presidential administration since Richard Nixon proclaimed a federal war on "drug abuse" in the early 1970s. Nixon also championed a "balanced approach" of public health rehabilitation for addict-victims and tough punishment for traffickers, and he signed comprehensive drug legislation that offset discretionary possession penalties (as leverage to coerce users into treatment) with lengthy mandatory sentences for "professional" suppliers. The major federal drug and crime control laws enacted during the Nixon era passed Congress with near unanimity, a pattern of bipartisan policymaking that continued with the Anti-Drug Abuse Act of 1986 and the Violent Crime Control and Law Enforcement Act of 1994, signed by Republican Ronald Reagan and Democrat Bill Clinton, respectively.[6] During his presidency, Barack Obama frequently criticized the "bipartisan cause to get tough on crime" during the 1980s and 1990s, especially the mandatory-minimum sentencing laws that exacerbated racial inequality and mass incarceration, but carving "smart on crime" exceptions for some nonviolent drug offenses did not disrupt the broader patterns of either drug prohibition or the carceral state.[7] While Obama and other key administration officials repudiated the martial discourse of a "war on drugs," they consistently opposed the transformative alternatives of legalization or decriminalization, even of marijuana, simultaneously labeling drug abuse and addiction a "disease" and advocating criminalization to compel offenders into treatment.[8] Despite some important reforms, the resilience of the federal war on drugs during the Obama administration reflects the bipartisan consensus that the criminal justice system should ultimately regulate the illicit drug market and the parallel refusal to acknowledge that prohibition itself creates the context for violence and crime, whether by traffickers or law enforcement, both domestically and internationally.

The Reform Debate: Balance versus Legalization

Barack Obama entered the White House after a quarter century of exponential growth in the American prison system resulting primarily from "get tough" political choices rather than rising crime rates, in particular the bipartisan policy commitment to increased mandatory-minimum sentences and harsher policing and prosecution tactics in the intertwined wars on crime and drugs. The Obama administration also encountered a more fluid political climate than at any point since the 1970s, with many state governments experimenting with diversion programs for nonviolent offenders, and civil rights and civil liberties organizations popularizing the concepts of "mass incarceration" and the "New Jim Crow."[9] The incarcerated population in the United States exceeded 2.3 million at the end of 2008, more than quadruple the total in the early 1980s. Federal and state correctional institutions held more than 1.6 million prisoners, with the remainder in local jails and 5 million more people on probation or parole. In the federal and state prison systems combined, 93 percent of inmates were male and the racial breakdown totaled 38 percent African American (triple the population rate), 20 percent Hispanic (1.2 times the population rate), and 34 percent white (half the population rate). One out of every one hundred American adults resided in a prison or jail during 2008, including one out of nine African American males between the ages of twenty and thirty-four. Half of all inmates in state prisons were serving time for violent crimes (including robbery), alongside about one-fifth each for property and drug convictions. In the federal system, conversely, slightly more than half of the 201,280 prisoners were serving sentences for drug felonies, a product of the increasing federalization of the war on drugs during and after the crack epidemic of the 1980s and a jurisdictional as well as political explanation for the Obama administration's primary reform focus on nonviolent drug criminals.[10]

From the start, the Obama White House portrayed its balanced philosophy of public health and public safety as a new departure in federal drug and crime control, with the second half of the "tough and smart" equation designed to neutralize the epithet of "soft" as a descriptor of medicalization and rehabilitation. President Obama named Gil Kerlikowske, the chief of the Seattle Police Department, as director of the Office of National Drug Control Policy, responsible for coordinating international interdiction and domestic enforcement, prevention, and treatment programs throughout the executive branch. Kerlikowske, the fifth consecutive "drug czar" from a law enforcement or military background (since 1991), did strike a different tone, declaring that the "metaphor and philosophy of a 'War on Drugs' is flawed" in a major 2009 speech to the International Association of Chiefs of Police. Because "addiction is a disease" rather than a "moral failing," the new drug czar explained, the administration's strategy would utilize public health resources on the demand side ("jail is not a solution") while continuing to deploy law enforcement aggressively to stop the production and distribution of illegal drugs. Kerlikowske then denounced advocates of legalization, asserting that this disastrous policy would not reduce crime and violence in American communities or save children from the tragedy of drug abuse.[11] In essence, the White House strategy sought to marginalize the growing legalization movement by portraying its own balanced approach as a public health corrective to prior administrations that prosecuted the war on drugs "as an all-or-nothing choice between demand reduction and supply reduction," a greatly exaggerated if not completely false interpretation of recent U.S. history. According to Kerlikowske, the Obama administration believed in "using the criminal justice system to spur people in need of treatment to get it," a benevolent phrase that justified the continued criminalization of the "disease" of addiction and the illicit recreational market more broadly.[12]

The administration's antilegalization stance faced its first major challenge in the area of marijuana policy, which pitted state-level reform movements against hardline drug warriors in the Drug Enforcement Administration (DEA) and the Department of Justice (DOJ). During the 2008 campaign, Barack Obama criticized the Bush administration for crackdowns on dispensaries in the thirteen states that had legalized medical marijuana, often by popular referendum. Soon after the election, the DEA launched another series of high-profile raids, but new attorney general Eric Holder then pledged that the Obama administration would only target growers and dispensaries that violated both state and federal law by using "medical marijuana laws as a shield." In October 2009, under pressure from the marijuana reform lobby, the Justice Department issued a directive to federal prosecutors that investigations should not prioritize activities "in clear and unambiguous compliance" with state medical marijuana laws. The DOJ memo reiterated, however, that marijuana remained a "core priority" of the federal war on drugs because of its dangers for consumers and status as the largest source of revenue for Mexican cartels.[13] The DEA, a bureaucracy with considerable autonomy, then released its own political manifesto condemning the medical marijuana movement as a smokescreen for legalization and labeling most dispensaries "fronts for drug dealers, not health facilities." The DEA also defended the continued classification of marijuana under Schedule 1 of the Controlled Substances Act, as a drug with "a high potential for abuse" and "no accepted medicinal value," and recycled the hype that pot-smoking teenagers risked serious health hazards and were likely to graduate to cocaine, heroin, or methamphetamine addiction.[14] During Obama's first term, DEA agents and federal prosecutors actually escalated raids and investigations of state-licensed growers and dispensaries, angering progressive and libertarian groups that criticized the "chasm between rhetoric and reality" in the administration's drug policies and labeled the president worse than George W. Bush on the medical marijuana issue.[15]

The Obama administration's opposition to marijuana legalization ultimately placed federal policy in conflict with a considerable anticriminalization shift in public opinion as well as reform initiatives approved in a majority of American states. In a series of pronouncements, drug czar Gil Kerlikowske blamed the marijuana legalization movement for increased rates of adolescent drug use and justified criminal enforcement (including 858,408 marijuana arrests nationwide in 2009) as part of the balanced collaboration between law enforcement and public health, the "surest route to reducing drug use and its consequences."[16] The administration's first *National Drug Control Strategy* (2010) confirmed that marijuana interdiction remained at the center of the federal war on drugs and strongly rejected legalization as a mistake that would encourage youthful experimentation—without mentioning that a system of alcohol-style regulation would undercut the international cartels and underground traffickers the blueprint promised to "eradicate."[17] The breakthrough for the marijuana reform movement came in 2012, when voters in Colorado and Washington approved referenda legalizing recreational possession and licensing the cultivation and sale of the drug. The DEA promptly announced its intention to "vigorously enforce" the federal prohibition against recreational marijuana providers, "even if such activities are permitted under state law."[18] But national opinion surveys revealed that a clear majority of Americans (58 percent in 2013) supported legalization, and twenty-five states had also established medical marijuana systems by the end of Obama's presidency.[19] Given these political realities, the Justice Department issued a new directive in mid-2013 that enumerated a policy of federal noninterference as long as states effectively regulated their legalized recreational or medical marijuana markets, while making clear the administration's commitment to enforce national law to prevent involvement by criminal enterprises and any distribution to minors.[20]

During Obama's second term, the stark racial disparities in marijuana enforcement increasingly moved to the center of the national debate because of the advocacy of human rights organizations and the growing protest movement against "stop-and-frisk" tactics and "broken windows" policing. The antimarijuana crusade, according to a 2013 report by the American

Civil Liberties Union, effectively operated as "a war on people of color," with African Americans 3.73 times more likely than whites to be apprehended despite nearly identical usage rates, and marijuana violations accounting for more than half of drug arrests nationwide during the previous decade. The ACLU blamed targeted policing in nonwhite neighborhoods, criticized federal law enforcement programs that incentivized local and state arrests of low-level offenders, and advocated legalization as the only solution to these systematic racial disparities.[21] That same year, a class action lawsuit against the City of New York succeeded in demonstrating unconstitutional racial profiling of young African American and Latino males, including massive discrepancies in marijuana arrest rates, as a deliberate "result of the NYPD's stop and frisk practices."[22] And in 2014, after the Michael Brown shooting in Ferguson, Missouri, the Black Lives Matter movement escalated its demands for the end of racial profiling, stop-and-frisk sweeps, and the "criminalization and over-policing of communities of color."[23] The pressure from below clearly influenced Barack Obama, who began publicly observing that "middle-class kids don't get locked up for smoking pot, and poor kids do," particularly nonwhite youth. But the president continued to reject marijuana legalization, despite conceding that smoking pot was probably "less dangerous" than drinking alcohol, based on a "where do you draw the line" argument about cocaine, methamphetamine, and heroin.[24]

Human rights organizations responded by moving beyond the popular marijuana reform stance to challenge the bipartisan federal support for a criminal justice approach to drug markets on public health, civil libertarian, and racial justice grounds. In a 2014 "Nation Behind Bars" report, Human Rights Watch labeled criminalization of adult recreational use of any drug to be a violation of the fundamental right to privacy and "counterproductive to the purpose of furthering public health." Combining a philosophical manifesto for comprehensive legalization with stark data on racial discrimination in drug enforcement, Human Rights Watch argued that absent direct harm to others, "government should not restrict the liberty and autonomy of individuals simply because some or even many members of the public find their choices offensive or immoral."[25] In 2016, the ACLU and Human Rights Watch jointly issued another exposé of the "human costs of criminalizing personal drug use" in the United States, including findings that racial disparities pervaded the drug prohibition regime at all levels and that law enforcement made more arrests for marijuana possession alone in 2015 than for all violent crimes combined.[26] The DEA forcefully counterattacked the legalization movement for promoting a dangerous policy that would "condemn tens of thousands of our fellow citizens to a life of dependency and horror and endanger the lives of countless innocent others."[27] And in 2016, the Department of Justice once again rejected a petition to remove marijuana from Schedule 1, citing established scientific knowledge about its hazards and lack of medical utility. After the November election, Barack Obama did imply that as a private citizen, he would speak out for the regulation of marijuana through a public health system, similar to the laws controlling alcohol and tobacco, but until the end the official policy of the Obama White House continued to "steadfastly oppose legalization of marijuana and other drugs."[28]

Race and Mandatory-Minimum Sentencing

During Obama's first term, the administration sought to reduce racial discrimination in the criminal justice system primarily by focusing on "equitable drug sentencing" rather than curbing police enforcement, addressing prosecutorial discretion, or reconsidering mandatory-minimum penalties for violent offenses.[29] The main achievement involved the Fair Sentencing Act, introduced in 2009 by a group of Senate Democrats to implement the repeated recommendations of the U.S. Sentencing Commission to eliminate the 100-to-1 disparity between crack and powder cocaine penalties established by the Anti-Drug Abuse Act of 1986, the bipartisan legislation that escalated the Reagan era war on drugs. The cocaine differential—a minimum five-year prison sentence for trafficking 500 grams of powder or 5 grams of crack—generated almost no controversy at the time but eventually came to epitomize racial inequality in federal drug enforcement. Critics such as the ACLU and the Sentencing Project publicized findings that the disparity lacked any pharmacological basis and "unjustly and disproportionately penalize(s) African American defendants," who accounted for 80 percent of those sentenced under the mandatory-minimum crack laws. Both groups also emphasized that although the Anti-Drug Abuse Act explicitly targeted "major" traffickers, police enforcement and federal prosecutions had mainly resulted in the incarceration of low-level street dealers and couriers. Senator Richard Durbin (D-Illinois), the lead sponsor of the Fair Sentencing Act, portrayed the "smart and fair" elimination of racial injustice as a necessary component of a "tough" policy that would "redirect federal resources toward large-scale, violent traffickers and increase penalties for the worst drug offenders." The Obama administration endorsed the bill to achieve "equity in penalties for cocaine-related crimes while retaining the tools needed by law enforcement to protect our communities from the violence associated with drug trafficking."[30]

In 2010, the U.S. Congress unanimously approved the Fair Sentencing Act, and President Obama signed the legislation with a bipartisan group of congressional leaders standing by his desk in the Oval Office. The White House's celebration of the new consensus for federal drug reform overshadowed the watering down of the final version, which rather than abolish only reduced the powder/crack disparity from a 100-to-1 to an 18-to-1 ratio, a compromise demanded by Republicans on the Senate Judiciary Committee. The Fair Sentencing Act did eliminate the five-year mandatory-minimum penalty for simple possession of 5 grams or more of crack cocaine, which Congress had added in 1988. The Sentencing Project warned that the 18-to-1 disparity would continue to institutionalize racial discrimination in the criminal justice system but also underscored that sentencing reform only began to address the issue, because targeted police enforcement and prosecutorial discretion meant that African Americans served almost as lengthy prison terms for drug convictions (58.7 months) as white defendants did for violent crimes (61.7 months). In addition to its limited scope, the Fair Sentencing Act of 2010 did not apply retroactively, meaning that about 15,000 federal prisoners continued to serve mandatory-minimum terms under a statutory mandate now widely acknowledged to be racially unjust.[31] In 2013, in an equal-protection case brought by two such black inmates, a federal appellate panel ruled that Congress's refusal to apply the Fair Sentencing Act retroactively represented unconstitutional racial discrimination, an indictment with radical potential. Placing "law and order" over collective justice, the Obama administration successfully appealed this decision, arguing that Supreme Court precedent only barred legislative action based on deliberate racial animus, not just racially disparate impact, even if foreseeable.[32]

During Obama's second term, the administration launched a more comprehensive initiative to reduce the impact of mandatory-minimum sentencing laws, again focused primarily on nonviolent drug offenders. The 2012 Democratic Party platform pledged to address the "disproportionate effects of crime, violence, and incarceration on communities of color," a much more visible acknowledgment of racial inequality in the criminal justice system than in the 2008 version.[33] The Obama administration recognized that criminal justice reform, especially if focused on nonviolent offenses and offset by tough policies toward violent crime, aligned with shifts in public opinion and would receive support from "people on the right," in the words of Attorney General Eric Holder. In a 2012 national survey, the Pew Charitable Trusts reported that a large majority believed that too many Americans were in prison; notably, policies promoting alternatives to incarceration for nonviolent offenders secured the approval of 91 percent of Democrats and 77 percent of Republicans.[34] In August 2013, Holder delivered one of the most consequential speeches of the Obama era to the American Bar Association, labeling the criminal justice system "in too many respects broken. . . . Too many Americans go to too many prisons for far too long and for no truly good law enforcement reason." The attorney general did not identify racially selective policing as the cause and instead decried the "harsher punishments" for African American and Latino males who broke the drug laws but should be diverted into treatment or community service. In Holder's vision, the federal government would become "both smarter and tougher on crime," reducing racial disparities in criminal justice while keeping "violent criminals off our streets" and "reserving the most severe penalties for serious, high-level, or violent drug traffickers."[35]

Following Holder's speech, the Department of Justice released a "Smart on Crime" blueprint that critically assessed the "nation's system of mass imprisonment" and acknowledged the "demographic disparities that have provoked questions about the fundamental fairness of the criminal justice system." In discursive terms, the DOJ's acceptance of the indictment of "mass incarceration" represented a major breakthrough for the progressive movement for criminal justice reform, even as its artfully worded acknowledgment of the perception of racial discrimination did not place blame on any ongoing actions by police, prosecutors, judges, or policymakers—just the "unfair sentencing disparities" locked in by antiquated mandatory-minimum laws. The DOJ's "Smart on Crime" program endorsed state-level reform efforts that had reduced incarceration and recidivism levels through the diversion of nonviolent drug offenders, singling out Texas and Arkansas as cost-effective models for national policy.[36] This strategy deliberately appealed to the conservative politicians and intellectuals in the Right on Crime coalition, a recently launched initiative that criticized excessive big-government spending on criminal justice programs, particularly the over-reliance on prison for nonviolent offenders.[37] As an initial bureaucratic measure, Holder issued a memo instructing U.S. prosecutors not to bring full charges under available mandatory-minimum statutes for nonviolent drug offenders who did not deal to minors, work in a criminal organization, or have multiple prior offenses.[38] As the next political step, the attorney general endorsed the Smarter Sentencing Act, a bipartisan Senate bill sponsored by Richard Durbin (D-Illinois) and Mike Lee (R-Utah) that would restore more judicial discretion in mandatory-minimum drug cases and apply the 2010 crack penalty revision retroactively.[39]

Between 2013 and 2016, the Obama administration pursued a two-part strategy of promoting mandatory-minimum sentencing reform in Congress and launching a clemency initiative for federal inmates serving lengthy prison terms for crack cocaine offenses punished "under an unfair system." President Obama announced the clemency program by criticizing the non-retroactivity of the Fair Sentencing Act of 2010 and calling on Congress to restore the "promise of equal treatment for all" by enacting the Smarter Sentencing Act.[40] In 2015, the Republican-controlled Senate Judiciary Committee approved a compromise version that retained the retroactive crack provision, exempted a narrow class of nonviolent drug felons from mandatory-minimum penalties, slightly lowered the required minimums for second and third convictions, and increased sentences for drug offenders with violent records. Families Against Mandatory Minimums, an influential lobby, criticized the revised package for continuing to subject low-level drug offenders and especially racial minorities to "harsh, expensive, one-size-fits-all sentences" and failing "to match the overwhelming support for reform that can be found across the political spectrum."[41] In the end, the polarized politics of the 2016 presidential election doomed even the diluted sentencing bill, leaving Eric Holder (after stepping down) to say that he was "ashamed of this nation" since Congress would not "simply do the right thing."[42] As a limited substitute, the DOJ's clemency program solicited applications from federal drug prisoners who were "not hardened criminals," had no record of violent crime or links to trafficking organizations, and had served at least ten years under outdated mandatory-minimum laws.[43] Criminal justice reformers criticized the restrictive selection criteria and urged categorical clemency for entire classes of drug offenders, similar to the 1970s amnesty for Vietnam draft resisters. Instead, President Obama ultimately commuted the sentences of almost 1,700 nonviolent drug offenders, an unprecedented number but also only 10 percent of total applicants.[44]

The Obama administration played a key role in repositioning nonwhite drug offenders as sympathetic victims of excessive criminal sanctions, a status generally reserved for "otherwise law-abiding" white youth in American political culture, but the "tough and smart" reform binary of violent versus nonviolent criminals constrained its critique of mass incarceration.[45] In 2015, President Obama delivered a major speech on criminal justice reform to the NAACP's annual conference, just a few days before visiting the Oklahoma prison, in a political climate transformed by the Black Lives Matter movement against police violence and racial overcriminalization. Obama started by indicting a criminal justice system "skewed by race and by wealth" but also told the audience that he would "be honest. There are a lot of folks who belong in prison.... Murderers, predators, rapists, gang leaders, drug kingpins.... Our communities are safer, thanks to brave police officers and hardworking prosecutors who put those violent criminals in jail." Then the president, inaccurately, singled out the "real reason our prison population is so high"—inflexible sentencing laws that sent nonviolent drug offenders away for far too long, where the "punishment simply does not fit the crime." In an expansion of the administration's critique, Obama also highlighted differential treatment based on race by police and prosecutors, citing research showing that "people of color are more likely to be stopped, frisked, questioned, charged, detained . . . [and] sentenced to more time for the same crime." As remedies for racially inequitable mass incarceration, Obama advocated social welfare investments rather than simply policing disadvantaged neighborhoods as "danger zones," reforming the school-to-prison pipeline of the juvenile justice system, improving carceral conditions to promote rehabilitation rather than recidivism, and "banning the box" to increase employment opportunities for released inmates. For the first time, he also called for legislative action to "get rid of" mandatory-minimum sentences for nonviolent drug crimes "entirely."[46]

The White House's reform emphasis on nonviolent drug offenders closely tracked the "New Jim Crow" critique of the war on drugs popularized by legal scholar Michelle Alexander, but other advocacy groups and criminologists argued that this agenda remained too narrow to reverse mass incarceration in significant and lasting ways.[47] In 2015, the Department of Justice announced that the combined federal and state prison population had declined for the first time in at least four decades, by 15,400 prisoners during the previous calendar year, or 1 percent of the total. The steady, decades-long reduction in the national rates of violent and property crime accounted for much of this decrease, combined with the modest effects of sentencing reforms and drug offender diversion programs. The data also revealed that in state prisons, which contained the vast majority of inmates, racial disproportionality in incarceration rates for violent crimes exceeded those for drug offenses for African Americans and Hispanics alike.[48] In a 2015 analysis, the Urban Institute found that sentencing reforms for nonviolent drug offenders "have helped stem the tide of prison growth, but they will not be sufficient to further cut the prison population dramatically," an outcome that would require policy decisions to reduce the severity of punishment for property and violent crimes as well.[49] The Department of Justice did accelerate its investigations of racially biased policing practices in the aftermath of Ferguson, but President Obama also continued to walk the line of "tough and smart" criminal justice reform. In a late 2015 speech to the International Association of Chiefs of Police, Obama highlighted racial disparities in arrests and sentencing policies but made clear that "I don't have sympathy for dangerous, violent offenders. . . . This is not some bleeding heart attitude here. . . . Those who peddle drugs need to be punished. I don't think decriminalization is some panacea."[50]

Interdiction and Drug Markets

In the areas of foreign policy and border interdiction, the Obama administration's commitment to the traditional supply-side suppression policies of the war on drugs differed little from its predecessors', as did the federal government's continuing inability to eradicate or even meaningfully impede an illicit global market that serves the demands of millions of American consumers. The bipartisan consensus around drug interdiction is most evident in international policy, where the bureaucratic autonomy of the State Department and the Drug Enforcement Administration is extensive. In the 2010 *National Drug Control Strategy*, the Obama administration pledged to disrupt the transnational drug cartels, primarily based in Mexico and Colombia, which "move large quantities of cocaine, heroin, methamphetamine, marijuana, and other illicit drugs into the United States." The main initiatives, as for the previous half-century of federal interdiction policy, included concentrated resources on the Southwest border, collaboration with "international partners . . . to protect the public health and safety of our citizens," crop eradication and promotion of "alternative livelihoods" for coca and opium farmers in supplier nations, and joint counternarcotics missions in source and transit countries from Latin America to the Middle East. The *National Security Strategy* labeled Plan Colombia, the U.S. military intervention and coca eradication program launched by the Clinton administration in 2000, a "dramatic success"—a stark contrast to Amnesty International's verdict that the initiative had escalated violence and human rights abuses, merged counternarcotics with American corporate imperialism and support for right-wing paramilitary organizations, and represented a "failure in every respect." The Obama administration also praised and doubled the funding for the Bush administration's Merida Initiative, a bilateral counternarcotics partnership with the government of Mexico that received $1.5 billion between 2007 and 2015.[51]

In 2009, the White House unveiled a comprehensive, multiagency strategy to "support the Mexican government's campaign against the violent cartels" and prevent the "spillover" of instability and bloodshed from the border cities of Tijuana and Juarez. The Obama administration also announced its commitment to halt not only the "flow of drugs and violence into the United States" but also the "illegal flows of weapons and bulk cash to Mexico."[52] The next month, in an unusual (and diplomatically essential) admission of American responsibility, Secretary of State Hillary Clinton traveled to Mexico City to acknowledge that "our insatiable demand for illegal drugs fuels the drug trade" and that guns smuggled from the U.S. facilitated much of the violence in northern Mexico. President Obama, in a joint appearance with President Felipe Calderón of Mexico, also conceded that American consumer demand and weapons were "helping to keep these cartels in business." But the immediate solution, according to both Clinton and Obama, required enhanced border security and increased military assistance to help the Mexican government succeed in "destroying and disrupting the cartels."[53] Escalation of the Merida Initiative produced extraordinary violence in northern Mexico, including an estimated 50,000 to 100,000 deaths between 2006 and 2015, with many civilians caught in the crossfire. Drug war opponents argued that the U.S. policies of prohibition and interdiction were themselves the fundamental causes of violence by generating an immensely profitable underground market policed by the military and law enforcement rather than an alternative system of legal regulations on production, distribution, and consumption.[54] Even the mainstream Council on Foreign Relations concluded in 2011 that the long war on drugs in Mexico had completely failed to curb either supply or demand in the illicit market, and the time had come for U.S. policymakers to recognize that "prohibition bestows enormous profits on traffickers" and interdiction had only "intensified" the violent competition among transnational cartels.[55]

As in domestic drug war politics, the U.S. government faced increasing pressure from international advocates of legalization and decriminalization during the Obama era, including unprecedented resistance from political leaders in Central and South America. Drug czar Gil Kerlikowske labeled the growing opposition to U.S.-financed interdiction from within these "strategic partner" nations to be a "profound mistake," while the DEA responded with an antilegalization manifesto insisting that drug prohibition reduces rather than "contributes to violence along the Southwest border."[56] Then in 2011, President Juan Manuel Santos of Colombia jolted the U.S.-led international drug control regime when he called for new "market alternatives" that would "take away the violent profit that comes with drug trafficking. . . . If that means legalizing, and the world thinks that's the solution, I will welcome it."[57] That same year, the Global Commission on Drug Policy concluded bluntly that "the war on drugs has not, and cannot, be won" and called for harm reduction policies to replace interdiction, including legal regulation of marijuana and licensing experiments with other prohibited drugs "to undermine the power of organized crime."[58] At the 2012 Summit for the Americas, held in Colombia, President Obama responded that "legalization is not the answer" and pledged that his administration would continue to pursue the balanced policies of demand-side reduction and supply-side interdiction, "for the sake of the health and safety of our citizens."[59] But pressure for a fundamental reorientation of international drug control policy continued to build throughout Obama's second term, culminating in a 2016 declaration, signed by more than one thousand world leaders, that the global war on drugs "has proven disastrous for global health, security and human rights. . . . It created a vast illicit market that enriched criminal organizations, corrupted governments, triggered explosive violence, distorted economic markets, and undermined basic moral values."[60]

During Obama's second term, the federal drug control system also faced a pronounced challenge from the deadly intersection of the legal market for prescription medication produced by the pharmaceutical industry and the illegal market of heroin and methamphetamine imported by Mexican cartels or manufactured by domestic sources. The division between legal and illegal drugs is a political one, not directly related to the pharmacological properties or the public health hazards of regulated or prohibited substances, whether public policy facilitates lucrative and licit markets for corporations that produce pharmaceuticals, alcohol, and tobacco or involuntarily creates profitable if illicit markets for international and domestic traffickers. In assessing the Obama administration's embrace of its "predecessors' militaristic counternarcotics policies in the Americas," foreign policy expert Suzanna Reiss argues that the international drug control regime has long rested on the "power of the United States to designate players in the drug trade as either legal or illegal," and that pharmaceutical companies in particular have extracted raw materials from developing nations designated as illegal suppliers and then recirculated these drugs as prescription medications for international and domestic consumers.[61] Between 1999 and

2014, the sale of pharmaceutical pain relievers quadrupled in the United States, leading to more than 165,000 overdose deaths during these years, a significant increase in heroin use by Americans who started out in the prescription market, and the declaration of an "unprecedented opioid epidemic" by federal public health agencies.[62] In 2007, Purdue Pharma pleaded guilty to felony charges and paid a $600 million fine, a small fraction of profits, for deliberately "misbranding" and marketing OxyContin as a safe painkiller with low potential for addiction and abuse.[63] The Obama administration's 2010 *National Drug Control Strategy* did include prescription drug abuse as a major federal priority but targeted "rogue" pain clinics and heroin smuggled by Mexican cartels rather than the "legitimate benefits" provided by pharmaceutical corporations.[64]

The overwhelming whiteness of the "opioid epidemic," and especially the media and political focus on the confluence of prescription drug abuse and new heroin markets in the Middle American heartland, increased the bipartisan push for medicalization rather than incarceration of the users caught up in the nation's latest drug crisis. A 2015 exposé in the *New York Times* portrayed a ruthless network of Mexican heroin traffickers who were exploiting the prescription painkiller epidemic in rural and suburban areas to provide illegal narcotics to a new group of "victims—mostly white, well-off and often young."[65] That same year, President Obama traveled to West Virginia, a mostly white state with the nation's highest overdose rate, for a highly publicized community forum on the rising tide of addiction to prescription painkillers and heroin. With universalistic language that echoed every president since Nixon, Obama portrayed a drug abuse epidemic that "doesn't discriminate. It touches everybody—from celebrities to college students, to soccer moms, to inner city kids. White, black, Hispanic, young, old, rich, poor, urban, suburban. . . . There is no 'us' and 'them.'" Obama's "tough and smart" resolution, however, only reinforced the administration's drug war binary between supply-side predators and demand-side victims. The president redoubled his call for treatment rather than "long prison sentences for nonviolent drug offenders" but reassured the crowd that the federal government would "go after the hardened criminals who are bringing drugs like heroin into our country," specifying Mexican cartels without mentioning the complicity of pharmaceutical corporations.[66] The U.S. Congress responded with the Comprehensive Addiction and Recovery Act of 2016, a bipartisan measure that passed overwhelmingly and provided additional funding for drug treatment and diversion programs. President Obama signed the legislation but criticized its only "modest steps to address the opioid epidemic" and called for a much greater federal commitment to public health solutions and treatment for drug abuse and addiction.[67]

The policies of criminalization and interdiction at the center of federal drug control are deeply embedded in American political culture and state-building processes. The Obama administration's "tough and smart" approach maintained the traditional merger of law enforcement and public health while seeking to shift the balance from incarceration toward medicalization and coercive rehabilitation, but only for deserving victims and low-level nonviolent offenders. During the second term, President Obama and Attorney General Holder more vocally embraced the cause of criminal justice reform and increasingly addressed racial disparities in drug war enforcement, an unprecedented although only partial alignment of top federal officials with the agenda of civil liberties, human rights, and grassroots racial justice organizations. The Obama administration continued to reject the policies of legalization or even decriminalization, promoting reforms of discriminatory policing and excessive sentencing rather than confronting the racial inequalities and imperialist violence inherent in drug war interdiction at home and abroad. After the November 2016 election, which unexpectedly returned a "law and order" Republican administration to power, Obama pledged to keep fighting for racial justice and expressed frustration with progressive critics and activists who did not acknowledge "the constraints of our political system and the constraints on this office."[68] Yet in the end, the Obama administration's policy preferences shaped its drug control agenda as much as the political calculations, bureaucratic obstacles, and legislative opposition encountered by the nation's first African American president. Obama's invitation to David Simon, the creator of *The Wire*, to visit the White House in 2015 captured the dissonance between the reform and antiprohibition positions most clearly. Simon, who had recently denounced the administration's continued "prosecution of our misguided, destructive, and dehumanizing" war on drugs, disparaged the arrest-first philosophy of criminalization. President Obama responded by lamenting racial disproportionality in incarceration rates, urging "smarter" treatment of nonviolent offenders arrested on drug charges, and championing the "tough" law enforcement mission of fighting trafficking and violent crime.[69]

12

A Promise Unfulfilled, an Imperfect Legacy

OBAMA AND IMMIGRATION POLICY

Sarah R. Coleman

When President Obama entered office, the content, scope, and partisan nature of immigration policy debates had been re-formed in the face of a profound demographic shift in the United States over the previous forty years largely due to immigration. As a result of these changes to the debates, the Obama administration's efforts at comprehensive immigration reform, a signature 2008 campaign issue, were blocked. Obama's legacy on the issue is marked by the contrasting policies of trying to bring unauthorized immigrants out of the shadows through executive action while at the same time removing unprecedented numbers of unauthorized immigrants. Policy toward refugees in the wake of the Arab Spring and subsequent upheaval in the Middle East was also heavily contested. The Obama administration contended with the need for security versus a commitment to addressing a humanitarian crisis. In both immigration and refugee policy development, President Obama's expansive vision of inclusion was frustrated by partisan political opposition.

Fulfilling the Promise

With the passage of the Hart-Celler Act in 1965, the United States entered a new era of immigration, both in terms of scale and in demographic profile. Migration from Latin America, Asia, and the Caribbean grew while European migration fell; by 1975 approximately 75 percent of immigrants to the United States were from the developing world. Immigration was also of a much larger scale than seen in previous decades, and by 1981, annual documented admissions were already double those of 1965. By 2000, new immigrants and their offspring accounted for half the total growth in the U.S. population during the previous decade.[1] Immigration, as a political issue, became more prominent over the period. As the boundaries of the physical nation-state seemed, in the eyes of many, to become infinitely more porous, social policies, such as access to health care, that impacted immigrants became central to the politics of immigration policy in a profound way. During the Obama administration net migration with Mexico actually fell in the wake of the Great Recession, with estimates showing a net loss of 140,000 from 2009 to 2014, but these figures were all but forgotten as the rising demographic trends of the previous decade and growing restrictionist sentiment continued to dominate the headlines and shape the political debate.[2]

The politics of immigration policy were also being remade. Immigration policy had long been an issue that divided the parties internally and policy changes were made by compromises among strange bedfellows.[3] When Obama came into office, immigration was moving from an issue that traditionally drew bipartisan alliances to an increasingly partisan issue.[4] Changes within both parties recast these debates with enormous consequences for Obama's immigration policy.

In earlier eras of mass immigration, organized labor had formed strong Democratic opposition to increased immigration, but over the previous two decades the growing influence of unions representing service workers led organized labor to support immigration reform with a path to legalization. In 2000, the AFL-CIO officially reversed its earlier opposition to liberalizing immigration policy, representing one of the most significant reversals of policy on the Democratic side.[5] By 2006, only one Democratic senator opposed a comprehensive immigration bill on grounds that it would be negative for labor.[6] Increasingly Democrats saw the service workers unions and growing Latino electorate as a key source of electoral support. For these groups, the liberalization of immigration policy was a key issue.

Within the GOP, there was a growing radicalization on immigration policy. The party had long been split between pro-immigration voices from business and agricultural industries and nativist conservative voices. While restrictionist sentiment began to gain footing in the Republican Party in the 1970s, during the Reagan administration pro-immigration forces had controlled the passage of the 1986 Immigration Reform and Control Act (IRCA), which included an expansive legalization and agricultural worker program. In the 1990s with the rise of social conservatism and the passage of anti-immigrant initiatives such as Proposition 187 in California, leaders supporting immigration restriction gained prominence within the party. President George W. Bush drew pro-immigration policies back to the forefront of the Republican Party but he was time and again opposed in his efforts by the growing restrictionist elements of his own party, which charged that immigrants were a threat to the nation by taking jobs from native-born Americans as well as draining the welfare and healthcare systems. These changes within both the Democratic and Republican parties created a new environment within which the Obama administration would attempt to shape dramatic reform.

With the ground beneath his feet having undergone a dramatic shift over the previous decades, President Obama came into office promising to rise above partisan posturing and Washington gridlock to address pressing policy needs. These imperatives included passing comprehensive immigration reform. The last comprehensive immigration reform legislation that had become law, IRCA, was a "grand bargain"–style law, which coupled restrictive employer sanctions that sought to stem the flow of immigration with a seasonal agricultural worker program that provided cheap labor for agricultural interests, and a large legalization program for unauthorized immigrants living in the country since 1982. The restrictionist elements of the bill had been ineffective at stemming the flow of immigration into the country, while the legalization elements had given citizenship status to approximately three million immigrants, fostering a cynicism among immigration restriction activists about "grand bargain"–style bills.

The two previous administrations had attempted to address an immigration system considered "broken" by many, tailoring their approaches in very different manners. President Bill Clinton did not propose any significant reform, instead responding to Republican-led initiatives in Congress and signing piecemeal legislation that boosted enforcement. President George W. Bush embraced a different, more proactive approach, making comprehensive reform a central part of his domestic agenda, and pushing "grand bargain"–style efforts in 2006 and 2007 that combined enforcement measures and a legalization measure. These proposals were met with stiff opposition from restrictionist members in Congress due to the failure of the earlier 1986 IRCA to stem immigration flows. Obama's approach was similar to Bush's. He proactively sought a liberalizing "grand bargain," and he would also run into congressional opposition that was even greater than Bush had faced, due to growing conservatism within the Republican Party with the rise of the Tea Party.

Beginning while he was on the campaign trail, Obama had signaled his commitment to tackling immigration, saying in 2008, "I think it's time for a President who won't walk away from something as important as comprehensive reform when it becomes politically unpopular. And that's the commitment I'm making to you."[7] He went even further and promised to make it a "top priority" in the first year of his administration. Obama's opponent that year, Arizona senator John McCain, had previously worked with Senator Ted Kennedy in an effort to pass comprehensive immigration reform that included a pathway to citizenship for unauthorized immigrants, but in his attempt to win the Republican primary, and reflecting the broader GOP turn toward conservatism on the issue, McCain embraced a tougher stance on immigration that focused on enforcement. Obama's immigration policy was a key part of his efforts to woo Latino voters. While George W. Bush had earned a record 44 percent of the Latino vote in 2004, many of those voters shifted in 2008 to the Democratic candidate; Obama won 68 percent of the Latino vote. Importantly, exit polls showed that Hispanic voters provided crucial margins in the battleground states of Colorado, New Mexico, and Nevada.[8]

Once in office, though, other political concerns began to weigh heavily on the new president. The bruising fight over health care, ongoing debates over financial regulatory reform, and the administration's energy policy proposal left the White House with little political capital left for a protracted battle over immigration reform. Despite the fact that Obama had promised to address it in his first year in office, in the summer of 2009, he demurred, saying, "Now, I've got a lot on my plate, and it's very important for us to sequence these big initiatives in a way where they don't all just crash at the same time."[9] While not the focus of the immediate comprehensive legislation, the issue of immigration still permeated the political debate through the president's first year in office. For example, the Affordable Care Act (ACA) specifically made unauthorized immigrants ineligible to buy marketplace health coverage, or for premium tax credits and other savings on marketplace plans. The contentiousness of the immigration issue was highlighted when Congressman Joe Wilson famously heckled the president about the ACA's provisions relating to unauthorized immigrants at a 2009 joint session of Congress, with Wilson shouting, "You lie!"

Although the administration delayed pushing a comprehensive immigration reform package, it engaged in a significantly expanded enforcement effort that drew sharp criticism from pro-immigration activists. In embracing this hardline approach on immigration enforcement, the White House hoped to gain credibility with skeptical conservatives and thereby lay the groundwork for a broad legalization push later. In order to carry out this ramped-up enforcement effort, the Obama administration turned to deportation tools initially established under President Clinton and enhanced under the second Bush administration. President Obama's efforts at deportation fit neatly into a two-decade trend toward greater enforcement.

In the early 1990s, with hundreds of thousands of unauthorized immigrants entering the country and rising anti-immigrant sentiment, and following the passage of the anti-immigrant Proposition 187 ballot initiative in California and the 1993 World Trade Center bombing, Washington began to consider harsher enforcement measures to assuage public concerns with unregulated immigration.[10] Seizing on the anxiety of these events, the new GOP majority elected in 1994 moved to work on legislation aimed at restricting immigration.

After watching the passage of Proposition 187, and fearing that a soft policy could cost President Bill Clinton votes in California and reelection more broadly, the White House looked to toughen its approach on immigration policy, and so worked with the new Republican majority to fashion immigration responses based on enforcement. The resulting bills passed by Congress and signed into law, the Illegal Immigration Reform and Immigrant Responsibility Act of 1996 (IIRIRA) and the Anti-Terrorism and Effective Death Penalty Act, were heavily focused on the restriction of unauthorized immigration. Among their toughest provisions were those making it easier to deport immigrants by radically expanding the crimes that made an immigrant eligible for deportation and by creating expedited deportation procedures that allowed for removal of certain noncitizens without a hearing before an immigration judge. These provisions were made even more aggressive in the wake of 9/11 as part of the USA Patriot Act. As a result of these changes to deportation law, while before 1996 internal enforcement activities had not played a very significant role in immigration enforcement, afterward, as sociologists Douglas Massey and Karen Pren have shown, internal enforcement rose "to levels not seen since the deportation campaigns of the Great Depression."[11]

Using the mechanisms established by the Clinton administration and embraced and expanded by the Bush administration, the Obama administration undertook a large-scale deportation effort. Current estimates suggest that between 2009 and 2015, the Obama administration removed more than 2.5 million people through immigration orders, a figure that does not include the number of people who "self-deported" or were "returned" or turned away to their home country at the border by U.S. Customs and Border Protection.[12]

The increasingly forceful way in which the Obama administration undertook these enforcement efforts needs to be understood in context. In the first term of the Bush administration, the majority of immigrants the United States sent home were "returned," meaning that they were sent, often by bus, back across the border with no fingerprints taken or a permanent mark on their immigration records. Toward the end of the Bush administration, the Department of Homeland Security (DHS) shifted policies to limit the number of "returns" and instead embrace a policy of formal "removals," a process that creates a permanent record, exposing those caught returning again illegally to prison time and prohibiting them from applying for legal status in the United States for at least five years.[13] The Obama administration embraced this more potent process of "removals." Whereas in the final year of the Bush administration more than a quarter of those caught in the United States with no criminal record were returned to their native countries without charges, by 2013 under the Obama administration formal "removal" charges were filed in more than 90 percent of those types of cases.[14] Obama's actions drew the ire of liberal immigration activists, and the head of the National Council of La Raza, the nation's largest Latino advocacy organization, publicly called President Obama "the deporter-in-chief."[15] In response, those supporting the administration reiterated that the increase in deportations was a way for Obama to show Republicans that he understood their concerns and was invested in comprehensive reform. Obama's actions aligned with the position of mainstream Republicans on the lawfulness of using the federal government to police the border and control the flow of people into the nation.

The Obama administration's tough stance on enforcement expanded upon the two previous administrations' approaches in many ways, but there was one way in which the administration made a distinct break in the enforcement arena, namely opposing and rolling back efforts to extend immigration enforcement powers to state and local governments. This move to reassert federal supremacy over immigration enforcement was a way for the administration to press back against growing restrictionist backlash in the states.

Although the overarching legal framework for federal control over immigration enforcement was established in the Constitution and detailed in the Supreme Court case *Chy Lung v. Freeman* in 1876, in the wake of federal inability to control immigration flows, states began during the 1990s and 2000s to make efforts to take immigration enforcement into their own hands, a trend that continued in the early Obama administration. In Arizona, the Republican legislature and Republican governor Jan Brewer passed and signed a piece of legislation, SB 1070, which made it a crime to fail to carry immigration documents and gave state and local police broad power to ask for immigration documentation and detain anyone suspected of being in the country without authorization. Obama immediately denounced the measure as "misguided" and shortly thereafter directed the Justice Department to sue the state of Arizona to challenge the law's constitutionality. The administration's opposition to immigration federalism, meaning a shift in the role of the states and localities in making and implementing immigration policy, was made clear by Attorney General Eric Holder's announcement that "setting immigration policy and enforcing immigration law is a national responsibility," arguing that allowing "a patchwork of state laws" would "create more problems than it solves."[16] Holder's statement, and the Justice Department's suit, signaled an enormous break in recent federal policy toward immigration. The Supreme Court largely sided with the administration's position, striking down three of the four key provisions of the Arizona statute, and the "show me your papers" provision was upheld only after the court attached provisions that sharply narrowed its scope.[17]

Obama's commitment to rolling back immigration federalism was further cemented later during the president's first term when the administration announced it would scale back on one of the more controversial arms of interior enforcement, the 287(g) program, which allowed the deputizing of state and local law enforcement to assist in federal immigration enforcement.[18] The 287(g) program was controversial as many argued it led to an increase in racial profiling by law enforcement as well as a shattering of the tenuous relationship between local law enforcement and the immigrant communities they were entrusted to protect.

In an effort to reassert federal authority over immigration enforcement, the Obama administration announced that it would not only subject the

287(g) program to greater federal oversight, but that it would increasingly invest in an initiative called Secure Communities as a preferable alternative. Established in 2008, Secure Communities directed state and local law enforcement to send fingerprints of those they detained to ICE officials who would make immigration status determinations and decide the appropriate action. The administration argued that moving from 287(g) to Secure Communities transferred the decision-making authority on immigration matters from state and local law enforcement back into the hands of federal immigration officials. By consolidating border enforcement under federal authority, the Obama administration opposed the growing restrictionist backlash fomenting in many states.

While the administration had at first demurred from taking action on comprehensive immigration reform, pressure to address immigration continued to grow from some on Capitol Hill and among immigration activists in advance of the 2010 midterm elections. Liberal immigration activists staged a large rally on the Mall that drew tens of thousands of supporters. In early 2010, Republican senator Lindsey Graham of South Carolina and Democratic senator Charles Schumer of New York began to work together on a bill that they revealed for the first time in the *Washington Post* on March 9, 2010. It included increased funding for border and workplace enforcement, a legalization program, an expanded visa program for high-skilled workers, and required that all workers, including authorized immigrants and American citizens, present a biometric identity card when they applied for jobs. But Graham withdrew his support for the bill in April, fearing that Democrats were only pushing the bill to gain support of Latinos before the 2010 midterms.[19] Graham's move reflected a larger movement within his party. Indeed, while many Republicans had joined liberal Democrats in support of comprehensive reform in 1986 during the passage of IRCA and during President Bush's failed efforts in 2006 and 2007, in Obama's first term, not a single Republican senator was willing to support comprehensive reform publicly.[20]

United opposition to any form of broad immigration reform action in Congress was even more apparent when Democrats in Congress with the support of the president pushed to move on the Development, Relief, and Education for Alien Minors (DREAM) Act in the fall of 2010. The DREAM Act would have given unauthorized immigrants who came to the United States as children a path toward legal status and perhaps eventually citizenship if they lived in the country for more than five years and attended college or served in the military. While different versions of the legislation had been exchanged across Capitol Hill for over a decade, often receiving some GOP support, in 2010 all but three Republicans in the Senate voted with five Democrats to filibuster the bill, blocking it from coming up for a vote on the floor. The cloture vote on the DREAM Act was significant for two reasons. First, it showed the depth of opposition to immigration reform even within the Democratic caucus, and second, with Republicans set to control the House in 2011, it virtually guaranteed that comprehensive immigration legislation was dead for the president's first term.

Hardline opposition to immigration reform had been growing since the early 2000s, but this opposition accelerated after the 2010 elections, which brought new members aligned with the Tea Party into Congress. Immigration was central to the Tea Party platform, as 80 percent of Tea Party activists saw illegal immigration as a very serious problem. Viewing unauthorized immigrants as "freeloading at the expense of hardworking Americans," those aligned with the Tea Party opposed any form of legalization or "grand bargain"–style immigration reform.[21]

In the summer of 2012, under pressure from party activists to show some effort on immigration reform before the November election and unable to rise above the partisanship that dominated Washington as he had hoped, President Obama turned to his executive powers and announced the creation of the Deferred Action for Childhood Arrivals (DACA) program. Obama's executive order targeted an approximately 1.5 million unauthorized immigrants thirty-one years of age or younger who had been in the United States for at least the previous five years and had been under the age of sixteen when they arrived in the United States, had graduated high school or served in the military, and had no significant criminal record. The policy allowed this segment of younger immigrants to apply for a two-year renewable reprieve on deportation.

The use of executive action was a significant move in immigration policy for the administration, as previously in 2011, the president had signaled his reticence on using executive action, commenting that immigration activists "wish I could just bypass Congress and change the law myself. But that's not how a democracy works. What we really need to do is to keep up the fight to pass genuine, comprehensive reform."[22] The administration defended its executive order by arguing it was a legal use of the authority of the federal government to exercise prosecutorial discretion with regard to unauthorized immigrants in order to prioritize deportation proceedings.[23] Obama's turn to executive action reflected a realistic assessment of how entrenched the majority Republican opposition was to any liberalizing immigration action.

Numerous presidents before Obama had turned to executive action to address immigration issues, but the targets had generally been smaller or more discrete populations, such as Reagan's executive action that protected from deportation an estimated 100,000 families with unauthorized minor children of parents legalized by IRCA, or Carter's executive action admitting Cuban and Haitian refugees after the Mariel boatlift.[24] President Obama's use of executive authority to create DACA in 2012 would be his administration's first broad measure of immigration reform, and at the time he called it at the announcement a "temporary, stop-gap measure." However, executive action would be a mechanism he would turn to again to get around the full-scale blockade of any reform in Congress as his administration progressed.

Although DACA drew support from many liberal immigration activists, Obama's failure to push for larger comprehensive immigration reform nonetheless continued to be an issue during the 2012 election, as many believed Obama had not done enough in his first term. This discontent was illustrated during Univision host Jorge Ramos's interview with the president in 2012. When asked by Ramos about his failure to push immigration reform, Obama attempted to focus on the pressing economic imperatives he had faced coming into office before blaming the failure on Republicans in Congress. Ramos retorted, "You promised that, and a promise is a promise. And with all due respect, you didn't keep that promise."[25]

Despite some reservations, Latino voters turned out in record numbers in 2012, supporting Obama over Mitt Romney by a margin of 71 percent to 27 percent.[26] In key states like Colorado, Nevada, and New Mexico, exit polls showed that Obama won the Hispanic vote by large percentages that well exceeded his margins of victory.[27] While the president had not moved on comprehensive immigration reform as he had promised he would in his first campaign, his late efforts with DACA were effective in securing Latino turnout, as a survey of Latino voters found that 58 percent said the DACA announcement had made them "more enthusiastic" about supporting the president's reelection.[28] In his election night speech, President Obama again specifically mentioned immigration as a priority for his second term.

Entering President Obama's second term, immigration reform seemed poised to move after the politics surrounding the issue changed—the GOP saw significant losses among Latino voters in the 2012 election. Jockeying to be in control over the immigration reform agenda, President Obama and a bipartisan group of senators unveiled comprehensive reform proposals within a day of each other in January 2013. Senator McCain, who was a lead architect of the Senate proposal, put it bluntly when asked what had changed the outlook for immigration reform in the new Congress. "Elections," he answered. As McCain noted, the "Republican Party is losing the support of our Hispanic citizens."[29]

The Senate plan was similar to the unsuccessful 2007 legislation. It included a path to citizenship for unauthorized immigrants, enhancements to border security, and a low-skilled guest worker program. The president's proposal included a faster citizenship process. Over the spring and early summer of 2013, the Senate passed its bipartisan comprehensive immigration legislation with support from both parties and the president endorsed the measure. While liberal immigration activists pushed the president to expand the DACA program to other groups of people in order to pressure Congress to pass a more expansive immigration overhaul, he refused, commenting, "If we start broadening that, then essentially I'll be ignoring the law in a way that I think would be very difficult to defend legally. . . . So that's not an option."[30]

Obama's aversion to taking further executive action began to change in 2014 when the effort to pass the Senate legislation faltered in the House, where conservatives dominated the leadership and played a strong role in determining immigration policy positions. The 2010 redistricting and gerrymandering of congressional districts created fewer, denser urban Democratic districts while at the same time giving Republicans greater margins in districts they controlled. This process also empowered a group of hardline anti-immigration Republican members of Congress from mostly white rural districts, like Congressman Steve King of Iowa. Majority Leader Eric Cantor's defeat in his primary by Tea Party member David Brat running on a platform of opposing "amnesty" further emboldened the restrictionist sentiment among House Republicans.

House Republican opposition to supporting a comprehensive reform bill grew during the spring of 2014 following a sudden surge at the southern U.S. border of unaccompanied minors and women with children from the "Northern Triangle" countries of Central America—Honduras, El Salvador, and Guatemala. Fleeing gang and cartel violence in their home nations and seeking refugee status in the United States, by the end of fiscal year 2014, over 68,541 unaccompanied minors had been apprehended at the border.

President Obama declared the issue a humanitarian crisis, and the administration struggled to address the detention of minors. Nationwide, this surge of migrants fueled calls for immigration restriction among conservative activists. As a result of these prevailing winds in the House, in June 2014 Speaker John Boehner informed the president that there would be no vote on immigration for the rest of the year.

Frustrated by the House's inaction, the following week President Obama announced in the Rose Garden a twofold shift in his immigration policy. Realizing that no deal on immigration legislation would be coming, Obama announced that he would again use his executive power to make changes to the nation's immigration system by the end of the summer. Specifically, he sought to expand opportunities for legalization and to slow down interior enforcement and deportations.

Though Obama noted in June that he would take action by the end of the summer, political interests intervened. Where Obama had pushed immigration to the backburner in order to pursue other legislative items on his agenda in 2009 and 2010, in 2014, the push for reform was again delayed as Democrats feared that too much emphasis on the issue could hurt the party in the year's midterm elections. As a result, Obama delayed announcing any additional new executive actions until after the November midterms. Two weeks after election day, Obama announced his series of executive actions related to immigration. He did so with a defiant statement that both rebuked the Republican-controlled Congress and sought to appeal to a nation's compassion. Obama noted that mass deportation of potentially millions is "not who we are," drawing on Scripture to admonish, "We shall not oppress a stranger for we know the heart of a stranger—we were strangers once, too." He voiced his frustration with Republican members of Congress who opposed his actions, saying, "To those members of Congress who question my authority to make our immigration system work better, or question the wisdom of me acting where Congress has failed, I have one answer: Pass a bill."[31]

His major announcement was an executive action aimed at deferral of deportation for parents of U.S. citizens or legal permanent residents as well as an expansion of the current DACA program. Under the Deferred Action for Parents of Americans (DAPA) program, parents of U.S. citizens or legal permanent residents would be able to apply for a grant of relief from deportation and be authorized to work provided they had lived in the United States for five years or more. Under the expansion of DACA, the administration eliminated the current age cut-off of thirty-one or under, and allowed immigrants to apply if they had lived in the United States since 2010, not 2007 as before.[32] Experts estimated that the changes to the DACA program would increase the number of people eligible for that program to about 1.5 million from 1.2 million, and combined with the DAPA program, would protect up to 5 million unauthorized immigrants from deportation. All of these programs combined would have the potential to benefit just under half of the nation's unauthorized immigrant population.[33]

The president's executive actions drew harsh rebuke from those opposed to immigration liberalization, with some like Congressman Steve King charging that it was an unconstitutional action that illegally granted "amnesty to millions." He urged his supporters to "to step up and guard a post," and to "refurbish the pillars of American Exceptionalism."[34] The president's use of executive action fueled the growing restrictionist movement within the Republican Party. The DAPA and expanded DACA programs were immediately challenged by Texas and twenty-five other states. In order to challenge the statute, Texas argued it suffered a concrete injury as a result of the DAPA program as the state would lose millions of dollars if it were required to provide driver's licenses to almost 600,000 eligible immigrants in the state. Texas also argued that in creating the program the administration bypassed a little-known federal statute, the Administrative Procedure Act, which requires the executive branch to seek public input when changing a significant rule. Finally and most significantly, the state argued that while the administration claimed DAPA was the president's decision on how to enforce laws created by Congress, the president had violated the "Take Care" clause of the Constitution because the president has allegedly changed the law rather than "tak[ing] care that the laws be faithfully executed."

A U.S. district judge in Brownsville, Texas, issued an injunction to prevent the programs from launching and agreed the state had standing to challenge the statute. This decision was later affirmed by the Fifth Circuit Court of Appeals and shortly thereafter the federal government appealed the case to the Supreme Court. On June 23, 2016, the Supreme Court announced it had deadlocked 4–4 in a decision that read, in its entirety, "The judgment is affirmed by an equally divided court." The ruling set no precedent on the larger questions at hand and simply left in place the lower court's preliminary injunction blocking the program. As Walter Dellinger, acting solicitor general in the Clinton administration, commented on the decision, "seldom have the hopes of so many been crushed by so few words."[35]

While the DACA and DAPA programs drew the most public attention and were the hallmark of President Obama's embrace of executive actions after the failure of comprehensive reform efforts, President Obama made several other changes to enforcement efforts in an effort to recalibrate the administration's immigration policy.

On this new path, the Obama administration quietly began to slow down interior enforcement, moving resources from the interior to the border, and providing a renewed emphasis on targeted removal of criminal aliens.[36] According to Immigration and Customs Enforcement (ICE), during fiscal year 2015 when the agency began implementing the Obama administration's "clearer and more refined" civil immigration enforcement priorities, with emphasis on the removal of convicted felons over noncriminals, there was a single-year decrease in removals of 25.5 percent.[37]

The administration's efforts to move away from interior enforcement in the second term went hand in hand with the president's commitment to reducing the role of state and local law enforcement involvement in immigration enforcement. In his first term, he sought to transition from the 287(g) policies to the Secure Communities program, and in November 2014 he announced that the Secure Communities programs too would be phased out completely.[38] While the administration had argued early on that the Secure Communities program would allow for more targeted interior enforcement toward the immigrants with long and violent criminal records, the program did not function that way and drew similar criticism to 287(g) with regard to racial profiling. ICE data on the program showed that it failed to prioritize those who had committed violent crimes for deportation. By ending the program, the administration sought to consolidate immigration enforcement efforts squarely in the jurisdiction of the federal government.

By the end of the Obama administration, a bifurcated image of immigration enforcement had emerged. At the border, unauthorized immigrants were more frequently subject to formal removal and criminal charges. At the same time in the interior, Obama moved in his second term to provide greater flexibility, with more emphasis placed on targeted removal.[39]

While the largest focus of immigration policy in the United States during the Obama administration was on migratory flows from Mexico and Central America, global events pushed the question of refugees from the Middle East into a prominent position later in his administration. In the years following 9/11, immigration to the United States has been increasingly framed as a security issue based on the idea that immigrants have the potential to threaten the nation's security through terrorism. This securitization of immigration was perhaps seen most clearly during the Obama administration in the debates over refugee admissions.

Following the arrest of two Iraqi refugees in Kentucky on suspicion of plotting a terrorist attack in 2011, these debates over the securitization of immigration and refugee admissions grew. As the bloody civil war in Syria in the wake of the Arab Spring spurred the movement of millions of refugees across Europe and the world, Obama's refugee policy became more contested. In response to the humanitarian crisis, the number of Syrian refugees resettled in the United States grew rapidly, from 31 in 2012 to 1,682 in 2015.[40] Under pressure from European allies and other countries addressing exploding growth in the number of Syrian refugees, in 2015 the administration announced a new plan to increase the limit on annual refugee visas from 75,000 to 85,000 for 2016 then to 100,000 in the following year.[41] Obama also raised the number of Syrian refugees who would be offered legal status to at least 10,000 in the 2016 fiscal year. In 2016 alone, the Obama administration ended up resettling 12,587 Syrian refugees.

These policies regarding Syrian refugees drew domestic criticism from the left and right. Liberals attacked the Obama administration for its meager admissions numbers, especially in contrast to the efforts seen in countries such as Germany. On the other side, the administration faced strong conservative opposition to the increasing number of refugees it sought to resettle each year. Conservatives charged that potential ISIS/ISIL terrorists could enter the United States as Syrian refugees. In the weeks following the terrorist attacks in Paris in November 2015, these calls to restrict refugees increased and members of the House voted to pass legislation further tightening the refugee screening process. Several conservative governors, such as Texas governor Greg Abbott, went so far as to remove their states from the Federal Refugee Resettlement Program.[42] As 2016 wound to a close, Obama's efforts to increase the number of Syrian refugees admitted to the United States became a flash point of the presidential election, with Hillary Clinton calling for the United States to do more by admitting a substantial number of refugees and Donald Trump calling for a severe restriction.

An Imperfect Legacy

With his plans for comprehensive immigration reform defeated by Congress, his efforts at executive action stymied by the courts, and a small but increasingly persistent commitment to refugee admissions, President Obama ended his two terms with few successes and a mixed legacy on immigration and refugee policy. As of September 2016, the Obama administration had granted 752,154 unauthorized immigrants DACA approval, granting them deportation action deferral and access to a work permit, but the administration had also removed a record number of immigrants, over 2.5 million, from the country.[43]

Failing to effectively read the changing politics of immigration policy and manage congressional opposition, Obama turned to executive action to achieve substantive reform, a move that lacked the consensus building required of comprehensive reform and fueled the growing anti-immigrant sentiment among conservatives. While the long-term impact of President Obama's actions on immigration remains unclear, in the immediate term, their role in fostering the restrictionist backlash that President Donald Trump harnessed in the 2016 campaign is clear.

13

Liberal Internationalism, Law, and the First African American President

Jeremi Suri

The election of the nation's first African American president was possible, in part, because of a failed war in Iraq. Barack Obama promised change in the way the country conducted itself at home and abroad. Speaking to a crowd of 200,000 enthusiastic German citizens in Berlin, he announced that his presidency would "build new bridges across the globe as strong as the one that bound us across the Atlantic. Now is the time to join together, through constant cooperation, strong institutions, shared sacrifice, and a global commitment to progress, to meet the challenges of the 21st century."[1]

Obama offered a liberal internationalist vision—emphasizing multilateralism, negotiation, and disarmament—after eight years of aggressive neoconservative militarism under President George W. Bush. He affirmed the standard defense of American power: "The United States of America has helped underwrite global security for more than six decades with the blood of our citizens and the strength of our arms." Yet, he emphasized, "adhering to standards, international standards, strengthens those who do, and isolates and weakens those who don't." The latter claim explained his early opposition to the Iraq war, the use of torture, and the incarceration of accused terrorists at Guantánamo Bay without due process. Obama aimed to fuse American power with collective security efforts, not unilateral efforts, and he sought to expand the reach of international law, not national vigilante efforts at "ending tyranny" in faraway lands.[2]

Although Obama flagrantly affirmed American exceptionalism and the indispensable role of the United States around the globe, he rejected the inherited justifications for continuous war against threatening powers and violent ideologies. He argued for engagement, diplomacy, and limited use of force to build peace and law in troubled areas. He spoke optimistically of persuading and converting adversaries, rather than trying to eliminate them. "The promotion of human rights cannot be about exhortation alone. At times, it must be coupled with painstaking diplomacy. I know that engagement with repressive regimes lacks the satisfying purity of indignation. But I also know that sanctions without outreach—condemnation without discussion—can carry forward only a crippling status quo. No repressive regime can move down a new path unless it has the choice of an open door."[3]

Continuous war closed opportunities for engagement that Obama wanted to open as part of an evolving liberal world order: "Agreements among nations. Strong institutions. Support for human rights. Investments in development. All these are vital ingredients." President Obama's menu of preferred policies emphasized cooperation, even with adversaries, over coercion. After the near global opposition to America's invasion of Iraq, Obama sought to make the United States once again a popular world leader.[4]

Referring to the expansive Global War on Terror, begun by his predecessor, the president explained: "This war, like all wars, must end. That's what history advises. That's what our democracy demands." Obama defined his liberal internationalism in stark contrast to Bush's aggressive unilateralism. And this contrast remained powerful, despite Obama's own violent antiterrorist policies.[5]

Law above Morality

Invoking the memory of the Marshall Plan and the Berlin Airlift after the Second World War, Obama renewed an American commitment to nation-building, as far as Afghanistan and as close as American cities:

> This is the moment when we must renew our resolve to rout the terrorists who threaten our security in Afghanistan, and the traffickers who sell drugs on your streets. No one welcomes war. I recognize the enormous difficulties in Afghanistan. But my country and yours have a stake

in seeing that NATO's first mission beyond Europe's borders is a success. For the people of Afghanistan, and for our shared security, the work must be done. America cannot do this alone. The Afghan people need our troops and your troops; our support and your support to defeat the Taliban and al Qaeda, to develop their economy, and to help them rebuild their nation. We have too much at stake to turn back now.[6]

Obama's vision was progressive and pragmatic, focused on American leadership through democratic alliances and common law that would underpin legitimate force. As a black man, he had credibility when he doubted the effectiveness of lawless power—executed by nonstate and state actors—in defending democracy. Moral self-righteousness was harmful, he argued, when used to justify violence that destroyed an alleged "evil" without attention to the humanity of those targeted, or the prospects for a better alternative. Moral self-righteousness corrupted power when undisciplined by the deliberative and consensus qualities of law.[7]

In his Nobel Peace Prize address and other speeches, Obama echoed the famous midcentury theologian Reinhold Niebuhr, who saw tragic "irony" in American efforts to marry power with righteousness, which often produced neither. Niebuhr, like Obama, counseled for more modesty, more attention to trade-offs, and more willingness to accept "lesser evils," rather than the dangerous illusions of perfection. The United States was exceptional, Niebuhr and Obama believed, but not above history or human folly.[8]

Motivated by the immoral consequences of hyper-moralistic rhetoric in recent American history, President Obama spoke from the heart when he criticized the passivity of privileged citizens in the face of injustice at home and abroad. Obama called for a broader and more creative foreign policy, less imprisoned by the atavistic reliance on overwhelming American military power, which had long proven less effective than it first appeared. He wanted more diverse partnerships and intelligent persuasion; less physical posturing and self-righteous certainty. Obama's international outlook mixed American muscle and dollars with advocacy for democratic ideals, assistance from friends, and openness to change—even from old enemies.[9]

The president obviously did not rule out military conflict, but he preferred targeted and limited force, with clear purpose. He opposed continuous and overwhelming warfare that promised, falsely, to translate American military superiority into political domination of distant societies. The wars of the Cold War (in Korea and Vietnam) and later (Yugoslavia,

Kuwait, and Iraq) proved that American strength was often insufficient and counterproductive for national goals. These wars also undermined American claims to democracy and justice, as well as the general standing of the United States in the world. At home and abroad, America's continuous string of military conflicts since 1950 had diminished the country and its ideals, according to Obama.[10]

He sought to tame war with law, and where possible, end American military conflicts (especially in the Middle East) that undermined the values of the nation and its allies. That was his clear and consistent rationale for withdrawing from Iraq, where he believed the U.S. invasion in 2003 had imperiled America's global standing, brutalized its politics, and overburdened its economy. He "surged" American forces in Afghanistan to defeat the remnants of Al-Qaeda and the Taliban, but the goal there was to withdraw soon and limit the material and idealistic costs of continuous fighting. Obama wanted to replace foreign occupations with multilateral nation-building, and he hoped to return resources to Americans, suffering from a debilitating economic recession at home. "America could best serve the cause of freedom," Obama wrote, "by concentrating on its development, becoming a beacon of hope for other nations and people around the globe."[11]

Use (and Non-Use) of Force

Obama's emphasis on law had contradictory effects, complicating any assessment of his foreign policy legacy. The president consistently sought to curtail costly military campaigns that included extensive death and destruction. He was skeptical about the legality or morality of war on a large scale. He also doubted the effectiveness of major military campaigns, explaining in part his hesitance and ultimate passivity in the face of genocide in Syria. Obama felt legally and practically constrained against undertaking extensive military action to stop the civil war in Syria, or at least balance the increasing advantage accruing to Syrian president Bashar al-Assad's Russian- and Iranian-supported forces. He painfully watched events in Syria, spoke forcefully for regime change, but did very little.

Despite his obvious reluctance to deploy troops in large numbers, Obama's emphasis on legality and his desire to use American power more effectively triggered a surprising increase in executive authority over the use of force. The president perceived terrorist groups—associated with Al-Qaeda, other networks, and later ISIS—as grave threats to the United States. He took his constitutional role as commander-in-chief very seriously. Searching for a legal and lethal mechanism to defeat terrorists, Obama turned to targeted assassinations of enemy combatants, ordered and approved by the president. He also stretched the writ of American intelligence agencies to investigate and disrupt alleged terrorist supporters—both at home and abroad. The Obama administration felt less empowered to start traditional wars, but the president was comfortable using law to justify alternative measures that were more proportional than overwhelming, and more controlled from the White House than from the battlefield or allied counsels. In this sense, the Obama "war doctrine," as some would call it, vastly increased the direct reach of presidential force at the cost of traditional institutions, especially Congress. When seeking approval for its actions, the administration looked to the courts, often in secret, rather than the public or the legislature.

We know the president thought deeply about these matters, and he had reservations about how his actions could empower a more reckless successor. As a good lawyer, he sought to nurture careful procedures for assessing targets, collateral damage, and regional reverberations. He consulted closely with leaders of the military and relevant civilian agencies. Nonetheless, Obama could not avoid the consequence of creating permanent and centralized war powers for the president that were less accountable to American democratic institutions than traditional acts of warfare. He affirmed, as no chief executive had before, the right of the president to kill enemies abroad without notice, based solely on the judgment of his closest advisors. Obama saw this as legal police power liberated from traditional Cold War assumptions about large armies and long occupations; critics at home, and especially abroad, saw it as covert warfare open to dangerous abuses previewed by prior CIA interventions in Iran, Guatemala, Indonesia, and Chile. To some, Obama looked like a new age imperialist, armed with manipulative legal rationalizations.[12]

Ending the Global War on Terror

Obama's predecessor had a more traditional Cold War mindset that emphasized battlefield force over aerial and other covert technologies—although he was happy to use the latter when he felt they reinforced, but did not substitute for, the human battlefield. George W. Bush's military traditionalism made his goals and actions much easier to understand for proponents and critics alike. Bush's military traditionalism was the "old" way of thinking that Obama was determined to escape.

Speaking to a shaken nation as rescue crews continued to remove mangled bodies from the smoldering remains of the World Trade Center on September 20, 2001, President George W. Bush had announced a Global War on Terror that, by 2008, had grown into a global war without end. Bush memorably explained that the war on terror "will not end until every terrorist group of global reach has been found, stopped, and defeated." Every single one, in all parts of the world: "Americans should not expect one battle, but a lengthy campaign, unlike any other we have ever seen. . . . Every nation, in every region, now has a decision to make. Either you are with us, or you are with the terrorists. From this day forward, any nation that continues to harbor or support terrorism will be regarded by the United States as a hostile regime."[13]

Bush's belligerent announcement of the global war on terror was emotional, expansive, and limitless. It reflected the profound anger, fear, and desire for revenge that characterized American attitudes after the September 11, 2001, terrorist attacks. Bush's words were a form of collective venting and public lashing out. They married Cold War muscle to a self-righteousness that fit Bush's religiosity, but not the next president's analytical attitude, and his skepticism of moralistic simplicity.[14]

The core problem, as Obama and others observed, was that the "Bush doctrine" extolled a permanent war against an abstract phenomenon in all corners of the globe for all time. The war would not end, according to Bush, until every terrorist was killed. This was a messianic vision more than a practical policy. The American military would set its sights on all groups that housed, supported, or even sympathized with a terrorist network. There could be no end, short of total victory. Three years later, in his second inaugural address, Bush spoke of "ending tyranny in our world" with a combination of religious exuberance and limitless ambition.[15]

Bush's call for a global war on terror echoed Cold War rhetoric about a global struggle against communism. Bush's plans for antiterrorist proxy wars replayed the logic of American anticommunist interventions across the world during the Cold War. Assumptions about American dominance, forward military action, regime change, and support for favorable dictators transferred smoothly from the repertoire of Henry Kissinger and other Cold Warriors to the late twentieth-century neoconservatives. It should be no surprise that Kissinger's influence, in particular, grew during Bush's presidency.[16]

Obama would have none of that. He thought of himself as the anti–Cold Warrior, the anti-neoconservative, even the anti-Kissinger. That self-definition deepened as the president's team took office and sought to define what they were about. In foreign policy, it is always easier to articulate what you are against, instead of what you are for. The president did not have a clear vision of the world he hoped to create, but he knew which mistaken American actions he wanted to reverse, especially in Iraq.

An Obama Doctrine?

Obama frequently criticized the foreign policy "establishment," including Bush, Kissinger, and other war hawks. He did not favor overwhelming American dominance, forward military action, regime change, or support for favorable dictators—standard patterns in American policymaking since 1945. The new president's preference for diplomacy and law defined his earliest actions to unwind his predecessor's failed, anachronistic policies. As Obama announced near the end of his time in the White House, his aim from the start was to "bury the last remnant of the Cold War" and "extend the hand of friendship" to a world eager to cooperate with the United States, not fight old battles.[17]

If anything, the president looked back to an early twentieth-century world, where American power was global, but less militarized and more multilateral. The early twentieth century was also a formative period for international law, when American figures like Elihu Root, Charles Evans Hughes, William Howard Taft, Henry Stimson, and Felix Frankfurter sought to build an international system governed by rules, consensus, and arbitration, rather than war. They favored multilateral sanctions and joint police actions—as in the cooperative response to China's Boxer Rebellion— over unfettered national competition. Although most of these earlier policymakers were Republicans, Obama embodied similar aspirations in his efforts to negotiate global reductions in nuclear weapons and carbon dioxide emissions, among other issues. He was not just a multilateralist, but a legal internationalist. He rejected the Democratic Party's more traditional emphasis on values (democracy and anticommunism) over international law and order.[18]

In defense of a more lawful global system, Obama began by banning torture, drawing down American forces in Iraq, and pledging to close the prison at Guantánamo Bay—all acts of war associated with the Bush administration. Obama made one of his first major foreign trips to Egypt, not Israel, where he intentionally redefined the American image abroad. Instead of dividing the world between those "with us" and those with the terrorists, he spoke of enduring connections across religious and ethnic lines. Obama called upon listeners "to join together on behalf of the world that we seek—a world where extremists no longer threaten our people, and American troops have come home; a world where Israelis and Palestinians are each secure in a state of their own, and nuclear energy is used for peaceful purposes; a world where governments serve their citizens, and the rights of all God's children are respected. Those are mutual interests. That is the world we seek. But we can only achieve it together."[19]

The president was serious about opening the United States to friendlier relations with the citizens of the Middle East, and he hoped to do this by negotiating mutually beneficial deals with their leaders, and those in other regions. Diplomacy was indeed his alternative to war. Secretary of Defense Robert Gates, initially appointed by George W. Bush after serving his father, stayed on to serve Obama as well, and he observed the seriousness of the new president's efforts: "I found the president quite pragmatic on national security and open to compromise on most issues—or, to put it more crassly, to cutting a deal. . . . Obama was the most deliberative president I worked for."[20]

That is high praise from a leading Republican policymaker. Working closely with Gates and his secretary of state, Hillary Clinton, Obama reached out to China, Russia, and Iran—perhaps the three most important American regional adversaries—seeking to build a working relationship with each. He refrained from the kind of threatening rhetoric that both Ronald Reagan and George W. Bush employed at the start of their presidencies. Obama was measured, discreet, and aspirational in his words. He dropped the aggressive Bush administration phrases that fired up Americans but frightened foreigner observers: "Global War on Terror," "axis of evil," "radical Islam," and "American preeminence." Instead, Obama spoke of cooperation and partnership. He backed his words with high-level messages of conciliation to leaders in Beijing, Moscow, Tehran, and other capitals.

Openings

Acting on behalf of the president's priorities, Secretary Clinton made Asia the destination for her first foreign trip in office. She pledged to pursue a firm but peaceful working relationship with Beijing that limited Chinese expansion in the region, but also showed respect for the sovereignty and security interests of the mainland. Obama and Clinton hoped to encourage

China to act as a "responsible stakeholder" through a mix of incentives and limits—the latter designed not to insult Beijing or challenge its standing. The new administration sought to become a more active "balancer" in the region, assuring Chinese neighbors of American commitments and engaging the Chinese in productive dialogues. A targeted increase of American force was included in this effort (the "pivot") designed to be big enough to strengthen American security guarantees to allies, but small enough not to provoke retaliation from Beijing. Obama wanted to increase his deal-making leverage with all actors in the Pacific region.[21]

Trade was a central issue for Washington and its longtime Pacific allies, particularly Japan, Singapore, Australia, and New Zealand. The United States led regional negotiations for a far-reaching free trade agreement in 2008, during the last year of the Bush administration. President Obama pushed forward, arguing that more open exchange of goods across countries, and the creation of a larger integrated Pacific market, would stimulate economic growth and political cooperation. It would also create a counterbalance in Asia to China's rapidly expanding economy.

The Obama administration and eleven other countries signed a final landmark agreement in February 2016, known as the Trans-Pacific Partnership (TPP). The document cemented closer relations among the signatories and it promised to embed the United States deeper in the Pacific as a promoter of trade, innovation, and collective security. Although Donald Trump withdrew from the TPP as one of his first acts as president in 2017, the agreement created the largest single trading bloc in Asia, and it continued to operate for the eleven other signatories, wedding them close to one another and continuing American trade interests. The TPP was an effective act of economic statecraft for the Obama administration in Asia—it increased American influence, counterbalanced China, but did not antagonize Beijing.[22]

In Russia the president also sought to replace the animosity of the last Bush years with more effective diplomacy. During the summer of 2008, Russian leader Vladimir Putin (then serving officially as prime minister) had orchestrated an invasion of the Russian-populated regions of Abkhazia and South Ossetia within the independent post-Soviet nation of Georgia. The Bush administration had condemned this aggression, and frozen relations with Moscow. Obama sought to reopen negotiations with Russia, focusing on mutual interests in combatting terrorism, stabilizing Afghanistan, and reducing nuclear arms—an issue close to the president's heart. Secretary Clinton famously called this a "reset" in U.S.–Russian relations, where

Washington would not forgive Moscow's recent aggression, but would continue to seek areas of cooperation around common interests. Obama hoped to make Moscow a responsible stakeholder, as he also assured Russia's neighbors of America's continued commitment to their defense.[23]

In Iran the president pursued his most radical peace initiative. From his first days in office, he set out to reverse the virtual war that had existed between the Islamic Republic and the United States since the Iranian Revolution of 1979. Millions of Americans could still remember, with anger, the seizure of the American Embassy in Tehran and the fifty-two diplomats held hostage by Iranian revolutionaries for 444 humiliating days. The history of U.S.–Iranian animosity, and the contemporary rivalry for influence in the Middle East, made cooperation especially difficult between Washington and Tehran.[24]

Obama was realistic about the challenges and the risks, but he reached out to Iran nonetheless. In May 2009 the president sent a personal letter to Iran's supreme leader, Ayatollah Ali Khamenei, proposing "cooperation in regional and bilateral relations," and encouraging an agreement to curtail Tehran's nuclear program. Obama also sent a videotaped message to the Iranian people at the time of their New Year celebrations, on March 20, 2009. He saw Iran as a necessary part of any peace settlement in the Middle East. On the eve of the failed "Green Revolution" in Iran (an event that kicked off the Arab Spring in other countries), he explored various possibilities, unsure of how Tehran would respond, but determined to pursue engagement above all.[25]

Although he expected Washington and Tehran to remain rivals, President Obama anticipated major internal changes in Iran that would encourage openings for American collaboration and the institutionalization of peace in the region. He hoped to wean the United States from its strategic dependence on Saudi Arabia, Israel, and Pakistan, creating a broader balance of power in the region with increased leverage for the United States. Obama wanted to build more partnerships focused on specific problems, including counterterrorism and economic development, as he withdrew American soldiers.

Mounting evidence of Tehran's efforts to deploy a nuclear weapon reinforced White House desires to negotiate, but they also motivated Congress and the president to impose severe sanctions on Iranian banking and trade. This was what Obama administration officials came to call a "dual track" — a mix of carrots and sticks aimed at encouraging Iranian compromise on American terms. Obama was adamant about wanting to prevent nuclear proliferation, especially in the Middle East. He increased American diplomatic options to pursue his ambitious goals of regional peace and "global zero"—elimination of all nuclear weapons.[26]

Those who alleged that the president had grown "soft" were contradicted by his rapid increase in targeted killings of terrorists through a mix of aerial drone strikes and U.S. special forces operations—including the famous May 2, 2011, raid on Al-Qaeda leader Osama bin Laden's compound in Pakistan. Obama's lawyers worked hard to create new legal authorizations to justify targeted killings, even as they claimed the country was coming out of war, and returning to more vigorous due process protections. As before, the president wanted more diplomatic and military tools for law enforcement and peace promotion overseas, not permanent war or occupation. He remained committed to international legal policing power, rather than arbitrary violence or unilateral power projection.[27]

Obama's first years in office marked a self-conscious shift away from the obsession with force and dominance in the Cold War and the Global War on Terror years. The president continued to use America's formidable military capabilities, but with more self-imposed legal, political, and strategic limitations. He wanted to make American power more targeted and balanced between military and nonmilitary dimensions. He aimed for precision above preponderance, lawfulness above moral self-righteousness. To his critics on the right, this seemed like too little forcefulness and too little assertion. To his critics on the left, Obama was justifying a permanent covert war president, with too much unilateral power. The White House was often caught between these two camps.

Obama sought to use his controversial powers by redoubling his cooperative efforts across the globe. He continued to push for American national interests in Asia, Europe, and the Middle East, but he worked vigorously to build alliances and negotiate with adversaries. Most of all, Obama avoided simple binaries between friends and enemies, or "us" versus "them." He spoke and acted as if there were possibilities for cooperation with a wide range of states, some of which supported terrorists. Obama even considered negotiations with the terrorists themselves.

The first black president was, in many ways, a classical liberal internationalist—perhaps more than any president since Franklin Roosevelt. Like Roosevelt, Obama was deliberative. He sought to win over challengers and achieve his aims, short of war. Obama had thought deeply about the prior seventy years of American foreign policy, and the permanent state of international crisis. He endeavored to avoid wars wherever possible, manage the

use of force tightly, and make certain that the full range of American resources were matched to clear and important political aims. Obama wanted
to erase the militaristic Cold War mentality that he saw in the Global War
on Terror. He made a compelling case for dialing back on military crises,
and dialing up on diplomacy and persuasion—even in a world filled with
anti-American aggressors.

Mixed Results

Looking back on Obama's time in office, one can see many important
achievements for his liberal internationalism. He reversed more than fifty-
five years of Cuban–American hostility, turning a powerful source of anti-
American hostility in the Western Hemisphere into an opportunity for
newfound American trade and travel. Even Obama's most vocal Republican
adversaries, including Texas governor Greg Abbott, have replaced their
Cold War threats toward Cuban aggression with a public embrace of new
openings on the island. The Cold War and the Global War on Terror froze
Cuban–American hostility, and increased the power of Fidel and Raúl Castro as anti-American icons. Obama's emphasis on diplomacy and engagement allowed him to make progress where ten previous presidents—from
Eisenhower to Bush—could not.

More controversially, President Obama negotiated and then implemented a comprehensive agreement with ten international signatories that
halted Iranian nuclear weapons development for at least a decade. Despite
organized (but not majority) opposition at home and abroad, the president
used all of his available leverage to craft an enforceable framework for veri-
fying that Iranian nuclear facilities were closed, while incentivizing broader
cooperation. As part of the deal, the United States returned Iranian money
seized in the United States after 1979, and it dropped some (but not all) of
the sanctions that crippled Iran's economic development. The full effects
of the Iranian nuclear deal remain uncertain, but President Obama succeeded—as his predecessors did not—in opening real possibilities for cooperation between Washington, Tehran, and other allies around regional
and global issues. He increased American leverage in Iran and other societies by giving the United States greater access to their people, as well as their
leaders.

The most obvious failure of Obama's foreign policy was in Russia. If
anything, the eight years of his presidency witnessed the poisoning of
what were still promising ties between the United States and Russia in

2008, and a return to Cold War hostilities. By the summer of 2016, Russia was following a Soviet script of challenging NATO forces in Europe, invading neighboring states (Ukraine, and especially the Ukrainian province of Crimea), aiding Middle Eastern strongmen (Bashar al-Assad in Syria), harboring spies with valuable American secrets (Edward Snowden), and attacking American information networks (cyber-warfare.) Vladimir Putin went a step beyond where even Soviet leaders feared to tread, intervening directly in an American presidential election to support a candidate (Donald Trump) strangely susceptible to the Russian president's influence. Marrying traditional KGB tactics to cyber-warfare and social media savvy, Putin helped to create a Manchurian Candidate bent on weakening American power from within. Putin also made Russia a recognized military and cyber-threat to the functioning of democratic elections throughout Europe and North America. He became a unifying strategic adversary for Western leaders, including members of the U.S. Congress who agreed on tightening sanctions, despite partisan differences and presidential opposition.[28]

In light of these troubling events, Obama's attempted "reset" with Russia looks naïve and potentially disastrous for American national interests. Washington's conciliatory moves appear to have encouraged Putin's aggression in Europe, the Middle East, and other regions. Divisions within the United States and NATO also appear to have reduced Putin's fears of retaliation. With increasing Russian boldness and aggression, the possibilities of a major war, including nuclear weapons, have grown considerably—either due to inadvertent crisis escalation, miscalculation, or misperception by decision-makers on one side of the escalating conflict.

Not only does the rhetoric echo the Cold War, so do the growing tensions surrounding Russian and American military forces deployed in Eastern Europe and Central Asia. Since 2014 Russian air and sea forces have conducted intentionally provocative moves near NATO-deployed planes and ships. Russia has ended all adherence to recent nuclear agreements, increasing the size of its nuclear stockpile and the number of available delivery vehicles.[29]

The nuclear arms race has returned, and Obama reluctantly made efforts to modernize the American arsenal in response. In 2015 the United States participated in a Cold War–style military exercise with its NATO allies—the largest since the collapse of the Soviet Union—simulating a war with Russia in Europe. In 2016 a second such exercise took place, with a focus on protecting Poland's integrity against a feared Russian invasion.

These were hardly the antiwar efforts that Obama hoped to lead when he announced an end to permanent war less than eight years earlier. Just the opposite.

The rise of the Islamic State (ISIS) followed a similar pattern. With the withdrawal of American soldiers from Iraq and Afghanistan, a new terrorist organization emerged, led by poorly educated Islamic leaders who were radicalized in American-run prisons, where they also formed new political networks. Released into collapsing societies, they organized a media-savvy transnational organization that mobilized adherents seeking to overturn Western power and build an alternative state. They used terror to intimidate enemies and they ran proto-state institutions in the Middle East to sell oil, collect taxes, and finance violent operations. Amid a civil war that fragmented Syria, ISIS exploited the cracks in that society and others to establish pockets of power. ISIS directed its violent efforts nearby, and as far as Belgium and Somalia. It inspired copy-cats even farther afield, including within the United States.[30]

Obama's attempts at Middle East reconciliation, beginning with his 2009 speech in Egypt, did not work. His military de-escalation might have enabled the rise of ISIS, despite American successes in killing Al-Qaeda leaders through targeted drone attacks and special forces operations. Without a fighting army on the ground, the United States left a vacuum that the most extreme and violent groups filled. ISIS exploited the militarization of the region, the resentments of so many residents, and the absence of a force capable of enforcing order. Obama's liberal internationalism failed to stop a Middle Eastern descent into Hobbesian "state of war" conditions, including public executions, mass emigration, and genocide.

Despite continuous urgings, the president did not intervene to stop the horror around ISIS because he did not see an exit strategy. The same was true for events in Russia. Obama and his European allies did not perceive a benefit in provoking war with Vladimir Putin. In both settings the president chose to curtail his hopes for cooperation. He acted to contain but not destroy threatening actors, as he avoided direct American embroilment on the ground.

In a famous set of interviews with journalist Jeffrey Goldberg, Obama threw up his hands: "There are going to be times where either because it's not a direct threat to us or because we just don't have the tools in our toolkit to have a huge impact that, tragically, we have to refrain from jumping in with both feet." Tragic indeed, and perhaps wise, but certainly not satisfying for a country that defines itself as the leader of the free world.[31]

The Tragedy of Obama's Foreign Policy

Obama's liberal internationalism did not reject force or idealism, but it cautiously avoided warfare at almost all costs. The first black president excavated an American sensibility from before the Second World War, when international thinkers like William Howard Taft and Herbert Hoover—as well as Jane Addams and W.E.B. Du Bois—argued that war could only be the very last resort for policy. Like Taft and Hoover, Obama accepted the tragedy of a terribly imperfect international system, he sought to improve it slowly through diplomacy and negotiation, and he avoided the whirlwind of full-scale military conflict, if at all possible.[32]

Although it seems cowardly to some, there is an admirable courage in acknowledging, as Carl von Clausewitz famously wrote, that war is stubbornly unpredictable and often deeply counterproductive, even for the modern Napoleon, or Bush, or Putin. A president who commands the most powerful modern military, but also identifies with the helplessness of citizens targeted for lynching, incarceration, and other frequent brutalities has reasons to doubt the efficacy of mass violence. Obama's hesitance in confronting Putin and ISIS was born of pessimism about not only the practicality of force, but also its broader implications. He doubted that fighting one set of bad guys with overwhelming force would really help the suffering who do not need more war, but instead more opportunity and law.[33]

The mixed and unsatisfying foreign policy legacy of such a thoughtful and "deliberative" president (as described by a Republican, Robert Gates) raises uncomfortable questions for observers. Is it possible to lead a powerful nation, with extensive international ambitions, and avoid military conflict? Can a global hegemon live by law, rather than war? Is non-intervention in the face of tragedy better than flawed but righteous action?[34]

The major achievement of Obama's foreign policy was that he tried to answer these questions by minimizing and targeting force, emphasizing law and nonmilitary tools wherever possible. This liberal internationalist approach allowed him to create openings in Cuba and Iran that ended longstanding Cold War conflicts. These openings have the potential to improve millions of lives and benefit the United States, among other nations.

The glaring failure of Obama's foreign policy was that even when he used force, through drone strikes or regime overthrow in Libya, his hesitations and tentativeness limited his ability to affect change on the ground. Adversaries like Putin and Assad discounted his attempts at deterrence. Often correctly, they assumed he would not retaliate effectively against their aggression. Allies (especially in the Middle East, but also in Asia and Europe) had their confidence in American commitments shaken. They were not as certain as they once were under Washington's security umbrella.

Bullies at home and abroad grew stronger, while Obama avoided direct confrontation. Violent and hateful actors lingered, ominously, on his watch. Shockingly, one of them replaced him as president.

The 2015 and 2016 NATO military exercises were necessary to reinforce alliance confidence, but they were not nearly enough after Putin's brutal invasion of Crimea and his escalating meddling in foreign elections. Russian aggression and the continuing genocidal violence in Syria, Iraq, and other parts of the Middle East will be as much a part of Obama's liberal internationalist legacy as his praise-worthy openings to Cuba and Iran. His foreign policy record was hopeful, tragic, and deeply contradictory. The same could be said of Obama's domestic record, inherited by President Donald Trump and a white nationalist Republican Party in control of Congress after 2016.[35]

The Irony of the First African American President

The irony is that for the first African American president, race mattered in his foreign policy, but not as anyone expected. Historians will not remember Obama as a president who democratized international affairs by opening policy to new ethnic groups, or expanding the dialogue about race and foreign affairs. He did some of that, but it was not his consistent priority. He was not a great liberator.

Obama will have enduring influence as the only U.S. leader since the Second World War to challenge the close connection between war and American policy. He personally felt the brutalizing consequences of American power as no other president had, at least since Abraham Lincoln. Obama worked throughout his two terms to remove the murderous "shock and awe," and replace it with precision, balance, and careful limitations. He wanted to tame American power, to make it lawful, which also meant to make it less abusive.

International politics, like domestic politics, are inherently violent, and the violence is often uncontrolled. American power in the last century has come largely from a preponderance of violent capabilities, and presidents have used that preponderance to pursue their foreign policy aims. That is why we refer to the "Cold War" and the "Global War on Terror."

President Obama moved away from these phrases and the preponderance of violence to seek authority in new controls, especially through law. He aimed to make American politics less violent and more inclusive—and that applied to citizens at home, and peoples abroad. Obama sought to discipline the corrupting and self-serving tendencies of dominant force. What else should we expect from someone who personally felt the perils of uncontrolled violence, and relied on the law for his safety? What else should we expect from a man who led a country where the fires of race hatred continued to burn (witnessed by recurring mass shootings in Charleston and Orlando, among other cities), and civility depended on constitutional institutions and habits, not any broad moral consensus among citizens? If anything, moral arguments about guns, abortion, immigration, and human rights divided Americans in Obama's time. Cold Wars were personal wars for Obama that he wanted to extinguish through law, even at the cost of deeply held convictions.

President Obama's sophisticated and sometime contradictory worldview failed to persuade many at home and abroad. The election of Donald Trump in 2016 and his aggressive advocacy of militaristic protectionism were stinging rejections of Obama's liberal internationalism. Trump also abandoned the Cold War consensus on alliances, deterrence, and Russian containment—embraced most proudly by the Republican Party before his election.

Trump and Obama shared dissatisfaction with what had been seventy years of conventional wisdom on American foreign policy. Future historians will define their presidencies as the abrupt end of the Cold War era. The future will be determined by the contest between liberal internationalism and militaristic protectionism that Obama's presidency opened. The first African American president began an international reconstruction moment—with all the partisanship, violence, and uncertainty of prior reconstructions.

14

Terror Tuesdays

HOW OBAMA REFINED BUSH'S COUNTERTERRORISM POLICIES

Kathryn Olmsted

On many Tuesdays during his presidency, Barack Obama convened an extraordinary meeting in the Oval Office. His national security aides would show him mug shots and short biographies of alleged terrorists. The suspects were Yemenis, Saudis, Afghans, and sometimes Americans; they included men, women, and teenagers. The president would look over these chilling "baseball cards," as one aide called them, and pick which subjects should be put on a kill list to be assassinated on his orders.

The decision by a liberal president—a former professor of constitutional law—to embrace an official program of targeted killing of suspected terrorists was one of the most surprising developments of the Obama presidency. Moreover, the assassination program was just one of several hardline Bush administration counterterrorism policies that Obama chose to continue. "Nothing else in Mr. Obama's first term has baffled liberal supporters and confounded conservative critics alike as his aggressive counterterrorism record," the *New York Times* reported in 2012.[1] His record in his second term remained the same.

Though his supporters thought he would bring new hope and wholesale change, Obama shared President George W. Bush's core beliefs about terrorism, and adopted remarkably similar policies. "I don't think it's even fair to call it Bush Lite. It's Bush," said one conservative defense expert, James Jay Carafano of the Heritage Foundation, in 2010. "It's really, really hard to find a difference that's meaningful and not atmospheric."[2] Obama failed to fulfill his campaign promise to shutter the prison at Guantánamo, increased the number of assassinations, extended Bush's surveillance programs, and prosecuted whistleblowers who tried to tell the American people about these policies. Although Obama generally preferred multilateral, negotiated solutions to foreign policy problems, he made an exception when dealing with terrorists.

Obama's counterterrorism policies did differ from those of Bush in one significant way: the new president was much more concerned that those policies should stay within U.S. and international law. Bush and his team had believed that the commander-in-chief could transcend the laws. Obama decided to normalize his predecessor's practices and make them legal— by tweaking the programs, or, if necessary, by changing the laws to fit the policies.

The Rule of Law

Obama's supporters believed that he would dramatically reform Bush's policies once he came into office. These hopes seemed justified early in Obama's first term. On his second day in office, the new president issued executive orders that banned abusive interrogation techniques and commanded the closure of the Guantánamo detention facility within a year.[3] Obama's supporters celebrated what they saw as the start of a new era. Jubilant defense attorneys at Guantánamo danced in a conga line, shouting "Rule of law, baby!"[4]

But the celebrants' hopes soon faded. Congress first refused to pay to shut down Guantánamo, estimated to cost $80 million, and then voted in 2010 to prohibit the Obama administration from bringing those prisoners to the United States for any reason—for prosecution or resettlement—and to make it difficult to send them to other countries as well. Some of his aides urged the president to fight Congress, but he decided against spending any more political capital on the issue. The administration beat a quick retreat when faced with congressional opposition.

It proved easier to stop torture. In April 2009, Obama's first Central Intelligence Agency (CIA) director, Leon Panetta, announced that the agency had fully implemented the president's executive order and ended the use of torture in interrogations. Panetta ordered his employees to "continue to conduct debriefings using a dialog style of questioning that is fully consistent with the interrogation approaches authorized and listed in the Army Field Manual"—that is, aligned with the Geneva Conventions—and to report any instances of abuse by American government employees or their allies. Moreover, he closed all the "black sites," or secret prisons in other countries where CIA officers and contractors had tortured their prisoners.[5] Also in April 2009, in response to a federal judge's order in a lawsuit brought by the American Civil Liberties Union, Obama released the Bush administration's infamous "torture memos," which set forth the legal justifications for interrogation methods such as waterboarding, sleep deprivation, and confinement in a box filled with insects.[6]

But President Obama refused to prosecute the officials who designed, justified, or carried out the torture program, saying that it was a "time for reflection, not retribution." Both Obama and Attorney General Eric Holder agreed that CIA agents who had followed the Bush administration's interrogation guidelines should not be punished for doing things that the government had told them were legal. Holder did order an investigation of interrogators who might have gone beyond Bush's torture rules. But Republicans in Congress charged that the inquiries would demoralize the nation's spies and make the CIA more reluctant to take risks—and thus expose the nation to more terrorist attacks.[7] In 2012, Holder decided against prosecuting any of these agents either, saying that there was not enough admissible evidence.[8] Human rights groups were bitterly disillusioned.[9]

But Obama's actions did not surprise many observers who were familiar with his thinking on terrorism and his views of Bush's second term policies. For one thing, the Bush administration had already begun moderating its counterterrorism programs before Obama took office. When Obama's advisers started to study the details of Bush's policies, they discovered that "most of them had already been rethought, changed, and largely legitimated," as legal scholar and former Bush-era Justice Department lawyer Jack Goldsmith explained.[10] Journalists, civil liberties groups, and government bureaucrats had pushed the Bush administration to order the eventual closing of the CIA's secret prisons and to accede to congressional demands to modify his surveillance programs and interrogation methods. Once the Bush counterterrorism programs were legitimized, Goldsmith argued, it became more difficult for Obama to change them, even if he had wanted to do so.[11]

Moreover, as a presidential candidate, Obama had indicated that he agreed with Bush's tough policies against terrorists, even as he opposed the Iraq war. "Rather than fight a war that does not need to be fought, we need to start fighting the battles that need to be won on the central front against al Qaeda, in Afghanistan and Pakistan," he said on the campaign trail.[12] Obama always supported a vigorous war on terrorists; he just wanted to conduct this war within the law.

The Drone Wars

Like his predecessor, the new president committed himself early on to aggressive pursuit of suspected terrorists. When an Al-Qaeda agent tried and failed to blow up an airliner on Christmas Day 2009, Obama made a speech that sounded very reminiscent of Bush. "We are at war," he said. "We are at war against al Qaeda, a far-reaching network of violence and hatred that attacked us on 9/11, that killed nearly 3,000 innocent people, and that is plotting to strike us again. And we will do whatever it takes to defeat them."[13] Even in his speech accepting the Nobel Peace Prize in December 2009, he signaled his intention to vanquish what he saw as an existential threat. "Evil does exist in the world," he said. "A nonviolent movement could not have halted Hitler's armies. Negotiations cannot convince al Qaeda's leaders to lay down their arms."[14]

But Obama wanted his war on terrorists to be more focused and less deadly for American forces. Armed drones gave Obama's CIA the capability to run a "cleaner" war. After all, with their decision to ban torture and their commitment to closing Guantánamo and the black sites, the Obama administration officials had few options for housing terrorists. John Rizzo, the CIA's acting general counsel, contended that Obama's advisers did not explicitly discuss the trade-offs. "They never came out and said they would start killing people because they couldn't interrogate them, but the implication was unmistakable," he told a journalist. "Once the interrogation was gone, all that was left was the killing."[15] In short, Obama's CIA chose to kill suspected terrorists rather than capture and interrogate them.

With the escalation of the targeted killing program, Obama completed a process of restoring the CIA's license to kill that had begun decades earlier. During its first thirty years, the CIA had targeted foreign leaders only at presidential insistence—or so it claimed. In 1975, a special Senate investigating committee headed by Idaho Democrat Frank Church examined alleged assassination plots by the CIA and reported that the agency had tried to kill at least five foreign leaders.[16] President Gerald Ford responded to the revelations by issuing an executive order that prohibited assassinations by U.S. government employees, and his successors reaffirmed the ban.[17] However, during the Reagan administration, government lawyers began interpreting the executive order to allow "*pre-emptive neutralization* of anti-American terrorist groups which plan, support, or conduct hostile terrorist acts against U.S. citizens, interests, and property overseas," as a 1984 directive explained.[18] Reagan's successors maintained and expanded the CIA's authority to "neutralize" terrorists. Shortly after the terrorist attacks on the World Trade Center and the Pentagon on September 11, 2001, President George W. Bush signed a directive giving the CIA explicit authority to assassinate terrorists.[19] The Bush administration began using Predator drones in 2002 to locate alleged terrorists and then fire missiles at them.

President Obama significantly expanded the targeted killing program, increasing both the number of strikes and their frequency outside of the war zones in Afghanistan and Iraq. In the first year of Obama's presidency, the CIA conducted fifty-two drone strikes in Pakistan, compared to forty-eight during the entire Bush administration. That number escalated to 122 in 2010, before declining to just a handful by 2016. As the Pakistan drone strikes declined, the Obama administration began ramping up its assassination program in Yemen, peaking at forty-seven hits in 2012. Obama's CIA had also launched nineteen drone attacks against terrorists in Somalia by September 2016 and one in Libya.[20]

Obama officials escalated the killings in part because they had greater numbers of more accurate drones at their disposal, as the second-generation Reaper drone allowed its pilots to survey targets for longer periods, while new missiles proved smaller and more accurate. But Obama's advisers also embraced the targeted killing program as a smarter, more efficient way to wage war against terrorists. The Obama administration argued that the targeted killing program allowed the United States to eliminate the terrorist networks and thus avoid protracted wars.

Like the CIA, the Pentagon's secretive Joint Special Operations Command also used drones to kill people they considered America's enemies. The military initially launched the strikes in areas of open combat, including Iraq, Afghanistan, and eventually Syria. But the lines between the CIA's drone strikes and those of the military grew increasingly blurred over the years. Though the Pentagon maintained sole authority for the open warfare areas, it set up a drone program in Yemen parallel to that of the CIA.

The Obama administration not only ordered more drone strikes, but it also started a vigorous campaign to defend their legality.[21] Harold Koh, the State Department's legal adviser and an eminent scholar of human rights and constitutional law, insisted in a widely reported speech in 2010 that the Obama administration differed from its predecessor in many ways, including its commitment to "living our values by respecting the rule of law." In the war with Al-Qaeda, he said, "The United States has the authority under international law, and the responsibility to its citizens, to use force, including lethal force, to defend itself, including by targeting persons such as high-level al-Qaeda leaders who are planning attacks." Koh argued that the strikes never specifically targeted civilians; but if it seemed inevitable that civilians would die in the attack, then U.S. officials would carefully weigh the potential military benefits against the cost of innocent lives. Obama was still following the decades-old ban on assassinations, he said: "The use of lawful weapons systems—consistent with the applicable laws of war—for precision targeting of specific high-level belligerent leaders when acting in self-defense or during an armed conflict is not unlawful, and hence does not constitute 'assassination.'"[22]

Koh told of his personal involvement in helping to compile the administration's "kill list." Like all the Obama administration officials involved in the drone program, he emphasized the research and analysis that went into each decision to target a terrorist. "As the dean of Yale Law School I spent many, many hours looking at the résumés of young twenty-year-olds, students in their twenties, trying to figure out which ones should be admitted," he told his fellow lawyers in one public speech. "I now spend a comparable amount of time studying the résumés of terrorists, same age. Reading about how they were recruited. Their first mission. Their second mission. Often I know their background as intimately as I knew my students'."[23] In subsequent major policy speeches, Counterterrorism (and later CIA) chief John Brennan, Attorney General Holder, and Defense Department General Counsel Jeh Johnson elaborated on the legal justifications and underlined the administration's commitment to the rule of law.[24]

The Obama administration lawyers worked even harder to justify the drone executions of American citizens. In 2011, the CIA targeted and killed Anwar al-Awlaki, a New Mexico–born mullah who had preached at mosques in San Diego and Virginia before joining Al-Qaeda in Yemen. The missile that killed al-Awlaki also hit another American, an Al-Qaeda propagandist named Samir Khan. Shortly afterward, a Pentagon drone strike in Yemen killed a third American, al-Awlaki's teenage son, by accident.

The Justice Department's Office of Legal Counsel (OLC) had spent months preparing the legal justification for targeting the senior al-Awlaki. In secret memos, the acting chief of the OLC, David Barron, argued that the government's responsibility to protect public safety outweighed al-Awlaki's individual rights as a citizen.[25] The ACLU and the *New York Times* sued to see Barron's memos, and they won a favorable court decision in 2014. Obama planned to appeal the ruling, but the president changed his mind when he nominated Barron for a seat on the U.S. Court of Appeals and the memo controversy threatened to derail the confirmation process. Some senators warned that they would bottle up Barron's nomination unless Obama bowed to the court's decision and released the memos. Once the administration promised to comply, the Senate voted 53–45 to confirm Barron; the critics had disagreed with the administration's lack of transparency, not necessarily with the substance of Barron's reasoning.[26] The CIA's congressional overseers strongly supported the administration's legal case, with Intelligence Committee vice chair Senator Dianne Feinstein of California dismissing the senior al-Awlaki as a "so-called" American.[27]

Feinstein's support for drone strikes reflected the opinions of most Americans. Obama's targeted killing program remained his most popular policy. In 2012, according to a *Washington Post*–ABC News poll, 83 percent of Americans approved of Obama's use of drones against suspected terrorists. Only 4 percent strongly disapproved.[28] Pollsters did not ask the respondents why they approved of the strikes, leaving it unclear whether the policy resonated with voters because they believed it helped avoid lengthy wars and avert future attacks, or because they got visceral satisfaction from the revenge murders of accused terrorists.

The targeted killing program also produced profits for defense contractors and jobs for their employees, and therefore generated fervent support in Congress. The U.S. military allocated more than $4.4 billion to spend on unmanned aerial vehicles (UAV) in Fiscal Year 2017.[29] The total did not include drones used by the CIA, whose budget is secret. House members who represented districts with UAV production formed a "drone caucus," which at one point counted sixty members. Drone manufacturers like General Atomics, Northrop Grumman, and Lockheed Martin spent millions every year to lobby Congress to approve more spending on unmanned vehicles.[30]

Though the drone strikes were initially shrouded in secrecy, the American public did learn many specifics about the program thanks to aggressive reporting by national security reporters at elite newspapers and specialized blogs. A study by the Joan Shorenstein Center on the Press, Politics, and Public Policy in 2013 found that annual coverage by five major media outlets increased dramatically in Obama's first term, from 326 stories on the drone program in 2009 to 625 articles in 2012.[31] These stories revealed key aspects of the program, including the criteria for assembling the kill list and the potentially large numbers of civilians who died in the strikes.[32]

The media revelations about the targeted killings forced the administration to disclose more details about them. To demonstrate a commitment to transparency, the president in 2016 released statistics on drone and cruise missile strikes outside of official war zones. He also issued an executive order codifying "best practices" for reducing civilian casualties and charged the director of national intelligence with issuing an annual report on noncombatant deaths.[33] He claimed that these strikes had killed somewhere between 2,372 and 2,581 terrorists and 64 and 116 civilians from the time he took office until the end of 2015.[34] The total number of casualties caused by the strikes, especially the number of civilian casualties, was hotly contested by the president's critics. Nongovernmental organizations counted a significantly higher number of noncombatant deaths, from two to four times as many as the administration claimed.[35] Critics noted that forty-one civilians were killed in one 2009 air strike in Yemen alone, so the administration's estimate that only twenty-three to seventy-four additional civilians had been killed in the ensuing six years scarcely seemed credible.[36]

Critics used anecdotal evidence to argue that the drone strikes actually encouraged more terrorism, as the surviving relatives of the dead civilians vowed to take revenge on the United States.[37] "What we know of the U.S. is this is what they do to people like me. They uproot us, they kill us, they target us, without any reason. They turn our lives upside down," Faheem Qureshi, who was wounded in Obama's first drone strike, told a journalist. "Of course the U.S. is hated in that part of the world, and it's hated more because of what they've done to people like me."[38] Even some of the CIA officers who planned and executed the drone strikes felt ambivalent about them. Bush's and Obama's lawyers "had drawn up semantic arguments carefully delineating the difference between a targeted killing and an assassination," wrote Elliot Ackerman, a former CIA paramilitary officer. "But when the picture of the person you were trying to kill sat on your desk; when you watched the Predator strikes light up the night sky just across the border; and then, when you took that same picture and moved it into a file for archiving, it sure felt like assassination."[39]

It was special forces commandos, not drones, who carried out the most famous assassination of Obama's presidency. By early 2011, the CIA strongly suspected that Osama bin Laden was hiding out in a compound in Abbottabad, Pakistan, just a mile from that nation's premier military academy. The president considered launching a drone strike on the house. However, he rejected this option because a missile might incinerate bin Laden's corpse, making it impossible for the United States to know for certain that he had been killed. Moreover, an air strike would kill many civilians and might miss the main target. Instead, Obama ordered Navy Seals to raid the compound in the middle of the night and shoot the 9/11 mastermind at close range.[40] Secretary of State Hillary Clinton strongly supported the president's decision, and sat with him to watch a live video feed from outside the compound as the operation took place.[41]

The special forces troops, who accomplished their mission without losing any American lives, were technically under the command of the CIA for the raid. The Obama administration sometimes "sheep-dipped" special forces in this manner. Since countries like Pakistan refused to allow U.S. combat operations within their borders, the White House would circumvent the objections by transforming the soldiers into spies for the night.[42]

The success of the bin Laden raid boosted the president's popularity and even briefly earned praise for the president from Republicans. Former president George W. Bush hailed the attack. "This momentous achievement marks a victory for America, for people who seek peace around the world, and for all those who lost loved ones on September 11, 2001," he said in a statement.[43] Administration insiders told reporters of President Obama's resolve throughout the planning for the operation. "I worked for a lot of these guys and this is one of the most courageous calls . . . that I think I've ever seen a president make," Secretary of Defense Robert Gates told *60 Minutes*.[44] Hundreds of people gathered in New York and outside of the White House, waving flags and chanting "U.S.A.! U.S.A.!"[45]

Liberty and Security

While Obama's assassination policy enjoyed broad support, his surveillance program proved more controversial. Candidate Obama had criticized the Bush administration's mass surveillance programs for presenting "a false choice between the liberties we cherish and the security we provide."[46] Civil libertarians had hoped that his presidency would mark a new period of governmental commitment to transparency. But there were already signs in 2008 that Obama would begin to abandon what he later called his "healthy skepticism" about surveillance programs.[47] That year, while campaigning for the presidency, Senator Obama voted for legislation—amendments to the Foreign Intelligence Surveillance Act (FISA)—that legalized and institutionalized the Bush administration's warrantless surveillance program.

Early in his administration, the new president signaled his intention to continue Bush's surveillance policies. In February 2009, the nation's top intelligence chiefs, including the heads of the National Security Agency (NSA) and Federal Bureau of Investigation (FBI), met with the president and his legal advisers to brief him on their domestic espionage program. Obama and his aides were surprised by the extent of the spying: the NSA was secretly vacuuming up the records of telephone calls and emails of all Americans and analyzing the metadata to search for possible terrorist links. Unlike Bush's wiretap program, which had targeted specific individuals, this program involved collecting the records of everyone who made phone calls in the United States. As the intelligence leaders explained, the congressional intelligence committees had been briefed on the new program, and the FISA court had approved it. All three branches of government believed it was necessary, legal, and constitutional.

Obama and his team quickly agreed to continue Bush's mass surveillance program. The president and attorney general wanted to make sure that the NSA complied with all the directives of the FISA court, and Holder assigned Justice Department lawyer Todd Hinnen to oversee a review of the program. When the reviewers uncovered potential legal problems, such as failure to protect the identity of innocent Americans, the Obama administration fixed them. Officials never considered ending the program as a whole. The lawyers' job, Hinnen explained, was "not to decide what the intelligence community needed. Our job was to help them bring the tool they said they needed up to conform with the rule of law."[48] As long as the program passed legal muster, Obama gave it his blessing.

Over the next few years, the NSA's metadata dragnet stayed secret as Congress passed and the president signed bills that continued the legal authority for Obama's surveillance programs. In 2011, the renewal of the Patriot Act included extensions of some of its most controversial provisions, including Section 215, which gave the government power to compel businesses, such as telecommunications companies, to release records that were "relevant" to an investigation. Obama also signed in 2012 an extension of the FISA amendments act.

But in March 2012, two of the intelligence community's congressional overseers began questioning whether the Obama administration's surveillance programs were legal and constitutional. As members of the Senate Intelligence Committee, Democrats Mark Udall of Colorado and Ron Wyden of Oregon had been briefed on the metadata vacuuming. They believed that secret courts had given too much power to the government's eavesdroppers. But because the briefings were classified, they could not disclose any specific information, and their complaints were somewhat opaque. "We believe," they wrote in an open letter to Attorney General Holder, "most Americans would be stunned to learn the details of how these secret court opinions have interpreted Section 215." Because of secret rulings, they said, there was a "significant gap between what most Americans *think* the law allows and what the government *secretly claims* the law allows."[49]

The senators' specific concerns remained mysterious until June 5, 2013, when the *Guardian* newspaper published one of the most significant national security leaks in American history. Under the headline "NSA Collecting Phone Records of Millions of Verizon Customers Daily," reporter Glenn Greenwald unveiled a secret FISA court order that compelled a subsidiary of the telecommunications giant to hand over all the phone records in its systems. "The document shows for the first time," the story read, "that under the Obama administration the communication records of millions of U.S. citizens are being collected indiscriminately and in bulk—regardless of whether they are suspected of any wrongdoing."[50] The next day, the *Washington Post* revealed that the program reached far beyond Verizon. Citing and publishing another top-secret document, writers Laura Poitras and Barton Gellman reported that the NSA and FBI were "tapping directly into the central servers of nine leading U.S. Internet companies, extracting audio and video chats, photographs, e-mails, documents, and connection logs that enable analysts to track foreign targets."[51] Edward Snowden, a former employee of an NSA contractor, soon emerged in Hong Kong and took credit for leaking the documents.

Obama responded to the stories at first by castigating Snowden and defending the program. "It's important to recognize that you can't have 100 percent security and also then have 100 percent privacy and zero inconvenience," he said. "We're going to have to make some choices as a society."[52] Because media coverage of the Snowden case focused on the personality and motivations of the leaker himself rather than on the substance of his leak, Obama initially found it easy to ignore or dismiss concerns about the surveillance program.[53] But civil liberties groups continued to pressure him to enact reforms to safeguard Americans' privacy. In response, he set up a presidential commission to review the program.

Obama's Review Group on Intelligence and Communications Technology recommended forty-six reforms, including a ban on NSA bulk collection of phone records. But the members also urged the Obama administration to find a way to give the NSA some access to the data without holding the records itself. A year and a half later, in June 2015, the USA Freedom Act extended the relevant section of the Patriot Act and adopted some reforms and controls on bulk data collection. Under the new act, the NSA could look through the telecommunications companies' metadata, but only after it identified specific phone numbers and individuals and obtained a court order.[54]

Civil liberties groups were unsure whether to celebrate the measure's reforms or condemn its compromises and equivocations. Jameel Jaffer, the American Civil Liberties Union's deputy legal director, hailed the passage of "the most important surveillance reform bill since 1978," but then cautioned that its reforms were hardly comprehensive. "The bill leaves many of the government's most intrusive and overbroad surveillance powers untouched," he said, "and it makes only very modest adjustments to disclosure and transparency requirements."[55] The USA Freedom Act compromise was a typical solution for the Obama administration: there were more safeguards for civil liberties, but the basic structure of the counterterrorism program remained unchanged.

The War on Leakers

Obama initially pledged that his administration would encourage, rather than punish, government whistleblowers who revealed abuses and incompetence within their agencies. His presidential transition webpage proclaimed in 2008: "We need to empower federal employees as watchdogs of wrongdoing and partners in performance. Barack Obama will strengthen whistleblower laws to protect federal workers who expose waste, fraud, and abuse of authority in government."[56]

Instead, civil libertarians were again disappointed by Obama's performance in office. Obama's Justice Department greatly increased the number of prosecutions of whistleblowers for violating the Espionage Act. Federal prosecutors charged eight leakers with espionage—more than all the previous presidential administrations combined.

The Espionage Act had been passed in 1917 with the goal of stopping the theft of government secrets and their transmittal to foreign powers. It was notably used against a whistleblower who leaked secret information to the media in 1971, when Daniel Ellsberg gave the Pentagon Papers to newspapers. The judge threw out Ellsberg's case because of prosecutorial misconduct. Federal prosecutors used the Espionage Act against leakers two more times over the next thirty-five years: in 1985, against Samuel Loring Morison, who leaked pictures of Soviet aircraft to reporters; and in 2005, when the Bush administration targeted Lawrence Franklin, a Pentagon analyst who disclosed intelligence on Iran to a pro-Israel lobbying group in the United States. Franklin eventually served ten months in jail on the charge.[57]

Then, in 2009, the president's new director of national intelligence, Dennis Blair, vowed to become much more aggressive in pursuing alleged leakers. "My background is in the Navy," retired admiral Blair told the *New York Times*, "and it is good to hang an admiral once in a while as an example to the others. We were hoping to get somebody and make people realize that there are consequences to this and it needed to stop."[58] Blair and other security officials worried that technological changes had made it much simpler and faster for whistleblowers to transmit huge troves of documents to the public. In the Internet age, leakers like Snowden could instantly download secrets and sneak them out of a secure facility, and later email them to confederates around the globe. The recipients of the documents could then post them online for the whole world to see. Given the ease of stealing secrets in the twenty-first century, government officials wanted to make potential leakers think twice before they loaded national secrets onto their flash drives.

Moreover, the president himself had little patience for those who went outside the law to pursue their own policy agendas. Despite Senator Obama's rhetorical commitment to protecting government employees who exposed fraud and abuse, President Obama saw the people who leaked the secrets of his administration as criminal leakers, rather than heroic whistleblowers, and resolved to hold them accountable.

Over the next several years, the Obama administration charged eight government employees or former employees with violating the Espionage Act. One of those accused, James Hitselberger, took classified documents for his own archival collection at the Hoover Institution. The rest allegedly leaked information on government malfeasance or illegality to the media. They included Thomas Drake of the NSA, who disclosed evidence of fraud and illegal surveillance at his former agency; John Kiriakou of the CIA, who confirmed the existence of the CIA's torture program and leaked the name of an officer who had been involved in it; Jeffrey Sterling of the CIA, who revealed to reporter James Risen of the *New York Times* the details of a U.S. program to sabotage Iran's nuclear facilities; and Stephen Jim-woo Kim, who leaked information on North Korea's nuclear tests to James Rosen of Fox News. The Obama Justice Department also initially pursued the recipients of some of this classified information, including reporters Rosen and Risen. The two biggest leak cases of the Obama administration featured Snowden, who took refuge in Russia to avoid extradition on Espionage Act charges, and Chelsea Manning, who was sentenced to thirty-five years in federal prison for giving hundreds of thousands of secret documents to WikiLeaks.[59]

In Manning's case, at least, President Obama decided that his administration had been overzealous in its determination to punish whistleblowers. On January 17, 2017, three days before the end of his presidency, Obama commuted Manning's sentence, paving the way for her release in May. Right before Obama's decision, White House spokesman Josh Earnest explained that the president believed that Manning's case was much different from that of Snowden. "Chelsea Manning is somebody who went through the military criminal justice process, was exposed to due process, was found guilty, was sentenced for her crimes, and she acknowledged wrongdoing," he said. "Mr. Snowden fled into the arms of an adversary and has sought refuge in a country that most recently made a concerted effort to undermine confidence in our democracy."[60] As President Obama left office, the government of Russia agreed to extend Snowden's asylum.

Normalizing the Unimaginable

Back in the 1970s, in the aftermath of the Vietnam War and Watergate, the CIA had defended itself against charges that it was a "rogue elephant on a rampage," recklessly trying to kill the nation's enemies without presidential approval. Richard Helms, the agency's former chief, insisted to the Church Committee that it did not occur to him to ask the president or his advisers for explicit authority to kill Cuba's Fidel Castro. "I didn't see how one would have expected that a thing like killing or murdering or assassination would become a part of a large group of people sitting around a table in the United States government," he testified. When Senator Church pressed Helms on whether the president had "clearly conveyed" a command to murder Castro, Helms protested that no intelligence chief would ask his president to leave a record of such an order: "I can't imagine anybody wanting something in writing saying I have just charged Mr. Jones to go out and shoot Mr. Smith."[61]

By 2010, Richard Helms's scenario had become not only imaginable but ordinary. A large group of people sat around a table in the U.S. government discussing assassination almost every week, and the U.S. president routinely put his orders to kill in writing. Under Barack Obama's leadership, American liberals embraced exactly the sort of national security policies that they had condemned in the aftermath of the Vietnam War. Obama continued to bring Bush's policies into alignment with U.S. and international law, but otherwise he came to terms with what he saw as the unpleasant necessities of the post-9/11 state.

15

A Hyphenated Legacy?

OBAMA'S AFRICA POLICY

Jacob Dlamini

After all, I have the blood of Africa within me.
—PRESIDENT BARACK OBAMA, 2009[1]

Of the three continents of which Barack Obama's cosmopolitan and peripatetic upbringing spoke, none loomed larger than Africa. Land of the father he barely knew but hankered after and home to hundreds of relatives whose (often bitter) life experiences meant that the world's second-largest continent could never be entirely an idealized and mythical fatherland, Africa constituted a complex part of Obama's hyphenated identity. Whereas the average African American, assuming she cared, could speak only in the abstract of her connection to Africa, Obama could speak in both emotional but also real terms of the places in which his immediate relatives lived or lay buried. No wonder, then, that when Obama was elected president in 2008, some expected that he would have a special relationship with Africa. He did not. As this chapter argues, it would not help to look to Obama's hyphenated identity in order to understand his Africa policy. In fact, any assessment of President Obama's Africa policy must contend with at least three factors: the nature and real-world effects of the Africa-related programs of the man whom Obama succeeded in the White House; the political and symbolic importance of the historic fact that Obama was the U.S.'s first

black president, and, third, the actual policies that guided Obama's relations with Africa.

Contending with the first factor means coming to terms with what it
meant for Obama to follow George W. Bush into the White House; engaging with the second factor means grappling with the role of race in Obama's
dealings with Africa; while examining the third means taking seriously
Obama's role as a historic agent with a range of policy tools at his disposal,
some of which he used and many of which he did not use. By looking at
these three factors in tandem, we are able to come to a balanced apprecia-
tion of Obama's Africa policy. We are able to see the extent to which Obama
was constrained by the contingencies of his office and context as well as
the extent to which he was able to strike out on his own, breaking with his
predecessor in the process. Obama treated the continent of his father only
in relation to what he saw as the strategic interests of the United States.
Africa did not hold any special racial purchase for America's first black
president.

If it was Obama's good fortune, at least on the domestic front, to succeed Bush as president, that benefit did not extend to the foreign front,
especially when it came to the two men's policies on Africa. In 2002, Bush
created the Millennium Challenge Account, a bilateral U.S. development
assistance program intended to reduce poverty and promote economic
growth in the world. In 2003, Bush launched the President's Emergency
Plan for AIDS Relief (PEPFAR), a five-year, $15 billion program to fight
AIDS in Africa and the Caribbean. Bush followed this up in 2004 with
World Bank reforms that led to the conversion of 45 percent of the loans
issued by the bank's International Development Agency into grants. In
2005, Bush pushed the G8 to support full debt relief for the world's most
heavily indebted countries, the majority of which were in Africa.[2] In 2008,
Bush appointed the first fulltime U.S. ambassador to the African Union
(AU), making the United States the first major Western country to have a
permanent diplomatic mission to Africa's premier political body. This came
a year after AFRICOM, one of six U.S. military commands around the
world, began operating from Germany. These, then, were some of the initiatives that defined Bush's Africa policy. For a man who began his campaign in 2000 for U.S. president by saying the United States had no vital
interests in Africa, they were substantial indeed.[3] In fact, in many assessments of the Bush presidency, Africa remains the one unblemished spot.[4]
Such was the positive legacy of Bush's Africa policy that Obama could not
better it. This is not to say that Obama could not have tried to do better than

his predecessor, even with the Republican opposition that he faced. But that would have required the allocation of what journalist Howard French called "policy bandwidth" to Africa.[5] Obama did not do that. Like Bush, Obama chose to see Africa through a security lens and the prism of Islamist terror; unlike Bush, he could not complement this with the kinds of largesse that Bush was able to offer.

How was Bush able to do this, effectively tripling U.S. aid to Africa to an estimated $8 billion by the time he left office in January 2009? As Princeton Lyman, a former U.S. ambassador to Nigeria and South Africa, said: "Bush was able to triple aid to Africa because he had a Republican Congress that did not care how much he spent."[6] Bush governed as a war president. As his administration said in its 2002 National Security Strategy, "The events of September 11, 2001, taught us that weak states, like Afghanistan, can pose as great a danger to our national interests as strong states."[7] Even Bush's support for debt relief was framed in terms of U.S. geopolitical interests. As Eric Helleiner and Geoffrey Cameron point out, "After Iraq had fallen to U.S. forces in April 2003, U.S. policymakers had immediately recognized that the economic reconstruction of Iraq would require a dramatic reduction in that country's external debt."[8] With Iraq owing foreign creditors about $120 billion, the United States pushed for full debt cancellation. But the country held only $4 billion of Iraq's debt. The rest belonged to Kuwait, Saudi Arabia, and G8 countries such as France, Germany, and Russia— which had opposed the Iraqi invasion.[9]

In truth, however, the U.S. Congress was also not as compliant as Lyman made it sound. In fact, it was largely because of Congress's refusal to pay for the reconstruction of Iraq that the Bush administration pushed for full debt relief for the world's most indebted countries. Having been shamed by French president Jacques Chirac at the G8 summit in June 2004 for pushing for Iraqi debt relief while ignoring that of other poor countries, the United States suddenly announced its support for full debt cancellation.[10] Bush was able to do this in part because there had developed a coalition on both the left and the right in support of debt relief. Anticapitalists on the left and Christian evangelicals on the right supported debt cancellation, giving Bush the leverage he needed to take the stance he took.

When Bush assumed the presidency in 2001, there were civil wars in Angola, the Congo-Kinshasa, Liberia, Sierra Leone, and the Sudan. By the end of Bush's first term, all but the conflict in the Congo had ended. The fighting in the Sudan, until then Africa's longest-running civil war, ended during Bush's second term in 2005 with a peace agreement. The deal set the stage for the independence of South Sudan, which came about toward the end of Obama's first term in 2011. Bush also increased funding for the U.S. Agency for International Development (USAID). Andrew Natsios, who ran the agency from 2001 to 2006, said: "[The U.S. Agency for International Development] went from $150 million when I started to $800 million by the time [Bush] left office in assistance, and much of that was to Africa. . . . When I started at [US]AID the total development program, not including food aid and or emergencies for civil wars, . . . it went from $1.2 billion when [Bush] started in early 2001 to $7 billion when he left office. So it was [a] 600 percent increase. That's a massive increase."[11]

However, by the time Obama succeeded Bush in January 2009, the U.S. economy was in a ditch and Obama faced a bloc of congressional Republicans not prepared to deal with him on any issue. Obama could not offer the kinds of lavish programs that Bush had offered. He could merely inherit (with substantial room for tweaks, for sure) what Bush had put in place. So PEPFAR stayed—but without the religious injunctions that emphasized abstinence; so too did the African Growth and Opportunity Act (AGOA), the trade deal first introduced by President Bill Clinton in 2000 and renewed by Bush to give select African countries preferential access to U.S. markets.

But the biggest continuity between Bush and Obama concerned Bush's War on Terror. Bush had responded to the 9/11 terrorist attacks in part by targeting the Sahel—that strip of the Sahara running from West to East Africa—for heightened surveillance and counterinsurgency. Believing that the region, majority Muslim, could become a breeding and training ground for Islamist insurgencies unless better managed through strong states, the Bush administration set up military alliances that Obama took over and extended when he became president. In fact, by the time Obama left office in January 2017, he had extended Bush's forays into the Sahel so extensively that the United States had military personnel in thirteen African countries. Such extensive presence made it easier for the United States to help Africans fight the Ebola epidemic that broke out in Sierra Leone in February 2014. However, absent from Obama's relations with Africa was any consideration of Africans as, first and foremost, "economic beings."[12] This is in contrast with China, for example, which Obama saw as both an economic and a military player.

It may be asked: How different were U.S. policies toward Africa compared to other regions of the world? Here is something that might help us answer that question: There are more Muslims in Africa than there are in all of Arabia. Until recently, Islam in Africa was defined by its openness, not its militancy. Whatever traces one finds of intolerance and outright terrorism among Muslims in Africa (notably in West, East, and North Africa), these have had to do more with the importation of intolerant strains, such as Saudi-inspired Wahhabism, into Africa. To be sure, these importations have taken on lives of their own to a point where terrorism by Muslim extremists in Africa cannot be blamed squarely on Saudi sponsorship. Starting with Al-Shabbab in Somalia, Boko Haram in Nigeria and Cameroon, and ISIS in North Africa, each of these insurgencies has drawn oxygen from a legitimate well of grievances in each place. Al-Shabbab owes its existence largely to the collapse of the authoritarian regime of Siad Barre in the 1990s and has continued to thrive in the gaps created by not simply the loss of territorial Somalia but also the incompetence of neighbors such as Kenya; Boko Haram—currently on the back foot in West Africa—would not be half the menace it has been had the Nigerian state taken its responsibilities, especially in the northeastern regions of Nigeria, seriously. As for ISIS in Africa, we must wonder if Obama's 2011 decision to support the British and the French in their drive to oust Libyan dictator Muammar Gaddafi was not, in fact, one of his more consequential mistakes in office.

Not only did the ouster of Gaddafi pit Obama against the rest of Africa, it also created a power vacuum in Libya, making it possible for ISIS to gain a North African foothold while also depriving European states such as Spain, Portugal, and Italy of an ally in the management of human smuggling across the Mediterranean. Almost to a man (only one of Africa's fifty-four countries is led by a woman), African leaders opposed the toppling of Gaddafi on the grounds that the United Nations mandate authorizing such a mission was obtained under false pretenses and that the mission itself showed Western disdain for African sovereignty. The Africans had a point. But so committed was Obama to the ousting of Gaddafi he did not listen to his African counterparts. In this sense, Obama's attitude toward Africa was no different from that of Bush when he ignored African protests (including by Nelson Mandela) to invade Iraq. However, the discord between Obama and his African peers did not prevent Obama from working with African leaders on a range of issues, especially security.

But it did bedevil U.S. efforts to find an African "home" for AFRICOM. Since it began operations in 2007, AFRICOM and its two-thousand-strong personnel have been based in Germany. No African country will host the command. South Africa, the dominant country in southern Africa, is not keen on the command and is definitely not keen on any of its neighbors playing host; the Kenyan government, which dominates East Africa, might be open to hosting the mission, but as one U.S. military official told me, the Kenyans can hardly protect themselves so how would they protect what would essentially be a massive gated community with its own schools, hospitals, and shops? Besides, East Africa is too close to Middle Eastern hot spots for U.S. comfort. Then there is Nigeria, the West African powerhouse, which also does not want AFRICOM in its backyard.

———

What, then, of race and Obama's relations with Africa? In August 2006, a South African newspaper editor based in Johannesburg asked S'Thembiso Msomi, one of his political correspondents, to fly down to Cape Town for a speech by a "little-known" U.S. senator named Barack Obama.[13] The senator, who was on a two-week tour of five African countries,[14] had already been talked about as a future U.S. president following his well-received speech at the Democratic convention in Boston in July 2004. But Msomi, a seasoned journalist who followed American politics, was skeptical about the hype surrounding Obama. Having observed Jesse Jackson fail twice in his bid to secure the Democratic Party's nomination for president, Msomi doubted that a black man could become president of the United States. Recalling his grandfather's claim that "America will never be ready for a Negro as president," Msomi passed on going to Cape Town. He had far more exciting stories to chase than travel 784 miles to listen to a U.S. politician on a "senatorial safari."[15] Obama's next stop was Kenya, where Kenyans treated him like a "rock star and returning 'son of the soil.'"[16] But when Obama spoke out against corruption in the East African country, the Kenyan government dismissed his criticism as the "very poorly informed" musings of a "junior senator."[17] However, the Kenyan government changed its tune in November 2008 when the junior senator from Illinois became the forty-fourth president of the United States. Mwai Kibaki, the Kenyan president, said, "The victory of Senator Obama is our own victory because of his roots here in Kenya. As a country, we are full of pride for his success."[18] Kenya declared a public holiday to celebrate Obama's victory.

Msomi's skepticism about the "little-known senator" and the disdain for Obama the "junior senator" shown initially by the Kenyan government are worth recalling, if only to remind ourselves that nothing about Obama's relationship with Africa was predetermined. When assessing Obama's Africa policy, we would do well to go beyond his blackness. We would be better served, in other words, by a postracial approach to an examination of President Obama's Africa policy.[19] Focusing narrowly on the racial aspect of Obama's relations with Africa would limit us to the merely symbolic—important as that is in a racialized world—without telling us much about how this child of a father from Kenya and a mother from Kansas related to Africa as president. What was Obama's Africa policy and what effect, if any, did his identity as a self-described African American have on this policy? What was the role of the hyphen between "African" and "American" in Obama's policy toward Africa? Did the hyphen serve as a bridge between Africa and America—there but not always easy to cross—or as the sign of a split? I would argue that any assessment of the racial aspect of Obama's Africa policy must begin with the observation that even though Obama identifies as African American, the "African" in that definition is adjectival, describing that which comes after: American. The stress always falls on "American." This is not to say that Africa did not matter to President Obama. It did. But it mattered only in relation to what President Obama saw as the strategic interests of the United States in Africa. Put yet another way: Africa did not hold any special place in the heart of the first black president of the United States. Of course, Obama cared about Africa and its people but that did not translate into any special policies. In fact, one U.S. government official said: "There was a significant vacuum in terms of Obama's engagement with Africa."[20] He paid the place no special attention.

By insisting that we take our assessment of Obama's Africa policy beyond questions of race, I do not mean to suggest that the two parts of his identity bear no historical weight, or that the fact that he was the first black president of the United States did not matter. Rather, I intend to caution us against readings of Obama's Africa policy that, ironically, would see those keen to emphasize Obama's "Africanness" mired in the same murky swamps as the birther movement, whose insistence on Obama's illegitimacy was founded on what this movement saw as his foreignness or, if you will, his "Kenyanness." This caution is necessary because it also serves as a useful counter to the right-wing cant advanced by the likes of Dinesh D'Souza and Boris Johnson: that President Obama harbored a secret anti-West agenda. D'Souza claimed that Obama, who barely knew his father, was "still trying to apply his father's discredited formulas from the 1950s even though they have no relevance to the world we live in today."[21] D'Souza had no evidence for this claim other than the fact of Obama's blackness. That is, D'Souza read a certain kind of politics onto Obama's skin. For D'Souza, it was enough that Obama was a black man and that he identified as such to assume that Obama could only ever relate to Africa through the prism of race.

Still, there is no denying that a wave of Obamamania swept across Africa when Obama was elected U.S. president in November 2008, making him one of the most popular figures on the continent.[22] There is also no denying Obama's adoption by Africans. Nelson Mandela, the former president of South Africa, said, "Your victory has demonstrated that no person anywhere in the world should not dare to dream of wanting to change the world for a better place."[23] Umaru Yar'Adua, the president of Nigeria, noted: "Obama's election has finally broken the greatest barrier of prejudice in human history. For us in Nigeria, we have a great lesson to draw from this historic event."[24] A BBC poll conducted during the 2008 election found that Obama was the preferred candidate of 71 percent of Nigerians.[25] A BBC poll in July 2016 found that 95 percent of Kenyans viewed Obama's election and two-term presidency positively.[26] This was up from the 87 percent of Kenyans who expressed preference for Obama when he first ran in 2008.[27]

To be sure, there were countries in Africa where support for Obama declined in his eight years in office. In Nigeria, Obama's approval rating dropped from 88 percent in 2012 to 74 percent in 2016, while in Ghana the number of people who approved of Obama dipped from 78 percent in 2012 to 70 percent in 2016.[28] However, with regard to Africa overall, Obama left the White House much as he entered it: widely popular and with high approval ratings. It would be easy to see in Obama's high approval ratings in Africa an expression of racial pride among Africans. But that would be a poor substitute for an assessment of Obama's Africa policy. For example, why did his support decline in Ghana, the first sub-Saharan country to gain independence (in 1957) and to be visited by President Obama in July 2009? Might the drop in support for Obama in Nigeria, Africa's most populous country and the scene of a protracted Islamic insurgency, have something to do with the thrust of Obama's counterterrorism policies in Africa? We cannot answer these questions correctly if we limit ourselves to questions of race. We can only answer them if we take seriously the fact that, despite his hyphenated identity, Obama was above all a U.S. president. This does not mean that we can or indeed must ignore Obama's African heritage.

What, then, of that heritage? Speaking about the divorce of Obama's mother Stanley Ann Dunham and father Barack Obama senior, the historian Ali Mazrui said that it could turn out to be "one of the most significant matrimonial breakups in history."[29] Mazrui said Obama would probably not have become U.S. president if his parents had stayed together, as he would have been raised more African than American. Mazrui did not explain the meaning of each category but gestured at the different life chances offered by each. Obama, in fact, might have been just "another African sending remittances to Kenya," Mazrui said.[30] Mazrui, himself a Kenyan, said Obama's parents might even have moved to Kenya to raise their family there. There is no mistaking Mazrui's cynicism about what might have happened to an "African" Obama. To understand Mazrui's cynicism, we must remember that Mazrui, who died in 2014, was a member of that generation of African intellectuals that came of age at the height of Africa's decolonization in the 1960s but was driven into exile by the failure of Africa to translate the promise of postcolonial freedom into reality. Like Obama's father, who moved to the United States to take advantage of a scholarship program for African students sponsored by the U.S. government, Mazrui came of age at a time when many people, including Barack Obama senior and Mazrui himself, believed that they could lead Africa into a bright postcolonial future. They were disappointed. Mazrui ended up teaching in the United States; Obama senior, after failing to find a job in independent Kenya in keeping with his status as a former Harvard University student, died at the young age of forty-six, an embittered, abusive drunk in a corrupt and tribalist Kenya.

As a number of African commentators have pointed out, some half in jest, if Obama had indeed been born and raised in his father's Kenya, he would still have had a better chance of being elected president of the United States than of his father's Kenya. Despite fifty-three years of independence, Kenya has yet to have a president from the Luo, the ethnic group to which Obama's father belonged. According to the historian Ibrahim Sundiata, "Government figures show that a Kenyan born in Luoland today can expect to live several years less than one born in Kikuyuland."[31] Kikuyuland is of course where three of Kenya's four presidents since independence come from. President Obama knows this Kenya intimately.[32] "When my cousin in Kenya complains that it's impossible to find work unless he's paid a bribe to some official in the ruling party, he hasn't been brainwashed by Western ideas," says Obama in his book *The Audacity of Hope*.[33] In his younger years, Obama might have looked to Africa as a "new promised land, full of ancient traditions and sweeping vistas, noble struggles and talking drums," but he had long been disabused of such romantic notions by the time he took the oath of office in January 2009.[34] Flying to Kenya in 1988 to visit his late father's grave, Obama wondered: What if the only tie binding him to his father and to Africa was a "name, a blood type, or white people's scorn?"[35] So what bound him to Africa? Was there something in his relationship with Africa that translated into U.S. policy on Africa during his time in office?

The one area that, for some observers, has drawn the sharpest contrast between Bush and Obama concerns each man's respective position on HIV/AIDS in Africa. Bush's President's Emergency Plan for AIDS Relief (PEPFAR) set aside a guaranteed $15 billion to be used over a five-year period to prevent, treat, and research HIV/AIDS.[36] About 100,000 people in sub-Saharan Africa were on antiretrovirals (ARVs) before Bush introduced PEPFAR; by the time he left office in 2009, an estimated two million Africans were on ARVs.[37] In 2005, Bush launched a $1.2 billion initiative to tackle malaria. "There's no reason for little babies to be dying of mosquito bites around the world," Bush said.[38] Even some of Bush's foes praised his policy on HIV/AIDS in Africa. Bono, the lead singer of the band U2, told *Daily Show* host Jon Stewart: "I know that's hard for you to accept but George kind of knocked it out of the park. I can tell you, and I'm actually here to tell you that America now has five million people being kept alive by these drugs. That's something that everyone should know."[39]

But Bush's HIV/AIDS policy was not without controversy. A precondition for the use of PEPFAR funds was that about 20 percent of the money be used on programs to promote abstinence. The money could also not be used to support needle-sharing schemes. Walter C. Carrington, who served as U.S. ambassador to Senegal in 1980–1981 and to Nigeria in 1993–1997, said, "A conventional wisdom has developed that George W. Bush's Africa policy was one of the most successful in American history. How could it be otherwise with three such accomplished blacks in the highest rungs of the Department of State and on the National Security Council. However, it is probably time to temper that nostalgia with a dose of reality."[40] Carrington went on:

> The number one example offered in support of an enlightened Bush policy is ... [PEPFAR]. ... However, it was hobbled by religion-driven requirements such as promoting abstinence and forbidding funds to be spent on condoms and safe-sex education. Despite the millions spent, a recent report in the *Annals of Medicine* reveals that the rate of new infections in the PEPFAR countries has not been slowed, but is in fact on the rise. Uganda, which had been the signal country for reducing the spread of AIDS, found its progress reversed after adopting the PEPFAR strictures.[41]

If Bush had both a pragmatic and a sentimental approach toward a poor hapless Africa verging on the abstract, Obama's Africa was an all-too-real place peopled by grandparents, aunts, and cousins; if Bush's policy toward Africa was founded in large part on his no-doubt sincere concern with the African body—as can be seen in the emphasis placed by his Africa AIDS policy on reforming the behavior of Africans through abstinence pro-grams—Obama's policy toward Africa was unsentimental, if a tad patron-izing at times. Obama could speak second-hand about the postcolonial frus-trations experienced by his Harvard-educated father in Kenya, but he could certainly speak first-hand about Africa's potential and the frustrations felt by his cousins and half-siblings in Kenya. Recall the passage in *Dreams from My Father* where, visiting Kenya in 1988, Obama lands at the airport in Nai-robi only to be told that the airline has misplaced his luggage. Airline offi-cials fail to return his luggage at the promised time. It is only when Obama is introduced to someone who knows the Big Man at the airline, a Mr. Ma-duri, that his suitcase reappears.[42] As Obama leaves Maduri's office, he sees the portrait of another Big Man hanging on a wall in the building. The Big Man is Jomo Kenyatta, independent Kenya's first president.

It was men like Kenyatta that Obama had in mind when he delivered his first major address in a sub-Saharan country as U.S. president. Addressing the Ghanaian Parliament on July 11, 2009, Obama declared the era of Big Men in Africa over, saying: "Africa's future is up to Africans."[43] Explaining why he had chosen Ghana for his first official trip to sub-Saharan Africa, Obama said: "I have come here to Ghana for a simple reason: The 21st century will be shaped by what happens not just in Rome or Moscow or Washington, but by what happens in Accra as well." Obama noted that for far too long the West had treated Africa more like a mendicant than a part-ner. But he also pointed out the many problems that could not be blamed simply on the West. "Countries like Kenya had a per capita economy larger than South Korea's when I was born. They have badly been outpaced. Dis-ease and conflict have ravaged parts of the African continent." He must have been too polite to mention Ghana by name because it, too, had been on par with South Korea in 1957.

A remarkable feature of Obama's Ghana speech was the absence of any sentimental tosh.[44] Yes, he told his hosts about his paternal grandfather who worked as a cook for the British in Kenya; he reminded them that he, too, had the blood of Africa coursing through his veins and that his family's story encompassed "both the tragedies and triumphs of the larger African story." But Obama's speech was not, to use a South African expression, a *boeti-boeti* story—a brotherly chat between siblings. He was there as a potential partner to offer Ghana and the rest of Africa a partnership "grounded in mutual responsibility and mutual respect." He was there to talk about what became a consistent theme of his Africa policy, namely the need for executive legitimacy, as well as impersonal and accountable institutions in Africa. Development, Obama the constitutional scholar said, needed good governance. "Africa doesn't need strong men; it needs strong institutions"— accountable and functional institutions. He said, with an implicit nod to the Iraq debacle created by his predecessor, that the United States would not impose any system of government on any country. "But what America will do is increase assistance for responsible individuals and responsible institutions."

In 2012, the White House published the U.S. Strategy toward Sub-Saharan Africa, setting out Obama's policy on Africa. As Obama explained in the preface, the policy built on the address he gave in Ghana in 2009. According to the document, there were four pillars to the U.S. strategy toward sub-Saharan Africa: strengthening democratic institutions in Africa; spurring economic growth, trade, and investment; advancing peace and security; and promoting opportunity and development. The policy statement was indeed an elaboration of the Ghana speech. In terms of the policy, the United States would support "key reformers and institutions of government at all levels to promote the rule of law, strengthen checks on executive power, and incorporate responsive governance practices." A good example of this in practice was the $500,000 that USAID gave to South Africa's Office of the Public Protector, a constitutional body set up in post-apartheid South Africa to keep the country's executive power in check. The money was intended to beef up the public protector's capacity to fight corruption.[45]

One of the most important initiatives of the Obama administration is the Kleptocracy Asset Recovery Initiative, launched in 2010 and led by teams from the Department of Justice and the Federal Bureau of Investigations. The initiative's focus is global but among those targeted so far are Teodoro Nguema Obiang Mangue, son of the president of Equatorial Guinea, one of the very few places in Africa colonized by Spain. Nguema, a minister on a $100,000 annual salary in his father's cabinet, spent more than $300 million on Ferraris, a Gulfstream jet, a California mansion, and Michael Jackson's jacket from the video for the hit song "Thriller." The U.S. government, which seized Obiang's U.S. possessions, announced in October 2015 that $30 million from the sale of these assets would be given to the citizens of Equatorial Guinea, a poverty-stricken country cursed with oil.[46] The same initiative has also gone after the family of Sani Abacha, the Nigerian dictator whose legendary looting of the Nigerian economy only ended when he died suddenly in office in 1998. Abacha had taken over in a coup in 1993.

As part of the Obama administration's commitment to the strengthening of democratic institutions and human rights, Obama also openly supported the rights of LGBTQ communities in Africa. Speaking during a state visit to Kenya in July 2015, Obama said, "When you start treating people differently, because they're different, that's the path whereby freedoms begin to erode. And bad things happen."[47] President Uhuru Kenyatta, Kenya's richest man and son of Kenya's first president, responded, "There are some things that we must admit that we don't share." David Bahati, an anti–gay rights activist and Ugandan legislator, was less diplomatic: "The good thing with the West is that we know that Obama can influence the world only up to 2016."[48] Lest we think that Bahati is some exotic African bigot, we must remember that he is, in fact, part of a global evangelical network that includes Sam Brownback, the Republican governor of Kansas, and Jim Inhofe, a Republican senator from Oklahoma. "I'm a Jesus guy, and I have a heart for Africa," Inhofe said.[49] It might also be worth reminding ourselves that U.S. evangelicals helped draft Uganda's draconian anti–gay rights laws.

Obama visited Africa four times during his presidency, his last visit coming in July 2015. While he certainly spoke out for LGBTQ rights and against corruption, he devoted the bulk of his African visits to economic and trade issues, which constitute the second pillar of his Africa policy. Here, Obama had a number of signature initiatives. His most substantial initiative is Power Africa. The program, launched in 2013, seeks to double access to electricity in sub-Saharan Africa. The White House said at the time of the launch that a $7 billion investment spread over five years would boost access to electricity in Africa by twenty million new homes and businesses.[50] In 2015, Obama "tripled those initial goals to 60 million electricity connections and 30,000 megawatts of energy."[51] Another key Obama project is Feed the Future. The project seeks to fight global hunger and to boost food security in nineteen countries, twelve of which are in Africa, by improving agricultural production, trade, and economic development.

Feed the Future is connected to the African Growth and Opportunity Act, which gave thirty-nine sub-Saharan African countries preferential access to the U.S. market in 2000 and was reauthorized by Obama in 2015. According to Florizelle Liser, the assistant U.S. trade representative for Africa, the act resulted in a fourfold increase (from $1.4 billion in 2001 to $4.1 billion in 2015) in non-oil trade between Africa and the United States.[52] Even though the increase looks impressive, Africa still accounts for only 2 percent of U.S. trade.[53] In 2015, two-way trade between Africa and the United States amounted to $37 billion. Goods exports totaled $18 billion (1.2 percent of total U.S. goods exports for 2015) and imports $19 billion (about 0.8 percent of total U.S. goods imports for 2015). The $19 billion-worth of imports for 2015 actually represents a 29.6 percent decrease from 2014, and was down 63 percent from 2005. In fact, just five African countries dominate Africa's trade with the United States: South Africa (which accounts for 39 percent), Angola (15 percent), and then Nigeria ($1.9 billion), Chad ($1.3 billion), and Côte d'Ivoire ($1.0 billion). The five largest import categories from Africa are crude oil ($6.6 billion), platinum and diamonds ($2.9 billion), vehicles ($1.5 billion), cocoa ($1.2 billion), and iron and steel ($662 million).[54]

Walter C. Carrington, the former U.S. ambassador critical of Bush's Africa policy, says: "Throughout his presidency, Bush viewed Africa mainly through the prism of terrorism."[55] The same charge can be leveled at Obama. In fact, the advancement of peace and security constitutes the third pillar of Obama's Africa policy. The key objectives of this pillar include the following: fighting Al-Qaeda and other terrorist groups, promoting regional security cooperation, combating transnational threats such as piracy off the coast of Somalia, preventing conflict and going after the perpetrators of mass atrocities, and working with the United Nations to support peace-building and peacekeeping operations on the continent. This is done through AFRICOM, whose sphere of operations covers all of Africa except Egypt. As explained above, the command is headquartered in Germany—a sign of its fraught relationship with many of the fifty-three African countries with which it works. The United States has troops stationed in thirteen African countries—a deployment that covers the Sahelian belt from West Africa to East Africa. Going from west to east, the thirteen countries are: Mali, Burkina Faso, Niger, Nigeria, Chad, the Central African Republic, the Democratic Republic of the Congo, South Sudan, Uganda, Ethiopia, Kenya, Djibouti, and Somalia.[56]

The deployments are not equal in size. For example, in Uganda, where the United States is helping the Ugandan military go after Joseph Kony and the Lord's Resistance Army, there are only a handful of advisers on the ground. Djibouti, on the other hand, hosts Camp Lemonnier, the only permanent U.S. military base in Africa. The base occupies about five hundred acres of land and houses an estimated three thousand U.S. troops, including hundreds of special forces. The U.S. military opened Camp Lemonnier, which is about one hundred miles from Yemen and five hundred miles from Somalia, in 2002 as part of President Bush's global strategy to combat terrorism. In 2014, President Obama and Ismail Omar Guelleh, his Djiboutian counterpart, signed a twenty-year lease extension for Camp Lemonnier. The United States pays $70 million a year in rent for the base, which is home to the U.S.'s Predator drones and F-15 fighter jets. The base serves as a jumping-off point for operations throughout the Horn of Africa and large parts of the Middle East. In fact, the base is where Navy Seals first took an American woman and a Danish man whom they rescued from Somali pirates in 2012.

In September 2016, investigative reporter Nick Turse reported that the U.S. military was building a $100 million drone base in Agadez, a town in the Sahara desert in Niger. According to Turse, when completed, the Agadez base would house the MQ-9 Reaper, a "newer, larger, and potentially more lethal model than the venerable Predator drone."[57] The military investment in Niger is neither isolated nor a singular feature of Obama's Africa policy. In 2002, the U.S. State Department launched the Pan-Sahel Initiative, a counterterrorism program that developed into the Trans Sahara Counterterrorism Partnership. The partnership, which spent about $288 million between 2009 and 2013, supports the military in Chad, Mali, Mauritania, and Niger, with Niger alone receiving $30 million of that.[58] U.S. largesse in the Sahel has done nothing for stability or even poverty reduction. Niger suffered a coup in 2010; Chad had a coup attempt in 2006 and 2013; Mauritania experienced coups in 2005 and 2008; and Mali's military usurped power in Mali in 2012.[59] Ambassador Carrington's reflections on the Mali case bear quoting at length:

> In most of Africa no institution is more distrusted by its people than their own military, which has so often carried out coups against lawfully constituted governments. AFRICOM particularly boasted of its successes in working with the Malian military to mold it into an effective fighting force against terrorists. The result was a disaster. What many of us feared came to pass. The Malian army, led by General Amadou Sanogo, who had been AFRICOM's poster child, staged a coup against one of Africa's oldest democracies. The situation fell apart and the north-

ern half of the country tried to break away. Mali's AFRICOM-trained army wilted in the face of secessionist and jihadist militias. French troops had to intervene to clean up the mess.[60]

The sad truth is that the Sahelian region and large parts of West Africa, which used to be relatively free of jihadist groups before 2001, are now hotbeds of Islamic insurgencies. Africa, which has more Muslims than all of Arabia, is now home to a range of jihadists sworn to the destruction of the West but who, because of Africa's size and their relative isolation from the West, take out their murderous schemes on fellow Africans who have neither the means nor the networks to escape. In Nigeria, a key variable in Obama's Africa policy, Boko Haram has waged a seemingly ceaseless insurgency. In fact, it is this, together with the United States' marginal involvement in Nigeria's counterinsurgency campaign against Boko Haram, that might explain the drop in Obama's popularity in the West African country. Traditionally, the United States has viewed Nigeria, Egypt (even though the United States considers it part of the Near East and not Africa as such), Kenya, and South Africa as anchors of its Africa policy, with Nigeria shoring up West Africa, Egypt North Africa, Kenya East Africa, and South Africa the southern region of the continent. But, given the mistrust that many African countries have for the United States, America's geopolitical assumption of these four countries as political and economic anchors has not always worked.

In the case of South Africa, the mistrust is largely an ideological holdover from the Cold War, during which the United States, especially under Ronald Reagan, supported apartheid South Africa. In the case of Nigeria and Kenya, the mistrust stems also from the instability of Nigeria—prone as it was, until recently, to coups—and the endemic corruption of Kenya. That is one reason why none of these countries has either offered or agreed to host AFRICOM. African governments worry that allowing AFRICOM to set up shop in their territories would be an open invitation to the United States to meddle in their internal affairs. This is not to say that these four states and African countries will not deal with the U.S. military. There is, for example, extensive military cooperation between the United States and a number of African countries, including South Africa. The U.S. military also conducted a number of joint military exercises with many African militaries during Obama's time in office. Nevertheless, fears of a too-cozy connection to the U.S. military remain. "Under Obama, initial fears of AFRICOM dragging Africa into the war on terrorism are being realized. Muslims who have long been comfortable with the concept of a secular state and democracy are apt to become more and more radicalized," said Carrington, perhaps putting too fine a point on it.[61] Regardless, his argument stands.

Obama did not choose to be a wartime president. But where his predecessor was a unilateralist, he was a multilateralist. However, that should not blind us to the fact that Obama's Africa policy, especially his counterterrorism strategy, has only ever been in the service of the national interest of the United States. Even where the Obama administration has worked closely with African governments and militaries, this has always been in pursuit of U.S. interests. Take the presence of U.S. military personnel in thirteen African countries. Many of these are involved in training their host militaries and in helping these militaries wage effective counterinsurgency campaigns. But the idea here has always been to neutralize the threat at the source. That is why we should not be scandalized by comments such as the following from a senior U.S. military officer attached to AFRICOM: "We don't want to see our guys going in and getting whacked. . . . We want Africans to go in."[62] In the few publicly known instances where U.S. military personnel did go in, the aim was to neutralize terrorists considered direct threats to the United States. Take the September 2009 killing by U.S. Navy Seals of Al-Qaeda terrorist Saleh Ali Nabhan in Somalia. Nabhan had been involved in the 1998 bombings of the U.S. embassies in Kenya and Tanzania.

The fourth pillar of Obama's Africa policy concerns the promotion of opportunity and development in Africa. This, in fact, is another area where we see more continuity than change between Obama's Africa policy and that of his predecessor. Obama's policy built on Bush's PEPFAR and malaria initiative. It is important to remember in connection with this that, even though Obama did continue initiatives first introduced by Bush, there were differences in style. When, for example, Obama went on his "senatorial safari" in Africa in 2006, one of the things he did was to hold public meetings with HIV/AIDS activists and people living with AIDS in South Africa; in Kenya he publicly took an HIV test—as part of an effort to promote testing and to help fight the stigma against people with HIV/AIDS. Would Bush have done this?

Bush's involvement with Africa did not extend to that level. The fourth pillar of Obama's Africa policy also promoted food security and sought to increase opportunities for women and youth. It also set out to respond to humanitarian crises in a timely fashion while helping African communities to become more resilient, and—in one notable departure from Bush's Africa policy—committed the Obama administration to combat the negative effects of climate change. This last bit of the policy included support for the adoption of low-emissions development strategies, financial aid for the development of clean energy, and the promotion of the sustainable use of Africa's natural resources. Obama's concern with climate change and the sustainable use of Africa's natural resources was not simply about the preservation of a public good. It was also about confronting China's maneuverings in Africa. Throughout Africa, China has struck deals that have seen it undertake massive infrastructure projects in return for unlimited access to Africa's natural resources. The most recent example of such projects is a 460-mile railway linking Ethiopia's capital Addis Ababa to the port in Djibouti. China, Africa's largest trading partner since 2009, built and paid for the $3.4 billion railway. It is not clear how Ethiopia is going to pay for this except through some sort of barter.

Conclusion

These, then, are the elements of Obama's Africa policy. As should be clear by now, one does not need a racial lens to make sense of this policy. Indeed, one does not even need to know that Obama is African American to see that the policy outlined above is that of an American president. He afforded Africa no special geopolitical considerations. The continent of his father, home still to hundreds of his relatives, occasioned no special consideration from Obama. He pushed for stronger and accountable institutions in Africa; he called for the protection of vulnerable groups, including the LGBTQ community; he promoted the interests of women and young people; he continued Bush's HIV/AIDS and malaria projects; he reauthorized the preferential trade accord with thirty-nine African countries; and he sought to promote greater access to electricity in Africa. But he also increased U.S. military presence in Africa, sending more military personnel to many more countries and getting U.S. troops involved in many more countries, and stationing many more drones in Africa than his predecessor did. The gambles that Obama took through AFRICOM's alliance with a number of militaries along the Sahel did not pay out. In fact, they collapsed and left in their wake jihadist insurgencies where there had been few or none before.

Writing shortly after Obama's first election in 2008, Nigerian scholar Adekeye Adebajo said: "In spite of the great expectations unleashed by his historic election, in some African quarters, that Obama will act as a Messiah by increasing U.S. support for Africa, even a black Gulliver will be held down by powerful Lilliputian legislators who control America's purse strings."[63] So it came to pass. But not only because Republican Lilliputians held the black Gulliver down. Obama treated with Africa where it suited his agenda; he dealt with the continent in pursuit of what he saw as the national interests of the United States. It is on the basis of that—his pursuit of America's national interests in relation to Africa—that we must assess his policy.

16

Criticize and Thrive

THE AMERICAN LEFT IN THE OBAMA YEARS

Michael Kazin

A Change Is Going to Come?

On election night in 2008, Bob Dylan happened to be giving a concert in Minneapolis, the same city where he began his career half a century earlier singing folk music at a scruffy coffeehouse. "I was born in 1941," he told the audience in a voice turned sandpapery with age. "That was the year they bombed Pearl Harbor. I've been living in darkness every since. It looks like things are going to change now."[1]

The icon of 1960s rebellion rarely speaks with such passion, at least in public. But that night, most of his fellow Americans on the liberal and radical left could second his emotion. Nearly seventy million voters had just chosen an eloquent, hip, youngish black man with a background as an anti-apartheid activist, community organizer, and opponent of the Iraq war to govern the most powerful nation on earth. Not since Franklin D. Roosevelt's reelection in 1936 had nearly everyone who identified with the quarrelsome, perpetually embattled American left given more than grudging support to a victorious presidential nominee. In Chicago's Grant Park, where forty years earlier police had beaten up antiwar demonstrators come to protest at the Democratic National Convention, an exuberant throng composed of people of all ages and races gathered to glory in what they believed would be a new dawn of progressive social change. "He stands on the shoulders of the crowds of four decades ago," commented Todd Gitlin, a professor of journalism who was a leader of radical students in the 1960s. "His rebellion takes the form of practicality. He has the audacity of reason." The president-elect was, if anything, more popular overseas than at home. As the French philosopher Pascal Bruckner, normally a critic of the multi-cultural left, put it, "*Barack Obama était le candidat du monde.*"[2] A confirmation of sorts arrived less than a year after the election when Obama was awarded the Nobel Peace Prize.

But in the United States, the celebration did not last that long. By the summer of 2009, many liberals were denouncing the new president's appointments of such Wall Street "insiders" as Lawrence Summers and Timothy Geithner and wondering why he had not broken up the banks and insurance companies they blamed for causing the Great Recession. That August, Katrina vanden Heuvel, editor of *The Nation*, faulted Obama for not emulating FDR in using "this moment of crisis . . . to restructure—not simply resuscitate—the smug financial sector." For their part, most radicals had already written Obama off as what Tariq Ali, the veteran British Marxist, damned as a "messenger-servant of the country's corporations . . . ensuring that no obstacles are placed in their way."[3]

Such harsh judgments from the left remained the norm as the president stumbled through his first term, then won reelection but saw his party lose control of the House and the Senate, as well as a majority of governorships and state legislatures. The most salient criticisms—whether voiced in sorrow or anger or contempt—included: Obama's failure to fight for a public option in the Affordable Care Act; his reluctance to boldly protest an upsurge in racist talk and police killings of unarmed black men; his refusal to pull U.S. forces out of Afghanistan and to abandon the surveillance regime accompanying the unending "war on terrorism"; his lack of support for legislation that would have made it easier for unions to organize or to do anything else of significance to attack economic inequality; and his persistent attempts to compromise with the same Republicans in Congress who—backed by a large and well-funded network of right-wing groups like the Tea Party—sought to defeat him at every turn. In August 2014, Cornel West, perhaps Obama's most prominent black critic, summed up the radical indictment: "He posed as a progressive and turned out to be counterfeit. We ended up with a Wall Street presidency, a drone presidency, a national security presidency.... [H]e's just another neoliberal centrist with a smile and a nice rhetorical flair."[4]

Yet the disappointments and cynicism helped produce an ironic result. The left revived in numbers, spirit, and creativity during the Obama years— due, in no small part, to the gap between what most liberals and radicals had hoped (and some expected) from his administration and what actually took place. With his bracingly progressive rhetoric and activist biography, the first African American president had raised expectations among leftists of nearly every stripe. Their frustrations proved to be productive ones: they helped fuel an upsurge of protest and organizing that propelled issues like police killings of black men and economic inequality to the forefront of national politics. They also did much to make what became a heated, two-person battle within Obama's party to succeed him a contest to prove who could sound more progressive than the other.

Something like this had happened twice before in modern U.S. political history. During the 1930s and 1960s, the left also mushroomed when avowedly liberal presidents were in office. There were, of course, significant differences between what occurred during Obama's presidency and those of Franklin D. Roosevelt, John F. Kennedy, and Lyndon B. Johnson. In the earlier periods, major social movements on the left enabled Democratic Congresses to pass and Democratic presidents to sign landmark pieces of legislation that became pillars of the liberal state. Not until late in the 1960s did conservatives gain the legitimacy and the resources to apply counter-pressure from the right. Still, in all three eras, the left responded to reform-ist chief executives in similar ways. Intellectuals and organizers found their voice on issues they could use to build their movements both in numbers and confidence.

However, those previous lefts used a mix of hope and discontent to build institutions that sustained their activism and won signal victories that altered the politics and, to a degree, the culture of the nation. The left that began to thrive during the Obama presidency did not develop into such a mature, enduring force. It is too early to know whether its spirited mobili-zation against the Trump administration and Republican Party's domi-nance of the federal government will produce that result.

A Half-Correct Critique

Before describing how the left grew, one first ought to evaluate its criti-cisms of Obama's presidency. Were the charges valid? The answer depends on what one thinks the president actually wanted to accomplish, how he went about it, and what, given the political context he inherited, Obama realistically could have done. Those who saw him as a stalwart progressive impatient to launch a New Deal or Great Society for the twenty-first century and to denounce and defy anyone who got in his way did not take an accurate measure of the man. As Gitlin suggested—and as historian James T. Kloppenberg argued in an intellectual biography written midway through Obama's first term—the president was an instinctive pragmatist who believed that only patient, empathetic deliberation could generate beneficent change. These qualities of mind had helped him become the first African American president of the *Harvard Law Review* and then a skillful community organizer in Chicago where he learned, in Kloppenberg's words, "to coax from groups a sense of what they shared, an awareness that proved sturdy because it was their doing, not his." Then, in the 2004 keynote at the Democratic Convention that vaulted Obama to national prominence, he famously declared while "there are those who are preparing to divide us, the spin masters and negative ad peddlers," the reality was "there's not a liberal America and a conservative America; there's the United States of America." Alas, when he got to the White House, this exponent of consensus-building took far too long to understand that neither he, nor any other president, could effectively govern that way. Driven by ideological conviction and electoral self-interest, his Republican opponents had no intention of making deals.[5]

Obama's left critics also ignored obstacles that would have confronted any serious reformer who moved into the White House near the beginning of an economic crisis severe enough to be compared to the Great Depression. When FDR took office in 1933, more than three years after the stock market crash, no one blamed him for the millions of unemployed or the thousands of banks that were in danger of going broke. But Obama had to weather the inevitable decline of the economy and so he reaped less credit from the slow recovery that followed. If Roosevelt had been elected in, say, 1930, he surely would have struggled mightily to enact the New Deal programs that became keystones of the modern liberal state.

Neither should one ignore, or quickly disparage, reforms that Obama and a Democratic Congress managed to enact during the first two years of his administration—reforms that the incoming Trump administration sought to dismantle. The economic stimulus plan, the ACA, the Dodd-Frank regulation of high finance, and the beginning of a serious effort to stall or reverse global warming were serious attempts to solve some of the nation's and one of the world's most serious problems. And, on climate change, the executive orders Obama issued, the international pacts he spearheaded, and the Keystone and North Dakota pipeline projects he halted (if only temporarily) were enough to cheer even most radical environmentalists. If these were the acts of a corporate "messenger-servant," why did the pro-corporate Republicans who blasted Obama as a "socialist" not get the message?[6]

Most of the president's left critics also neglected the fact that he had to cope with much smaller majorities in Congress than FDR and LBJ enjoyed—and unbending opposition from nearly every GOP lawmaker in both houses. This was a stark contrast with the relative bipartisanship that prevailed during earlier liberal heydays. A sizable minority of Republicans had voted for such signature programs of the New Deal as Social Security and the G.I. Bill as well as for such pillars of the Great Society as Medicare and the Civil Rights Act.[7]

Yet, Obama's left critics were certainly correct about one big thing: the president did not live up to the image of a bold movement leader that had done much to win him both his party's nomination and, perhaps, the general election. As the recession predictably worsened in 2009, he stuck to managing the crisis from the White House instead of traveling around the nation to empathize with Americans who had lost their homes, their jobs, and their life savings. As Theda Skocpol commented, in an otherwise positive evaluation of Obama's first two years in office, the president's "failure to engage more consistently in high-profile public leadership on the economy constitutes, in an important sense, democratic political malpractice." Organizing for America (OFA), the group Democrats created just before the inauguration to harness the momentum of the Obama campaign to their legislative program, failed to keep the party's young, multicultural base mobilized against the Republican onslaught that followed.[8]

How Black Lives Matter Mattered

Members of that base in communities around the nation soon began to mobilize themselves. The most impressive effort was made by young African Americans who had celebrated Obama's election but quickly realized the president would or, perhaps, could do little to dismantle racist practices in government and the economy. Criminal justice became their primary target. Activists rallied first in the summer of 2013 under the twitter hashtag #BlackLivesMatter after a jury in Florida acquitted George Zimmerman for the killing of Trayvon Martin. Over the next three years, the protests grew, in decentralized fashion, from smartphone to smartphone, and city to city, as the murders of individual black men were caught on amateur videos and then viewed everywhere.

In a trajectory familiar from the black freedom movement of the 1960s, activists moved swiftly from protesting specific outrages (lack of civil and voting rights then, police killings now) to a bold assault on the norms and structures of American society itself. The three young individuals who launched the original presence on social media proudly identified themselves as "queer Black women" and insisted the new freedom movement "affirm the lives" of African Americans of all genders, sexualities, and national origins. Their language testified to the remarkable legitimacy and influence the cause of LGBTQ rights and identity had gained in the early years of this century. The trio roundly condemned both "hetero-patriarchal society" and a "narrow" black nationalism of the past that had taken those norms for granted.[9]

In the summer of 2016, some fifty black-led groups, assembled under the Movement for Black Lives (MBL), issued a platform of demands and policies on taxes, reparations, the military budget, education, incarceration, and, of course, police conduct that was as sweepingly radical as any group on the left—aside from dogmatic sects—had issued since the 1960s. Some of its planks were borrowed from the think-tank Demos and other liberal organizations. Still, the platform writers made clear their distance from Obama and his party. Their movement might be "focused on domestic policies." But nothing short of an international uprising would repair "the ravages of global capitalism and anti-Black racism, human-made climate change, war, and exploitation."[10]

To have an African American as president gave the new black freedom movement both a sense of hope and a target on which to train its frustrations with the slow pace of change. Many lashed out at the president and other members of the black elite, in and out of government, for preaching to young African Americans in poor communities a gospel of "respectable" speech and dress instead of enacting policies that would give them a good education and secure jobs at living wages.[11]

At the same time, the enthusiasm for Obama's presidency, which never flagged among most non-activist African Americans, did help gain the black left a nationwide audience for the first time in decades. The organizers of mass protests could point to the gap between Obama's rhetoric about racism and his lack of progress in combatting the suffering it caused. A month after Trayon Martin was killed in Florida, the president declared, "If I had a son, he'd look like Trayvon. . . . When I think about this boy, I think about my own kids." But Obama had also made clear that he could not do more to address and remedy the problems of African Americans than he would for the concerns of other citizens. Black Lives Matter thus became the latest progressive movement to advance when it could challenge a president who either did not, or could not, fulfill his promises—instead of having to combat one who had no sympathy at all with its cause.[12]

There was a critical difference, however, between this upsurge and that of the large black reform and radical left whose actions did much to shape the history of postwar America. No equivalent of the NAACP, SCLC, CORE, or SNCC emerged to raise money and plan strategy for Black Lives Matter; no facsimile of Martin Luther King Jr., Malcolm X, Stokely Carmichael, Angela Davis, or Fannie Lou Hamer thrilled mass rallies with his or her rhetoric and became a familiar name in the mass media. The young activists who spearheaded the new movement did not attempt to build a durable local or national organization or choose leaders who could represent their cause to the country at large. They were sharply critical of the "old guard" of men like Jesse Jackson Sr. and Al Sharpton who seldom showed up at street protests they did not initiate. The "new guard" also had little faith their elders were sincerely committed to "intersectionality"—a determination to fight all forms of oppression, which quickly became a cherished goal for young leftists of all races. As a group called Ferguson Action explained late in 2014, "We are decentralized, but coordinated. . . . We do not cast any one of ours to the side in order to gain proximity to perceived power. Because this is the only way we will win." Such a "horizontalist" approach seemed only natural for a movement launched and diffused on social media.[13]

However, a movement that eschews durable organizations and depends on police murders to sustain itself may also speed its own decline. As the sociologist Jo Freeman warned decades ago during the upsurge of radical feminism, "The more unstructured a movement is, the less control it has over the directions in which it develops and the political actions in which it engages. . . . Diffusion of [its] ideas does not mean they are implemented; it only means they are talked about."[14]

With Trump as president, it is quite unlikely that Black Lives Matter, with its combination of local protests and a radical vision, will spur statutory change, much less anything as far-reaching as the Civil Rights and Voting Rights Acts of the 1960s. But the brash, independent spirit of the new black movement certainly inspired a national debate about policing and incarceration, in which the 2016 presidential nominees of both major parties engaged. No meaningful change in politics occurs without a catalyst that, in most cases, does not endure.

The Limits of Occupy

The Occupy uprising launched in September 2011 provided a similar jolt from the left without building a structure equipped to organize for systemic reform. Responding to the call of *Adbusters*, a Canadian anticorporate magazine, several dozen radicals began camping out in Zuccotti Park in lower Manhattan. They declared themselves the tribunes of the 99 percent of the people against the 1 percent who ruled the global economy and whose reckless investment schemes had, they charged, brought on the Great Recession. Within days, the group in the renamed Liberty Park swelled into the thousands. Soon, protesters inspired by their example were occupying parks and other locations in dozens of other cities; suddenly, thanks to blanket media coverage, "economic inequality" had become as inescapable an issue as civil rights had been during the 1960s.[15]

However, unlike any antiracist movement past or present, Occupy really did express the sentiments of most Americans, if not quite 99 percent of them. A poll that November reported that six-tenths of the public "supported government efforts to reduce disparities in wealth"; another survey taken that same month found that the same proportion of registered voters agreed it was necessary "to reduce the power of major banks and corporations" and give neither "financial aid to corporations" nor "provide tax breaks to the rich." For decades, labor union officials and left-wing journalists and academics had been demanding changes in a status quo that favored the wealthy. But it took an unplanned protest by a group composed mainly of young, middle-class whites without steady jobs to make a dent in what the historian Steve Fraser dubbed "the Age of Acquiescence."[16]

How Occupy activists viewed Barack Obama also tended to differ from how their counterparts in Black Lives Matter regarded the president. Many of the African Americans who took to the streets of Ferguson, Baltimore, and other cities complained that the first black chief executive was too much of a bystander to their cause. But they could not realistically accuse him of abetting the crimes they were protesting. In contrast, those who kept the Occupy encampments going—what Todd Gitlin called "the inner movement"—viewed Obama as yet another shill for the "neoliberal" order, decidedly part of the problem instead of the solution, to borrow a phrase favored by the New Left of the 1960s.[17]

Besides a loathing for finance capitalism and its political enablers, the Occupiers articulated no specific ideology. Yet some of the most vocal among them embraced an updated form of anarchism—one refashioned to embrace the strict environmentalism, multiculturalism, and gender neutrality that nearly every young leftist now takes for granted. They were the cyber-clever progeny of Henry David Thoreau and Emma Goldman, streaming video and organizing flash mobs instead of penning essays about the wilderness or traveling around the country touting feminism and free love. The horizontal nature of a movement brought to life and sustained by social media fit snugly inside the anarchist vision of a future in which autonomous, self-governing communities would link up with one another— voluntarily of course.[18]

But the quite un-anarchistic resident of the White House had helped set the stage for the radicals who condemned him. In the later months of 2008, Obama had the ironic good fortune to be running in the midst of an economic debacle. In his acceptance speech at the Democratic convention in Denver, he set aside his bent for compromise to blame the "old, discredited Republican philosophy" of "trickle-down economics" for causing millions of Americans to lose their jobs, their homes, and enough money to pay credit card bills and college tuition. The attack was reminiscent of that which Franklin D. Roosevelt, accepting the Democratic nomination, had hurled at the Hoover administration seventy-six years before.[19]

Yet, in both cases, presidential practice lagged behind campaign rhetoric. When they took office, neither FDR nor Obama had a strategy for winning higher wages, enhanced bargaining power, or job security for wage-earners. Instead, both concentrated on restoring the health of a badly ailing macroeconomy. Roosevelt vowed to cut federal spending and expended most of his energies on rescuing banks and manufacturing firms from the abyss. Although Obama in 2008 had the support of nearly every union in the country, he made no attempt to get Congress to enact the Employee Free Choice Act, labor's main legislative priority. Even when, in December 2011, the president devoted an entire speech to the issue of economic inequality—an implicit nod to Occupy—he addressed it to a politically safe demographic, "the middle class," and essentially repeated the critique of conservative economics he had made during his 2008 campaign.[20]

Midway through his own first term, Franklin Roosevelt had benefited from, and began to appeal to, a larger and far better organized class-conscious left. From the mass strike wave of 1934 to the sit-down strikes of 1936–37, working-class activists—some of whom belonged to one or another Marxist party—nurtured an environment in which the president and Democrats from industrial states could win more votes by supporting unions than they lost to Americans who feared social unrest. At the same time, non-left figures like Francis Townsend were gaining a mass following with the demand to create a federal pension for the elderly. Demagogues Huey Long and Charles Coughlin rose to national prominence with calls to redistribute the wealth. The ability to channel this resistance into legislation and Democratic majorities in Congress and industrial states was a vital element in the construction of the New Deal order.[21]

In contrast, Occupy mainly generated a shift in political rhetoric. Many local unions did hail the encampments and supplied them with food and other resources. But labor was hardly the vigorous, growing force it had been from the 1930s through the 1950s. In the wake of Occupy, the Service Employees International Union (SEIU)—the largest private-sector union in America—organized one-day strikes among fast-food workers for a wage of $15 an hour. Soon, Bernie Sanders and other left Democrats took up the demand as well. But by the time Obama left office, it had not led to a rebirth of unions among the men and women who need them most.

How Marriage Equality Won

The most successful movement on the broad left during Obama's presidency—that of LGBTQ activists—managed to appear less radical in its key demand and was far better equipped to win it. During his 2008 campaign, the Democratic nominee had affirmed the position on legal matrimony taken by nearly every politician from both major parties: "*I believe marriage is between a man and a woman. I am not in favor of gay marriage.*" However, back in 1996, when he was running for a seat in the Illinois Senate, Obama had endorsed such unions and even told a gay magazine that he "would fight efforts to prohibit" them. Running for reelection in 2012, he changed his mind again or, more likely, decided to help increase the speed at which the winds of politics were already blowing. In June 2016, by a 5–4 decision, the Supreme Court, in *Obergefell v. Hodges*, agreed, and marriage equality became the law of the land.[22]

This remarkable victory was not merely the result of an increased tolerance of sexual diversity in American culture; it depended upon a shrewd strategy LGBTQ activists carried out with persistence and an acute sense of how to shift public opinion their way. In the 1990s, gay rights attorneys filed suit in liberal states like Hawaii and Vermont where they could establish precedents. Then, they challenged the Defense of Marriage Act, easily passed in 1995 by Congress and signed by President Bill Clinton, and were able to convince Obama's Justice Department not to defend the law in court. Accompanying these legal maneuvers was a change of message: instead of talking about marriage as a "right," the movement's literature stressed that same-sex couples wanted to get married for the same reasons that straight couples did: for "love and commitment." That helped break down the resistance of people who had bridled at the idea of overturning a legal norm as old as civilization itself.[23]

Although Barack Obama's gradual "evolution" toward backing same-sex marriage frustrated its supporters, his change of position accelerated the pace of their victory. The president's new stance immediately became that of his party. It helped win over black church-goers as well as bind most young people of all races to the Democrats—when they bothered to vote. By 2015, it had become inconceivable to imagine that the administration would side with the four conservative justices who dissented from the landmark ruling. No major expansion of individual freedom in U.S. history has occurred without a presidential blessing, however tardy it may be.

Why the Antiwar Movement Disappeared

In sharp contrast, few leftists of any stripe devoted much effort to opposing Obama's continuation of military intervention or proposed alternatives of their own. During the 1960s, protest against the U.S war in Indochina had been a signature cause for radicals, and eventually, for most liberals too. By 2014, opinion polls showed that most Americans opposed the ongoing U.S. war against the Taliban in Afghanistan; support had been declining steadily since Obama took office.[24] But no protest was large or creative enough to gain the attention of anyone outside a small circle of activists. In the spring of 2015, on the twelfth anniversary of the invasion of Iraq, a nationally advertised Spring Rising Anti-War Intervention attracted only a few hundred demonstrators to Washington, D.C., and received no coverage at all in the mainstream media and barely any mention in left-wing outlets.

Perhaps the most obvious, and most significant, reason for the absence of a large and persistent antiwar movement is the nature of the enemies the United States has been fighting since the fall of 2001. There are, of course, many distinctions between Al-Qaeda and the Taliban, Saddam Hussein's regime and ISIS. But nearly all Americans sensibly regard each of these groups (Hussein's, retrospectively) with loathing. So antiwar activists sensibly sought to focus on innocent victims: how U.S. military actions kill and maim large numbers of civilians, particularly with drones often directed from buildings located in northern Virginia.

But the flourishing of the peace movement during the 1960s did not depend solely on having an unpopular war to stop. Many of its most talented and committed activists came from other movements on the broad left—against poverty, for civil liberties, for nuclear disarmament, and especially for black liberation. They had learned to define their politics as a moral undertaking that could transform the world. Slogans like SNCC's "One Man, One Vote—Mississippi, Vietnam," and Muhammad Ali's statement, "I ain't got no quarrel with them Viet Cong. No Viet Cong ever called me nigger," when he applied to be a conscientious objector, helped forge the link between black freedom and antiwar movements. For both groups, a passionate internationalism was taken for granted.

Contemporary foes of U.S. action in the Muslim world did not have such an expansive, optimistic vision. Most feminist and LGBTQ activists objected to the size of the military budget, but few drew connections between the violence in the Mideast and the injustices they combat at home. After all, misogynistic groups like ISIS and the Taliban burn to reverse every achievement that activists for gender equality hold dear. Neither did any spokesperson for Black Lives Matter or the movement to halt climate change link his or her cause to that of pulling all foreign troops out of Afghanistan. The one exception to this pattern is the Boycott, Divestment, Sanctions (BDS) campaign to punish Israel for its occupation of Palestinian lands—which became the left's anti-imperialist cause of choice. But no U.S. soldiers are patrolling the West Bank.

Perhaps one reason few leftists spent their time agitating against U.S. military intervention abroad is that issue was not the property of the left alone. Rand Paul and other libertarians on the right spoke out against "imperial overreach" and NSA surveillance as consistently as did anyone on the left. In his 2016 campaign, Donald Trump sometimes echoed their views and vowed to take care of America First. All opponents of intervention, whatever their ideology, agree that U.S. military power does little or no good in the world; they do not agree about why. Meanwhile, President Obama often seemed apologetic about committing U.S. forces. In foreign affairs, the president showed more enthusiasm for recognizing the communist regime in Cuba—a step universally applauded on the left. With such ambiguous realities and contradictory motivations, any hope for mass antiwar protest fizzled. The result was that, by the end of Obama's term, left internationalism had become close to an oxymoron on any issue other than climate change. As the political theorist Michael Walzer puts it, "The default position of the left is that the best foreign policy is a good domestic policy."[25]

The Bernie Boom

The best evidence that a left focused on domestic concerns was thriving with Obama in the White House emerged during the final year of his presidency—in the extraordinary campaign for the Democratic nomination by an independent senator in his seventies who had criticized the president for not following through on his progressive promises. An avowed socialist, Bernie Sanders received 45 percent of the vote in his 2016 run and won an overwhelming majority of votes cast by people of all races under thirty years old. His popularity was a testament both to his principled "authenticity" and to the hunger for egalitarian change stoked by the left upsurge that began during the final years of George W. Bush's administration but accelerated greatly under Barack Obama—whom many conservatives accused of being a "socialist" too.

Ironically, Sanders might be the most unchangeable politician in America. By the time he announced for president, Sanders had spent over half a century advocating a reform agenda that would turn the United States into a social-democratic nation—a Finland with a lot more people and much warmer summers. His rhetoric rarely altered from his tenure as mayor of the largest city in Vermont in the 1980s to his campaign for the White House more than thirty years later. Sanders bashed millionaires and billionaires for corrupting democracy and strongly supported labor unions and public health insurance; he paid less attention to racial inequality and the degradation of the environment. Like his hero, Eugene Victor Debs, he viewed every political issue through the lens of class injustice. Unlike Obama, Sanders never abandoned the passionate leftism of his youth.[26]

Inevitably, this led him to disparage the president during his first term in office. "I think that there are millions of Americans who are deeply disappointed" in Obama, Sanders claimed in 2011, "who believe that with regard to Social Security and a number of other issues, he has said one thing as a candidate and is doing something very much else. . . . [They] cannot believe how weak he has been . . . in negotiating with Republicans." Sanders even mused, at the time, about challenging the president in several primaries. In the summer of 2016, after losing to Hillary Clinton in the Democratic race, he refreshed his critique: "After Obama became president," Sanders told an interviewer, "he severed his ties with the grassroots that got him elected."[27]

Despite losing the nomination, Sanders and his followers wielded a good deal of influence over the party the senator had never actually joined. Hillary Clinton seconded his opposition to the Trans-Pacific Partnership bill backed by President Obama and embraced Sanders's call for a big boost in the minimum wage, debt-free tuition in public colleges, and a reversal of the Supreme Court ruling in the *Citizens United* case. As a result, the platform adopted by the Democratic Party in 2016 leaned further leftward than any since the days when most party leaders were proud to wear the liberal label.

What Future for the Left?

Where does the left go from here? In 2017, its resurgence during Obama's tenure helped prepare both Democrats shattered by Hillary Clinton's defeat and radicals who had grudgingly supported her, if at all, to organize a sizable movement of "resistance" to President Donald Trump and his policies. In the first months after the celebrity billionaire was inaugurated, they staged an impressive variety of protests—on the streets, in airports, and at congressional town halls—on a scale not seen on the broad left since the heyday of the antiwar movement at the end of the 1960s. Young "millennials" who voted for Sanders were playing a prominent role in the movement. They were also challenging the elected leaders of the Democrats in Congress and at the Democratic National Committee to embrace a sweeping platform that would include single-payer health insurance, higher taxes on the rich, and other stands the Vermont senator had taken during his 2016 campaign. It seems likely that the Democratic presidential field for 2020 will be crowded, at least initially, by aspirants eager to run to the left, including Sanders himself.

Yet, it would be naïve to assume that the prospects of contemporary leftists are as bright as were those of their predecessors in the 1930s and the 1960s. During those eras, the Democratic Party was a more truly national party than it is today when its strength lies in big cities, nearby suburbs, and the states of the Northeast and West Coast. And the "resistance" to President Trump and the GOP majority in Congress is hardly the equivalent of the industrial labor upsurge of the 1930s or the black freedom movement of the early to mid-1960s, each of which gave left activists a sense of common purpose and helped elect liberal Democratic majorities in Congress and many key states. Today, the left's reluctance to or inability to build institutions that might unite its different constituent groups means that "intersectionality" is, at least for now, more a trendy catchphrase than a strategy inspired by popular will and the resources to back it up.

As ever, a president is an ally of the left only when the left makes it difficult for him (or someday, she) not to be so. During the 2008 campaign, a black community organizer from New Orleans remarked that Obama "is a man who can be accommodated by America, he is not my hero, because a politician, by nature, has to surrender."[28] The question, as always, is which forces the president will bargain with, whose rhetoric and demands he will amplify, and which he will surrender to.

17

Civic Ideals, Race, and Nation in the Age of Obama

Gary Gerstle

Barack Obama's victory in the presidential election of 2008 thrilled millions. Most Americans had assumed that they would never witness an African American ascending to the nation's highest office. Obama's election was seen as evidence that the American dream worked and that the country's civic nationalist tradition could triumph. Perhaps the United States was finally fulfilling its commitment to the proposition that all men are created equal. Perhaps it was on the cusp of establishing a racially more perfect union.

An America fully committed to its civic nationalist creed had seemed within reach before: not just at the moment of the country's eighteenth-century founding, but also during the hopeful years of Reconstruction (1865–1877) and during the civil rights heyday of the 1960s. But these early episodes of civic nationalist progress had crested and then receded before full equality between the races had been achieved. Could Obama's 2008 election break this earlier pattern, and finally lay to rest America's potent and resilient racial nationalist tradition? In 2008 and 2009, many believed that this outcome was within America's grasp. Many hoped that their era would be one to usher in America's "postracial" age. They were wrong.

Reconstruction's advances in the 1860s and the civil rights legislation in the 1960s had become occasions for remobilizing racial nationalist sentiment. Obama's election unleashed a similar dynamic, this time propelled by a powerful conviction forming among millions of whites: namely, that no black man, even one who was half-white, had a right to sit in the White House. White fears about Obama in the years after 2008 were magnified by what people's eyes and the nation's demographers were telling them: the country was in the process of becoming nonwhite. Not just the White House but also the country was in the process of being "lost." The hope and despair coursing through Obama's America revealed how much the two contrary nationalist traditions that had defined the country since its beginning still mattered, and how much they still organized the country's political and cultural life.

"The American Dream Come True Tonight"

Civic nationalism expresses the belief that all Americans are fundamentally equal and are endowed with unalienable rights to life, liberty, and the pursuit of happiness. The creed countenances no discrimination on the basis of race or any other ascriptive characteristic. It proclaims that America is open to the talents of anyone willing to work hard, obey the law, and declare fealty to America's core egalitarian and democratic ideals. It has a universal character, in that aspirations for equality and inalienable rights fire the imagination of humans everywhere. But because civic nationalist principles are central to the Declaration of Independence, they are thought to have particular meaning in the American republic.[1]

If one were to design the perfect civic nationalist, he or she would look a lot like Barack Obama. Obama believed intensely in the American dream, and in his own life as an embodiment of civic ideals. His was a story of one man's rise from obscurity to prominence across a terrain strewn with obstacles. He was not the beneficiary of wealth, family connections, or other privilege. He was black, of course. He was abandoned as a baby by his Kenyan father, whom he would never come to know. He was raised by a single mother, a white Kansas girl from humble middle-class circumstances. His smarts, ambition, and discipline propelled his ascent through elite Occidental College, Columbia University, and Harvard Law School. His political rise was equally meteoric: Illinois state senator in 1996, U.S. senator in 2002, U.S. presidential nominee in 2008. Obama understood, of course, that the civil rights revolution had opened institutions and careers to him in ways they had not been for generations of blacks who preceded him. But the very success of this revolution demonstrated to him that America was delivering on what Martin Luther King Jr. had once called its promissory note: that America would overcome its racial nationalist tradition and embrace fully its civic creed. A new era of civic nationalism had dawned in America. Obama would be the one to announce its arrival.[2]

Taking notice of this rising star and his deep belief in America's civic creed, the Democratic Party selected Obama to make a prime-time speech to the country at its 2004 National Convention in Boston. Obama used the moment to take his stand with the country's civic nationalist tradition, and to call Democrats back to a faith that major segments of the party had found difficult to embrace in the wake of the disappointments of the 1960s and 1970s. "In no other country on Earth," Obama declared in his national debut, was his own "story even possible." "Tonight," he added, "we gather to affirm the greatness of our nation," a greatness rooted in the country's original declaration that "'all men are created equal . . . [and] endowed by their Creator with certain inalienable rights.'"[3]

The African American experience, of course, had never fit comfortably within the narrative of American freedom that was so central to the civic nationalist tradition. For most of American history it was simply not true that a black man or woman who worked hard, obeyed the law, and espoused patriotic sentiment could count on getting ahead. Obama mostly preferred to ease past this uncomfortable truth, an inclination that became stronger once he decided to run for president in 2008. But his longtime pastor and friend, the Reverend Jeremiah Wright, made it impossible for him to ignore the issue.

Jeremiah Wright's Christianity and politics had been fired in the black nationalist crucible of the 1960s and 1970s.[4] Wright thundered forth in his weekly sermons from his pulpit at Chicago's Trinity United Church of Christ like an Old Testament truth-teller, his words, like those of the prophet Isaiah, uncompromising and frequently condemnatory.[5] In one sermon, given in 2003, Wright cataloged the offenses that the government had committed against African Americans: it "put them outside the equal protection of the law, kept them out of their racist bastion of higher education, and locked them into positions of hopelessness and helplessness." Shifting from the past to the present, Wright condemned America in terms that made his words indistinguishable from Malcolm X's sternest. "The government gives them drugs, builds bigger prisons, passes a three-strike law, and then wants us to sing 'God Bless America.' No, no, no. Not God Bless America. God Damn America."[6] In early 2008, enterprising journalists unearthed a video of this sermon, which was soon being shown on what

seemed like an interminable loop on Fox News and other cable and network TV outlets.[7]

As a member of Trinity United for more than twenty years, Obama had
listened to Wright's sermons on countless Sundays. He was close to the man
himself and admired his social conscience and pastoring skills. He had
asked Wright to officiate at his and Michelle's wedding and to baptize their
daughters. The community that Wright offered Obama, then, was sustaining to Obama on a deeply personal level. It had nourished him on his long
journey from the distant periphery of African American life—growing up
in a white family from Kansas on an island in the middle of the Pacific—to
its core in Chicago, one of the great black metropolises. Obama's association with Wright and with Trinity United was thus not one he could easily
renounce. And yet, to save his presidential campaign, he had to condemn
Wright. And he had to do something more: he had to explain to white
America how he could associate with this man for so long and still be regarded as an individual who believed deeply in America, and in its promise.
This is the background for Obama's "More Perfect Union" speech, delivered from the new Constitution Center in Philadelphia to a national television audience on March 18, 2008. It is arguably one of the most profound
meditations on race and the American experience ever spoken in a formal
and public setting by an American.

Obama's first words were those with which the Constitution begins:
"We the people, in order to form a more perfect union." He could not have
made his affiliation with the civic nationalist tradition more clear. Obama
acknowledged the Constitution's great flaw, the "original sin of slavery,"
which the framers failed to eradicate. But Obama was equally quick to insist
that redemption from this sin was already contained within the Constitution, which promised all Americans liberty and justice "and a union that
could be and should be perfected over time."[8]

Obama's successful association of the struggle for black freedom with
the core message of the Constitution was one of the speech's key achievements. Another was Obama's ability to show that his own biracialism gave
him a unique ability to comprehend the aspirations and frustrations of both
black and white America and to find a way to bring the two together. "I am
the son of a black man from Kenya and a white woman from Kansas,"
Obama declared. "I was raised with the help of a white grandfather who
survived a Depression to serve in Patton's Army during World War II." Yet
I "am married to a black American who carries within her the blood of
slaves and slaveowners—an inheritance we pass on to our two precious
daughters."[9]

Obama demanded that the hurt of black Americans—as given expression by Wright—be recognized: originating in slavery, it was sustained by more than sixty years of Jim Crow, and unending forms of post–Jim Crow exclusion and discrimination. Though many blacks "scratched and clawed their way to get a piece of the American Dream," Obama remarked, many were defeated in their attempts, passing a "legacy of defeat . . . on to future generations" still haunted by "memories of humiliation and doubt and fear." It was inevitable, Obama observed, that some of that anger would find its way into the black church, the repository of so much of the black community's hope and fear. "That anger is not always productive," but it is "real; it is powerful" and cannot be wished away.[10]

But, Obama asserted, neither could the anger and resentment of whites. This was the most startling move that Obama made in this speech, emboldened to do so by his belief that his biracialism had given him as much insight into—and authority to speak about—whites as blacks. "A similar anger exists within segments of the white community" who do not feel "privileged by their race." They, too, have had to scratch for everything. They, too, "are anxious about their futures, and feel their dreams slipping away." And when they are described as simpleminded bigots because they do not want their children bussed across town, or because "their fears about crime in urban neighborhoods" are attributed to racial bias, "resentment builds." As with black anger, white resentment could focus on the wrong targets. "And yet, to wish away the resentments of white Americans, to label them as misguided or even racist, without recognizing they are grounded in legitimate concerns . . . widens the racial divide," and blocks "the path toward understanding."[11]

Having argued for a kind of parity of hurt and misunderstanding among blacks and whites, Obama asked both groups to find a common faith in the American dream. "The profound mistake of Reverend Wright's sermons," Obama suggested, "is not that he spoke about racism in our society. It's that he spoke as if our society was static; as if no progress had been made; as if this country . . . is still irrevocably bound to a tragic past. But what we know—what we have seen—is that America can change. That is [the] true genius of this nation. What we have already achieved gives us hope—the audacity to hope—for what we can and must achieve tomorrow."[12] The joining together of two racial nations under circumstances of equality and understanding was the ultimate meaning of a more perfect union.

Rarely had a major politician spoken so forthrightly and eloquently of the pain and hurt in both of America's two major racial communities, or suggested that a reckoning with anger and resentment on both sides of the

FIGURE 17.1. Obama and Civic Nationalism Triumphant. Obama waving to his supporters, 200,000 of whom had gathered at Grant Park in Chicago the evening of November 5, 2008, to celebrate his election to the presidency. (Courtesy John Gress/Reuters Pictures)

racial divide could allow the country to resume its march to a more perfect union. The spirit Obama summoned on that March 2008 Philadelphia evening carried him to victory first in June, when he amassed enough delegates to best Hillary Clinton in the contest for the Democratic Party nomination, and then in the fall when he defeated John McCain for the presidency. Obama had not won a majority of white votes, but exit polls indicated he had won more of them (43 percent) than John Kerry had won in 2004 (41 percent).[13] And the turnout for him in black and other minority communities had been overwhelming.

More than 200,000 Chicago residents turned up in Grant Park the night of Obama's November election to celebrate his historic victory. At 10 P.M. central time, a journalist reported, "the crowd just went crazy . . . people were jumping up and down," as "giant television screens ... declared Mr. Obama the projected winner."[14] From New York to LA, and from Miami to Cleveland, Obama supporters "danced in the streets, wept, lifted their voices in prayer and brought traffic to a standstill." In Philadelphia, people streamed toward City Hall. "Under a light rain, they danced to the music blaring from car radios. Drivers stopped in the middle of the street, opened their car doors and broadcast Obama's acceptance speech. 'Barack is in the house!'" exclaimed one Pamela Williams. "'I'm ecstatic,'" declared a thirty-three-year-old business owner in South LA. In a black church in Chicago, worshippers "bowed their heads" and then lifted them to shout "'Thank you, Lord!'" One of the worshippers was Mattie Bridgewater, a public school teacher in Chicago who had attended the same school as Emmett Till, the Chicago boy brutally murdered in 1955 Mississippi for allegedly whistling at a white woman. She admitted she had never expected to live to see this day: "'I'm sitting here in awe. . . . I just thank my God I was allowed to live long enough to see it.'" She and her ninety-two-year-old mother had both voted for Obama earlier that day.[15] Jesse Jackson was an equally important witness to the occasion. He had gone to Grant Park to honor Obama. The event had temporarily rendered this loquacious pioneer of the civil rights movement speechless. Tears poured down his face as he struggled to absorb the momentousness of the occasion.[16]

The joy came forth again on Inauguration Day, January 20, 2009. "Two million people," reported the *Telegraph*, "covered almost every square foot of Washington's two-mile grass runway from the Capitol to the Lincoln Memorial . . .—a restless sea of red, white, and blue flags that barely stopped waving from freezing dawn to chilly dusk."[17] People had come from all over the country, and braved the bitter cold, to make this assembly the largest inauguration in American history. Neither the cold nor the formidable police presence managed to subdue the spirits of the crowd. And everyone, on this day, seemed to partake of the spirit of American civic nationalism, most evident in the sea of flags and the numbers dressed in red, white, and blue. Aretha Franklin sang "My Country, 'Tis of Thee" at the swearing-in ceremony.[18] That evening, the celebration continued at myriad balls unfolding across the capital. At the hip-hop Youth Ball, Kanye West rewrote the lyrics to his song "Heartless" to honor both the new president and the American dream: "From miles around they came to see him speak / The story that he told / to save a country that's so blue / that they thought had lost its soul / the American dream come true tonight."[19] A CNN poll taken shortly after the November elections seemed to back up West's declaration,

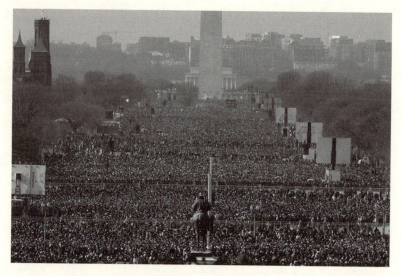

FIGURE 17.2. Obama's Inauguration. This shot captures many of the estimated 2 million people who attended Obama's inauguration on January 20, 2009, filling the Mall in Washington, D.C., from the Capitol to the Washington Monument. (Courtesy PA Images)

finding that 80 percent of African Americans agreed with the statement that "'Obama's election was a dream come true.'"

But another CNN poll had unearthed a more ominous sentiment: "Among white Americans," CNN noted, "only 28 percent said Obama's victory in the race for the White House was a dream come true, with the vast majority, 70 percent, saying it was not."[20] If the numbers of this CNN poll were to be believed, a large majority of white Americans saw no reason to be jubilant about an African American moving into the White House.

"Multiculturalist Ideology Be Damned"

At its core, racial nationalism is the belief that America is a land meant for white people, or Europeans, and their descendants. It has been a part of the American inheritance since the moment of the country's founding. It provided justification for enslaving Africans and subsequently subjecting them to second-class citizenship on account of their alleged racial inferiority. One of its earliest and most powerful iterations was the 1790 Naturalization Law that limited citizenship to immigrants who were free and who were white. Through this law, in force for three-quarters of the country's history, America revealed its aspiration to be a white nation.[21]

This law was finally repealed in 1952, as the civil rights revolution was gathering steam and as anticolonial revolts occurring abroad among non-white populations were further signaling the end of centuries of white supremacy. By the 1960s and 1970s, the frank expression of racial superiority in the United States was more and more associated with white southern "rednecks," bigots whom a majority had become embarrassed to call Americans. As the civil rights revolution advanced, as equal rights for blacks and other racial minorities under the law became the goal to which all mainstream politicians had to subscribe, racial nationalism lost considerable legitimacy. Explicit talk of racial superiority and inferiority was banished from polite public conversation and from mainstream politics. This was a substantial achievement.

But the sentiments that fueled racial nationalism did not go away. Republican depictions of blacks in the 1970s and 1980s first as "welfare queens" and then as an "underclass" rested on unspoken convictions that blacks were inferior to whites, and that they were incapable of sustaining a strong work ethic or family values.[22] Also unspoken in public, but felt among many, was the belief that blacks were more violent than whites; this belief, in turn, justified draconian policing strategies meant to bring law and order and civility to urban areas. By the 1990s and the first decade of the twenty-first century, racially discriminatory drug laws had filled prisons with minorities and given America one of the highest rates of incarceration in the world.[23]

White supremacist hate groups, such as David Duke's Ku Klux Klan and the Aryan Brotherhood, did make their racial thinking—and racial nationalism—plain. But a much larger group of mostly white Americans shared some of these sentiments, even as they would never have regarded themselves as Klan material. Many were devoted followers of Rush Limbaugh and other conservative shock radio jockeys. Here again, explicit racial talk of the sort that was so common in pre–civil rights America was rare. But anger at minorities thought to have been given undeserved privileges and rights was palpable, as was anger at the growing influence of minorities, women, and others in the workplace and in politics. Those who harbored this anger argued that it was not fair to label their behavior as "racist"; rather, they were opposed to what they castigated as "political correctness"—the policing of language to the point where it became impermissible to use any word thought to convey even a hint of racial, ethnic, or sexual insult or humor. Meanwhile, the numbers of minorities seemed to be growing all the time, fueled by a seemingly unstoppable flow of immigrants, legal and illegal, from Mexico. In the early years of the twenty-first century, demographers had begun to proclaim that by midcentury America would be a majority-minority nation.[24]

The advance of this demographic transformation impelled a portion of America's conservative punditry to unleash apocalyptic warnings about America's impending demise. Thus did Patrick Buchanan declare in 2006 that "America is being invaded" by hordes similar to the barbarian ones that had destroyed Rome. "If this [invasion] is not stopped," Buchanan warned, "it will mean the end of the United States," the end of "our civilization." The signs of racial decline were everywhere: in "the death of faith, the degeneration of morals, contempt for the old values, collapse of the culture, paralysis of the will."[25]

The apocalyptic moment Buchanan returned to again and again was 2050, when America would be composed, for the first time, of a majority of people with no blood connection to Europe. Buchanan included Mexicans and other Latinos, as well as Asians and Africans in this majority. "It is not true that all creeds and cultures are equally assimilable in a First World nation born of England, Christianity, and Western civilization," Buchanan intoned.[26] Only certain races and ethnicities could be assimilated to the American culture of liberty and freedom. "Race matters. Ethnicity matters. History matters. Nationality matters," Buchanan declared in staccato bursts. "Multiculturalist ideology be damned, this is what history teaches."[27] Through such rhetoric and argument, Buchanan and other conservatives were rehabilitating racial nationalism for a new century. In the figure of Barack Obama, the country's first nonwhite president, they found an irresistible target.

The key charge against Obama—that as a black man, he had no right to occupy the White House, and no right to lead America—could never be uttered directly. After the civil rights revolution, such statements could no longer be made in public. Hence ostensibly race-neutral grounds had to be found for challenging Obama's legitimacy to occupy the Oval Office. None proved more powerful than the charge that Obama had not been born in the United States. This was a fantastical claim, as it was rather easy to show that he had been born in Hawaii after it had become a state—and therefore fully a part of the United States. But the will on the part of majorities of Republicans to believe the allegation about Obama's foreign birth was so strong that for years it overcame every fact or reality check. If the claim could be shown to be true, then Obama's illegitimacy as president would be plainly revealed. The Constitution had made clear, after all, that every president had to be "a natural born citizen" of the United States. If Obama was not, he would have to be removed from office. Here was a way of bringing America's first—and hopefully last—black presidency to a quick and decisive end.

The most common foreign-birth fantasy was that Obama's father had whisked his pregnant Kansan wife off to Kenya so that she would give birth on his native, African soil. In 2008, the Obama campaign thought the charge so ridiculous that it had trouble taking it seriously. When the allegation persisted, the campaign released "a certification of live birth" from the Hawaii Department of Health showing that Obama had indeed been born in that state in 1961. The campaign posted the document online; two independent groups, FactCheck.org and PolitiFact, vouched for its authenticity.[28] But this did not satisfy Obama's critics, now increasingly known as "birthers," who wanted to know why Obama had not released his so-called long-form Hawaiian birth certificate. The reason was simple: the state of Hawaii regarded the long form as a private record; it had no public, and therefore no legal, standing.[29] But Obama's "decision" to keep the public from accessing this private form was now taken as evidence that he was hiding something—perhaps that he had in fact been born in Kenya or that the form had identified him as Muslim.[30]

The birthers kept their accusations in the public eye for three long years. In 2011, Donald Trump, in one of his first political interventions, jumped aboard the birthers' bandwagon, alleging that "there's something on that birth certificate that he [Obama] doesn't like."[31] That charge finally faded in 2012, only to be replaced by another equally damaging accusation: that Obama was a secret practitioner of the Muslim faith. Deceit on Obama's part was once again invoked: Obama's mother had allegedly enrolled him in a madrassa during their time in Indonesia, and Obama had been a secret Muslim ever since. Suggesting that he had attended a madrassa, of course, was a way to tie Obama to radical Islam, for these Muslim schools were thought by Americans to be the sites where youngsters were indoctrinated in the virtues of jihad, of holy war against non-Muslims.[32] And America could not tolerate a jihadist-sympathizer in the White House.

The charge that Obama was a Muslim actually gained in resonance across the two terms of his presidency. In 2009, relatively small minorities, 11 percent of Americans and 18 percent of Republicans, believed this about him. By 2010, the numbers had climbed to 18 percent and 31 percent, respectively. By 2015, they had more than doubled from their 2009 levels, with almost a third of Americans and nearly half of Republicans believing that Obama was a Muslim.[33] That Obama had attended church at Trinity United for twenty years now seemed not to matter.

Occasionally the true nature of the animus against Obama—that, as a black man, he had no right to occupy the White House—came into clear view. Such was the case with sentiments expressed at the Tea Party's March on Washington on September 12, 2009. The Tea Party erupted into American politics only a few months after Obama's election. Tea Party members regarded themselves as heirs to the Sons of Liberty of 1773 who had tossed boatloads of tea into Boston Harbor as an act of defiance against British taxation and tyranny. Twenty-first-century Tea Partiers opposed with fury two signature legislative initiatives of the Obama administration: the near trillion-dollar stimulus package of 2009 meant to revive the economy in the aftermath of the 2008 crash and the even more ambitious Affordable Care Act (ACA) that aimed to provide insurance to millions of Americans who could not afford health care.[34]

The ranks of the Tea Party were overwhelmingly white and middle-aged to elderly. Many members were concerned that Obama's healthcare plan would undermine the integrity of Medicare, a massive and highly respected government program that provided health care to those sixty-five and older. Much fun was poked at Tea Partiers who demanded that the government "keep its hands off their Medicare," as though Medicare were something other than a government-sponsored and -funded program. But the deeper anxiety being expressed was about a new, and nonwhite, America taking shape under Obama that would unfairly lay claim to resources and privileges that had long been rightfully reserved for true (read white) Americans.

The Tea Party's September 2009 March on Washington shocked everyone with its size: as many as 100,000 protesters came to Washington to take their stand. The crowd made its sentiments known through all kinds of signs, many of them comparing Obama to Hitler or to a hammer-and-sickle socialist. Another theme came up again and again, however: Obama's identity as an African. The signs were not kind to Obama's paternal heritage. "The Zoo Has an African [lion—represented by an image], and the White House has a Lyin' African!" proclaimed several signs held aloft that day. "OBAMA[,] GO BACK HOME TO KENYA AND TAKE YOUR RADICAL LEFT COMMY FRIENDS WITH YA," screamed another.[35] A third proclaimed, "Somewhere in Kenya a Village Is Missing an Idiot."[36] A fourth offered this lost-in-America idiot a "FREE TICKET BACK TO KENYA!!"[37]

That someone born in Hawaii could be portrayed with such conviction as having been born in Kenya spoke to the powerful influence of the birther

OBAMA CARE

Coming soon to a clinic near you

FIGURE 17.3. Obama as Witch Doctor. This image circulated through Tea Party email lists in summer 2009 and appeared on a full-scale poster held aloft by a participant in the Tea Party March on Washington on September 12, 2009. The creator of this image is unknown.

canard about Obama's foreign and African birth. To Tea Partiers, Obama's insistence that he had not been born abroad only confirmed that he was a deceiver, a man never to be trusted. And "the fact" that he had been born abroad rendered his occupancy of the White House illegal, much as undocumented immigrants occupied a place in America to which they had no right. The illegality and deception that had overwhelmed American politics and culture had now engulfed the White House itself. America was in deep peril. It needed the Tea Party to bring it to its senses.

That Obama's deception was of an African cast, of course, made things worse. Any Tea Partier sixty years of age or older had likely been reared on a steady diet of Johnny Weissmuller Tarzan films in his or her youth. Though made in the 1930s and 1940s, these films were cycled endlessly through TV programming in the 1950s and 1960s, often on lazy Saturday

FIGURE 17.4. Obama as Chimpanzee. This image of Obama and "his family" was shared in an email by GOP and Tea Party activist Marilyn Davenport in April 2011. The creator of this image is unknown.

afternoons when they were a cheap way for the networks to keep themselves on the air. These movies are laced with images of the alternately savage and childlike African other.[38] One popular sign from the 2009 march could have been pulled straight out of a Tarzan movie: it depicted Obama as a witch doctor, his temple crowned by a wild feather headdress and his nose pierced twice by a fearsome-looking bone. Its creator is unknown, but it had been making the rounds in Tea Party email circles and popping up on Tea Party websites for weeks before the September march. It is hardly surprising, then, that someone thought to reproduce it on a poster-size scale for the Washington march itself.[39]

Tea Party leaders banned such images of Obama from future marches, worried that such vicious caricatures would give their organization a bad name. But this ban had little effect on Tea Party member behavior on the Internet, where images of Obama as a primitive African and, even worse, as a monkey continued to surface for years. These images were the work of battalions of Photoshopping "artists" who were using spare time, at home or at work, to attack the American president in the most offensive way possible. Many did not think of their work as racist. Such was the case with Tea Party activist Marilyn Davenport who, in April 2011, circulated a shot of Barack Obama superimposed on the head of a baby chimpanzee alongside "mom" and "dad" chimpanzees, the three arranged in a "lovely" family pose. The tagline: "Now you know why—No birth certificate!" When accused even by fellow Republicans of circulating an image "dripping with racism," Davenport retorted that "she was not a racist" and "simply found it amusing."[40] She and her friends were simply having a good laugh. Perhaps Davenport did not attach much significance to her racist Photoshopping because for her, as for many Americans, dehumanizing Obama via Internet pictures and comments had become routine. Evidence shows that even white police officers were exchanging samples of this art and its associated commentary with each other.[41]

Though the Tea Party failed to dislodge Obama from the presidency in 2012, it did strip him of his majorities first in the House (2010) and then in the Senate (2014). Its supporters paralyzed the federal government, ensuring that Obama and the Democrats would have no major legislative accomplishments during his final six years in office. The country suffered from this paralysis, its effects most evident in Congress's inaction on a number of critical fronts: millions of undocumented immigrants living in the shadows; the poor condition of large portions of the country's transportation infrastructure; an epidemic of gun ownership and killing; and slow progress on climate control. Whatever Obama accomplished, he did more and more by executive order, a limited decree-issuing power given to presidents to advance laws passed by Congress that required some modification—usually in the form of refining mechanisms of implementation and enforcement—in order to accomplish the original legislative aim.[42]

The intensity and constancy of conservative attacks across the years of his presidency charred Obama, making him more reluctant than he had been to share himself and his dreams with the American people. The "keep hope alive" crusader of the 2008 campaign, the one so ready to use personal details of his family's life and journey as evidence that the American dream still lived, disappeared somewhere in the first term and, except for brief flashes, never really returned. Obama dared not show any anger, lest he be categorized and demeaned as an "angry black man," in the manner of Jesse Jackson. Plain speaking on race questions was also, he learned, a perilous act. When Obama offered sympathy for the family of Trayvon Martin, an innocent black teenager killed by white vigilante George Zimmerman in Florida in 2012, the president drew an outraged response from white conservatives who accused him of taking the side of blacks and of attempting to exert undue influence on the legal process. Obama's offensive words had been anodyne: "If I had a son he'd look like Trayvon. And I think they [his parents] are right to expect that all of us as Americans are going to take this with the seriousness it deserves."[43]

Obama's cautiousness, however, won him little credit from his critics, who now began complaining that he was remote, hard to read, and inaccessible. Obama's reticence confirmed the suspicions of many whites that he was indeed an alien presence in the White House. Obama had been damned when he expressed some sympathy for the predicament of blacks tangling with police forces predisposed to seeing them as criminals, and damned again when he clammed up, determined to reveal nothing about his feelings at all. Race had boxed him in.[44]

Race also required that Obama constrain himself in terms of domestic policy. He rarely proposed or endorsed legislation meant to address problems particular to the black community and requiring a remedy that could be interpreted as race specific. His reluctance to do so recalled the strategy of FDR. Obama's legislation, like that of the New Deal, would focus on the economic needs of ordinary Americans for jobs, health care, and protection against predatory lending practices. Like FDR, Obama hoped to draw Americans of all colors, religions, and nationalities into his coalition.

Obama rarely acknowledged the closeness of his legislative approach to that of FDR. In part this was due to Roosevelt's poor record on racial matters; Obama did not want his reluctance to support policies meant to benefit blacks to be interpreted as a tacit acceptance of Rooseveltian racial nationalist beliefs.[45] But Obama's reluctance to invoke FDR was also likely driven by Obama's fear that his reform agenda relative to Roosevelt's would be found wanting. No president has matched—or is ever likely to match—FDR's First Hundred Days, nor the magnitude of his two greatest achievements: recovery from the Great Depression and victory in World War II. During his four terms, Roosevelt also transformed America with dams, airports, roads, bridges, post offices, school buildings, and electrification; during Obama's two terms, the country's once state-of-the-art infrastructure continued its long-term decline. Obama's achievement in health care, if it survives the current Republican presidency and Congress, will one day come to be seen as rivaling FDR's achievement with Social Security. But the Obama administration's record, overall, cannot match what the Roosevelt administration accomplished across its four terms. That Obama never found an evocative label, such as the "New Deal," to encompass his reform ambitions further underscores the fragmentary nature of his accomplishments.

The achievement gap between the two administrations, however, should not be attributed solely, or even primarily, to Obama's limitations as a leader. Obama had to operate in political circumstances that were far more difficult than what Roosevelt had had to manage. Roosevelt never had to contend with charges that he was racially unfit for the White House; to the contrary, he was an American blueblood. Roosevelt had also benefited from the emergence of a powerful left, manifest in the multimillion-member labor movement, populist insurgencies such as Huey Long's "Share the Wealth" campaign, and a strong Communist Party. This progressive uprising won for FDR huge and left-leaning majorities in Congress in 1934 and 1936. That electoral upheaval, in turn, pushed New Dealers, and Roosevelt himself, to do more for the common people—in the form of jobs programs and redistributionist taxation, labor, and welfare policies—than they otherwise would have done. By contrast, no left insurgency filled Obama's sails; none even existed for most of his first term. Instead, Obama had to contend every day with racially inflected populist fury on the right. That right undercut Obama's support in Congress every bit as quickly and effectively as the left insurgency of the 1930s had given the Roosevelt coalition extraordinary legislative influence. The weakness of the left in the early twenty-first century constrained the Obama administration in profound ways.[46]

Voices on the left did emerge near the end of Obama's first term, when young people, gathering under the banner "We are the 99%," occupied parks and squares in New York and other cities to protest the concentration of wealth and power in the "1%." Taking the name "Occupy Wall Street," after the site of the first protest in September 2011, these protesters eventually coalesced into significant left movements, such as Black Lives Matter and socialist Bernie Sanders's 2016 campaign for the presidency. But these movements acquired heft only in late 2014 and 2015, too late in Obama's presidency to be useful to him.[47] Like all presidents in their last two years in office, Obama had become a lame duck, with little chance of getting significant legislation through Congress. Obama did turn toward executive orders and foreign policy in his last two years—arenas in which he could pursue policy goals without having to worry much about congressional support. In foreign affairs, he made the United States a signatory to the Paris climate accords and the Iran nuclear deal. In the United States he signed executive orders to allow four million undocumented immigrants to remain legally in the United States, to give America a more robust clean power energy regime, and to ensure citizens' privacy. But because none of these foreign or domestic acts were secured through congressional legislation or treaties, each can be reversed by the stroke of a subsequent president's pen.[48] Hillary Clinton, had she been elected, would no doubt have preserved Obama's executive orders and foreign policy initiatives. Donald Trump, by contrast, wants to erase Obama's legacy.

Obama's accomplishments look more substantial once we grasp the hostile political environment in which he had to operate. He superintended an economic recovery much more robust than what Europe achieved during those years. He brought a half-century campaign for national health insurance to a successful conclusion. The ranks of the African American middle class expanded substantially under him. His vision of civic nationalism inspired tens of millions of young nonwhites to believe that they could find opportunity and liberty, and democracy, in America. That nonwhite Americans could make this hope their own is what made the musical *Hamilton: An American Musical*, a celebration of America's founding written, staged, and performed by Americans of color, the smash Broadway hit of 2015.[49]

As we get distance on the events of these years, Obama will come to be seen as having guided America to its 2050 demographic date with destiny when a majority of the country will be nonwhite. Obama's contribution will have been to show that the country could change dramatically in population terms and yet still be American in its dreams and aspirations, in its regard for democracy and for the Constitution. He has demonstrated that the country's civic nationalist dream remains a dynamic force—and a North Star—amid the demographic, economic, and political turbulence of the early decades of the twenty-first century.

And yet Obama's presidency has also demonstrated the tenacity of America's racial nationalist tradition. Tens of millions of white Americans were simply unable to accept him as their president. The amount of energy they dedicated to discrediting him, often on charges that any reasonable person would immediately recognize as ludicrous, has been staggering. That Obama exited the presidency without blemish in his personal life is itself an impressive accomplishment. Obama's knowledge of his moral rectitude will likely give him little comfort, however, as he contemplates what he was never given a chance to do: transcend racial division, create a path toward citizenship for millions of illegal immigrants, rebuild the country's infrastructure, and give the country a chance to recover from its addiction to guns and violence. And then there are the matters that, as a black man, he could not, and would not, touch at all: most important, the tangle of poverty, police violence, and prison that has shaped the lives of too many of the country's black poor.

America elected its first black president in the early twenty-first century and then told him that he, as a black man, should not be allowed to govern the white nation over which he presided. The Obama campaign for the presidency reinvigorated America's civic nationalist tradition like no other event of the last fifty years. And yet it also stirred the racial nationalist anxieties of millions of white Americans who simply could not become comfortable with the idea that a black man was commander-in-chief.

Donald Trump's victory in November 2016 owed a great deal to his ability to become the instrument through which white Americans expressed their unease about America's accelerating transformation into a society no longer recognizable as white and European. Trump delighted in unlocking the box into which white Americans had stuffed two generations' worth of racial grievance. Already in Obama's first term, he had grasped how much he could advance his own political career by embracing the birther canard that a black man born on African soil had ascended illegally to the White House. In 2015 he calculated correctly that vicious rhetorical attacks on Mexicans and Muslims would propel him to the forefront of those vying for the 2016 Republican nomination. The undulating sea of white faces that populated every one of his rallies in 2015 and 2016 underscored the racial meaning of his slogan "Make America Great Again."

President Trump will not succeed in eradicating America's diversity any more than Obama succeeded in uprooting its racism. Both civic nationalism and racial nationalism will continue to shape American life and politics. Both traditions still constitute the paradox that is America.

NOTES

Chapter 1: Policy Revolution without a Political Transformation: The Presidency of Barack Obama

1. Jennifer Schuessler, "Historians Assess Obama's Legacy under Trump's Shadow," *New York Times*, November 13, 2016.

2. James T. Kloppenberg, *Reading Obama: Dreams, Hope, and the American Political Tradition* (Princeton, NJ: Princeton University Press, 2010); David J. Garrow, *Rising Star: The Making of Barack Obama* (New York: William Morrow, 2017).

3. The single best biographical treatment of Obama remains David Remnick, *The Bridge: The Life and Rise of Barack Obama* (New York: Knopf, 2010).

4. See, for instance, Lily Geismer, *Don't Blame Us: Suburban Liberals and the Transformation of the Democratic Party* (Princeton, NJ: Princeton University Press, 2015); and Mark Foley, *Front Porch Politics: The Forgotten Heyday of American Activism in the 1970s and 1980s* (New York: Hill and Wang, 2013).

5. Michael Grunwald, *The New New Deal: The Hidden Story of Change in the Obama Era* (New York: Simon & Schuster, 2012); Jonathan Chait, *Audacity: How Barack Obama Defied His Critics and Created a Legacy That Will Prevail* (New York: Custom House, 2017); Peter Baker, *Obama: The Call of History* (New York: New York Times and Calloway, 2017); Theda Skocpol and Lawrence Jacobs, *Reaching for a New Deal: Ambitious Governance, Economic Meltdown, and Polarized Politics in Obama's First Two Years* (New York: Russell Sage, 2011).

6. Theda Skocpol and Vanessa Williamson, *The Tea Party and the Remaking of Republican Conservatism* (New York: Oxford University Press, 2012).

7. Micah L. Sifry, "Obama's Lost Army," *New Republic*, February 9, 2017, https://new republic.com/article/140245/obamas-lost-army-inside-fall-grassroots-machine.

8. David Daley, *Ratf**ked: The True Story behind the Secret Plan to Steal America's Democracy* (New York: Liveright, 2016).

9. Josh Saul and Max Kutner, "FBI Director James Comey Tried to Reveal Russian Tampering Months before Election," *Newsweek*, March 29, 2017, http://www.newsweek.com/fbi -director-james-comey-russian-tampering-election-576417.

10. Chas Danner, "Obama Rejected Comey Op-Ed on Russia's Election Meddling," *New York*, April 22, 2017, http://nymag.com/daily/intelligencer/2017/04/report-obama-rejected -comey-op-ed-on-russian-interference.html.

11. David Remnick, "Obama Reckons with a Trump Presidency," *New Yorker*, November 28, 2016.

Chapter 2: Tea Partied: President Obama's Encounters with the Conservative-Industrial Complex

1. Barack Obama, Keynote address to the Democratic National Convention, Boston, MA, 2004, http://www.washingtonpost.com/wp-dyn/articles/A19751-2004Jul27.html.

2. James T. Kloppenberg, *Reading Obama: Dreams, Hope, and the American Political Tradition* (Princeton, NJ: Princeton University Press, 2010).

3. Lisa McGirr, *Suburban Warriors: The Origins of the New American Right* (Princeton, NJ: Princeton University Press, 2001); Kevin Kruse, *White Flight: Atlanta and the Making of Modern Conservatism* (Princeton, NJ: Princeton University Press, 2005). In recent years, historians have been focusing on the next phase of conservatism, in which conservative leaders confronted the challenges of governance and depended on deep-rooted organizations and institutions to promote their ideas. For a review of the historiography of conservatism, see Julian E. Zelizer, *Governing America: The Revival of Political History* (Princeton, NJ: Princeton University Press, 2012), 68–89; Kimberly Phillips-Fein, "Conservatism: A State of the Field," *Journal of American History* 98, no. 3 (2011): 723–43.

4. Meg Jacobs and Julian E. Zelizer, *Conservatives in Power: The Reagan Years* (Boston: Bedford Books, 2010).

5. Quoted in David Remnick, "Going the Distance," *New Yorker*, January 27, 2014.

6. Julian E. Zelizer, *Pirate Politics: Newt Gingrich, the Speaker Wright Scandal, and the Origins of Our Polarized Times* (work in progress).

7. Thomas A. Mann and Norman J. Ornstein, *It's Even Worse Than It Looks: How the American Constitutional System Collided with the New Politics of Extremism* (New York: Basic Books, 2012).

8. Steven S. Smith, "The Senate Syndrome," *Issues in Governance Studies*, no. 35 (June 2010): 1–30.

9. "Senate Action on Cloture Motions," U.S. Senate, Senate.gov, 2016.

10. Nolan McCarty, "The Policy Effects of Political Polarization," in *The Transformation of American Politics: Activist Government and the Rise of Conservatism*, ed. Paul Pierson and Theda Skocpol (Princeton, NJ: Princeton University Press, 2007), 223–55; Jacob Hacker, "Privatizing Risk without Privatizing the Welfare State: The Hidden Politics of Social Policy Retrenchment in the United States," *American Political Science Review* 98, no. 2 (2004): 243–60.

11. Theda Skocpol and Vanessa Williamson, *The Tea Party and the Remaking of Republican Conservatism* (New York: Oxford University Press, 2012).

12. Paul Krugman, "Not Enough Audacity," *New York Times*, June 25, 2009.

13. Glenn Kessler, "When Did Mitch McConnell Say He Wanted to Make Obama a One-Term President," *Washington Post*, January 11, 2017.

14. David Daley, *Ratf**ked: The True Story Behind the Secret Plan to Steal America's Democracy* (New York: Liveright, 2016), 21.

15. Tim Dickinson, "Meet the Right-Wing Rebels Who Overthrew John Boehner," *Rolling Stone*, October 6, 2015.

16. Theda Skocpol and Alexander Hertel-Fernandez, "The Koch Network and Republican Party Extremism," *Perspectives on Politics* 14 (2016): 681–99; Jane Mayer, *Dark Money: The Hidden History of Billionaires behind the Rise of the Radical Right* (New York: Doubleday, 2016).

17. Daley, *Ratf**ked*.

18. For two new histories of the conservative media, see Nichole Hemmer, *Messengers of the Right: Conservative Media and the Transformation of American Culture* (Philadelphia: University of Pennsylvania Press, 2016); and Brian Rosenwald, *Mount Rushmore: The Rise of Talk*

Radio and Its Impact on Politics and Public Policy (Cambridge, MA: Harvard University Press, forthcoming).

19. Hemmer, *Messengers of the Right*.

20. Julian E. Zelizer, "The End of the Fairness Doctrine in the 1980s," in *Media Nation: The Political History of News in Modern America*, ed. Bruce J. Schulman and Julian E. Zelizer (Philadelphia: University of Pennsylvania Press, 2017).

21. For the best history of Fox News, see Gabriel Sherman, *The Loudest Voice in the Room: How the Brilliant, Bombastic Roger Ailes Built Fox News—and a Divided Country* (New York: Random House, 2014).

22. Matt Grossman and David Hopkins, *Asymmetric Politics: Ideological Republicans and Group Interest Democrats* (New York: Oxford University Press, 2016).

23. Jess Henig, "Born in the U.S.A.," Factcheck.org, August 28, 2008, http://www.factcheck.org/2008/08/born-in-the-usa/.

24. Sara Olkon and James Janega, "Tax Activist's Ad Challenges Obama's Eligibility for Office," *Chicago Tribune*, December 3, 2008.

25. Quoted in Gabrial Winant, "The Birthers in Congress," *Salon*, July 28, 2009, http://www.salon.com/2009/07/28/birther_enablers/.

26. Willoughby Mariano, "Liberal Bloggers Say Candidate for Governor Nathan Deal 'Dabbled' in Birther Conspiracies," *Politifact Georgia*, August 20, 2010, http://www.politifact.com/georgia/statements/2010/aug/20/liberal-bloggers/liberal-bloggers-say-candidate-governor-nathan-dea/; Eric Kleefled, "Vitter: 'I'm Not a Birther' and 'Liberal Thought Police' Oppose Access to Courts," *TPM*, July 15, 2010, http://talkingpointsmemo.com/dc/vitter-i-m-not-a-birther-and-liberal-thought-police-oppose-access-to-courts; Ashley Powers, "On the Case: Sheriff Joe Arpaio Probes Obama Birth Certificate," *Los Angeles Times*, March 1, 2012, http://www.latimes.com/news/nation/nationnow/la-na-nn-joe-arpaio-obama-birther-2012030 1,0,5437098.story.

27. Ashley Parker and Steven Eder, "Inside the Six Weeks Donald Trump Was a Non-Stop Birther," *New York Times*, July 2, 2016.

28. Adam Gopnik, "Trump and Obama: A Night to Remember," *New Yorker*, September 12, 2015.

29. Joel B. Pollak, "The Vetting," Breitbart.com, May 17, 2012.

30. Parker and Eder, "Inside the Six Weeks Donald Trump Was a Non-Stop Birther."

31. J. Eric Oliver and Thomas J. Wood, "Conspiracy Theories and the Paranoid Style(s) of Mass Opinion," *American Journal of Political Science* 58, no. 4 (2014): 952–66.

32. Robert Draper, "Inside the Power of the N.R.A.," *New York Times*, December 12, 2013.

33. Marc Maron, *WTF?*, episode 613, June 22, 2015.

34. President Barack Obama, "Transcript and Analysis: Obama Addresses the Nation in Farewell Address," January 10, 2017, NPR.org.

Chapter 3: Neither a Depression nor a New Deal: Bailout, Stimulus, and the Economy

1. David Leonhardt, "Top Priority Is Stabilizing the Patient," *New York Times*, November 6, 2008, B1.

2. Jackie Calmes, "In Candidates, Two Approaches to Wall Street," *New York Times*, September 16, 2008, 1; Michael Cooper, "For the Nominees, New Roles and New Risks," *New York Times*, September 25, 2008, A24.

3. Patrick Healy, "On Bailouts, Candidates Were Surely Themselves," *New York Times*, September 29, 2008, A16.

4. Timothy F. Geithner, *Stress Test: Reflections on Financial Crisis* (New York: Crown, 2014), 208–9.

5. David M. Herszenhorn, "Bailout Plan Wins Approval; Democrats Vow Tighter Rules," *New York Times*, October 4, 2008, A1; Henry M. Paulson Jr., *On the Brink: Inside the Race to Stop the Collapse of the Global Financial System* (New York: Business Plus, 2010), 328.

6. Paulson, *On the Brink*, 238; Ben S. Bernanke, *The Courage to Act: A Memoir of a Crisis and Its Aftermath* (New York: W. W. Norton, 2015), 218.

7. Geithner, *Stress Test*, 338; Steven Perlberg, "Rick Santelli Started the Tea Party with a Rant Exactly 5 Years Ago Today," *Business Insider*, February 19, 2014, http://www.businessinsider .com/rick-santelli-tea-party-rant-2014-2; Theda Skocpol and Vanessa Williamson, *The Tea Party and the Remaking of Republican Conservatism* (New York: Oxford University Press, 2012), 7; Jill Lepore, *The Whites of Their Eyes: The Tea Party's Revolution and the Battle Over American History* (Princeton, NJ: Princeton University Press, 2011), 3.

8. Matt Taibbi, "Secrets and Lies of the Bailout," *Rolling Stone*, January 4, 2013, http:// www.rollingstone.com/politics/news/secret-and-lies-of-the-bailout-20130104.

9. Mike Webb, "Paul Kiel and Karen Weise Discuss the Stars and Slackers of the Bailout," ProPublica, October 5, 2010, https://www.propublica.org/podcast/item/paul-kiel-and-karen -weise-discuss-the-stars-and-slackers-of-the-bailout; Paul Kiel and Dan Nguyen, "Bailout Tracker," ProPublica, October 17, 2016, https://projects.propublica.org/bailout/.

10. Pepper D. Culpepper and Raphael Reinke, "Structural Power and Bank Bailouts in the United Kingdom and the United States," *Politics and Society* 42, no. 4 (2014): 427–54.

11. Ibid., esp. 428 and 440; Andrew Ross Sorkin, *Too Big To Fail: The Inside Story of How Wall Street and Washington Fought to Save the Financial System—and Themselves* (New York: Penguin, 2010), 525.

12. Barrie A. Wigmore, "A Comparison of Federal Financial Remediation in the Great Depression and 2008–2009," *Research in Economic History* 27 (2010): 255–303.

13. Christina D. Romer, "What Ended the Great Depression?" *Journal of Economic History* 52, no. 4 (December 1992): 757–84; Ben S. Bernanke, *Essays on the Great Depression* (Princeton, NJ: Princeton University Press, 2000).

14. *The Daily Show with Jon Stewart*, October 13, 2008 (Comedy Central), http://www.cc .com/video-clips/7q1f73/the-daily-show-with-jon-stewart-amity-shlaes.

15. Romer, "What Ended the Great Depression?" 757; Gauti B. Eggertsson, "Great Expectations and the End of the Depression," *American Economic Review* 98, no. 4 (September 2008): 1476–1516, esp. 1477; Amity Shlaes, *The Forgotten Man: A New History of the Great Depression* (New York: HarperCollins, 2007), 397; David R. Weir, "A Century of U.S. Unemployment, 1890–1990: Revised Estimates and Evidence for Stabilization," *Research in Economic History* 14 (1992): 301–46, esp. 322; Eric Rauchway, "New Deal Denialism," *Dissent* 57, no. 1 (Winter 2010): 68–72. For the standard series on unemployment, see Susan B. Carter, Scott Sigmund Gartner, Michael R. Haines, Alan L. Olmstead, Richard Sutch, and Gavin Wright, eds., *Historical Statistics of the United States, Earliest Times to the Present: Millennial Edition* (Cambridge: Cambridge University Press, 2006), vol. 2, 82–84, table Ba470–77, "Labor force, employment, and unemployment, 1890–1990."

16. Jonathan Chait, "Wasting Away in Hooverville," *New Republic*, March 17, 2009, https:// newrepublic.com/article/63351/wasting-away-hooverville; *CNN Larry King Live*, "Is America Broken?" March 3, 2009, http://www.cnn.com/TRANSCRIPTS/0903/03/lkl.01.html; Amity Shlaes, "FDR Was a Great Leader, But His Economic Plan Isn't One to Follow," *Washington Post*, February 1, 2009, B1; Anne Henderson, "Tax Cuts Work Better Than Public Stimulus," *The Australian*, December 29, 2010, http://www.theaustralian.com.au/news/world/tax-cuts-work-better -than-public-stimulus/story-e6frg6ux-1225977407766.

17. Geithner, *Stress Test*, 241; Shlaes, *Forgotten Man*, 142.

18. John Maynard Keynes, "From Keynes to Roosevelt: Our Recovery Plan Assayed," *New York Times*, December 31, 1933, XX2.

19. E. Cary Brown, "Fiscal Policy in the 'Thirties: A Reappraisal," *American Economic Review* 46, no. 5 (December 1956): 857–79, esp. 866; Thomas M. Renaghan, "A New Look at Fiscal Policy in the 1930s," *Research in Economic History* 11 (1988): 171–83.

20. Noam Scheiber, *The Escape Artists: How Obama's Team Fumbled the Recovery* (New York: Simon & Schuster, 2011), 27, 43.

21. Ibid., 40–42.

22. Brian Beutler, "Obama Was Right About Republican Extremism All Along," *New Republic*, October 25, 2016, https://newrepublic.com/article/138114/obama-right-republican-extremism-along.

23. Norm Ornstein, "Tribal Politics, the Stimulus, and the Right," *Atlantic*, February 20, 2014, http://www.theatlantic.com/politics/archive/2014/02/tribal-politics-the-stimulus-and-the-right/283961/; Ornstein on *The Rachel Maddow Show*, MSNBC, July 25, 2012, http://www.msnbc.com/transcripts/rachel-maddow-show/2012-07-25; Senate vote: http://www.senate.gov/legislative/LIS/roll_call_lists/roll_call_vote_cfm.cfm?congress=111&session=1&vote=00061; House vote: http://clerk.house.gov/evs/2009/roll046.xml.

24. Scheiber, *Escape Artists*, 15–16, 140–41.

25. Robert Kuttner, *A Presidency in Peril: The Inside Story of Obama's Promise, Wall Street's Power, and the Struggle to Control Our Economic Future* (White River Junction, VT: Chelsea Green, 2010), 75–76; Scheiber, *Escape Artists*, 134.

26. Jeffrey Frankel, "The Obama Stimulus and the 5-Year Anniversary of Market Turnaround," *Econbrowser*, February 26, 2014, http://econbrowser.com/archives/2014/02/guest-contribution-the-obama-stimulus-and-the-5-year-anniversary-of-market-turnaround; U.S. Bureau of Labor Statistics, Civilian Unemployment Rate, FRED, Federal Reserve Bank of St. Louis, https://fred.stlouisfed.org/series/UNRATE; Yuliya Demyanyk, Elena Loutskina, and Daniel Murphy, "Does Fiscal Stimulus Work When Recessions Are Caused by Too Much Private Debt?" *Economic Commentary* 2016–08, August 10, 2016, Federal Reserve Bank of Cleveland; Daniel J. Wilson, "Fiscal Spending Jobs Multipliers: Evidence from the 2009 American Recovery and Reinvestment Act," *American Economic Journal: Economic Policy* 4, no. 3 (2012): 251–82, esp. 277–78.

27. Michael Grunwald, *The New New Deal: The Hidden Story of Change in the Obama Era* (New York: Simon & Schuster, 2012), 435–48.

28. Benjamin Wallace-Wells, "Cass Sunstein Wants to Nudge Us," *New York Times*, May 16, 2010, SM38.

29. Eric Morath and Ben Leubsdorf, "U.S. Economy Roars Back, Grew 2.9% in Third Quarter," *Wall Street Journal*, October 28, 2016, http://www.wsj.com/articles/u-s-economy-grew-2-9-in-third-quarter-1477657992.

30. Mark Blyth, "Paradigms and Paradox: The Politics of Economic Ideas in Two Moments of Crisis," *Governance* 26, no. 2 (April 2013): 197–215, esp. 208; Paul Krugman, "Myths of Austerity," *New York Times*, July 2, 2010, A25.

31. Jack Bao, Maureen O'Hara, and Alex Zhou, "The Volcker Rule and Market-Making in Times of Stress," Finance and Economics Discussion Series 2016–102 (Washington, DC: Board of Governors of the Federal Reserve System, 2016), https://www.federalreserve.gov/econresdata/feds/2016/files/2016102pap.pdf.

32. Thomas E. Mann and Norman J. Ornstein, *It's Even Worse than It Was: How the American Constitutional System Collided with the New Politics of Extremism* (New York: Basic Books, 2016); Grunwald, *The New New Deal*, 448.

33. Barry Eichengreen and Kevin H. O'Rourke, "What Do the New Data Tell Us?" *Vox*, March 8, 2010, http://voxeu.org/article/tale-two-depressions-what-do-new-data-tell-us-february -2010-update#jun09; Kevin H. O'Rourke, "It Has Finally Happened," *Irish Economy*, November 29, 2015, http://www.irisheconomy.ie/index.php/2015/11/29/it-has-finally-happened/.

34. Ray C. Fair, July 20, 2016, comment on the vote-share equation, https://fairmodel.econ .yale.edu/vote2016/index2.htm.

35. Alan de Bromhead, Barry Eichengreen, and Kevin H. O'Rourke, "Political Extremism in the 1920s and 1930s: Do German Lessons Generalize?" *Journal of Economic History* 73, no. 2 (June 2013): 371–406, esp. 392.

36. Results of the 2014 European Elections, European Parliament, http://www.europarl .europa.eu/elections2014-results/en/country-results-el-2009.html.

Chapter 4: Achievement without Credit:
The Obama Presidency and Inequality

1. Thomas Piketty, *Capital in the Twenty-First Century*, trans. Arthur Goldhammer (Cambridge, MA: Belknap Press of Harvard University Press, 2014).

2. "Remarks by the President on the Economy in Osawatomie, Kansas," https://obama whitehouse.archives.gov/the-press-office/2011/12/06/remarks-president-economy-osawatomie -kansas.

3. Larry M. Bartels, *Unequal Democracy: The Political Economy of the New Gilded Age*, 2d ed. (New York: Russell Sage Foundation/Princeton University Press, 2016), 4, 34, 59.

4. Congressional Budget Office, "The Distribution of Household Income and Federal Taxes, 2013" (2016).

5. The confusion arises partly from Piketty's use of the term "total income" to refer to labor plus capital income, which invites misunderstanding from readers who think "total income" includes transfers and taxes. See, for example, the chart on page 299 of Piketty's *Capital in the Twenty-First Century*, which shows the share of the top decile in the early 2000s returning to the peak of the 1920s.

6. Christopher Jencks points out that the growth in the EITC and noncash benefits from 1996 to 2011 offset about four-fifths of the decline in extremely poor families' pretax money income. See Kathryn J. Edin and H. Luke Shaefer, *$2 a Day: Living on Almost Nothing in America* (Boston: Houghton Mifflin, 2015); Christopher Jencks, "Why the Very Poor Have Become Poorer," *New York Review of Books*, June 9, 2016.

7. Suzanne Mettler, "Reconstituting the Submerged State: The Challenges of Social Policy Reform in the Obama Era," *Perspectives on Politics* 8 (2010): 803–26.

8. Alan S. Blinder and Mark Zandi, "How the Great Recession Was Brought to an End," July 27, 2010, https://www.economy.com/mark-zandi/documents/End-of-Great-Recession.pdf.

9. Timothy M. Smeeding, Jeffrey P. Thompson, Asaf Levanon, and Esra Burak, "Poverty and Income Inequality in the Early Stages of the Great Recession," in *The Great Recession*, ed. David B. Grusky, Bruce Western, and Christopher Wimer (New York: Russell Sage Foundation, 2011), 97–98; Jason DeParle and Robert Gebeloff, "Food Stamp Use Soars, and Stigma Fades," *New York Times*, November 28, 2009.

10. Some research does find that fiscal relief increased employment (and therefore probably did limit increases in inequality): Gabriel Chodorow-Reich, Laura Feiveson, Zachary Liscow, and William Gui Woolston, "Does State Fiscal Relief during Recessions Increase Employment? Evidence from the American Recovery and Reinvestment Act," *American Economic Journal: Economic Policy* 4, no. 3 (2012): 118–45.

11. Executive Office of the President of the United States [Council of Economic Advisers],

"The Economic Record of the Obama Administration: Progress Reducing Inequality," September 2016 [referred to hereafter as "CEA Report on Inequality"], https://obamawhitehouse.archives.gov/sites/default/files/page/files/20160923_record_inequality_cea.pdf.

12. Justin Wolfers, "What Debate? Economists Agree the Stimulus Lifted the Economy," *New York Times*, July 29, 2014; Blinder and Zandi, "How the Great Recession Was Brought to an End"; Congressional Budget Office, "Estimated Impact of the American Recovery and Reinvestment Act on Employment and Economic Output in 2014," February 2015.

13. Gary Burtless and Tracy Gordon, "The Federal Stimulus Programs and Their Effects," in *The Great Recession*, ed. Grusky, Western, and Wimer, 249–93.

14. "CEA Report on Inequality."

15. Ibid.

16. By 2016, U.S. GDP was up 10 percent from the precrisis peak, whereas it was nearly flat in both the Euro area and Japan. See Organization for Economic Cooperation and Development, "OECD Economic Surveys: The United States, 2016," 17, www.oecd.org/eco/surveys/economic-survey-united-states.htm.

17. CNN Opinion Research, Poll, press release, January 25, 2010, http://i2.cdn.turner.com/cnn/2010/images/01/25/rel1g.pdf; "Polls: Stimulus Unpopular, but Its Uses have Broad Support," February 1, 2010, http://www.cnn.com/2010/POLITICS/01/29/stimulus.poll/.

18. Brandon L. Garrett, *Too Big to Jail: How Prosecutors Compromise with Corporations* (Cambridge, MA: Harvard University Press, 2014).

19. Michael Grunwald, *The New New Deal: The Hidden Story of Change in the Obama Era* (New York: Simon & Schuster, 2012), 125–26.

20. Ibid., 338.

21. Lydia Saad, "Americans Back More Stimulus Spending to Create Jobs," Gallup, June 17, 2010, http://www.gallup.com/poll/140786/americans-back-stimulus-spending-create-jobs.aspx; Grunwald, *The New New Deal*, 338.

22. For a more extended analysis, see my book *Remedy and Reaction: The Peculiar American Struggle over Health Care Reform*, rev. ed. (New Haven: Yale University Press, 2013).

23. For a summary of these and other points about the ACA's impact, see Barack Obama, "United States Health Care Reform: Progress to Date and Next Steps," *JAMA*, July 11, 2016, E1–E8; for the 2016 data, see *Poverty in the United States: 2016* (U.S. Bureau of the Census, September 2017), 60259.

24. Jon R. Gabel et al., "More Than Half of Individual Health Plans Offer Coverage That Falls Short of What Can Be Sold Through Exchanges as of 2014," *Health Affairs* 31 (2012),: 1339–48.

25. Sara R. Collins, Munira Gunja, Michelle M. Doty, and Sophie Beutel,"Americans' Experiences with ACA Marketplace and Medicaid Coverage: Access to Care and Satisfaction: Findings from the Commonwealth Fund Affordable Care Act Tracking Survey, February–April 2016," http://www.commonwealthfund.org/~/media/files/publications/issue-brief/2016/may/1879_collins_americans_experience_aca_marketplace_feb_april_2016_tb.pdf.sis.

26. Benjamin D. Sommers, Robert J. Blendon, E. John Orav, and Arnold M. Epstein, "Changes in Utilization and Health among Low-Income Adults after Medicaid Expansion or Expanded Private Insurance," *JAMA Internal Medicine* 176, no. 10 (2016):1501–9; Benjamin D. Sommers, Munira Z. Gunja, Kenneth Finegold, and Thomas Musco, "Changes in Self-Reported Insurance Coverage, Access to Care, and Health under the Affordable Care Act," *JAMA* 314, no. 4 (2015): 366–74; N. Dussault, M. Pinkovskiy, and B. Zafar, "Is Health Insurance Good for Your Financial Health?" Federal Reserve Bank of New York, June 6, 2016, at http://libertystreeteconomics.newyorkfed.org /2016/06/is-health-insurance-good-for-your -financial-health.html.

27. Stacey McMorrow and John Holahan, "The Widespread Slowdown in Health Spending

Growth," Urban Institute, June 20, 2016, http://www.rwjf.org/content/dam/farm/reports/issue _briefs/2016/rwjf429930.

28. Michelle Long, Matthew Rae, Gary Claxton, and Anthony Damico, "Trends in Employer-Sponsored Insurance Offer and Coverage Rates, 1999–2014" (Kaiser Family Foundation, March 2016), 5. Although the impact on the proportion of Americans with employer-sponsored coverage has been small, the decline in offer rates by small business has continued. See Paul Fronstin, "Fewer Small Employers Offering Health Coverage; Large Employers Holding Steady," *Notes* (Employee Benefit Research Institute), July 2016.

29. Ashley Kirzinger, Elise Sugarman, and Mollyann Brodie, "Kaiser Health Tracking Poll: June 2016," June 30, 2016, http://kff.org/global-health-policy/poll-finding/kaiser-health -tracking-poll-june-2016/.

30. Ashley Kirzinger, Bryan Wu, and Mollyann Brodie, "Kaiser Health Tracking Poll: September 2016," September 29, 2016, http://kff.org/health-costs/report/kaiser-health-tracking -poll-september-2016/.

31. Gary Claxton, Larry Levitt, and Michelle Long, "Payments for Cost-Sharing Increasing Rapidly over Time," Peterson-Kaiser Health System Tracker, April 12, 2016, http://www.health systemtracker.org/insight/payments-for-cost-sharing-increasing-rapidly-over-time/.

32. Jason Cherkis, "Kentucky Health Workers Pitch Obamacare at State Fair Alongside Corn Dogs, Fried Kool-Aid," *Huffington Post*, August 22, 2013, http://www.huffingtonpost .com/2013/08/22/kentucky-obamacare_n_3801054.html.

33. Of course, once the problems were fixed, the news media lost interest. For a reflection on the general pattern, see Jonathan Cohn, "When Public Silence Meets Government Success," *American Prospect* (Spring 2015): 22–25.

34. Kirzinger, Sugarman, and Brodie, "Kaiser Health Tracking Poll: June 2016."

35. U.S. Department of the Treasury, "Reducing Income Inequality through Progressive Tax Policy: The Effects of Recent Tax Changes on Inequality," September 26, 2016, https:// www.treasury.gov/resource-center/tax-policy/Documents/Report-Obama-Distribution -Changes.pdf.

36. Ibid.

37. Chuck Marr and Nathaniel Frentz, "Federal Income Taxes on Middle-Income Families Remain Near Historic Lows," Center on Policy and Budget Priorities, April 15, 2014, http:// www.cbpp.org/research/federal-income-taxes-on-middle-income-families-remain-near -historic-lows; Urban-Brookings Tax Policy Center (TPC), "Average and Marginal Federal Income Tax Rates for Four-Person Families at the Same Relative Position in Income Distribution, 1955–2014," July 1, 2015, http://www.taxpolicycenter.org/sites/default/files/legacy/taxfacts /content/PDF/family_inc_rates_hist.pdf.

38. Gallup organization, "Taxes," http://www.gallup.com/poll/1714/taxes.aspx.

39. Mettler, "Reconstituting the Submerged State."

40. See, for example, Annie Lowrie, "The Rich Get Richer through the Recovery," *New York Times*, September 10, 2013.

41. Binyamin Appelbaum, "U.S. Household Income Grew 5.2 Percent in 2015, Breaking Pattern of Stagnation," *New York Times*, September 13, 2016.

42. Jessica L. Semega, Kayla R. Fontenot, and Melissa A. Kollar, *Income and Poverty in the United States: 2016, P60-259* (U.S. Bureau of the Census, September 2017).

Chapter 5: Obama's Fight against Global Warming

1. Stephen Ansolabehere and David Konisky, *Cheap and Clean: How Americans Think About Energy in the Age of Global Warming* (Cambridge, MA: MIT Press, 2014).

2. Ryan Lizza, "As the World Burns," *New Yorker*, October 11, 2010.

3. Theda Skocpol, "Naming the Problem: What It Will Take to Counter Extremism and Engage Americans in the Fight Against Global Warming" (Paper presented at the Symposium on the Politics of America's Fight against Global Warming, Harvard University, Cambridge, MA, February 14, 2013).

4. Ibid.

5. D. W. Brady, M. P. Fiorina, and R. D. Rivers, "The Road to (and from) the 2010 Elections," *Policy Review* 165 (2011): 3–14.

6. Coral Davenport and Eric Lipton, "How G.O.P. Leaders Came to View Climate Change as Fake Science," *New York Times*, June 3, 2017.

7. Quoted in Jane Mayer, "New Koch," *New Yorker*, January 25, 2016.

8. Stephen Kretzmann and Matthew Malorana, "How Citizens United Paved the Way for Big Oil's Bribes," *Grist*, January 22, 2015.

9. Davenport and Lipton, "How G.O.P. Leaders Came to View Climate Change as Fake Science."

10. Juliet Eilpern, "White House Delayed Enacting Rules Ahead of 2012 Election to Avoid Controversy," *Washington Post*, December 14, 2013.

11. Quoted in Ryan Lizza, "The President and the Pipeline," *New Yorker*, September 16, 2013.

12. Quoted in ibid.

13. Elena Schor and Sarah Wheaton, "How Obama's Waiting Game Killed Keystone," *Politico*, November 6, 2015.

14. Chris Peak, "What 15 Experts Think of President Obama's Record on the Environment," *Nationswell*, September 18, 2015.

15. Quoted in Schor and Wheaton, "Keystone."

16. Bill McKibben, "Obama and Climate Change," *Rolling Stone*, December 2013.

17. Quoted in Matthew C. Nisbet, "Environmental Advocacy in the Obama Years: Assessing New Strategies for Political Change," in *Environmental Policy: New Directions for the Twenty-first Century*, ed. N. Vig and M. Kraft, 9th ed. (Washington, DC: Congressional Quarterly Press, 2015), 158.

18. McKibben, "Obama and Climate Change."

Chapter 6: Obama's Court?

1. Megan Ming Francis, *Civil Rights and the Making of the Modern American State* (New York: Cambridge University Press, 2014), 170; Barack Obama, "Why Organize? Problems and Promise in the Inner City" (1988) in *Community Organizing and Community Building for Health and Welfare*, ed. Meredith Minkler, 3rd ed. (New Brunswick, NJ: Rutgers University Press, 2012), 27, 28.

2. See, e.g., *United States v. Carolene Prods. Co.*, 304 U.S. 144 (1938).

3. *Brown v. Board of Education of Topeka*, 347 U.S. 483 (1954).

4. Clare Cushman, "Rookie on the Bench: The Role of the Junior Justice," *Journal of Supreme Court History* 32 (2007): 282.

5. See Office of Legal Policy, U.S. Department of Justice, Report to the Attorney General, *The Constitution in the Year 2000: Choices Ahead in Constitutional Interpretation* (Washington, DC: 1988); Jefferson Decker, *The Other Rights Revolution: Conservative Lawyers and the Remaking of American Government* (New York: Oxford University Press, 2016); Steven Teles, *The Rise of the Conservative Legal Movement: The Battle for Control of the Law* (Princeton, NJ: Princeton University Press, 2008).

6. Douglas H. Ginsburg, "Delegation Running Riot," *Regulation* (Winter 1995): 83 (reviewing David Schoenbrod, *Power Without Responsibility: How Congress Abuses the People Through*

Delegation [1993]); "Constitution in Exile: Cass Sunstein and Randy Barnett Debate," *Legal Affairs: Debate Club* (May 2, 2005), http://legalaffairs.org/webexclusive/debateclub_cie0505 .msp#Monday; William W. Van Alstyne, "The Constitution in Exile: Is It Time to Bring it In from the Cold?" *Duke Law Journal* 51 (2000): 1.

7. For a discussion of the Affordable Care Act and its effects, see Starr's chapter 4 in this volume.

8. *United States v. Lopez*, 514 U.S. 549 (1995); *United States v. Morrison*, 529 U.S. 598 (2000).

9. See Starr (chapter 4) and Zelizer (chapter 2) in this volume.

10. *National Federation of Independent Business v. Sebelius*, 567 U.S. 519 (2012).

11. Ibid.

12. Kenneth K. Ching, "Roberts on Obamacare: Liar, Lunatic, or Legitimate," *Journal of Law and Politics* 28 (2013): 335.

13. See Starr, chapter 4 in this volume.

14. Laurence Tribe and Joshua Matz, *Uncertain Justice: The Roberts Court and the Constitution* (New York: Holt, 2014), 52–54, 64–71.

15. See Allan Berube, *Coming Out under Fire: The History of Gay Men and Women in World War II* (New York: Free Press, 2000); Margot Canaday, *The Straight State: Sexuality and Citizenship in Twentieth-Century America* (Princeton, NJ: Princeton University Press, 2009); John D'Emilio and Estelle Freedman, *Intimate Matters: A History of Sexuality in America*, 3rd ed. (Chicago: University of Chicago Press, 2012).

16. *Bowers v. Hardwick*, 478 U.S. 186 (1986).

17. *Romer v. Evans*, 517 U.S. 620 (1996).

18. *Lawrence v. Texas*, 539 U.S. 558 (2003).

19. *Goodridge v. Dept't Pub. Health*, 798 N.E.2d 941 (Mass. 2003); *Baehr v. Miike*, 910 P.2d 112 (Haw. 1996).

20. Justin McCarthy, "Americans' Support for Gay Marriage Remains High, at 61%," Gallup, May 19, 2016, http://www.gallup.com/poll/191645/americans-support-gay-marriage-remains -high.aspx.

21. *United States v. Windsor*, 133 S.Ct. 2675 (2013).

22. *Obergefell v. Hodges*, 135 S.Ct. 2584 (2015).

23. Ibid.

24. *Obergefell*, 135 S.Ct. at 2593–94.

25. Stewart-Winter, chapter 7 in this volume.

26. Stephanie Francis Ward, "After *Obergefell*," *ABA Journal* (September 2015): 17.

27. *Burwell v. Hobby Lobby Stores, Inc.*, 134 S.Ct. 2751 (2014).

28. *Roe v. Wade*, 410 U.S. 113 (1973).

29. *Whole Woman's Health v. Hellerstedt*, 136 S.Ct. 2292 (2016).

30. Ibid.

31. For a discussion, see Risa Goluboff, *Vagrant Nation: Police Power, Constitutional Change, and the Making of the 1960s* (New York: Oxford University Press, 2016).

32. See generally Risa Goluboff, *The Lost Promise of Civil Rights* (Cambridge, MA: Harvard University Press, 2007).

33. Nancy Mclean, *Freedom Is Not Enough: The Opening of the American Workplace* (Cambridge, MA: Harvard University Press, 2008) (discussing the shift from massive resistance to color-blindness).

34. *Shelby County, Ala. v. Holder*, 133 S.Ct. 2612 (2013).

35. Ibid., at 2631.

36. Transcript of Oral Argument at 47, *Shelby County, Ala. v. Holder*, 133 S. Ct. 2612 (2013) (No. 12–96); Jess Bravin, "Scalia Calls Voting Act a 'Racial Preferment,' " *Wall Street Journal*, April 19, 2013, A3.

37. *Grutter v. Bollinger*, 539 U.S. 306 (2003).

38. *Gratz v. Bollinger*, 539 U.S. 244 (2003).

39. *Parents Involved in Community Schools v. Seattle School District No. 1*, 551 U.S. 701 (2007).

40. Ibid., at 748.

41. *Fisher v. University of Texas at Austin*, 133 S.Ct. 2411 (2013).

42. *District of Columbia v. Heller*, 554 U.S. 570 (2008).

43. Julie Creswell, "More Bang for the Investor's Buck, Spotting Gold in Gun Makers," *New York Times*, January 7, 2016, A1.

44. *Citizens United v. Federal Election Commission*, 558 U.S. 310 (2010).

45. Steven Rosenfeld, "The Hard Truth About *Citizens United*," *Salon*, January 21, 2012, http://www.salon.com/2012/01/21/the_hard_truth_of_citizens_united/.

46. *West Coast Hotel Co. v. Parrish*, 300 U.S. 379 (1937); *United States v. Carolene Prods. Co.*, 304 U.S. 144, 152 n.4 (1938).

47. Paul Krugman, "Why We're in a New Gilded Age," *New York Review of Books*, May 8, 2014 (reviewing Thomas Piketty, *Capital in the Twenty-First Century* [Cambridge, MA: Harvard University Press, 2014]); Steve Fraser, "The Gilded Age, Past and Present," *Salon* (April 28, 2008), http://www.salon.com/2008/04/28/gilded_age/.

48. Angela Monaghan, "US Wealth Inequality—Top 0.1% Worth as Much as the Bottom 90%," *Guardian: Economics Blog*, May 13, 2014, https://www.theguardian.com/business/2014/nov/13/us-wealth-inequality-top-01-worth-as-much-as-the-bottom-90 (citing Emmanuel Saez and Gabriel Zucman, *Wealth Inequality in the United States Since 1913: Evidence from Capitalized Income Tax Data* [Nat'l Bureau of Econ. Research, Working Paper No. 20625, 2014]).

49. "The U.S. Chamber of Commerce Continues Its Winning Ways," *Constitutional Accountability Center: Text & History Blog*, June 30, 2014, http://theusconstitution.org/text-history/2753/us-chamber-commerce-continues-its-winning-ways.

50. *Rent-A-Center, W., Inc. v. Jackson*, 561 U.S. 63 (2010); *AT&T Mobility v. Concepcion*, 563 U.S. 333 (2011); *Philip Morris USA v. Williams*, 549 U.S. 346 (2007); *Goodyear Dunlop Tires Operations, SA v. Brown*, 564 U.S. 915 (2011); *J. McIntyre Mach., Ltd. v. Nicastro*, 564 U.S. 873 (2011). See also Dan Dudis, *The Chamber of Litigation* (Washington, DC: Public Citizen, 2016), 4; U.S. Chamber Litigation Center, http://www.chamberlitigation.com/.

51. For similar observations, see Zelizer, chapter 2 this volume.

52. Michael Collins, "Trump Victory Is the End of the Line for Obama Judicial Nominees," *USA Today*, November 11, 2016, http://www.usatoday.com/story/news/politics/2016/11/11/trump-victory-end-line-obama-judicial-nominees/93615006/; Carl Tobias, "Confirming Circuit Judges in a Presidential Election Year," *George Washington Law Review Arguendo* 84 (2016): 160, 171n64.

53. "Obama's Judges Leave Liberal Imprint on U.S. Law," Reuters, August 26, 2016, http://www.reuters.com/article/us-usa-court-obama-idUSKCN1110BC.

54. *Friedrichs v. California Teachers Assc.*, 136 S.Ct. 1083 (2016); *United States v. Texas*, 136 S.Ct. 2271 (2016).

55. *Washington v. Trump*, No. 17–35105, 2017 WL 526497 (9th Cir. Feb. 9, 2017) (per curiam).

Chapter 7: The Gay Rights President

1. "Remarks at a Reception Honoring Lesbian, Gay, Bisexual, and Transgender Pride Month," June 29, 2009, in *Public Papers of the Presidents: Barack H. Obama* (2009, Book 1), (Washington, DC: GPO, 2011), 928–29 (also at https://www.gpo.gov/fdsys/pkg/PPP-2009-book1/pdf/PPP-2009-book1-Doc-pg927.pdf).

2. "Gay and Lesbian Rights," http://www.gallup.com/poll/1651/gay-lesbian-rights.aspx;

Dawn Michelle Baunach, "Changing Same-Sex Marriage Attitudes in America from 1988 through 2010," *Public Opinion Quarterly* 76, no. 2 (June 2012): 364–78; Gregory B. Lewis, "The Friends and Family Plan: Contact with Gays and Support for Gay Rights," *Policy Studies Journal* 39, no. 2 (May 2011): 217–38.

3. Lauren Sanders, "Effects of EEOC Recognition of Title VII as Prohibiting Discrimination Based on Transgender Identity," *Duke Journal of Gender Law and Policy* 23 (2016): 263–81.

4. Stephen A. Berry et al., "Healthcare Coverage for HIV Provider Visits Before and After Implementation of the Affordable Care Act," *Clinical Infectious Diseases* 63, no. 3 (August 2016): 387–95; Lindsay Dawson, Jennifer Kates, Michael Perry, and Kathleen Perry, "The ACA and People with HIV: An Update," May 4, 2016, http://kff.org/health-reform/issue-brief/the-aca-and-people-with-hiv-an-update/. For a critique of the rulemaking process, see Joanna V. Theiss, "It May Be Here to Stay, But Is It Working? The Implementation of the Affordable Care Act Through an Analysis of Coverage of HIV Treatment and Prevention," *Journal of Health & Biomedical Law* 12 (July 2016): 109–67.

5. U.S. Congress, Senate, Committee on Expenditures in the Executive Departments, *Employment of Homosexuals and Other Sex Perverts in Government*, Senate Doc. 241, 81st Cong., 2nd sess., 1950, 4; Margot Canaday, *The Straight State: Sexuality and Citizenship in Twentieth-Century America* (Princeton, NJ: Princeton University Press, 2009), 217; David K. Johnson, *The Lavender Scare: The Cold War Persecution of Gays and Lesbians in the Federal Government* (Chicago: University of Chicago Press, 2004); John D'Emilio, William B. Turner, and Urvashi Vaid, eds., *Creating Change: Sexuality, Public Policy, and Civil Rights* (New York: St. Martin's Press, 2000).

6. Quoted in Marc Stein, "Boutilier and the U.S. Supreme Court's Sexual Revolution," *Law and History Review* 23 (Fall 2005): 525.

7. Timothy Stewart-Winter, "Revisiting the Historical Record on HIV/AIDS, From Reagan to Clinton," *Slate*, March 14, 2016, http://www.slate.com/blogs/outward/2016/03/14/clintons_comments_on_regan_and_aids_were_a_missed_opportunity.html; Jennifer Brier, *Infectious Ideas: U.S. Political Responses to the AIDS Crisis* (Chapel Hill: University of North Carolina Press, 2011).

8. On municipal government as the key arena for gay mobilization before the 1990s, see Timothy Stewart-Winter, *Queer Clout: Chicago and the Rise of Gay Politics* (Philadelphia: University of Pennsylvania Press, 2016).

9. George Chauncey, *Why Marriage? The History Shaping Today's Debate Over Gay Equality* (New York: Basic Books, 2004).

10. David W. Dunlap, "Fearing a Toehold for Gay Marriages, Conservatives Rush to Bar the Door," *New York Times*, March 6, 1996.

11. Marc Solomon, *Winning Marriage: The Inside Story of How Same-Sex Couples Took On the Politicians and Pundits—and Won* (Lebanon, NH: ForeEdge, 2014).

12. "Beyond Marriage: A New Strategic Vision for All Our Families & Relationships," August 6, 2008, https://mronline.org/2006/08/08/beyond-same-sex-marriage-a-new-strategic-vision-for-all-our-families-relationships/; Molly Ball, "How Gay Marriage Became a Constitutional Right," *Atlantic*, July 1, 2015, http://www.theatlantic.com/politics/archive/2015/07/gay-marriage-supreme-court-politics-activism/397052/; Solomon, *Winning Marriage*.

13. Solomon, *Winning Marriage*, 270.

14. Tracy Baim, "Obama's Marriage Views Changed"; and Timothy Stewart-Winter, "Putting Obama's Questionnaire in Context," both in *Windy City Times*, January 14, 2009.

15. Barack Obama, response to IMPACT questionnaire, September 3, 1996, in 1996 general election questionnaires binder, box 4, IMPACT Records, Gerber/Hart Library and Archives, Chicago.

16. Helene Cooper, "Obama Will Back Repeal of Law Restricting Marriage," *New York Times*, July 20, 2011.

17. Pam Belluck, "Hundreds of Same-Sex Couples Wed in Massachusetts," *New York Times*, May 18, 2004.

18. Jesse McKinley, "Across U.S., Big Rallies for Same-Sex Marriage," *New York Times*, November 16, 2008.

19. Adam Liptak, "California Court Overturns a Ban on Gay Marriage," *New York Times*, May 16, 2008. Proposition 8 also clouded perceptions of the relationship between black and gay politics. In fact, the measure still would have passed even if *every* black voter in California had stayed home, and a widely reported exit poll probably overstated the proportion of African Americans who voted for the measure. Hendrik Hertzberg, "Eight Is Enough," *New Yorker*, December 1, 2008, http://www.newyorker.com/magazine/2008/12/01/eight-is-enough; Patrick Egan and Ken Sherrill, "Proposition 8: What Happened and Where Do We Go from Here?" (January 2009), report released by the National Gay and Lesbian Task Force Policy Institute, http://www.thetaskforce.org/downloads/issues/egan_sherrill_prop8_1_6_09.

20. "A Bad Call on Gay Rights," *New York Times*, June 16, 2009.

21. Julia Preston, "Obama Lifts a 22-Year Ban on Entry into U.S. by H.I.V.-Positive People," *New York Times*, October 31, 2009.

22. Lillian Faderman, *The Gay Revolution: The Story of the Struggle* (New York: Simon & Schuster, 2015), 516.

23. Nathaniel Frank, "The President's Pleasant Surprise: How LGBT Advocates Ended Don't Ask, Don't Tell," *Journal of Homosexuality* 60 (2013): 170–75.

24. Ibid., 164.

25. Faderman, *Gay Revolution*, 525–28.

26. Frank, "President's Pleasant Surprise."

27. Elisabeth Bumiller, "Pentagon Steps Up Talks on Ending 'Don't Ask, Don't Tell,'" *New York Times*, January 15, 2010.

28. Sheryl Gay Stolberg, "Deal Reached for Repealing Law on Gays in Military," *New York Times*, May 25, 2010.

29. Rick Valelly, "Making a Rainbow Military: Parliamentary Skill and the Repeal of 'Don't Ask, Don't Tell,'" in *Congress and Policy Making in the 21st Century*, ed. Jeffery A. Jenkins and Eric M. Patashnik (New York: Cambridge University Press, 2016), 75–105.

30. John Schwartz, "Awaiting the Next Step on Policy of Gay Service," *New York Times*, October 14, 2010.

31. John Schwartz, "Military Policy on Gays to Stand, Pending Appeal," *New York Times*, November 2, 2010.

32. Valelly, "Making a Rainbow Military," 90–91.

33. Quoted in Valelly, "Making a Rainbow Military," 94.

34. Barney Frank, *Frank: A Life in Politics from the Great Society to Same-Sex Marriage* (New York: Farrar, Straus and Giroux, 2015), 328; CNN Wire Staff, "Senate Passes 'Don't Ask, Don't Tell' Repeal; DREAM Act Fails," December 18, 2010, http://www.cnn.com/2010/POLITICS/12/18/dadt.dream.act/index.html.

35. Sheryl Gay Stolberg, "After Fall of 'Don't Ask,' Pushing for 'I Do,'" *New York Times*, December 21, 2010.

36. James Dao, "Same-Sex Marriage Faces Military Limits," *New York Times*, July 17, 2011.

37. John Schwartz, "Gay Couples Begin Attack on U.S. Marriage Law," *New York Times*, November 9, 2010.

38. Robert Pear, "Gay Workers Will Get Time to Care for Partner's Sick Child," *New York Times*, June 22, 2010.

39. Sheryl Gay Stolberg, "One Battle Finished, Activists Shift Sights," *New York Times*, December 20, 2010.

40. Dan Savage, "A Gay Agenda for Everyone," *New York Times*, January 23, 2011.

41. Jackie Calmes and Peter Baker, "Obama Endorses Same-Sex Marriage, Taking Stand on Charged Social Issue," *New York Times*, May 10, 2012; "Transcript: Robin Roberts ABC News Interview with President Obama," http://abcnews.go.com/Politics/transcript-robin-roberts-abc -news-interview-president-obama/story?id=16316043.

42. Dalina Castellanos, "NAACP Endorses Same-Sex Marriage, Saying It's a Civil Right," *Los Angeles Times*, May 19, 2012, http://articles.latimes.com/2012/may/19/nation/la-na-nn -naacp-gay-marriage-20120519.

43. Dan Eggen, "Obama's Gay Marriage Announcement Followed by Flood of Campaign Donations," *Washington Post*, May 10, 2012; Jackie Calmes, "Obama Heads West for Dollars and Thanks from Gay Supporters," *New York Times*, June 6, 2012; Associated Press, "Who Are Top 5 Donors to Obama, Romney Campaigns?" October 19, 2012, http://www.politico.com/news /stories/1012/82637.html; and Chris Geidner, "Senate Approves Several Out Gay Nominees, with No Opposition," *BuzzFeed*, August 1, 2013, http://www.buzzfeed.com/chrisgeidner/senate -approves-several-out-gay-nominees-with-no-opposition.

44. Micah Cohen, "Gay Support Buoyed Obama, as the Straight Vote Split," *New York Times*, November 16, 2012.

45. Michael D. Shear, "Obama's Pen May Shape Scope of Marriage Ruling," *New York Times*, June 14, 2013.

46. *Obergefell v. Hodges*, https://www.supremecourt.gov/opinions/14pdf/14-556_3204.pdf, 4.

47. Liam Stack, "Activist Removed after Heckling Obama at L.G.B.T. Event at White House," *New York Times*, June 24, 2015.

48. "U.S. Departments of Justice and Education Release Joint Guidance to Help Schools Ensure the Civil Rights of Transgender Students," May 13, 2016, https://www.justice.gov/opa /pr/us-departments-justice-and-education-release-joint-guidance-help-schools-ensure-civil -rights; Jennifer Rizzo and Zachary Cohen, "Pentagon Ends Transgender Ban," CNN.com, June 30, 2016, http://www.cnn.com/2016/06/30/politics/transgender-ban-lifted-us-military.

49. Liam Stack, "Trump Drops Defense of Obama Guidelines on Transgender Students," *New York Times*, February 11, 2017, https://www.nytimes.com/2017/02/11/us/politics/trump -transgender-students-injunction.html.

50. Abby Phillip, Thomas Gibbons-Neff, and Mike DeBonis, "Trump Announces That He Will Ban Transgender People from Serving in the Military," *Washington Post*, July 26, 2017, https://www.washingtonpost.com/world/national-security/trump-announces-that-he-will -ban-transgender-people-from-serving-in-the-military/2017/07/26/6415371e-723a-11e7-803f -a6c989606ac7_story.html.

51. CNN Wire Staff, "Senate Passes 'Don't Ask, Don't Tell' Repeal; DREAM Act Fails"; Timothy Stewart-Winter, "The Price of Gay Marriage," *New York Times*, June 26, 2015.

Chapter 8: Education in the Age of Obama: The Paradox of Consensus

1. "The Every Student Succeeds Act versus No Child Left Behind: What's Changed?" *USA Today*, December 11, 2015; "President Obama Signs into Law a Rewrite of No Child Left Behind," *New York Times*, December 10, 2015.

2. Valerie Strauss, "Arne Duncan: 'White Suburban Moms' Upset That Common Core Shows Their Kids Aren't 'Brilliant,'" *Washington Post*, November 16, 2013.

3. Quoted in Jonathan Alter, *The Promise: President Obama, Year One* (New York: Simon & Schuster, 2010), 338. On the continued low visibility of education in Washington, see Morton Keller, *Obama's Time: A History* (New York: Oxford University Press, 2015), 127–28; Lorraine M. McDonnell, "Surprising Momentum: Spurring Education Reform in States and Localities," in *Reaching for a New Deal: Ambitious Governance, Economic Meltdown, and Polarized Politics in Obama's First Two Years*, ed. Theda Skocpol and Lawrence R. Jacobs (New York: Russell Sage, 2011), 258.

4. Quoted in Steven Brill, *Class Warfare: Inside the Fight to Fix America's Schools* (New York: Simon & Schuster, 2011), 131.

5. See, e.g., Brill, *Class Warfare*, 217–18; Alter, *The Promise*, 91; Robert Maranto and Michael Q. McShane, *President Obama and Education Reform: The Personal and the Political* (New York: Palgrave, 2012), 1; Michael Q. McShane, "Turning the Tides: President Obama and Education Reform," *Education Outlook*, no. 6 (September 2012): 1, 6.

6. Barack Obama, *Dreams from My Father: A Story of Race and Inheritance* (New York: Random House, 1995), 235; idem, *The Audacity of Hope: Thoughts on Reclaiming the American Dream* (New York: Crown, 2006), 162; Brill, *Class Warfare*, 3.

7. Alter, *The Promise*, 90–91; Brill, *Class Warfare*, 4; Seyward Darby, "Old School," *New Republic*, December 24, 2008.

8. Alter, *The Promise*, 61–62, 90; Brill, *Class Warfare*, 4, 225.

9. Brill, *Class Warfare*, 240–42; Alter, *The Promise*, 91–92; "TIME Poll Results: Americans' Views on Teacher Tenure, Merit Pay, and Other Education Reforms," *Time*, September 9, 2010.

10. McDonnell, "Surprising Momentum," 236–37; "Common Core: Myths and Facts," *U.S. News and World Report*, March 4, 2014.

11. Brill, *Class Warfare*, 277, 414; Michael J. Petrilli, "No Child Left Behind: The Carrot That Feels Like a Stick," *Thomas Fordham Institute*, July 23, 2009; Joseph P. Viteritti, "The Federal Role in School Reform: Obama's 'Race to the Top,'" *Notre Dame Law Review* 87, no. 5 (2012): 2103; Michael Grunwald, "The Nation He Built," *Politico*, January/February 2016.

12. Frederick M. Hess, "The Real Obama Education Legacy," *National Affairs*, no. 25 (Fall 2015); Alter, *The Promise*, 62; Kevin G. Welner, "Free-Market Think Tanks and the Marketing of Education Policy," *Dissent* 58, no. 2 (Spring 2011): 39–40; David Brooks, "Getting Obama Right," *New York Times*, March 11, 2010; "Gingrich and Sharpton: Unlikely Pair Go on Tour," *National Public Radio*, September 12, 2009.

13. Maranto and McShane, *President Obama and Education Reform*, 65; Ashley Jochim, "A Reform at Risk? The Political Realities," in *Common Core Meets Education Reform*, ed. Frederick M. Hess and Michael Q. McShane (New York: Teachers College Press, 2014), 189; Michael J. Petrilli and Tyson Eberhardt, "Obama's Education Record," *Education Next* 12, no. 2 (Spring 2012): 239; William Hayes, *Consensus: Education Reform Is Possible* (Lanham, MD: Rowman and Littlefield, 2013), 40, 137; Jay Mathews, "Why Romney, Obama Are Education Twins," *Washington Post*, May 27, 2012.

14. Frederick M. Hess, "Why LBJ Is Smiling: The Bush Administration, 'Compassionate Conservatism,' and No Child Left Behind," in *Building Coalitions, Making Policy: The Politics of the Clinton, Bush, and Obama Presidencies*, ed. Martin A. Levin, Daniel DiSalvo, and Martin M. Shapiro (Baltimore: Johns Hopkins University Press, 2012), 63; "What GOP Candidates Got Wrong—and Right—about Common Core," *Washington Post*, March 14, 2016; Petrilli, "No Child Left Behind: The Carrot That Feels Like a Stick"; McShane, "Turning the Tides," 5; Hayes, *Consensus*, 49–50, 59; Jochim, "A Reform at Risk?" 189.

15. Brill, *Class Warfare*, 264; Hayes, *Consensus*, 39; Viteritti, "The Federal Role in School Reform," 2107; Paul Peterson, Michael Henderson, and Martin R. West, *Teachers versus the Pub-*

lic: What Americans Think About Schools and How to Fix Them (Washington, DC: Brookings Institution, 2014), 1–2.

16. Viteritti, "The Federal Role in School Reform," 2106; Diane Ravitch, *Reign of Error: The Hoax of the Privatization Movement and the Danger to America's Public Schools* (New York: Vintage, 2014), 28; Jason B. Cook, "The Impact of Charter Schools on District School Budgets," National Center for the Study of Privatization in Education, Working Paper no. 229 (May 17, 2016); Brian P. Gill and Kevin Booker, "School Competition and Student Outcomes," in *Handbook of Research in Education Finance and Policy*, ed. Helen F. Ladd and Margaret E. Goertz (New York: Routledge, 2015), 211–28; Jonathan Zimmerman, "He Transformed the Schools, but . . . ," *New York Review of Books*, March 5, 2015.

17. Diane Ravitch, *The Death and Life of the Great American School System* (New York: Basic Books, 2011), 195–222; Viteritti, "The Federal Role in School Reform," 2107–8; Welner, "Free-Market Think Tanks," 42.

18. Jonathan Zimmerman, "Uncle Sam at the Blackboard: The Federal Government and Education," in *To Promote the General Welfare: The Case for Big Government*, ed. Steven Conn (New York: Oxford University Press, 2012), 44–64; Viteritti, "The Federal Role in School Reform," 2088–89.

19. Lawrence R. Jacobs and Desmond King, "Varieties of Obamaism: Structure, Agency, and the Obama Presidency," in *Obama at the Crossroads: Politics, Markets, and the Battle for America's Future*, ed. Lawrence R. Jacobs and Desmond King (New York: Oxford University Press, 2012), 20; "Obama Wants to Limit Class Time Devoted to Standardized Tests," *Associated Press*, October 24, 2015; "Twenty Percent of New York State Students Opted Out of Standardized Tests This Year," *New York Times*, August 12, 2015.

20. Laura Moser, "Obama's Education Legacy Is More of a Mixed Bag Than He'd Like to Admit," *Slate*, January 13, 2016; Alicia Wong, "The Bloated Rhetoric of No Child Left Behind's Demise," *Atlantic*, December 9, 2015.

21. Viteritti, "The Federal Role in School Reform," 2089; Zimmerman, "Uncle Sam at the Blackboard," 45–46, 54–55; Suzanne Mettler, *The Submerged State: How Invisible Government Policies Undermine American Government* (Chicago: University of Chicago Press, 2011).

22. Obama, *Audacity of Hope*, 160–61; Peterson, Henderson, and West, *Teachers versus the Public*, 46.

23. Suzanne Mettler, "Eliminating the Market Middle-Man: Redirecting and Expanding Support for College Students," in *Reaching for a New Deal*, Skocpol and Jacobs, 111–12; Grunwald, "The Nation He Built"; Suzanne Mettler, "Obama and the Challenge of Submerged Politics," in *Obama and America's Political Future*, ed. Theda Skocpol (Cambridge, MA: Harvard University Press, 2012), 134.

24. Grunwald, "The Nation He Built"; Mettler, "Obama and the Challenge of Submerged Politics," 106.

25. Wong, "The Bloated Rhetoric of No Child Left Behind's Demise."

Chapter 9: Barack Obama and the Movement for Black Lives: Race, Democracy, and Criminal Justice in the Age of Ferguson

1. Peniel E. Joseph, *Dark Days, Bright Nights: From Black Power to Barack Obama* (New York: Basic Books, 2012). See also Peniel E. Joseph, *Waiting 'Til the Midnight Hour: A Narrative History of Black Power in America* (New York: Holt, 2007) and idem, *Stokely: A Life* (New York: Basic Books, 2014). Some of the most important works on what I have characterized as the civil rights movement's "heroic period" include David Garrow, *Bearing the Cross: Martin Luther King Jr. and the Southern Christian Leadership Conference* (New York: Quill, 1999); Clayborne Carson,

In Struggle: SNCC and the Black Awakening of the 1960s (Cambridge, MA: Harvard University Press, 1981); Taylor Branch, *Parting the Waters: America in the King Years, 1954–1963* (New York: Simon & Schuster, 1987); idem, *Pillar of Fire: America in the King Years, 1963–1965* (New York: Simon & Schuster, 1998); idem, *At Canaan's Edge: America in the King Years, 1965–1968* (New York: Simon & Schuster, 2006); Barbara Ransby, *Ella Baker and the Black Freedom Movement: A Radical Democratic Vision* (Chapel Hill: University of North Carolina Press, 2003); Thomas J. Sugrue, *Sweet Land of Liberty: The Forgotten Struggle for Civil Rights in the North* (New York: Random House, 2008).

2. Barack Obama, *Dreams from My Father: A Story of Race and Inheritance* (New York: Crown Books, 2004).

3. David Remnick, *The Bridge: The Life and Rise of Barack Obama* (New York: Knopf, 2010), 13. For a substantial treatment of Obama's early years see David Maraniss, *Barack Obama: The Story* (New York: Simon & Schuster, 2012).

4. "Barack Obama's New Hampshire Primary Speech," transcript, *New York Times,* January 8, 2008, http://www.nytimes.com/2008/01/08/us/politics/08text-obama.html.

5. Craig Steven Wilder, *Ebony and Ivy: Race, Slavery, and the Troubled History of America's Universities* (New York: Bloomsbury Press, 2013); Walter Johnson, *River of Dark Dreams: Slavery and Empire in the Cotton Kingdom* (Cambridge, MA: Harvard University Press, 2013); Edward E. Baptist, *The Half Has Never Been Told: Slavery and the Making of American Capitalism* (New York: Basic Books, 2014); Sven Beckert, *Empire of Cotton: A Global History* (New York: Knopf, 2014); Ira Katznelson, *When Affirmative Action Was White: An Untold History of Racial Equality in Twentieth-Century America* (New York: W. W. Norton, 2004); Richard Rothstein, *The Color of Law: A Forgotten History of How Our Government Segregated America* (New York: W. W. Norton, 2017).

6. Joseph, *Stokely: A Life,* 186–87.

7. Sociologist Monique W. Morris offers up a panoramic statistical overview of the way in which blacks are overrepresented among negative social economic indicators and underrepresented on virtually all measures of positive access to liberal democratic capitalist institutions, both public and private, in American society. See Monique W. Morris, *Black Stats: African Americans by the Numbers in the Twenty-First Century* (New York: New Press, 2014).

8. The literature on the historical roots of mass incarceration and its contemporary manifestations is vast. See for example, Elizabeth Hinton, *From the War on Poverty to the War on Crime: The Making of Mass Incarceration in America* (Cambridge, MA: Harvard University Press, 2016); James Forman Jr., *Locking Up Our Own: Crime and Punishment in Black America* (New York: Farrar, Straus, Giroux, 2017); Heather Ann Thompson, *Blood in the Water: The Attica Prison Uprising of 1971 and Its Legacy* (New York: Pantheon, 2016); Michael Javen Fortner, *Black Silent Majority: The Rockefeller Drug Laws and the Politics of Punishment* (Cambridge, MA: Harvard University Press, 2015); Barry Friedman, *Unwarranted: Policing without Permission* (New York: Farrar, Straus and Giroux, 2017). See also Baz Dreisinger, *Incarcerated Nations: A Journey to Justice in Prisons Around the World* (New York: Other Press, 2016).

9. Michelle Alexander, *The New Jim Crow: Mass Incarceration in the Age of Colorblindness* (New York: New Press, 2010); William Julius Wilson, *The Truly Disadvantaged: The Inner City, the Underclass, and Public Policy* (Chicago: University of Chicago Press, 1993).

10. The BLM movement's policy vision has been articulated in "A Movement for Black Lives" agenda comprised of a consortium of over fifty nonprofit groups working in the areas of criminal justice reform, voting rights, environmental and health policy, LGBTQ justice, antipoverty, and school and neighborhood desegregation. https://policy.m4bl.org/.

11. "Attorney General Eric Holder Delivers Remarks at the Annual Meeting of the American Bar Association's House of Delegates," *Justice News,* U.S. Department of Justice, August 12, 2013,

https://www.justice.gov/opa/speech/attorney-general-eric-holder-delivers-remarks
-annual-meeting-american-bar-associations.

12. Alexander, *The New Jim Crow*.

13. Wesley Lowery, *"They Can't Kill Us All": Ferguson, Baltimore, and a New Era in America's Racial Justice Movement* (Little, Brown: New York, 2016), 4–5.

14. See Hinton, *From the War on Poverty to the War on Crime*.

15. Phillip Agnew, "What President Obama Told Me about Ferguson's Movement: Think Big, but Go Gradual," *The Guardian*, December 5, 2014.

16. Agnew, "What President Obama Told Me about Ferguson's Movement." The lack of data on police shootings in the United States led the British-based *Guardian* newspaper to begin an online record, "The Counted," documenting police shootings in America. See https://www.the guardian.com/us-news/series/counted-us-police-killings. See also Peniel E. Joseph, "The Number of Times African Americans Were Brutalized by Police This Year? Unknown," Reuters.com, June 11, 2015, http://www.reuters.com/article/idUS130507368320150611.

17. Ta-Nehisi Coates, *Between the World and Me* (New York: Spiegel & Grau, 2015); Christopher J. Lebron, *The Making of Black Lives Matter: A Brief History of an Idea* (New York: Oxford University Press, 2017).

18. Michael Eric Dyson, *The Black Presidency: Barack Obama and the Politics of Race in America* (New York: Houghton Mifflin Harcourt, 2016), 193–95.

19. Ibid., 196–99.

20. Peniel E. Joseph, "The Struggle for Black Dignity Continues," CNN.com, August 12, 2016; and U.S. Department of Justice, Civil Rights Division, "Investigation of the Baltimore City Police Department," August 10, 2016, http://s3.documentcloud.org/documents/3009471/Bpd -Findings-8-10-16.pdf.

21. See special issue of *Time*, April 30, 2015.

22. Peniel E. Joseph, "The Passion of a President," TheRoot.com, March 7, 2015.

23. Quoted in ibid.

24. Dyson, *The Black Presidency*, 265.

25. Ibid., 249.

26. Peniel E. Joseph, "President Calls for Racial Justice and Prison Reform," TheRoot.com, July 14, 2015.

27. Sari Horwitz and Juliet Eilpern, "Obama Commutes Sentences of 46 Nonviolent Drug Offenders," *Washington Post*, July 13, 2015, https://www.washingtonpost.com/world/national -security/obama-commutes-sentences-of-46-non-violent-drug-offenders/2015/07/13/b533f61e -2974-11e5-a250-42bd812efc09_story.html?utm_term=.07f0932451e9.

28. Scott Horsley, "Obama Visits Federal Prison; a First for a Sitting President," *NPR News*, July 16, 2015, http://www.npr.org/sections/itsallpolitics/2015/07/16/423612441/obama-visits -federal-prison-a-first-for-a-sitting-president; Sari Horwitz and Wesley Lowery, "Obama's Crusade against a Criminal Justice System Devoid of 'Second Chances,'" *Washington Post*, April 22, 2016, https://www.washingtonpost.com/graphics/national/obama-legacy/racial-profiling -criminal-justice-reform.html.

29. Peniel E. Joseph, "Elizabeth Warren's Embrace of Black Lives Matter Is an Example of Moral Leadership," TheRoot.com, September 29, 2015, http://www.theroot.com/elizabeth -warren-s-embrace-of-black-lives-matter-is-an-1790861227.

30. Wesley Lowery, "Elizabeth Warren Just Gave the Speech that Black Lives Matter Activists Had Been Waiting For," *Washington Post*, September 27, 2015, https://www.washingtonpost .com/news/post-politics/wp/2015/09/27/elizabeth-warren-just-gave-the-speech-that-black -lives-matter-activists-have-been-waiting-for/?utm_term=.63efa15f22bf.

31. Attorney General Loretta Lynch's Remarks at the Eighth Annual Judge Thomas Flan-

nery Lecture, Washington, D.C., November 15, 2016, https://www.justice.gov/opa/speech
/attorney-general-loretta-e-lynch-delivers-remarks-eighth-annual-judge-thomas-flannery.

32. Peniel E. Joseph, "Dallas Shootings: The Latest Chapter in a Painful Racial History,"
Guardian, July 9, 2016, https://www.theguardian.com/commentisfree/2016/jul/09/police
-killings-dallas-shooting-racism-american-history.

33. For an important history of the black freedom movement's relationship with the crimi-
nal justice system in Atlanta during the civil rights era see Tomiko Brown-Nagin, *Courage to
Dissent: Atlanta and the Long History of the Civil Rights Movement* (New York: Oxford University
Press, 2011).

34. Peniel E. Joseph, "Our National Postracial Hangover," *Chronicle of Higher Education*,
July 27, 2009, http://www.chronicle.com/article/Our-National-Postracial/47462/.

35. Bryan Stevenson, *Just Mercy: A Story of Redemption* (New York: Spiegel & Grau, 2015).

36. "A Movement for Black Lives," https://policy.m4bl.org/.

37. See for an insightful example Keeanga-Yamahtta Taylor, *From #BlackLivesMatter to
Black Liberation* (Chicago: Haymarket Books, 2016).

Chapter 10: A Decent-Sized Foundation: Obama's Urban Policy

This chapter was written with the support of the Carnegie Corporation of New York. Thanks
to Andrew Diamond, Gary Gerstle, Nick Guyatt, Alice O'Connor, and Julian Zelizer for their
comments on this chapter, and to participants in workshops at Princeton, Paris-7-Diderot, and
Cambridge for their feedback.

1. Executive Order 13,503, 74 *Federal Register* 8139, February 19, 2009. For a mostly optimistic early assessment see "Obama's Urban Policy: A Symposium," *City and Community* 9, no. 1
(January 2010): 3–60.

2. Richard Florida, *The Rise of the Creative Class and How It's Transforming Work, Leisure,
and Everyday Life* (New York: Basic Books, 2002); Alan Berube, Bruce Katz, and Robert Lang,
Redefining Urban and Suburban America: Evidence from Census 2000 (Washington, DC: Brook-
ings Institution, 2005); Edward Glaeser, *The Triumph of the City: How Our Greatest Invention
Makes Us Richer, Smarter, Greener, Healthier, and Happier* (New York: Penguin, 2011); Alan
Ehrenhalt, *The Great Inversion and the Future of the American City* (New York: Knopf, 2012).

3. Jacob Rugh and Douglas S. Massey, "Segregation in Post–Civil Rights America: Stalled
Integration or End of the Segregated Century?" *Du Bois Review* 11, no. 2 (October 2014): 205–
32; Patrick Sharkey, *Stuck in Place: Urban Neighborhoods and the End of Progress toward Racial
Equality* (Chicago: University of Chicago Press, 2013); Gary Orfield, John Kucsera, and Gene-
vieve Siegel-Hawley, *E Pluribus . . . Separation* (Los Angeles: UCLA Civil Rights Project/
Proyecto Derechos Civiles, September 2012).

4. Sean F. Reardon and John T. Yun, "Integrating Neighborhoods, Segregating Schools:
The Retreat from School Desegregation in the South, 1990–2000," *North Carolina Law Review*
81 (2003): 1563–96; Gary Orfield, *Schools More Separate: Consequences of a Decade of Resegrega-
tion* (Cambridge, MA: Harvard University Civil Rights Project, 2001).

5. Heather Ann Thompson, "Why Mass Incarceration Matters: Rethinking Crisis, Decline,
and Transformation in Postwar American History," *Journal of American History* 97 (2010): 703–
34. See also chapters by Matthew Lassiter and Peniel Joseph in this volume.

6. In 2006, more than half of subprime loans went to African Americans, who comprised
only 13 percent of the population. And a recent study of data from the Home Mortgage Disclosure Act found that 32.1 percent of blacks, but only 10.5 percent of whites, got higher priced
mortgages—those with an interest rate three or more points higher than the rate of a Treasury
security of the same length. See Debbie Gruenstein Bocian, Wei Li, Carolina Reid, and Roberto

G. Quercia, *Lost Ground, 2011: Disparities in Mortgage Lending and Foreclosures* (Durham, NC: Center for Responsible Lending, 2011), http://www.responsiblelending.org/mortgage-lending /research-analysis/Lost-Ground-2011.pdf; Matthew Desmond, *Evicted: Poverty and Profit in the American City* (New York: Crown, 2016).

7. Roger Biles, *The Fate of Cities: Urban America and the Federal Government, 1945–2000* (Lawrence: University Press of Kansas, 2011); Michael B. Katz, *The Price of Citizenship: Redefining the American Welfare State* (Philadelphia: University of Pennsylvania Press, 2008); Jamie Peck, "Pushing Austerity: State Failure, Municipal Bankruptcy, and the Crises of Fiscal Federalism in the USA," *Cambridge Journal of Regions, Economics, and Society* 7, no. 1 (2014): 17–44.

8. On Obama's background, see Thomas J. Sugrue, *Not Even Past: Barack Obama and the Burden of Race* (Princeton, NJ: Princeton University Press, 2010); David Remnick, *The Bridge: The Life and Rise of Barack Obama* (New York: Simon & Schuster, 2010); David Maraniss, *Barack Obama: The Story* (New York: Simon & Schuster, 2011). See also Obama's own memoir, *Dreams from My Father* (New York: Times Books, 1995).

9. Andrew J. Diamond, *Chicago on the Make: Power and Inequality in a Modern City* (Berkeley: University of California Press, 2017); Sugrue, *Not Even Past*, esp. chap. 1.

10. Costas Spirou and Dennis R. Judd, *Building the City of Spectacle: Mayor Richard M. Daley and the Remaking of Chicago* (Ithaca, NY: Cornell University Press, 2016).

11. Andrew J. Diamond, "Chicago: A City on the Brink," *Books and Ideas*, May 15, 2012, http://www.booksandideas.net/Chicago-A-City-on-the-Brink.html.

12. I served as a mostly passive member of the campaign's Urban Advisory Committee; my comments are based on my reading of the hundreds of messages that came through the listserv.

13. Fredrick C. Harris, *The Price of the Ticket: Barack Obama and the Rise and Decline of Black Politics* (New York: Oxford University Press, 2012); Sugrue, *Not Even Past*, chap. 3.

14. For examples, see Barack Obama, "Remarks in Spartanburg, SC," June 15, 2007, http:// www.presidency.ucsb.edu/ws/index.php?pid=77003; "Remarks in Washington, DC: 'Changing the Odds for Urban America,'" July 18, 2007, http://www.presidency.ucsb.edu/ws/index .php?pid=77007; "Remarks to the U.S. Conference of Mayors," Miami, Florida, June 21, 2008, http://www.presidency.ucsb.edu/ws/index.php?pid=77555&st=urban&st1=; and "Democratic Convention: Obama Promotes Plan for Urban Development," *Wall Street Journal*, August 25, 2008.

15. Barack H. Obama, "Remarks to the National Association of Education Annual Meeting in Philadelphia," July 5, 2007, http://www.presidency.ucsb.edu/ws/index.php?pid=77006; "Remarks to the U.S. Conference of Mayors"; Bruce Katz, "Obama's Metro Presidency," *City and Community* 9, no. 1 (January 2010): 23–31.

16. Executive Order 13,503; Thomas J. Sugrue, "Carter's Urban Policy Crisis," in *The Carter Presidency*, ed. Gary Fink and Hugh Davis Graham (Lawrence: University Press of Kansas, 1997).

17. For details on the staff, programs, and initiatives of the White House Office of Urban Affairs, see https://obamawhitehouse.archives.gov/urbanaffairs.

18. "National Conversation of America's Cities and Metropolitan Areas," "Urban Tours," and "Urban Policy Working Groups," Office of Urban Affairs Initiatives, https://obamawhite house.archives.gov/administration/eop/oua/initiatives.

19. Quoted in "New White House Office to Redefine What Urban Policy Encompasses: Agenda May Address Suburbs Too," *Washington Post*, July 3, 2009.

20. "Obama to Cities: Drop Dead—The Life and Death of a Great American Urban Policy," *New York Observer*, February 15, 2012, http://observer.com/2012/02/obama-to-cities-drop -dead-the-life-and-death-of-a-great-american-urban-policy/; Theda Skocpol and Lawrence Jacobs, eds., *Reaching for a New Deal: Ambitious Governance, Economic Meltdown, and Polarized*

Politics in Obama's First Two Years (New York: Russell Sage, 2011). It is also notable that none of the essays in the book focused on civil rights, a topic that is, in many respects, closely related to urban policy.

21. "Obama's Urban Affairs Office Brings Hope but Not Much Change," *Huffington Post*, July 26, 2013.

22. The American Recovery and Reinvestment Act of 2009 (Pub. L. 111–5); for an overview, see the White House information pages and blogs about ARRA: https://www.whitehouse.gov /recovery/about. On the impact of the stimulus on education employment, see ED Recovery Act Report, Summary of Programs and State-by-State Data, http://www2.ed.gov/policy/gen /leg/recovery/spending/index.html.

23. For general overviews, see Paul Starr's chapter in this volume; Michael Grunwald, *The New New Deal: The Hidden Story of Change in the Obama Era* (New York: Simon & Schuster, 2012), Van Jones quoted on p. 305; Hilary Silver, "Obama's Urban Policy: A Symposium," *City and Community* (March 2010): 5, calls the ARRA a "stealth" urban program.

24. For details, see American Recovery and Reinvestment Act of 2009. Generally on the impact of healthcare spending on cities, see Daniel Gitterman, Joanne Spetz, and Matthew Fellowes, "The Other Side of the Ledger: Federal Health Spending in Metropolitan Economies," *Discussion Paper*, Brookings Institution Metropolitan Policy Program, September 2004, http:// www.brook.edu/metro/pubs/20040917_gitterman.htm; Margaret Pugh O'Mara, *Cities of Knowledge* (Princeton, NJ: Princeton University Press, 2005); Guian McKee, *Health-Care Policy as Urban Policy: Hospitals and Community Development in the Postindustrial City* (Charlottesville: University of Virginia, Miller Center for Public Affairs, 2010).

25. The Patient Protection and Affordable Care Act of 2010 (Pub. L. 148): https:// www.gpo.gov/fdsys/granule/PLAW-111publ148/PLAW-111publ148/content-detail.html. "Since Obamacare Was Passed Fifty Months Ago, Healthcare Has Gained One Million Jobs," *Forbes*, June 6, 2014; "Obamacare Is Creating More Jobs Now: Will There Be More Health Care Costs Later?" *Forbes*, July 2, 2015. The most substantial healthcare job growth occurred after the expansion of healthcare enrollment in 2014, and cannot be attributed entirely to the ACA. The population continued to age and the economy had been rebounding from recession since late 2009.

26. Gregory D. Squires and Derek S. Hyra, "Foreclosures—Yesterday, Today, and Tomorrow," *City & Community* 9, no. 1 (March 2010): 50–60; Algernon Austin, "Subprime Mortgages Are Nearly Double for Hispanics and African Americans," Economic Policy Institute, June 11, 2008, http://www.epi.org/economic_snapshots/entry/webfeatures_snapshots_20080611/; Andrew Jakabovics and Jeff Chapman, "Unequal Opportunity Lenders? Analyzing Racial Disparities in Big Banks' Higher Priced Lending," Center for American Progress, September 2009, http://www.americanprogress.org/issues/2009/09/pdf/tarp_report.pdf; Jennifer Wheary, Tatjana Meschede, and Thomas M. Shapiro, "The Downside before the Downturn: Declining Economic Security among Middle-Class African Americans and Latinos, 2000–2006," Brandeis University, Institute on Assets and Social Policy and Demos, n.d., http://www.demos.org/pubs /bat_5.pdf; Douglas S. Massey and Jacob S. Rugh, "Racial Segregation and the American Foreclosure Crisis," *American Sociological Review* 75 (2010): 629–51.

27. Squires and Hyra, "Foreclosures." For the Department of Treasury's ongoing evaluation of MHA and HAMP, see https://www.treasury.gov/initiatives/financial-stability/TARP -Programs/housing/mha/Pages/Surveys.aspx. For critical overviews of the program, see David Dayen, "Obama Program That Hurt Homeowners and Helped Big Banks Is Ending," *The Intercept*, December 28, 2015, https://theintercept.com/2015/12/28/obama-program-hurt-home owners-and-helped-big-banks-now-its-dead/; and Dayen, "Obama Failed to Mitigate America's Foreclosure Crisis," *Atlantic*, December 14, 2016.

28. Rakesh Kochhar, Richard Fry, and Paul Taylor, *Twenty-to-One: Wealth Gaps Rise to Record Highs between Whites, Blacks and Hispanics*, Pew Research Center, Social and Demographic Trends, July 26, 2011, http://www.pewsocialtrends.org/2011/07/26/wealth-gaps-rise-to-record-highs-between-whites-blacks-hispanics/.

29. Obama, "Remarks in a Discussion on Urban and Metropolitan Policy," June 13, 2009, http://www.presidency.ucsb.edu/ws/?pid=86417. On the history of efforts at executive branch reorganization, see Brian Balogh, Joanna Grisinger, and Philip Zelikow, *Making Democracy Work: A Brief History of Twentieth Century Executive Reorganization*, Miller Center of Public Affairs, University of Virginia, Working Paper (July 2002). On Carter's effort to coordinate urban policy across federal agencies (which Obama alluded to in his 2009 speech), see Sugrue, "Carter's Urban Policy Crisis."

30. Margery Austin Turner, "New Life for US Housing and Urban Policy," *City and Community* 9, no. 1 (January 2010): 35–36.

31. David Rusk, *Cities without Suburbs* (Baltimore: Johns Hopkins University Press, 1993); Myron Orfield, *Metropolitics: A Regional Agenda for Community and Stability* (Washington, DC: Brookings Institution, 1997); Bruce Katz, ed., *Reflections on Regionalism* (Washington, DC: Brookings Institution, 2000); Bruce Katz and Robert Puentes, *Taking the High Road: A Metropolitan Agenda for Transportation Reform* (Washington, DC: Brookings Institution, 2005); and especially Bruce Katz and Jennifer Bradley, *The Metropolitan Revolution: How Cities and Metros Are Fixing Our Broken Politics and Fragile Economy* (Washington, DC: Brookings Institution, 2013). For a comprehensive overview, including an archive of reports, see Brookings Metropolitan Policy Program, https://www.brookings.edu/program/metropolitan-policy-program/.

32. See, especially, Obama, "Remarks to the U.S. Conference of Mayors."

33. Ibid.

34. Obama, "Remarks in a Discussion on Urban and Metropolitan Policy." U.S. Conference of Mayors, "DOT Secretary Ray LaHood, HUD Secretary Shaun Donovan, and EPA Administrator Lisa Jackson Announce Interagency Partnership for Sustainable Communities," July 13, 2009, http://www.usmayors.org/usmayornewspaper/documents/07_13_09/pg10_lahood.asp.

35. Stanley Kurtz, *Spreading the Wealth: How Obama Is Robbing the Suburbs to Pay for the Cities* (New York: Sentinel, 2012); Ben Adler, "Urban Nation: How Stanley Kurtz Is Defending the Suburbs from His Own Doomsday Fantasy," *Next City*, August 22, 2012. On GOP opposition to Obama's policies generally, see Zelizer, chapter 2 in this volume.

36. Timothy P. R. Weaver, *Blazing the Neoliberal Trail: Urban Political Development in the United States and the United Kingdom* (Philadelphia: University of Pennsylvania Press, 2016).

37. Obama, "Changing the Odds for Urban America." Few urban ventures appealed to Obama more than the Harlem Children's Zone. For an overview, see Paul Tough, *Whatever It Takes: Geoffrey Canada's Quest to Change Harlem and America* (Boston: Houghton Mifflin, 2008). Obama was on a program with Canada in 2009, and favorably mentioned Canada and the Harlem Children's Zone in several speeches. Barack H. Obama, "Remarks on Community Service Programs," June 30, 2009, http://www.presidency.ucsb.edu/ws/index.php?pid=86358.

38. Obama, "Remarks in a Discussion on Urban and Metropolitan Policy."

39. Barack H. Obama, "Remarks on the 20th Anniversary of the Points of Light Institute," College Station, Texas, October 16, 2009, http://www.presidency.ucsb.edu/ws/index.php?pid=86756; Barack H. Obama, "Remarks at the Congressional Black Caucus Foundation Dinner," September 26, 2009, http://www.presidency.ucsb.edu/ws/index.php?pid=86693.

40. See Jonathan Zimmerman, chapter 8 in this volume.

41. "Obama to Cities, Drop Dead."

42. Thomas J. Sugrue, *Sweet Land of Liberty: The Forgotten Struggle for Civil Rights in the North* (New York: Random House, 2008), chap. 13; Davison M. Douglas, *Reading, Writing, and*

Race: The Desegregation of the Charlotte Schools (Chapel Hill: University of North Carolina Press, 1995); Matthew Lassiter, " 'Socioeconomic Integration' in the Suburbs: From Reactionary Populism to Class Fairness in Metropolitan Charlotte," in *The New Suburban History*, ed. Kevin M. Kruse and Thomas J. Sugrue (Chicago: University of Chicago Press, 2005), 140–43; *Milliken v. Bradley*, 418 U.S. 717 (1974); *Capacchione v. Charlotte-Mecklenburg Schools*, 57 F. Supp. 2d 228 (1999); *Parents Involved in Community Schools v. Seattle School District No. 1*, 551 U.S. 701 (2007).

43. Promise Neighborhoods Act of 2011 (*H.R. 2098* and *S. 1004*); David Raskin, "Revisiting the Hope VI Public Housing Program's Legacy," *Governing* (May 2012), http://www.governing .com/topics/health-human-services/housing/gov-revisiting-hope-public-housing-programs -legacy.html; "Fighting Poverty and Creating Opportunity: The Choice Neighborhoods Initiative," Department of Housing and Urban Development, *PD&R Edge Magazine*, https://www .huduser.gov/portal/pdredge/pdr_edge_frm_asst_sec_101911.html.

44. Weaver, *Blazing the Neoliberal Trail*, 281; White House, Office of the Press Secretary, "Fact Sheet: President Obama's Promise Zone Initiative," https://obamawhitehouse.archives .gov/the-press-office/2014/01/08/fact-sheet-president-obama-s-promise-zones-initiative; Barack H. Obama, "Remarks on the Promise Zones Initiative," January 20, 2014, http://www .presidency.ucsb.edu/ws/index.php?pid=104576.

45. White House, Office of the Press Secretary, "Obama Administration Releases Final Round of Promise Zone Designations," June 6, 2016, https://obamawhitehouse.archives.gov/the -press-office/2016/06/06/obama-administration-announces-final-round-promise-zone -designations.

Chapter 11: "Tough and Smart": The Resilience of the War on Drugs during the Obama Administration

1. *Vice Special Report: Fixing the System* (HBO, September 27, 2015); Barack Obama, "Remarks after Visit at El Reno Federal Correctional Institution," July 16, 2015, https://www .whitehouse.gov/the-press-office/2015/07/16/remarks-president-after-visit-el-reno-federal -correctional-institution; Obama, *Dreams from My Father: A Story of Race and Inheritance* (New York: Times Books, 1995), 93–94.

2. Michael D. Shear and Yamiche Alcindor, "Jolted by Deaths, Obama Found His Voice on Race," *New York Times*, January 14, 2017.

3. Obama, "Remarks at Howard University Convocation," September 28, 2007, *American Presidency Project*, http://www.presidency.ucsb.edu/ws/?pid=77014.

4. Democratic Party Platform, August 25, 2008, *American Presidency Project*, http://www .presidency.ucsb.edu/ws/?pid=78283.

5. *National Drug Control Strategy 2010*, https://www.whitehouse.gov/sites/default/files /ondcp/policy-and-research/ndcs2010.pdf.

6. Richard Nixon, "Statement about the Drug Abuse Office and Treatment Act of 1972," March 21, 1972, *American Presidency Project*, http://www.presidency.ucsb.edu/ws/?pid=3782; Naomi Murakawa, *The First Civil Right: How Liberals Built Prison America* (New York: Oxford University Press, 2014), 113–43.

7. Shane Smith, "Fixing the System: An Interview with President Obama on Prison Reform," *Vice* (October 2015), http://www.vice.com/read/fixing-the-system-0000760-v22n10.

8. *National Drug Control Strategy 2010*, 7.

9. Michelle Alexander, *The New Jim Crow: Mass Incarceration in the Age of Colorblindness* (New York: New Press, 2010); *The Growth of Incarceration in the United States: Exploring Causes and Consequences* (Washington, DC: National Academies Press, 2014).

10. Bureau of Justice Statistics, *Bulletin: Prisoners in 2008* (December 2009), https://www

.bjs.gov/content/pub/pdf/p08.pdf; Pew Center on the States; *One in 100: Behind Bars in America 2008* (February 2008), http://www.pewtrusts.org/~/media/legacy/uploadedfiles/wwwpew trustsorg/reports/sentencing_and_corrections/onein100pdf.pdf.

11. "White House Announces New Director of the Office of National Drug Control Policy," March 11, 2009, https://www.whitehouse.gov/the-press-office/white-house-announces-new -director-office-national-drug-control-policy; R. Gil Kerlikowske, "Speech to the International Association of Chiefs of Police Conference," October 6, 2009, https://dadonfire.files.wordpress .com/2009/10/100309_iacp.pdf.

12. Kerlikowske, "Remarks at the George Washington University Conference on 'Hemispheric Security,'" February 28, 2011, https://www.whitehouse.gov/ondcp/news-releases-remarks /remarks-by-gil-kerlikowske-at-the-george-washington-university-conference.

13. Holder quotation in Josh Meyer and Scott Glover, "Medical Marijuana Dispensaries Will No Longer Be Prosecuted, U.S. Attorney General Says," *Los Angeles Times*, March 19, 2009; David W. Ogden/DOJ, "Memorandum: Investigations and Prosecutions in States Authorizing the Medical Use of Marijuana," October 19, 2009, https://www.justice.gov/sites/default/files /opa/legacy/2009/10/19/medical-marijuana.pdf.

14. Drug Enforcement Agency, "The DEA Position on Marijuana" (July 2010, updated April 2013), https://www.ncjrs.gov/App/Publications/abstract.aspx?ID=254295.

15. Tim Dickinson, "Obama's War on Pot," *Rolling Stone*, February 16, 2012, http://www .rollingstone.com/politics/news/obamas-war-on-pot-20120216; Jacob Sullum/Cato Institute, "Bummer: Barack Obama Turns Out to Be Just Another Drug Warrior," *Reason*, September 12, 2011, http://reason.com/archives/2011/09/12/bummer/print.

16. Kerlikowske, "Californians Seeking Treatment for Marijuana at Higher Rates," October 20, 2010, https://www.whitehouse.gov/ondcp/news-releases-remarks/californians-seeking-treat ment-for-marijuana-at-higher-rates; Kerlikowske, "Why Marijuana Legalization Would Compromise Public Health and Public Safety," March 4, 2010, https://www.whitehouse.gov/sites /default/files/ondcp/issues-content/directors_cal_chiefs_remarks.pdf; DrugWarFacts.org, "Marijuana," http://www.drugwarfacts.org/cms/Marijuana#Total.

17. *National Drug Control Strategy 2010*, 8–9, 72.

18. "DEA Position on Marijuana" (2010/2013).

19. Gallup, "For First Time, Americans Favor Legalizing Marijuana," October 22, 2013, http://www.gallup.com/poll/165539/first-time-americans-favor-legalizing-marijuana.aspx; Pew Research Center, "Support for Marijuana Legalization Continues to Rise," October 12, 2016, http://www.pewresearch.org/fact-tank/2016/10/12/support-for-marijuana-legalization -continues-to-rise/.

20. James M. Cole/DOJ, "Memorandum: Guidance Regarding Marijuana Enforcement," August 29, 2013, https://www.justice.gov/iso/opa/resources/3052013829132756857467.pdf.

21. ACLU, "The War on Marijuana in Black and White," June 2013, https://www.aclu.org /files/assets/aclu-thewaronmarijuana-rel2.pdf.

22. Center for Constitutional Rights, "Landmark Decision: Judge Rules NYPD Stop and Frisk Practices Unconstitutional, Racially Discriminatory," August 12, 2013, https://ccrjustice .org/home/press-center/press-releases/landmark-decision-judge-rules-nypd-stop-and-frisk -practices.

23. Campaign Zero, "Solutions," 2015, http://www.joincampaignzero.org/solutions/ #solutionsoverview.

24. David Remnick, "Going the Distance: On and Off the Road with Barack Obama," *New Yorker*, January 27, 2014, http://www.newyorker.com/magazine/2014/01/27/going-the-distance -david-remnick; Obama, "Remarks in Town Hall with Young Leaders of the Americas," April 9,

2015, https://www.whitehouse.gov/the-press-office/2015/04/09/remarks-president-obama-town-hall-young-leaders-americas.

25. Human Rights Watch, "Nation Behind Bars: A Human Rights Solution," 2014, https://www.hrw.org/sites/default/files/related_material/2014_US_Nation_Behind_Bars_0.pdf.

26. Human Rights Watch and ACLU, "Every 25 Seconds: The Human Toll of Criminalizing Drug Use in the United States," October 2016, https://www.hrw.org/report/2016/10/12/every-25-seconds/human-toll-criminalizing-drug-use-united-states.

27. DEA, "Speaking Out against Drug Legalization," 2010, https://www.dea.gov/pr/multimedia-library/publications/speaking_out.pdf.

28. Chuck Rosenberg/DEA to Gina Raimondo and Jay Inslee, August 11, 2016, https://www.dea.gov/divisions/hq/2016/Letter081116.pdf; Office of National Drug Control Policy, "Marijuana Resource Center," https://www.whitehouse.gov/ondcp/marijuanainfo; Jann S. Wenner, "The Day After: Obama on His Legacy, Trump's Win, and the Path Forward," *Rolling Stone*, November 29, 2016, http://www.rollingstone.com/politics/features/obama-on-his-legacy-trumps-win-and-the-path-forward-w452527.

29. *National Drug Control Strategy 2010*, 55.

30. ACLU, "Cracks in the System: Twenty Years of the Unjust Federal Crack Cocaine Law" (October 2006), https://www.aclu.org/files/pdfs/drugpolicy/cracksinsystem_20061025.pdf; The Sentencing Project, "Federal Crack Cocaine Sentencing" (October 2010), http://www.sentencingproject.org/wp-content/uploads/2016/01/Federal-Crack-Cocaine-Sentencing.pdf; Senator Dick Durbin, Press Release, "Durbin Introduces Bill to Eliminate Sentencing Disparity between Crack and Powder Cocaine," October 15, 2009, http://www.durbin.senate.gov/newsroom/press-releases/durbin-introduces-bill-to-eliminate-sentencing-disparity-between-crack-and-powder-cocaine; *National Drug Control Strategy 2010*, 55.

31. "President Obama Signs the Fair Sentencing Act," August 3, 2010, https://www.whitehouse.gov/blog/2010/08/03/president-obama-signs-fair-sentencing-act; Sentencing Project, "Federal Crack Cocaine Sentencing."

32. *U.S. v. Blewett*, Nos. 12–5226/5582, Sixth Circuit Court of Appeals, December 3, 2013; "United States' Petition for Hearing En Banc," May 31, 2013, http://sentencing.typepad.com/files/blewett_petition-for-rehearing.pdf.

33. 2012 Democratic National Platform, "Moving America Forward," September 2012, *American Presidency Project*, http://www.presidency.ucsb.edu/papers_pdf/101962.pdf.

34. Eric Holder, interview, *PBS Frontline*, February 23, 2016, http://www.pbs.org/wgbh/frontline/article/eric-holder-if-sentencing-reform-dies-id-be-ashamed/; Pew Charitable Trusts, "Public Opinion on Sentencing and Corrections Policy in America," March 2012, http://www.pewtrusts.org/~/media/assets/2012/03/30/pew_nationalsurveyresearchpaper_final.pdf.

35. Holder, "Remarks to American Bar Association," August 12, 2013, https://www.justice.gov/opa/speech/attorney-general-eric-holder-delivers-remarks-annual-meeting-american-bar-associations.

36. Department of Justice, "Smart on Crime: Reforming the Criminal Justice System for the 21st Century," August 2013, https://www.justice.gov/sites/default/files/ag/legacy/2013/08/12/smart-on-crime.pdf; "Smarter Sentencing: Attorney General's Call to Reduce the Prison Population Is a Critical and Overdue Step," *New York Times*, August 14, 2013.

37. Right on Crime, "Statement of Principles," http://rightoncrime.com/statement-of-principles/.

38. Holder, "Memo: Department Policy on Charging Mandatory Minimum Sentences and Recidivist Enhancements in Certain Drug Cases," August 12, 2013, https://www.justice.gov/sites/default/files/oip/legacy/2014/07/23/ag-memo-department-policypon-charging-mandatory-minimum-sentences-recidivist-enhancements-in-certain-drugcases.pdf.

39. Durbin Press Release, "Durbin and Lee Introduce Smarter Sentencing Act," August 1, 2013, http://www.durbin.senate.gov/newsroom/press-releases/durbin-and-lee-introduce-smarter-sentencing-act; Holder, "Remarks to American Bar Association."

40. "Statement by the President on Clemency," December 19, 2013, http://www.whitehouse.gov/the-press-office/2013/12/19/statement-president-clemency.

41. Sentencing Reform and Corrections Act of 2015 (S.2123), https://www.congress.gov/bill/114th-congress/senate-bill/2123; Julie Stewart/FAMM, "Sentencing Reforms in the 114th Congress: They Simply Aren't Good Enough," November 17, 2015, http://famm.org/famm-president-julie-stewart-on-sentencing-reforms-in-the-114th-congress/.

42. Holder, interview (2016).

43. Department of Justice, "Announcing New Clemency Initiative," April 23, 2014, https://www.justice.gov/opa/pr/announcing-new-clemency-initiative-deputy-attorney-general-james-m-cole-details-broad-new; Julie Hirschfeld Davis and Gardiner Harris, "Obama Commutes Sentences for 46 Drug Offenders," *New York Times*, July 13, 2015.

44. "Commutations Granted by President Obama," https://www.justice.gov/pardon/obama-commutations; Marc Mauer, Nancy Gertner, and Jonathan Simon, "Time for a Broad Approach to Clemency," *The Hill*, June 3, 2016, http://thehill.com/blogs/congress-blog/judicial/282117-time-for-a-broad-approach-to-clemency.

45. Matthew D. Lassiter, "Impossible Criminals: The Suburban Imperatives of America's War on Drugs," *Journal of American History* 102, no. 1 (June 2015): 126–40.

46. Obama, "Remarks to NAACP Conference," July 14, 2015, https://www.whitehouse.gov/the-press-office/2015/07/14/remarks-president-naacp-conference.

47. Alexander, *New Jim Crow*.

48. Bureau of Justice Statistics, "Prisoners in 2014," September 2015, https://www.bjs.gov/content/pub/pdf/p14.pdf.

49. Urban Institute, "Reducing Mass Incarceration Requires Far-Reaching Reforms," August 2015, http://webapp.urban.org/reducing-mass-incarceration/index.html.

50. Obama, "Remarks at International Association of Chiefs of Police Annual Conference," October 27, 2015, *American Presidency Project*, http://www.presidency.ucsb.edu/ws/index.php?pid=110995; President's Task Force on 21st Century Policing, *Final Report* (Washington, DC, May 2015).

51. *National Drug Control Strategy 2010*, 63–88; Amnesty International, "U.S. Policy in Colombia," http://www.amnestyusa.org/our-work/countries/americas/colombia/us-policy-in-colombia; Clare Ribando Seelke and Kristin Finklea, "U.S.-Mexican Security Cooperation: The Merida Initiative and Beyond," *Congressional Research Service* (February 22, 2016), https://www.fas.org/sgp/crs/row/R41349.pdf.

52. "Administration Officials Announce U.S.-Mexico Border Security Policy: A Comprehensive Response and Commitment," March 24, 2009, https://www.whitehouse.gov/the-press-office/administration-officials-announce-us-mexico-border-security-policy-a-comprehensive-.

53. Mark Landler, "Clinton Says Demand for Illegal Drugs in the U.S. 'Fuels the Drug Trade' in Mexico," *New York Times*, March 26, 2009; Obama, "News Conference with President Felipe de Jesus Calderon Hinojosa of Mexico in Mexico City," April 16, 2009, *American Presidency Project*, http://www.presidency.ucsb.edu/ws/index.php?pid=86014.

54. Seelke and Finklea, "U.S.-Mexican Security Cooperation"; Suzanna Reiss, "Beyond Supply and Demand: Obama's Drug Wars in Latin America," *NACLA Report on the Americas* (January/February 2010), https://nacla.org/node/6429.

55. David A. Shirk, *The Drug War in Mexico: Confronting a Shared Threat* (Council on Foreign Relations, March 2011), http://i.cfr.org/content/publications/attachments/Mexico_CSR60.pdf.

56. Kerlikowske, "Remarks at George Washington University Conference on 'Hemispheric Security'"; DEA, "Speaking Out against Drug Legalization."

57. Juan Manuel Santos, "It Is Time To Think Again about the War on Drugs," *Guardian*, November 12, 2011, http://www.theguardian.com/world/2011/nov/13/colombia-juan-santos -war-on-drugs.

58. Global Commission on Drug Policy, "War on Drugs," June 2011, http://www.global commissionondrugs.org/wp-content/themes/gcdp_v1/pdf/Global_Commission_Report _English.pdf.

59. Jackie Calmes, "Obama Says Legalization Is Not the Answer on Drugs," *New York Times*, April 15, 2012.

60. Drug Policy Alliance, "A Public Letter to UN Secretary General Ban Ki-Moon," April 14, 2016, http://www.drugpolicy.org/ungass2016.

61. Reiss, "Beyond Supply and Demand."

62. DHHS, "The Opioid Epidemic: By the Numbers," June 2016, http://www.hhs.gov/sites /default/files/Factsheet-opioids-061516.pdf; Centers for Disease Control and Prevention, "Understanding the Epidemic," https://www.cdc.gov/drugoverdose/epidemic/.

63. U.S. Attorney for Western District of Virginia, "Statement on the Guilty Plea of the Purdue Frederick Company and Its Executives for Illegally Misbranding OxyContin," May 10, 2007, https://assets.documentcloud.org/documents/279028/purdue-guilty-plea.pdf; Barry Meier, "Narcotic Maker Guilty of Deceit over Marketing," *New York Times*, May 11, 2007.

64. *National Drug Control Strategy 2010*, 30, 33.

65. Sam Quinones, "Serving All Your Heroin Needs," *New York Times*, April 19, 2015.

66. Obama, "Remarks at Community Forum at East End Family Resource Center," October 21, 2015, https://www.whitehouse.gov/the-press-office/2015/10/21/remarks-president-com munity-forum-east-end-family-resource-center; Lassiter, "Impossible Criminals."

67. Comprehensive Addiction and Recovery Act of 2016 (S.524), https://www.govtrack .us/congress/bills/114/s524; Emmarie Huetteman, "Senate Approves Bill to Combat Opioid Addiction Crisis," *New York Times*, July 13, 2016; Obama, "Statement on the Comprehensive Addiction and Recovery Act of 2016," July 22, 2016, https://www.whitehouse.gov/the-press -office/2016/07/22/statement-president-comprehensive-addiction-and-recovery-act-2016.

68. Barack Obama Interview by Ta-Nehisi Coates, *Atlantic*, December 21, 2017, https:// www.theatlantic.com/politics/archive/2016/12/ta-nehisi-coates-obama-transcript-ii/511133/.

69. Jelani Cobb, "The Home Front," *New Yorker*, August 29, 2016; "The President Interviews the Creator of 'The Wire' about the War on Drugs," March 26, 2015, https://www.white house.gov/blog/2015/03/26/watch-president-sits-down-creator-wire-talk-about-war-drugs.

Chapter 12: A Promise Unfulfilled, an Imperfect Legacy: Obama and Immigration Policy

1. Aristide Zolberg, *Nation by Design: Immigration Policy in the Fashioning of America* (Cambridge, MA: Harvard University Press, 2006) 336–37, 439.

2. Ana Gonzalez-Barrera, *More Mexicans Leaving Than Coming to the U.S.* (Washington, DC: Pew Research Center, November 19, 2015), http://www.pewhispanic.org/2015/11/19 /more-mexicans-leaving-than-coming-to-the-u-s/, accessed January 31, 2017.

3. Daniel Tichenor, "Strange Bedfellows: The Politics and Pathologies of Immigration Reform," Labor 5, no. 2 (2008): 39–60.

4. Bradley Jones, *Americans' View of Immigrants Marked by Widening Partisan and Generational Divides* (Washington, DC: Pew Research Center, April 15, 2015), http://www.pewresearch

.org/fact-tank/2016/04/15/americans-views-of-immigrants-marked-by-widening-partisan-generational-divides, accessed January 31, 2017.

5. AFL-CIO Executive Council Statement on Immigration, February 16, 2000, http://www.aflcio.org/About/Exec-Council/EC-Statements/Immigration2, accessed January 31, 2017.

6. Gary Miller and Normal Schofield, "The Transformation of the Republican and Democratic Party Coalitions in the US," *Perspectives on Politics* 6, no. 3 (September 2008): 233–50.

7. Barack Obama, "Remarks at the 2008 National Council of La Raza Annual Meeting in San Diego, California," July 13, 2008, *The American Presidency Project*, http://www.presidency.ucsb.edu/ws/?pid=77652.

8. Julia Preston, "In Big Shift, Latino Vote was Heavily for Obama," *New York Times*, November 6, 2008.

9. Transcript of Press Conference by President Obama, President Calderon of Mexico, and Prime Minister Harper of Canada, August 10, 2009, https://obamawhitehouse.archives.gov/the-press-office/press-conference-president-obama-president-calderon-mexico-and-prime-minister-harpe, accessed January 31, 2017.

10. The unauthorized immigrant population was estimated to have grown from 3.5 million in 1990 to 5.7 million by 1995. Jeffery A. Passel and D'Vera Cohn, *Unauthorized Immigrant Population Stable for Half a Decade* (Washington, DC: Pew Hispanic, September 21, 2016).

11. Douglas S. Massey and Karen A. Pren, "Unintended Consequences of U.S. Immigration Policy: Explaining the Post-1965 Surge from Latin America," *Population and Development Review* 38, no. 1 (March 2012): 1–29.

12. Serena Marshall, "Obama Has Deported More People Than Any Other President," *ABC News*, August 29, 2016, http://abcnews.go.com/politics/obamas-deportation-policy-numbers/story?id=41715661, accessed January 31, 2017.

13. Nora Caplan-Bricker, "Who's the Real Deporter-in-Chief: Bush or Obama?" *New Republic*, April 17, 2015, https://newrepublic.com/article/117412/deportations-under-obama-vs-bush-who-deported-more-immigrants, accessed January 31, 2017.

14. Ginger Thompson and Sarah Cohen, "More Deportations Follow Minor Crimes, Records Show," *New York Times*, April 6, 2014.

15. Reid J. Epstein, "NCLR Head: Obama 'Deporter-in-Chief,'" *Politico*, March 4, 2014, http://www.politico.com/story/2014/03/national-council-of-la-raza-janet-murguia-barack-obama-deporter-in-chief-immigration-104217, accessed January 31, 2017.

16. David G. Savage, "Obama Administration Sues to Block Arizona Immigration Law," *Los Angeles Times*, July 6, 2010.

17. Adam Liptak, "Blocking Parts of Arizona Law, Justices Allow Its Centerpiece," *New York Times*, June 25, 2012.

18. Immigration and Customs Enforcement Press Release, December 20, 2012, https://www.ice.gov/news/releases/fy-2012-ice-announces-year-end-removal-numbers-highlights-focus-key-priorities-and.

19. John M. Broder, "Graham Pulls Support for Major Senate Climate Bill," *New York Times*, April 24, 2010.

20. John D. Skrentny, "Obama's Immigration Reform: A Tough Sell for a Grand Bargain," in *Reaching for A New Deal: Ambitious Governance, Economic Meltdown, and Polarized Politics in Obama's First Two Years*, ed. Theda Skocpol and Lawrence R. Jacobs (New York: Russell Sage, 2009), 292.

21. Vanessa Williamson, Theda Skocpol, and John Coggin, "The Tea Party and the Remaking of Republican Conservatism," *Perspectives on Politics* 9, no. 1 (2012): 25–43.

22. Barack Obama, "Remarks by the President on Comprehensive Immigration Reform,"

May 10, 2011, https://obamawhitehouse.archives.gov/the-press-office/2011/05/10/remarks -president-comprehensive-immigration-reform-el-paso-texas?Source=GovD, accessed January 31, 2017.

23. Janet Napolitano, "The Truth About Young Immigrants and DACA," *New York Times*, November 30, 2016.

24. Drew Desilver, *Executive Actions on Immigration Have a Long History* (Washington, DC: Pew Research Center, November 21, 2015), http://www.pewresearch.org/fact-tank/2014/11/21 /executive-actions-on-immigration-have-long-history/, accessed September 22, 2017.

25. "Remarks by the President at Univision Town Hall with Jorge Ramos and Maria Elena Salinas," September 20, 2012, https://www.whitehouse.gov/the-press-office/2012/09/20/remarks -president-univision-town-hall-jorge-ramos-and-maria-elena-salina, accessed September 22, 2017.

26. Mark Hugo Lopez and Paul Taylor, *Latino Voters in the 2012 Election* (Washington DC: Pew Research Center, November 7, 2012), http://www.pewhispanic.org/files/2012/11/2012 _Latino_vote_exit_poll_analysis_final_11-09.pdf, accessed January 31, 2017.

27. Julia Preston and Fernanda Santos, "A Record Latino Turnout, Solidly Backing Obama," *New York Times*, November 7, 2012.

28. June 2014 Latino Decisions/Center for American Progress Poll, http://www.latino decisions.com/files/2814/0415/0459/CAP_Poll_Results_Release_-_July_2014.pdf. accessed September 22, 2017.

29. Michael A. Memoli, Noam N. Levey, Brian Bennett, "Senators Unveil Bipartisan Immigration Plan but Opposition Looms," *Los Angeles Times*, January 28, 2013.

30. David Nakamura, "Obama, on Telemundo, Rules Out Freezing Deportations of Most Illegal Immigrants," *Washington Post*, September 17, 2013.

31. "Remarks by the President in Address to the Nation on Immigration," November 20, 2014, https://obamawhitehouse.archives.gov/the-press-office/2014/11/20/remarks-president -address-nation-immigration, accessed January 31, 2017.

32. Michael D. Shear, "Obama, Daring Congress, Acts to Overhaul Immigration," *New York Times*, November 20, 2014.

33. Haeyoun Park and Alicia Parlapiano, "Immigration Case Affects Millions of Unauthorized Immigrants," *New York Times*, June 23, 2016.

34. Steve King, "Protecting The Constitutional Balance of Power From Executive Amnesty," *Breitbart*, November 13, 2014, http://www.breitbart.com/big-government/2014/11/13 /rep-steve-king-protecting-the-constitutional-balance-of-power-from-executive-amnesty/, accessed January 31, 2017.

35. The Court was down to eight justices due to the unfilled vacancy caused by Antonin Scalia's death. Adam Liptak and Michael D. Shear, "Supreme Court Tie Blocks Obama Immigration Plan," *New York Times*, June 23, 2016.

36. Caitlin Dickerson "Obama Administration Is Quietly Delaying Thousands of Deportation Cases," *New York Times*, October 6, 2016.

37. Miriam Valverde, "Interior Deportations Down, at 9-Year Low, Border Group Says," *Politifact*, http://www.politifact.com/truth-o-meter/statements/2016/aug/05/national-border -patrol-council/interior-deportations-down-9-year-low/, accessed January 31, 2017.

38. Jeh Johnson Secure Communities Memo, November 20, 2014, https://www.dhs.gov /sites/default/files/publications/14_1120_memo_secure_communities.pdf, accessed January 3, 2017.

39. Marc R. Rosenblum and Doris Meissner, *The Deportation Dilemma: Reconciling Tough and Humane Enforcement* (Washington DC: Migration Policy Institute, April 2014).

40. Jie Zong and Jeanne Batalova, *Refugeees and Asylees in the United States* (Washington

DC: Migration Policy Institute, November 28, 2015), http://www.migrationpolicy.org/article/refugees-and-asylees-united-states, accessed January 31, 2017.

41. Michael R. Gordon, Alison Smale, and Rick Lyman, "U.S. Will Accept More Refugees as Crisis Grows," *New York Times*, September 20, 2015.

42. Jonathan Tilove, "Texas Withdraws from Federal Refugee Resettlement Program," *Austin American-Statesman*, September 30, 2016, http://www.statesman.com/news/state—regional-govt—politics/texas-withdraws-from-federal-refugee-resettlement-program/QynFVtQzgzde MSLILXgFIM/, accessed January 31, 2017.

43. USCIS Consideration of Deferred Action for Childhood Arrivals Data as of September 30, 2016, https://www.uscis.gov/sites/default/files/USCIS/Resources/Reports%20and%20 Studies/Immigration%20Forms%20Data/All%20Form%20Types/DACA/daca_performance data_fy2016_qtr4.pdf, accessed September 22, 2017.

Chapter 13: Liberal Internationalism, Law, and the First African American President

1. Transcript of presidential candidate Barack Obama's speech in Berlin, Germany, July 24, 2008, http://edition.cnn.com/2008/POLITICS/07/24/obama.words/.

2. Transcript of President Barack Obama's Nobel Peace Prize Address, Oslo, Norway, December 10, 2009, https://www.whitehouse.gov/the-press-office/remarks-president-acceptance-nobel-peace-prize.

3. Ibid.

4. Ibid.

5. "Remarks by President Barack Obama, National Defense University," May 23, 2013, https://www.whitehouse.gov/the-press-office/2013/05/23/remarks-president-barack-obama.

6. Obama's speech in Berlin, Germany. See also Jeremi Suri, *Liberty's Surest Guardian: American Nation-Building from the Founders to Obama* (New York: Free Press, 2011), chap. 6.

7. For a revealing account of Obama's evolving thinking about race, law, and power, see Thomas J. Sugrue, *Not Even Past: Barack Obama and the Burden of Race* (Princeton, NJ: Princeton University Press, 2010).

8. Obama was deeply moved by his reading of Niebuhr's most influential book, *The Irony of American History* (New York: Scribner's, 1952).

9. This analysis of the president's pragmatic liberal internationalism matches James T. Kloppenberg's analysis of Obama's intellectual roots in pragmatic political philosophy. See Kloppenberg, *Reading Obama: Dreams, Hopes, and the American Political Tradition* (Princeton, NJ: Princeton University Press, 2011). See also David Milne, *Worldmaking: The Art and Science of American Diplomacy* (New York: Farrar, Straus, and Giroux, 2015), 457–513.

10. Andrew Bacevich makes a similar argument. See *The New American Militarism: How Americans Are Seduced by War* (New York: Oxford University Press, 2005).

11. Barack Obama, *The Audacity of Hope: Thoughts on Reclaiming the American Dream* (New York: Broadway Books, 2006), 281. Obama drew on John Quincy Adams and other early American thinkers in writing these words, and he criticized the excessive interventionism of Cold War and post–Cold War American policymakers.

12. For good discussions of these issues that capture Obama's search for an alternative legal doctrine, and its dangers, see, among others: David J. Barron, *Waging War: The Clash between Presidents and Congress, 1776 to ISIS* (New York: Simon & Schuster, 2016); Charlie Savage, *Power Wars: Inside Obama's Post-9/11 Presidency* (New York: Little, Brown, 2015); David E. Sanger, *Confront and Conceal: Obama's Secret Wars and Surprising Use of American Power* (New York: Crown, 2012).

13. Transcript of President George W. Bush's address to a joint session of Congress, September 20, 2001, https://georgewbush-whitehouse.archives.gov/news/releases/2001/09/20010920-8.html.

14. For a sympathetic but still critical account of Bush's foreign policy, see Peter Baker, *Days of Fire: Bush and Cheney in the White House* (New York: Random House, 2013), 119–54.

15. Transcript of President George W. Bush's Second Inaugural Address, January 20, 2005, http://www.presidency.ucsb.edu/ws/?pid=58745.

16. See James Mann, *Rise of the Vulcans: The History of Bush's War Cabinet* (New York: Penguin, 2004); Jeremi Suri, *Henry Kissinger and the American Century* (Cambridge, MA: Belknap Press of Harvard University Press, 2007), chap. 6.

17. "Remarks by President Obama to the People of Cuba," March 22, 2016, https://www.whitehouse.gov/the-press-office/2016/03/22/remarks-president-obama-people-cuba.

18. On international and American foreign policy in the early twentieth century, see, among many others, Martti Koskenniemi, *The Gentle Civilizer of Nations: The Rise and Fall of International Law, 1870–1960* (New York: Cambridge University Press, 2004); Akira Iriye, *Cultural Internationalism and World Order* (Baltimore: Johns Hopkins University Press, 1997).

19. Transcript of "Remarks by President Barack Obama at Cairo University," June 4, 2009, https://www.whitehouse.gov/the-press-office/remarks-president-cairo-university-6-04-09.

20. Robert M. Gates, *Duty: Memoirs of a Secretary at War* (New York: Knopf, 2014), 298–99.

21. See Derek Chollet, *The Long Game: How Obama Defied Washington and Redefined America's Role in the World* (New York: Public Affairs, 2016), 57–61; John Lee, "Reaching the Limits: China as a Responsible Stakeholder," July 5, 2016, Project 2049 Institute, http://www.project2049.net/documents/160705_Lee_Reaching%20the%20Limits_China_Responsible%20Stakeholder.pdf.

22. See Robert D. Blackwill and Jennifer M. Harris, *War By Other Means: Geoeconomics and Statecraft* (Cambridge, MA: Belknap Press of Harvard University Press, 2016), esp. 220–50; Kurt M. Campbell, *The Pivot: The Future of American Statecraft in Asia* (New York: Hachette, 2016), esp. 251–76.

23. See Chollet, *The Long Game*, 64–66.

24. See David Farber, *Taken Hostage: The Iran Hostage Crisis and America's First Encounter with Radical Islam* (Princeton, NJ: Princeton University Press, 2005).

25. See Ewen MacAskill, "Obama Sent Letter to Khamenei before the Election, Report Says," *Guardian*, June 24, 2009; Gates, *Duty*, 327.

26. On "global zero," see Philip Taubman, *The Partnership: Five Cold Warriors and Their Quest to Ban the Bomb* (New York: HarperCollins, 2012), 285–393.

27. See, among others, Mark Mazzetti, *The Way of the Knife: The C.I.A., a Secret Army, and a War at the Ends of the Earth* (New York: Penguin, 2013); Jack Goldsmith, *Power and Constraint: The Accountable Presidency after 9/11* (New York: W. W. Norton, 2012).

28. See Robert Legvold, *Return to Cold War* (Malden, MA: Polity Press, 2016); Chollet, *The Long Game*, 159–79.

29. On recent Russian foreign policy, see Fiona Hill and Clifford G. Gaddy, *Mr. Putin: Operative in the Kremlin* (Washington, DC: Brookings Institution, 2015).

30. See Daniel Byman, *Al Qaeda, the Islamic State, and the Global Jihadist Movement* (New York: Oxford University Press, 2015), 163–86; Joby Warrick, *Black Flags: The Rise of ISIS* (New York: Doubleday, 2015); Andrew Thompson and Jeremi Suri, "How America Helped ISIS," *New York Times*, October 1, 2014.

31. Jeffrey Goldberg, "The Obama Doctrine," *The Atlantic*, April 2016, 85.

32. On Taft, Hoover, and early twentieth-century American antiwar internationalism, see

Alan Dawley, *Changing the World: American Progressives in War and Revolution* (Princeton, NJ: Princeton University Press, 2003); Christopher McKnight Nichols, *Promise and Peril: America at the Dawn of a Global Age* (Cambridge, MA: Harvard University Press, 2011); Emily S. Rosenberg, *Spreading the American Dream: American Economic and Cultural Expansion, 1890–1945* (New York: Hill and Wang, 1982).

33. On the unpredictability of war, Clausewitz remains essential reading, especially for Americans. Carl von Clausewitz, *On War*, ed. and trans. Michael Howard and Peter Paret (Princeton, NJ: Princeton University Press, 1976). Although he rejects pacifism, Obama is, of course, deeply influenced by the historical legacy of Dr. Martin Luther King Jr. and other nonviolent American civil rights activists. See Kloppenberg, *Reading Obama*, 243–44.

34. On Obama's seriousness, intelligence, and deliberative depth, see Gates, *Duty*, 298–99.

35. See Jeremi Suri, *The Impossible Presidency: The Rise and Fall of America's Highest Office* (New York: Basic Books, 2017), chap. 9 and epilogue.

Chapter 14: Terror Tuesdays: How Obama Refined Bush's Counterterrorism Policies

1. "Secret 'Kill List' Proves a Test of Obama's Principles and Will," *New York Times*, May 29, 2012.

2. Quoted in Peter Baker, "Obama's War Over Terror," *New York Times Magazine*, January 4, 2010.

3. "Executive Order: Review and Disposition of Individuals Detained at the Guantánamo Bay Naval Base and Closure of Detention Facilities," January 22, 2009, http://www.globalsecurity .org/security/library/policy/national/090122-exec-order_guantanamo-bay.htm; "Executive Order: Ensuring Lawful Interrogations," January 22, 2009, http://media.washingtonpost.com /wp-srv/politics/documents/interrogation_012209.pdf, accessed June 13, 2017.

4. "Guantánamo Bay: How the White House Lost the Fight to Close It," *Washington Post*, April 23, 2011.

5. "Message from the Director: Interrogation Policy and Contracts, Statement to Employees by Director of the Central Intelligence Agency Leon E. Panetta on the CIA's Interrogation Policy and Contracts," April 9, 2009, https://www.cia.gov/news-information/press-releases -statements/directors-statement-interrogation-policy-contracts.html, accessed June 13, 2017.

6. American Civil Liberties Union, Press Release, April 16, 2009, "Justice Department Releases Bush Administration Torture Memos," https://www.aclu.org/news/justice-department -releases-bush-administration-torture-memos, accessed June 13, 2017.

7. Charlie Savage, *Power Wars: Inside Obama's Post-9/11 Presidency* (New York: Little, Brown, 2015), 145; Jack Goldsmith, *Power and Constraint: The Accountable Presidency after 9/11* (New York: W. W. Norton, 2012), 111.

8. "Obama's Justice Department Grants Final Immunity to Bush's CIA Torturers," *Guardian*, August 31, 2012.

9. "No Charges Filed on Harsh Tactics Used by the C.I.A.," *New York Times*, August 30, 2012.

10. Goldsmith, *Power and Constraint*, 39.

11. Ibid.; Trevor McCrisken, "Ten Years On: Obama's War on Terrorism in Rhetoric and Practice," *International Affairs* 87, no. 4 (2011): 781–801.

12. Quoted in "New President, New Battlefield," *Los Angeles Times*, February 1, 2009.

13. Transcript: "Obama Outlines Steps to Prevent Terrorism," January 7, 2010, http://www .cnn.com/2010/POLITICS/01/07/transcript.obama.terror.report/index.html, accessed June 13, 2017.

14. Nobel lecture by Barack Obama, December 10, 2009, https://www.nobelprize.org/nobel_prizes/peace/laureates/2009/obama-lecture_en.html, accessed June 13, 2017.

15. Mark Mazzetti, *The Way of the Knife* (New York: Penguin, 2013), 219.

16. The five were Cuba's Fidel Castro, Patrice Lumumba of Congo, Ngo Dinh Diem of South Vietnam, Rafael Trujillo of the Dominican Republic, and Rene Schneider of Chile. On the Church committee, see Loch Johnson, *A Season of Inquiry: The Senate Intelligence Investigation* (Lexington: University Press of Kentucky, 1985); and Kathryn S. Olmsted, *Challenging the Secret Government: The Post-Watergate Investigations of the CIA and FBI* (Chapel Hill: University of North Carolina Press, 1996).

17. For a detailed discussion of the evolution of legal authority for targeted killing, see Jonathan Ulrich, "The Gloves Were Never On: Defining the President's Authority to Order Targeted Killing in the War Against Terrorism," *Virginia Journal of International Law* 45 (2005): 1029.

18. National Security Decision Directive 138, April 3, 1984, https://fas.org/irp/offdocs/nsdd/nsdd-138.pdf, accessed June 13, 2017. Emphasis added. For a discussion of NSDD 138, see Markus Gunneflo, *Targeted Killing: A Legal and Political History* (Cambridge: Cambridge University Press, 2016), chap. 3.

19. "CIA Told to Do 'Whatever Necessary' to Kill Bin Laden," *Washington Post*, October 21, 2001; "Bush Has Widened Authority of CIA to Kill Terrorists," *New York Times*, December 15, 2002.

20. See the New America Foundation, "Drone Wars Pakistan: Analysis," http://securitydata.newamerica.net/drones/pakistan-analysis.html; "Drone Wars Yemen: Analysis," http://securitydata.newamerica.net/drones/yemen-analysis.html; "Drone Wars Somalia: Analysis," http://securitydata.newamerica.net/drones/somalia-analysis.html, all accessed June 13, 2017.

21. See Robert M. Chesney, "Beyond the Battlefield, Beyond al-Qaeda: The Destabilizing Legal Architecture of Counterterrorism," *Michigan Law Review* 11, no. 163 (November 2013): 176–77.

22. Harold Koh, "Speech to the American Society of International Law," March 25, 2010, in Kenneth Anderson and Benjamin Wittes, *Speaking the Law: The Obama Administration's Addresses on National Security Law* (Stanford, CA: Hoover Institution Press, 2015), 357, 365, 368.

23. December 2011 speech quoted in Mazzetti, *Way of the Knife*, 301.

24. For the speeches by these and other Obama-era officials, see Anderson and Wittes, *Speaking the Law*.

25. David Barron, Memorandum for the Attorney General, February 19, 2010, http://nsarchive.gwu.edu/NSAEBB/NSAEBB529-Anwar-al-Awlaki-File/documents/15)%20OLC%20Barron-Lederman%20February%202010%20Awlaki%20memo.pdf; and David Barron, Memorandum for the Attorney General, July 16, 2010, https://www.aclu.org/sites/default/files/field_document/2014-06-23_barron-memorandum.pdf, accessed June 13, 2017.

26. See Ryan Lizza, "The Lawyer and the Kill-List Memo," *New Yorker*, May 22, 2014.

27. Amy Davidson, "John Brennan and the 'So-Called' Americans," *New Yorker*, February 8, 2013.

28. *Washington Post /ABC News* Poll, February, 1–4, 2012, *Washington Post*, http://www.washingtonpost.com/wp-srv/politics/polls/postabcpoll_020412.html, accessed June 13, 2017.

29. Center for the Study of the Drone, Bard College, "Drone Spending in the Fiscal Year 2017 Defense Budget," February 2016, http://dronecenter.bard.edu/files/2016/02/DroneSpendingFy17_CSD_1-1.pdf, accessed June 13, 2017.

30. "Defense Contractors Take to the Hill to Lobby on Drones," September 25, 2013, Center for Responsive Politics, OpenSecrets.org, https://www.opensecrets.org/news/2013/09/defense-contractors/, accessed June 13, 2017.

31. Tara McKelvey, "Media Coverage of the Drone Program," Shorenstein Center, February

2013, https://shorensteincenter.org/media-coverage-of-the-drone-program/, 21, accessed June 13, 2017.

32. See, for example, Mark Hosenball, "Secret Panel Can Put Americans on 'Kill List,'" *Reuters*, October 5, 2011; and Scott Shane, "CIA Is Disputed on Civilian Toll in Drone Strikes," *New York Times*, August 11, 2011.

33. "FACT SHEET: Executive Order on the U.S. Policy on Pre & Post-Strike Measures to Address Civilian Casualties in the U.S. Operations Involving the Use of Force & the DNI Release of Aggregate Data on Strike Outside Area of Active Hostilities," July 1, 2016, https://www.whitehouse.gov/the-press-office/2016/07/01/fact-sheet-executive-order-us-policy-pre-post-strike-measures-addresss, accessed June 13, 2017.

34. "Summary of Information Regarding U.S. Counterterrorism Strikes Outside Areas of Active Hostilities," https://www.dni.gov/files/documents/Newsroom/Press%20Releases/DNI+Release+on+CT+Strikes+Outside+Areas+of+Active+Hostilities.PDF, accessed June 13, 2017.

35. New America Foundation: http://securitydata.newamerica.net/world-drones.html; Long War Journal, http://www.longwarjournal.org/archives/2016/07/us-government-releases-data-on-counterterrorism-strikes-outside-areas-of-active-hostilities.php; Bureau of Investigative Journalism, https://www.thebureauinvestigates.com/category/projects/drones/, accessed June 13, 2017.

36. Fred Kaplan, "Reading Between the Lines of Obama's Drone-Casualty Report," *Slate*, July 5, 2016, http://www.slate.com/articles/news_and_politics/war_stories/2016/07/obama_s_drone_casualty_report_is_a_good_first_step.html, accessed June 13, 2017.

37. Although some drone strikes were followed by retaliatory terrorist attacks, experts are divided on whether the targeted killing program prompts more terrorist acts than it stops. For a thorough discussion of the conflicting evidence, see "The Civilian Impact of Drones: Unexamined Costs, Unanswered Questions," Center for Civilians in Conflict and Human Rights Clinic at Columbia Law School, 2012, http://www.law.columbia.edu/human-rights-institute/counterterrorism/drone-strikes/civilian-impact-drone-strikes-unexamined-costs-unanswered-questions, accessed June 13, 2017.

38. "Victim of Obama's First Drone Strike," *Guardian*, January 23, 2016. See also James Risen, *Pay Any Price: Greed, Power, and Endless War* (Boston: Mariner Books, 2015), 61–62.

39. Elliot Ackerman, "Assassination and the American Language," *New Yorker*, November 20, 2014.

40. Legendary investigative journalist Seymour Hersh reported that much of the official narrative about the killing of bin Laden is untrue. His major source was "a retired senior intelligence official." See "The Killing of Osama Bin Laden," *London Review of Books*, May 2015, 3–12. Other journalists dispute Hersh's revisionist account. See, for example, Savage, *Power Wars*, 724n72. For an account of the controversy that is sympathetic to Hersh, see Jonathan Mahler, "What Do We Really Know About Osama Bin Laden's Death?" *New York Times Magazine*, October 15, 2015.

41. Hillary Rodham Clinton, *Hard Choices* (New York: Simon & Schuster, 2014), 193–96.

42. Mazzetti, *Way of the Knife*, 133.

43. Quoted in "Bin Laden Is Dead, Obama Says," *New York Times*, May 1, 2011.

44. Quoted in Daniel Klaidman, *Kill or Capture: The War on Terror and the Soul of the Obama Presidency* (Boston: Mariner Books, 2013), 248.

45. "Outside the White House, A Celebration of Osama Bin Laden's Death," *Atlantic*, May 2, 2011.

46. "Obama on Surveillance, Then and Now," *New York Times*, June 7, 2013.

47. "Remarks by the President on Review of Signals Intelligence," January 27, 2014, https://

obamawhitehouse.archives.gov/the-press-office/2014/01/17/remarks-president-review
-signals-intelligence, accessed June 13, 2017.

48. Quoted in Savage, *Power Wars*, 168.

49. Mark Udall and Ron Wyden to Eric Holder, March 15, 2012, https://www.docu
mentcloud.org/documents/325953-85512347-senators-ron-wyden-mark-udall-letter-to.html,
accessed June 13, 2017. Emphasis in original.

50. Glenn Greenwald, "NSA Collecting Phone Records of Millions of Verizon Customers
Daily," *Guardian*, June 6, 2013.

51. Laura Poitras and Barton Gellman, "U.S., British Intelligence Mining Data from Nine
U.S. Internet Companies in Broad Secret Program," *Washington Post*, June 7, 2013.

52. Statement by the President, June 7, 2013, https://www.whitehouse.gov/the-press-office
/2013/06/07/statement-president, accessed June 13, 2017.

53. See "These Charts Show How the Edward Snowden Story Is Overwhelming the NSA
Story," *Washington Post*, July 3, 2013.

54. See Savage, *Power Wars*, 616–26.

55. Press release, "Senate Passes U.S.A. Freedom Act," June 2, 2015, https://www.aclu.org
/news/senate-passes-usa-freedom-act, accessed June 13, 2017.

56. "Joe Davidson's Federal Diary: Whistleblowers May Have Friend in Oval Office," *Washington Post*, December 11, 2008.

57. Savage, *Power Wars*, 366–67.

58. "Math behind Leak Crackdown: 153 Cases, 4 Years, 0 Indictments," *New York Times*,
July 20, 2013.

59. On the leak cases, see Savage, *Power Wars*, chap. 8; and Lloyd C. Gardner, *The War on
Leakers: National Security and American Democracy, from Eugene V. Debs to Edward Snowden*
(New York: New Press, 2016).

60. "Chelsea Manning to be Released Early as Obama Commutes Sentence," *New York
Times*, January 17, 2017.

61. Senate Select Committee to Study Governmental Operations with Respect to Intelligence Activities, *Alleged Assassination Plots Involving Foreign Leaders* (Washington, DC: Government Printing Office, 1975), 151.

Chapter 15: A Hyphenated Legacy? Obama's Africa Policy

1. President Obama's speech to the Ghanaian Parliament, July 11, 2009, whitehouse.gov, accessed October 6, 2016.

2. Matthew S. Williams, "The Bush Administration, Debt Relief, and the War on Terror:
Reforming the International Development System as Part of the Neoconservative Project," *Social Justice* 35, no. 3 (2008–9): 49.

3. Walter C. Carrington, "Preface," in *African Americans in U.S. Foreign Policy*, ed. Linda
Heywood, Allison Blakely, Charles Stith, and Joshua C. Yesnowitz (Urbana: University of Illinois
Press, 2015), xx.

4. See Gary Gerstle's essay "Minorities, Multiculturalism, and the Presidency of George W.
Bush," in *The Presidency of George W. Bush: A First Historical Assessment*, ed. Julian E. Zelizer
(Princeton, NJ: Princeton University Press, 2010), 258.

5. Howard French, "Remarks at African Studies Association Roundtable: Assessing
Obama's Foreign Policy Legacy in Africa," Washington DC, December 3, 2016.

6. Princeton Lyman, "Remarks at African Studies Association Roundtable: Assessing
Obama's Foreign Policy Legacy in Africa," Washington DC, December 3, 2016.

7. Quoted in Lawrence MacDonald, "President Bush's Second Term and Development: Five Issues Worth Watching," Center for Global Development, https://www.cgdev.org/doc/commentary/Second%20Term.pdf, accessed February 18, 2017.

8. Eric Helleiner and Geoffrey Cameron, "Another World Order? The Bush Administration and HIPC Debt Cancellation," *New Political Economy* 11, no. 1 (2006): 129.

9. Ibid.

10. Ibid., 131.

11. Quoted in Teresa Welsh, "A Complicated Legacy," *U.S. News & World Report*, July 28, 2015, http://www.usnews.com/news/the-report/articles/2015/07/28/obamas-legacy-on-africa-lacks-compared-to-bush, accessed October 25, 2016.

12. Howard French, "Remarks at African Studies Association Roundtable: Assessing Obama's Foreign Policy Legacy in Africa," Washington DC, December 3, 2016.

13. S'Thembiso Msomi, *Mmusi Maimane: Prophet or Puppet?* (Johannesburg: Jonathan Ball Publishers, 2016).

14. Obama's tour included stops in South Africa, Kenya, Djibouti, Ethiopia, and Chad. Planned stops in the Democratic Republic of the Congo and Rwanda were cancelled over safety fears.

15. Adekeye Adebajo, *The Curse of Berlin: Africa after the Cold War* (London: Hurst, 2010), 290.

16. Ibid.

17. Quotation from Ibrahim Sundiata's essay "Obama, African Americans, and Africans: The Double Vision," in *African Americans in U.S. Foreign Policy*, ed. Linda Heywood, Allison Blakely, Charles Stith, and Joshua C. Yesnowitz (Urbana: University of Illinois Press, 2015), 207.

18. Adebajo, *The Curse of Berlin*, 288.

19. I am, of course, being facetious here by miscasting the idea of postracialism, which some observers saw as the greatest promise of Obama's presidency when he assumed office in January 2009.

20. Jendayi Frazer, assistant secretary of state for Africa in the Bush presidency, said, "Obama visited Italy and Russia before his visit to Ghana yet did not talk about corruption until he was in Ghana." "Remarks at African Studies Association Roundtable: Assessing Obama's foreign policy legacy in Africa," Washington DC, December 3, 2016.

21. Quoted in Ibrahim Sundiata, "Obama, African Americans, and Africans," 206.

22. Adebajo, *The Curse of Berlin*, 288.

23. Ibid.

24. Ibid., 288–89.

25. Ibrahim Sundiata, "Obama, African Americans, and Africans," 202.

26. BBC, "Obama's Eight-Year Presidency Rated Well, Shows Global Poll for BBC World Service," July 8, 2016, www.bbc.co.uk, accessed October 8, 2016.

27. Sundiata, "Obama, African Americans, and Africans," 202.

28. BBC, "Obama's Eight-Year Presidency Rated Well."

29. Quoted in Adebajo, *The Curse of Berlin*, 292.

30. Quoted in ibid.

31. Sundiata, "Obama, African Americans, and Africans," 207.

32. Quoted in Ibrahim Sundiata, "Obama, African Americans, and Africans," 206.

33. Barack Obama, *The Audacity of Hope: Thoughts on Reclaiming the American Dream* (New York: Broadway Books, 2006), 315–16.

34. Barack Obama, *Dreams from My Father: A Story of Race and Inheritance* (New York: Three Rivers Press, 2004).

35. Ibid., 302.

36. Dana Hughes, "George W. Bush's Legacy on Africa Wins Praise, Even from Foes," http://abcnews.go.com/blogs/politics/2013/04/george-w-bushs-legacy-on-africa-wins-praise-even-from-foes/, accessed October 25, 2016.

37. Ibid.

38. Quoted in ibid.

39. Quoted in ibid.

40. Carrington, "Preface," xix. Carrington is referring to the three most prominent blacks in the first Bush administration: Colin Powell, President Bush's first secretary of state; National Security Advisor Condoleezza Rice; and Jendayi Frazer, U.S. assistant secretary of state for African affairs.

41. Ibid.

42. Obama, *Dreams from My Father*, 304–22.

43. Obama's address to Ghanaian Parliament, July 11, 2009, https://obamawhitehouse.archives.gov., accessed October 8, 2016.

44. This is not to say he did not patronize his audience or Africans in general. As Jendayi Frazer, assistant secretary of state for Africa in the Bush presidency, said, Obama visited Italy and Russia before his visit to Ghana yet did not talk about corruption until he was in Ghana. "Remarks at African Studies Association Roundtable: Assessing Obama's Foreign Policy Legacy in Africa," Washington DC, December 3, 2016.

45. However, USAID support for the Office of the Public Protector exposed the incumbent, Thuli Madonsela, to claims of treason. Mahlatse Gallens, "Foreign Funding Claims a 'Blatant Lie'—Madonsela," www.news24.com, October 20, 2016, http://m.news24.com/news24/South Africa/News/foreign-funding-claims-a-blatant-lie-madonsela-20161020, accessed October 26, 2016.

46. Leslie Wayne, "Wanted by U.S.: The Stolen Millions of Despots and Crooked Elites," http://www.nytimes.com/2016/02/17/business/wanted-by-the-us-the-stolen-millions-of-despots-and-crooked-elites.html?_r=0, accessed February 16, 2016.

47. Quoted in David Smith, "Obama Tells African States to Abandon Anti-gay Discrimination," *Guardian*, July 25, 2015, www.guardian.co.uk, accessed October 26, 2016.

48. Quoted in Sundiata, "Obama, African Americans, and Africans," 209.

49. Quoted in ibid.

50. Welsh, "A Complicated Legacy."

51. Ibid.

52. Quoted in Biznis Africa, "US Trade Rep Credits AGOA with Boost in Africa-US Non-oil Trade," https://agoa.info/news/article/6293-us-trade-rep-credits-agoa-with-boost-in-africa-us-non-oil-trade.html, accessed October 26, 2016.

53. Ibid.

54. The figures are taken from the official website of the Office of the U.S. Trade Representative, https://ustr.gov/countries-regions/africa, accessed October 26, 2016.

55. Carrington, "Preface," xx.

56. Adam Taylor, "Map: The U.S. Military Currently Has Troops in These African Countries," *Washington Post*, May 21, 2014, https://www.washingtonpost.com/news/worldviews/wp/2014/05/21/map-the-u-s-currently-has-troops-in-these-african-countries/, accessed October 27, 2016.

57. Nick Turse, "U.S. Military Building a $100 Million Drone Base in Africa," *Intercept*, September 29, 2016, https://theintercept.com/2016/09/29/u-s-military-is-building-a-100-million-drone-base-in-africa/, accessed October 27, 2016.

58. Ibid.

59. Ibid.

60. Carrington, "Preface," xxi.

61. Ibid.

62. Daniel Volman, "Obama Expands Military Involvement in Africa," *Inter-Press Service*, April 2, 2016, http://ipsnorthamerica.net/news.php?idnews=2965, accessed October 27, 2016.

63. Adebajo, *The Curse of Berlin*, 292.

Chapter 16: Criticize and Thrive: The American Left in the Obama Years

1. Andrea Swensson, "Bob Dylan: 'Things Are Going to Change Now,'" *CityPages* (Minneapolis), http://www.citypages.com/music/bob-dylan-things-are-going-to-change-now-6632216.

2. John M. Broder and Monica Davey, "Celebration and Sense of History at Chicago Party," *New York Times*, November 5, 2018, http://www.nytimes.com/2008/11/05/us/politics/05chicago .html?_r=0; Eric Collier, "Un 11-Septembre à l'envers," *Le Monde*, November 5, 2008, http:// www.lemonde.fr/elections-americaines/article/2008/11/05/un-11-septembre-a-l-envers _1114930_829254.html.

3. Katrina vanden Heuvel, "Let's Get Real About Obama," *Nation*, a column published August 13, 2009. Reprinted in Vanden Heuvel, *The Change I Believe In: Fighting for Progress in the Age of Obama* (New York: Nation Books, 2011), 17. Of course, the title of her book is a variation on Obama's 2008 campaign slogan, "Change We Can Believe In." Tariq Ali, *The Obama Syndrome: Surrender at Home, War Abroad* (London: Verso, 2010), 75.

4. Cornel West interview with Thomas Frank, *Salon*, August 24, 2014, http://www.salon. com/2014/08/24/cornel_west_he_posed_as_a_progressive_and_tur ned_out_to_be_counterfeit _we_ended_up_with_a_wall_street_presidency_a_drone_presidency/. By the summer of 2016, the tone of criticism from the far left had not changed. See the introduction by C. J. Polychroniou to his interview with Noam Chomsky, in which he labels Obama's regime "a neoliberal regime in overdrive." Chomsky, himself, was a bit more ambivalent. *Truthout*, June 2, 2016, http://www .truth-out.org/news/item/36260-a-mixed-story-ranging-from-criminal-to-moderate-improve ment-noam-chomsky-on-obama-s-legacy.

5. Brad Berenson quoted in David Remnick, *The Bridge: The Life and Rise of Barack Obama* (New York: Knopf, 2010), 207; James T. Kloppenberg, *Reading Obama: Dreams, Hope, and the American Political Tradition* (Princeton, NJ: Princeton University Press, 2011), 28–29; "Transcript: Barack Obama, Keynote Address to Democratic National Convention," *Washington Post*, July 27, 2004, http://www.washingtonpost.com/wp-dyn/articles/A19751-2004Jul27.html. For a splendid analysis of the institutional obstacles to a new New Deal, see Eric Alterman, *Kabuki Democracy: The System vs. Barack Obama* (New York: Nation Books, 2011).

6. In a 2015 interview, Naomi Klein acknowledged that Obama "sounds like a climate leader." *Democracy Now*, November 30, 2015, http://www.democracynow.org/2015/11/30/video _naomi_klein_extended_interview_on.

7. Theda Skocpol, *Obama and America's Political Future* (Cambridge, MA: Harvard University Press, 2012), 8.

8. Ibid., 37–38. In part, the failure of OFA was due to the changing makeup of the ACA as its backers struggled to gain support for it in Congress. But Skocpol also makes the cogent point that "grassroots activism works better when it is relatively spontaneous and at most loosely linked to official institutions." Ibid., 32.

9. "A Herstory of the #BlackLivesMatter Movement," http://blacklivesmatter.com/herstory/. The three women are Alicia Garza, Patrisse Cullors, and Opal Tometi.

10. "Platform," Movement for Black Lives, https://policy.m4bl.org/platform/. For a friendly

analysis, see Vann R. Newkirk II, "The Permanence of Black Lives Matter," *Atlantic*, August 3, 2016, http://www.theatlantic.com/politics/archive/2016/08/movement-black-lives-platform /494309/.

11. See Fredrick C. Harris, "The Rise of Respectability Politics," *Dissent* (Winter 2014): 33–37.

12. For a left-wing critique of Obama's presidency that understands his enduring appeal, see Keeanga-Yamahtta Taylor, *From #BlackLivesMatter to Black Liberation* (Chicago: Haymarket Books, 2016), 135–52.

13. Quoted in ibid.

14. Jo Freeman, "The Tyranny of Structurelessness," originally published in 1970: http://struggle.ws/pdfs/tyranny.pdf.

15. For a list of and documents from Occupations in the United States and abroad, see Occupy Archive, http://occupyarchive.org/items.

16. Polls quoted in Todd Gitlin, *Occupy Nation: The Roots, the Spirit, and the Promise of Occupy Wall Street* (New York: ItBooks, 2012), 37; Steve Fraser, *The Age of Acquiescence: The Life and Death of American Resistance to Organized Wealth and Power* (New York: Little, Brown, 2015).

17. Gitlin, *Occupy Nation*, 28.

18. This paragraph is adapted from a *New Republic* column I wrote in early November 2011: "Anarchism Now: Occupy Wall Street Revives an Ideology," *New Republic*, November 7, 2011, https://newrepublic.com/article/97114/anarchy-occupy-wall-street-throwback.

19. Transcript of Obama's speech at the Democratic National Convention, *Fox News*, September 6, 2012, http://www.foxnews.com/politics/2012/09/06/transcript-obama-speech-at -dnc.html; Transcript of FDR's speech at the Democratic National Convention, July 2, 1932, http://www.presidency.ucsb.edu/ws/?pid=75174.

20. Transcript of Obama speech in Osawatomie, Kansas, December 6, 2011, http://articles .latimes.com/2011/dec/06/news/la-pn-text-obama-speech-kansas-20111206/2.

21. Fraser, *The Age of Acquiescence*, 410–11.

22. Becky Bowers, "President Barack Obama's Shifting Stance on Gay Marriage," *Politifact*, May 11, 2012, http://www.politifact.com/truth-o-meter/statements/2012/may/11/barack-obama /president-barack-obamas-shift-gay-marriage/.

23. Most of this paragraph is based on David Cole, *Engines of Liberty: The Power of Citizen Activists to Make Constitutional Law* (New York: Basic Books, 2016), 15–93.

24. "More Americans Now View Afghanistan War as a Mistake," *Gallup News*, February 19, 2014, news.gallup.com/poll/167471/americans-view-afghan-war-mistake.aspx.

25. Jon Lee Anderson, "The Cuba Play," *New Yorker*, October 3, 2016, 53. The previous section on the absence of protest against U.S. wars is adapted from my article, "Why Is There Not Antiwar Movement?" *Dissent* (Summer 2015): https://www.dissentmagazine.org/article /michael-kazin-why-no-antiwar-movement-iraq; Michael Walzer, "A Foreign Policy for the Left," *Dissent* (Spring 2014), https://www.dissentmagazine.org/article/a-foreign-policy-for-the -left.

26. For a rather critical narrative of Sanders's career during the 1970s and 1980s, see Greg Guma, *The People's Republic: Vermont and the Sanders Revolution* (Shelburne, VT: New England Press, 1989). Sanders quoted in Eric Bates, "Bernie Looks Ahead," *New Republic*, November 2016, 32.

27. Evan McMorris-Santoro, "The Obama Campaign Remembers 2012 Very Differently Than Bernie Sanders," *BuzzFeed*, November 8, 2015, https://www.buzzfeed.com/evanmcsan /the-obama-campaign-remembers-2012-very-differently-from-bern?utm_term=.wbreRGIIq# .lhaM07yyZ; Bates, "Bernie Looks Ahead," 31.

28. Quoted in my review-essay, "Too Many Obamas?" *Raritan* 30 (Winter 2011): 93.

Chapter 17: Civic Ideals, Race, and Nation in the Age of Obama

1. Gary Gerstle, *American Crucible: Race and Nation in the Twentieth Century*, rev. ed. (Princeton, NJ: Princeton University Press, 2017), introduction.

2. Barack Obama, *Dreams from My Father: A Story of Race and Inheritance* (New York: Crown, 1995); Barack Obama, *The Audacity of Hope: Thoughts in Reclaiming the American Dream* (New York: Crown, 2006); David Remnick, *The Bridge: The Life and Rise of Barack Obama* (New York: Knopf, 2010); James T. Kloppenberg, *Reading Obama: Dreams, Hope, and the American Political Tradition* (Princeton, NJ: Princeton University Press, 2012); Thomas J. Sugrue, *Not Even Past: Barack Obama and the Burden of Race* (Princeton, NJ: Princeton University Press, 2010).

3. Barack Obama, "Transcript," Democratic National Convention Speech of Illinois Senate Candidate Barack Obama, *Washington Post*, July 27, 2004, http://www.washingtonpost.com/wp-dyn/articles/A19751-2004Jul27.html, accessed June 8, 2016.

4. Fredrick C. Harris, *The Price of the Ticket: Barack Obama and the Rise and Decline of Black Politics* (New York: Oxford University Press, 2012).

5. Ben Wallace-Wells, "Destiny's Child," *Rolling Stone*, February 22, 2007. According to MRC Newsbusters, *Rolling Stone* initially published this article under the title "The Radical Roots of Barack Obama." Only later was the title changed to "Destiny's Child." http://www.newsbusters.org/blogs/warner-todd-huston/2008/03/15/rolling-stone-changes-headline-obamas-radical-roots-destinys-chi, accessed June 6, 2016.

6. "Reverend Wright Transcript," abcnews.go.com, April 25, 2008, http://abcnews.go.com/Blotter/story?id=4719157&page=1, accessed June 8, 2016.

7. Harris, *Price of the Ticket*, 72.

8. Barack Obama, "A More Perfect Union," *Washington Post*, March 18, 2008, http://blogs.wsj.com/washwire/2008/03/18/text-of-obamas-speech-a-more-perfect-union/, accessed September 14, 2015. See also *The Speech: Race and Barack Obama's "A More Perfect Union,"* ed. Tracey Sharpley-Whiting (New York: Bloomsbury, 2009); and Barack Obama, "On My Faith and My Church," *Huffington Post*, March 14, 2008, http://www.huffingtonpost.com/barack-obama/on-my-faith-and-my-church_b_91623.html, accessed September 15, 2015.

9. Obama, "A More Perfect Union."

10. Ibid.

11. Ibid.

12. Ibid.

13. Robert Barnes and Michael D. Shear, "Obama Makes History: US Decisively Elected First Black President; Democrats Expand Control of Congress," *Washington Post*, November 5, 2008. Obama also won more white votes than Al Gore did in 2000 (42 percent), and his 43 percent of white votes was the third highest for a Democratic presidential candidate since 1976. Domenico Montanaro, "Obama Performance with White Voters on Par with Other Democrats," firstread.nbcnews.com, November 19, 2012, http://firstread.nbcnews.com/_news/2012/11/19/15282553-obama-performance-with-white-voters-on-par-with-other-democrats?lite, accessed June 8, 2016; Michael Tesler and David O. Sears, *Obama's Race: The 2008 Election and the Dream of a Post-Racial America* (Chicago: University of Chicago Press, 2010).

14. Andrew Mihalek, "First-Hand Report from Chicago," *Santa Barbara Independent*, November 5, 2008, http://www.independent.com/news/2008/nov/05/first-hand-report-chicago/, accessed June 8, 2016; Monica Davey, "Celebrating Obama in Grant Park," thecaucus.blogs.nytimes.com, November 5, 2008, http://thecaucus.blogs.nytimes.com/2008/11/05/waiting-for-obama-in-grant-park/, accessed June 8, 2016; John M. Broder and Monica Davey, "Celebration and Sense of History at Chicago Party," *New York Times*, November 5, 2008, http://www.nytimes.com/2008/11/05/us/politics/05chicago.html?_r=0, accessed May 10, 2016.

15. "'Yes We Did': Black Americans Rejoice," CBSNews.com, November 5, 2008, http://www.cbsnews.com/news/yes-we-did-black-americans-rejoice/, accessed June 8, 2016.

16. "Jesse Jackson Explains His Tears for Obama," *Huffington Post*, December 6, 2008, http://www.huffingtonpost.com/2008/11/05/jesse-jackson-explains-hi_n_141626.html, accessed March 24, 2016. For Obama's speech at Grant Park, see Barack Obama, "Full Text: Obama's Victory Speech," news.bbc.co.uk, November 5, 2008, http://news.bbc.co.uk/1/hi/world/americas/us_elections_2008/7710038.stm, accessed June 8, 2016.

17. Tom Leonard, "Barack Obama Inauguration: Two Million Turn Out to Greet Their New President," *Telegraph*, January 21, 2009, http://www.telegraph.co.uk/news/worldnews/barack obama/4300880/Barack-Obama-inauguration-Two-million-turn-out-to-greet-their-new -president.html, accessed June 10, 2016.

18. Jon Pareles, "Music for Many Firsts at Inauguration Events," *New York Times*, January 21, 2009, http://www.nytimes.com/2009/01/22/arts/music/22conc.html, accessed June 10, 2016.

19. Ibid.

20. Paul Steinhauser, "In Poll, African-Americans Say Election a 'Dream Come True,'" CNN.com, June 11, 2008, http://edition.cnn.com/2008/POLITICS/11/11/obama.poll/, accessed June 8, 2016.

21. Gerstle, *American Crucible*, introduction.

22. Leo Sands, "Governor Ronald Reagan and the Assault on Welfare" (undergraduate thesis, University of Cambridge, 2016).

23. Michelle Alexander, *The New Jim Crow: Mass Incarceration in the Age of Colorblindness* (New York: New Press, 2010); Marie Gottschalk, *Caught: The Prison State and the Lockdown of America's Politics* (Princeton, NJ: Princeton University Press, 2015); Ruth Wilson Gilmore, *Golden Gulag: Prisons, Surplus, Crisis, and Opposition in Globalizing California* (Berkeley: University of California Press, 2007); Heather Ann Thompson, *Blood in the Water: The Attica Prison Uprising of 1971 and Its Legacy* (New York: Pantheon, 2016); Elizabeth Hinton, *From the War on Poverty to the War on Crime: The Making of Mass Incarceration in America* (Cambridge, MA: Harvard University Press, 2016).

24. Gabriel Sherman, *The Loudest Voice in the Room: How the Brilliant, Bombastic Roger Ailes Built Fox News—and Divided a Country* (New York: Random House, 2014); Gary Gerstle, "The GOP in the Age of Obama: Will the Tea Party and the Republican Establishment Unite or Fight?" *New Labor Forum* 19 (Fall 2010): 23–31.

25. Patrick J. Buchanan, *State of Emergency: The Third World Invasion and Conquest of America* (New York: Thomas Dunne Books, St. Martin's Press, 2006), 3–7, 11–12.

26. He added, "Race, faith, ethnicity, and history leave genetic fingerprints no 'proposition nation' can erase." Ibid., 248.

27. Ibid., 246, 248, 250, 252. On the demographic future of America in 2050, see Jeffrey S. Passel and D'Vera Cohn, "U.S. Population Projections: 2005–2050," Pew Research Center, February 11, 2008, http://www.pewhispanic.org/2008/02/11/us-population-projections-2005-2050/, accessed June 10, 2016.

28. Amy Hollyfield, "Obama's Birth Certificate: Final Chapter," *PolitiFact*, June 27, 2008, http://www.politifact.com/truth-o-meter/article/2008/jun/27/obamas-birth-certificate -part-ii/, accessed June 8, 2016; Jess Henig, "Born in the U.S.A.," FactCheck.org, August 21, 2008, http://www.factcheck.org/2008/08/born-in-the-usa/, accessed June 8, 2016.

29. "Trump on Obama's Birth Certificate: 'Maybe It Says He's a Muslim,'" *Fox Nation*, March 30, 2011, http://nation.foxnews.com/donald-trump/2011/03/30/trump-obama-maybe -hes-muslim, accessed September 21, 2015; Sheryl Gay Stolberg, "Hawaii's Governor Takes on 'Birthers,'" *New York Times*, December 24, 2010, http://www.nytimes.com/2010/12/25/us/25 hawaii.html, accessed June 8, 2016.

30. Ben Smith, "Palin: Obama Birth Certificate a 'Fair Question,'" *Politico*, December 3, 2009, http://www.politico.com/blogs/ben-smith/2009/12/palin-obama-birth-certificate-a-fair-question-023233, accessed September 22, 2015; Gabriel Winant, "The Birthers in Congress," *Salon*, July 28, 2009, http://www.salon.com/2009/07/28/birther_enablers/, accessed May 16, 2016.

31. Trump seized headlines by announcing that he had sent his own investigators to Hawaii to determine the truth and that "they cannot believe what they are finding." The media interest that Trump stirred up embarrassed the Obama administration and compelled it to release the long form to the public. Even this release failed to quiet the tempest. Former speaker of the house Newt Gingrich, feigning incredulity, asked, "Why did it take so long? The whole thing is strange." In 2011 and 2012, Republicans in more than a dozen state legislatures introduced bills that, if passed, would have required Obama to submit proof of his birth on American soil as a condition for getting on the 2012 ballot. No hard evidence of Obama's foreign birth ever appeared. Obama's decisive victory over Mitt Romney in 2012 finally seemed to quash the birther challenge. Adam Caparell, "Show Me! Donald Trump Wants to See President Obama's Birth Certificate with His Own Eyes," *New York Daily News*, March 24, 2011, http://www.nydailynews.com/news/politics/show-donald-trump-president-obama-birth-certificate-eyes-article-1.118369, accessed September 21, 2015; Jeff Greenfield, "Donald Trump's Birther Strategy," *Politico*, July 22, 2015, http://www.politico.com/magazine/story/2015/07/donald-trumps-birther-strategy-120504, accessed June 8, 2016; Joshua Green, "What Donald Trump's Birther Investigators Will Find in Hawaii," *Atlantic*, April 12, 2011, http://www.theatlantic.com/politics/archive/2011/04/what-donald-trumps-birther-investigators-will-find-in-hawaii/237198/, accessed September 22, 2015; "Obama Releases 'Long Form' Birth Certificate," *BBC News*, April 27, 2011, http://www.bbc.co.uk/news/world-us-canada-13212230, accessed September 21, 2015. Both PolitiFact and FactCheck.org verified the authenticity of Barack Obama's birth certificate, this time the long-form version. Bill Adair, "PolitiFact's Guide to Obama's Birth Certificate," *PolitiFact*, April 27, 2011, http://www.politifact.com/truth-o-meter/article/2011/apr/27/politifacts-guide-obamas-birth-certificate/, accessed June 8, 2016; Lori Robinson, "Indeed, Born in the U.S.A.," FactCheck.org, April 27, 2011, http://www.factcheck.org/2011/04/indeed-born-in-the-u-s-a/, accessed June 8, 2016; Michael D. Shear, "Mixed Reaction to Release of Obama Birth Certificate," thecaucus.blogs.nytimes.com, April 27, 2011, http://thecaucus.blogs.nytimes.com/2011/04/27/mixed-reaction-to-release-of-obama-birth-certificate/, accessed June 8, 2016. See Ta-Nehisi Coates, "Fear of a Black President," *Atlantic*, September 2012, http://www/theatlantic.com/magazine/archive/2012/09/fear-of-a-black-president/309064/, accessed June 9, 2016.

32. Angie Drobnic Holan, "Obama Attended an Indonesian Public School," *PolitiFact*, December 20, 2007, http://www.politifact.com/truth-o-meter/statements/2007/dec/20/chain-email/obama-attended-an-indonesian-public-school/, accessed June 9, 2016; Angie Drobnic Holan, "Obama Sworn in on His Bible," *PolitiFact*, December 20, 2007, http://www.politifact.com/truth-o-meter/statements/2007/dec/20/chain-email/obama-sworn-in-on-his-bible/, accessed June 9, 2016; Steven Waldman, "Republicans Fuel Rumor That Obama Is Muslim," *Wall Street Journal*, October 21, 2016, http://blogs.wsj.com/capitaljournal/2008/10/21/republicans-fuel-rumor-that-obama-is-muslim/, accessed June 9, 2016; Brian Montopoli, "Huckabee Again Attacks Obama Worldview, Evokes Madrassas," CBSNews.com, March 3, 2011, http://www.cbsnews.com/news/huckabee-again-attacks-obama-worldview-evokes-madrassas/, accessed June 9, 2016; "Growing Numbers of Americans Say Obama Is a Muslim," Pew Research Center, August 18, 2010, http://www.pewforum.org/2010/08/18/growing-number-of-americans-say-obama-is-a-muslim/, accessed June 8, 2016.

33. Sarah Pulliam Bailey, "A Startling Number of Americans Still Believe President Obama

Is a Muslim," *Washington Post*, September 14, 2015, https://www.washingtonpost.com/news /acts-of-faith/wp/2015/09/14/a-startling-number-of-americans-still-believe-president-obama -is-a-muslim/, accessed June 8, 2016. The actual percentages in 2015 were 29 percent of Americans and 43 percent of Republicans.

34. On the Tea Party, see Theda Skocpol and Vanessa Williamson, *The Tea Party and the Remaking of American Conservatism* (New York: Oxford University Press, 2013). On the fury of Tea Partiers at Obama, see the following accounts of town hall meetings sponsored by the Tea Party in August 2009: Jessica Rinaldi, "When Protesters Disrupt Town Hall Healthcare Talks," Reuters, July 27, 2009, http://www.reuters.com/article/us-usa-healthcare-townhalls-idUSTRE 5765QH20090808, accessed March 24, 2016; Kevin Hechitikopf, "Rally Interrupts Dem Rep.'s Health Care Town Hall," CBSNews.com, August 3, 2009, http://www.cbsnews.com/news/rally -interrupts-dem-reps-health-care-town-hall, accessed March 24, 2016/; Ian Urbina, "Beyond Beltway, Health Debate Turns Hostile," *New York Times*, August 7, 2009, http://www.nytimes .com/2009/08/08/us/politics/08townhall.html?_r=0&mtrref=www.google.co.uk&gwh=78FB E4E211C423033E3096984A6D2F17&gwt=pay, accessed March 24, 2016.

On the battle over health care, see Lawrence R. Jacobs and Theda Skocpol, *Health Care Reform and American Politics: What Everybody Needs to Know* (New York: Oxford University Press, 2010); Paul Starr, *Remedy and Reaction: The Peculiar American Struggle over Health Care Reform* (New Haven: Yale University Press, 2013); Steven Brill, *America's Bitter Pill: Money, Politics, Backroom Deals, and the Fight to Fix Our Broken Healthcare System* (New York: Random House, 2015).

35. On the September 12, 2009, Tea Party rally in Washington, see Jeff Zeleny, "Thousands Rally in Capital to Protest Big Government," *New York Times*, September 12, 2012, http://www .nytimes.com/2009/09/13/us/politics/13protestweb.html, accessed April 7, 2016; Asha Beh, "Thousands of Anti-Obama Protestors March in D.C.," NBCWashington.com, September 12, 2009, http://www.nbcwashington.com/news/local/Taxpayer-Protestors-Get-Party-Started-Early -59126782.html, accessed March 24, 2016; Toby Harnden, "Thousands of 'Tea Party' Protestors March against Barack Obama in Washington," *Telegraph*, September 13, 2009, http://www .telegraph.co.uk/news/worldnews/barackobama/6184800/Thousands-of-tea-party-protesters -march-against-Barack-Obama-in-Washington.html, accessed April 7, 2016. For racist signs, see Ryan Grim and Luke Johnson, "Is the Tea Party Racist? Ask Some Actual, Out-of-the-Closet Racists," *Huffington Post*, October 24, 2013, http://www.huffingtonpost.com/2013/10/24/tea-party-racist_n_4158262.html, accessed May 26, 2016; Justin Berrier and Brooke Obie, "Right-Wing Media Attempt to Erase 'Bigoted Statements' from Tea-Party Movement," MediaMatters .org, July 15, 2010, http://mediamatters.org/research/2010/07/15/right-wing-media-attempt -to-erase-bigoted-state/1677160, accessed May 26, 2016. See also Anti-Defamation League, "Rage Grows in America: Anti-Government Conspiracies, ADL.org, November 2009, http:// www.adl.org/combating-hate/domestic-extremism-terrorism/c/rage-grows-in-america.html, 10, and http://www.adl.org/assets/pdf/combating-hate/Rage-Grows-In-America.pdf, accessed June 1, 2016; and Shannon Travis, "GOP Passes Resolution Blasting Tea Party 'Racism,'" CNN .com, July 16, 2010, http://edition.cnn.com/2010/POLITICS/07/14/naacp.tea.party/, accessed September 22, 2016.

36. Anti-Defamation League, "Rage Grows in America," 10.

37. Douglas Christian, "Absolutism vs Compromise and the Power of Words," *Baltimore Post-Examiner*, October 22, 2013, http://baltimorepostexaminer.com/absolutism-vs-compromise -power-words/2013/10/22, accessed September 14, 2015.

38. On the racial politics of Tarzan movies, see Kevin Dunn, "Lights . . . Camera . . . Africa: Images of Africa and Africans in Western Popular Films of the 1930s," *African Studies Review* 39

(April 1996), 149–75; Barbara Creed, *Pandora's Box: Essays in Film Theory* (Victoria: Australian Centre for the Moving Image, 2004), chap. 3 ("Me Jane: You Tarzan! Race and Gender in the Jungle"); Richard Dyer, *White* (London: Routledge, 1997).

39. The version of the image shown in figure 17.3 is taken from the Talking Points Memo website, July 23, 2009, http://talkingpointsmemo.com/muckraker/conservative-activist -forwards-racist-pic-showing-obama-as-witch-doctor, accessed September 21, 2016. For a shot of the poster version of this image held aloft at the march, see Ashley Fantz, "Obama as a Witch Doctor: Racist or Satirical?" CNN.com, September 18, 2009, http://edition.cnn.com/2009 /POLITICS/09/17/obama.witchdoctor.teaparty/, accessed May 18, 2016.

40. Alex Spillius, "Tea Party Activist Sends E-mail Depicting Barack Obama as a Chimpanzee," *Telegraph*, April 17, 2011, http://www.telegraph.co.uk/news/worldnews/us-election/8457101 /Tea-Party-activist-sends-email-depicting-Barack-Obama-as-a-chimpanzee.html, accessed June 9, 2016.

41. United States Department of Justice, Civil Rights Division, Investigation of the Ferguson Police Department, March 4, 2015 (Washington, DC: Government Printing Office, 2015), 72. This report notes that an "April 2011 email depicted President Barack Obama as a chimpanzee." This was the same month and year that Davenport posted and circulated her chimpanzee picture of the Obama "family."

42. Max Ehrenfreund, "Your Complete Guide to Obama's Immigration Executive Action," *Washington Post*, November 20, 2014, https://www.washingtonpost.com/news/wonk/wp/2014 /11/19/your-complete-guide-to-obamas-immigration-order/, accessed June 10, 2016.

43. Martin's "crime" had been walking to his father's home in Sanford from a local 7-Eleven store where he had gone to purchase a bag of Skittles and an iced tea for his sister and him to enjoy as they sat watching TV. Lizette Alvarez and Michael Cooper, "Prosecutor Files Charge of 2nd-Degree Murder in Shooting of Martin," *New York Times*, April 11, 2012, http://www .nytimes.com/2012/04/12/us/zimmerman-to-be-charged-in-trayvon-martin-shooting.html, accessed June 9, 2016; Greg Botelho, "What Happened the Night Trayvon Martin Died," CNN .com, May 23, 2012, http://edition.cnn.com/2012/05/18/justice/florida-teen-shooting-details/, accessed June 9, 2016; "The Trayvon Martin Case: A Timeline," *The Week*, July 17, 2012, http:// theweek.com/articles/476855/trayvon-martin-case-timeline, accessed June 9, 2016; David A. Graham, "Quote of the Day: Obama: 'If I Had a Son, He'd Look Like Trayvon,'" *Atlantic*, March 23, 2012, http://www.theatlantic.com/politics/archive/2012/03/quote-of-the-day-obama-if-i -had-a-son-hed-look-like-trayvon/254971/, accessed June 9, 2016.

44. On the continuing force of racism during the Obama years, see Dyson, *The Black Presidency*; Michael Tesler, *Post-Racial or Most Racial? Race and Politics in the Obama Era* (Chicago: University of Chicago Press, 2016); and Desmond S. King and Rogers M. Smith, *Still a House Divided: Race and Politics in Obama's America* (Princeton, NJ: Princeton University Press, 2011).

45. On Roosevelt's racial nationalist beliefs, and on the politics of his administration more generally, see Gerstle, *American Crucible*, chap. 4; Ira Katznelson, *Fear Itself: The New Deal and the Origins of Our Time* (New York: Liveright, 2013)

46. On the significance of the labor, the socialist (and communist) left, and left populism in the 1930s, see Gerstle, *Liberty and Coercion: The Paradox of American Government from the Founding to the Present* (Princeton, NJ: Princeton University Press, 2016), chap. 7; Alan Brinkley, *Voices of Protest: Huey Long, Father Coughlin, and the Great Depression* (New York: Knopf, 1982); Michael Kazin, *The Populist Persuasion: An American History* (New York: Basic Books, 1995), chaps. 5 and 6.

47. The absence of a left in 2008 was partly a matter of timing. Obama entered office at the moment when the economic crisis first broke, much as Herbert Hoover had in 1929. The onset of

a large economic calamity often generates disorientation; it takes time for oppositional movements to coalesce. Thus serious protest against living circumstances during the Great Depression only began in 1933 and 1934, four years after the stock market crashed. Had Obama first come into office in 2012, he would have benefited, as FDR had, from a left surge; his reform agenda would probably have had greater amplitude.

48. Obama's Executive Action on immigration was declared unconstitutional by the courts in 2016. See Adam Liptak and Michael D. Shear, "Supreme Court Tie Blocks Obama Immigration Plan," *New York Times*, June 23, 2016, http://www.nytimes.com/2016/06/24/us/supreme-court-immigration-obama-dapa.html?_r=0, accessed August 9, 2016.

49. Lin-Manuel Miranda, *Hamilton: An American Musical* (2015).

CONTRIBUTORS

SARAH R. COLEMAN is a postdoctoral fellow at the Center for Presidential History at Southern Methodist University. She received her PhD in history from Princeton University in 2016. Her dissertation was awarded the Outstanding Dissertation Award from the Immigration and Ethnic History Society.

JACOB DLAMINI is an assistant professor of history at Princeton University. He works on the cultural, social, and political history of Africa. He was a journalist for twenty years, working in South Africa and in the UK, and is the author of *Askari: A Story of Collaboration and Betrayal in the Anti-Apartheid Struggle*.

GARY GERSTLE is the Paul Mellon Professor of American History at the University of Cambridge. His books include *The Rise and Fall of the New Deal Order, 1930–1980*, and two prizewinners, *American Crucible: Race and Nation in the Twentieth Century* and *Liberty and Coercion: The Paradox of American Government from the Founding to the Present*. A revised edition of *American Crucible*, with a new chapter, "The Age of Obama, 2000–2016," was published in 2017.

RISA GOLUBOFF is the dean of the School of Law, Arnold H. Leon Professor of Law, and a professor of history at the University of Virginia. She has written *The Lost Promise of Civil Rights* and *Vagrant Nation: Police Power, Constitutional Change, and the Making of the 1960s*.

MEG JACOBS is a senior research scholar of history and public affairs at Princeton University. Her most recent book is *Panic at the Pump: The Energy Crisis and the Transformation of American Politics in the 1970s*. She is currently writing a book about the New Deal and World War II.

PENIEL E. JOSEPH is the Barbara Jordan Chair in Ethics and Political Values at the LBJ School of Public Affairs and a professor of history and the founding director of the Center for Study of Race and Democracy at

328 LIST OF CONTRIBUTORS

the University of Texas, Austin. A frequent national commentator on issues of race, democracy, and civil rights, he is the author of the award-winning *Waiting 'Til the Midnight Hour: A Narrative History of Black Power in America*; *Dark Days, Bright Nights: From Black Power to Barack Obama*; and *Stokely: A Life*.

MICHAEL KAZIN is a professor of history at Georgetown University and editor of *Dissent*. His most recent books are *War Against War: The American Fight for Peace, 1914–1918* and a new edition of *The Populist Persuasion: An American History*. He is a regular contributor to the *New York Times*, *Foreign Affairs*, the *Nation*, the *Daily Beast*, and other publications and websites.

MATTHEW D. LASSITER is a professor of history at the University of Michigan and the author of *The Silent Majority: Suburban Politics in the Sunbelt South* and *The Suburban Crisis: Crime, Drugs, and White Middle-Class America* (forthcoming).

KATHRYN OLMSTED is a professor of history at the University of California, Davis. She is the author of four books: *Right Out of California: The 1930s and the Big Business Roots of Modern Conservatism*; *Real Enemies: Conspiracy Theories and American Democracy, World War I to 9/11*; *Red Spy Queen: A Biography of Elizabeth Bentley*; and *Challenging the Secret Government: The Post-Watergate Investigations of the CIA and FBI*. She has also coedited a book on the history of the Central Intelligence Agency and published journal articles and book chapters that highlight her overlapping areas of expertise: conspiracy theories, government secrecy, espionage, counterintelligence, and anticommunism.

ERIC RAUCHWAY is professor of history at the University of California, Davis, and the author of several books on U.S. history including most recently *The Money Makers: How Roosevelt and Keynes Ended the Depression, Defeated Fascism, and Secured a Prosperous Peace*.

RICHARD SCHRAGGER is the Perre Bowen Professor and Joseph C. Carter Research Professor at the University of Virginia School of Law. He is the author of *City Power: Urban Governance in a Global Age*.

PAUL STARR is a professor of sociology and public affairs at Princeton University and cofounder and coeditor of *American Prospect*. Among his books are *The Social Transformation of American Medicine*, which won the Pulitzer Prize for General Nonfiction and the Bancroft Prize in American History; *The Creation of the Media: The Political Origins of Modern Communications*; and *Freedom's Power: The History and Promise of Liberalism.*

TIMOTHY STEWART-WINTER is an associate professor of history at Rutgers University–Newark. He is the author of *Queer Clout: Chicago and the Rise of Gay Politics*, which was awarded the 2017 John Boswell Prize. His writing has appeared in the *Journal of American History*, the *Journal of Urban History*, the *New York Times*, and *Dissent*.

THOMAS J. SUGRUE is a professor of social and cultural analysis and history at New York University, where he directs the Program in American Studies and also the Collaborative on Global Urbanism. He is author and editor of many books, including *The Origins of the Urban Crisis,* which won the Bancroft Prize, and *Not Even Past: Barack Obama and the Burden of Race.*

JEREMI SURI holds the Mack Brown Distinguished Chair for Leadership in Global Affairs at the University of Texas at Austin, where he is also a professor in the Department of History and the Lyndon B. Johnson School of Public Affairs. Suri is the author and editor of nine books, most recently *The Impossible Presidency: The Rise and Fall of America's Highest Office*. His writings appear widely in popular newspapers and magazines, and he is a frequent guest on radio and television shows.

JULIAN E. ZELIZER is the Malcolm Stevenson Forbes, Class of 1941 Professor of History and Public Affairs at Princeton University and a CNN Political Analyst. He is the author and editor of eighteen books on American political history, including *The Fierce Urgency of Now: Lyndon Johnson, Congress, and the Battle for the Great Society*. He has written over eight hundred op-eds, including his popular columns for CNN.com and *The Atlantic*. He appears frequently on radio and television shows.

JONATHAN ZIMMERMAN is a professor of history of education at the University of Pennsylvania. Zimmerman is the author of *The Case for Contention: Teaching Controversial Issues in American Schools* and six other books. He is also a frequent op-ed contributor to the *New York Times*, the *New York Review of Books*, and other popular newspapers and magazines.

INDEX

A NOTE ON THE TYPE

This book has been composed in Adobe Text and Gotham. Adobe Text, designed by Robert Slimbach for Adobe, bridges the gap between fifteenth- and sixteenth-century calligraphic and eighteenth-century Modern styles. Gotham, inspired by New York street signs, was designed by Tobias Frere-Jones for Hoefler & Co.